EXPLICATIONS

EXPLICATIONS

The Technique of French Literary Appreciation

BY

W. D. HOWARTH

Professor of Classical French Literature
University of Bristol

and

C. L. WALTON

Head of the Modern Languages Department
Harrow School

OXFORD UNIVERSITY PRESS

1971

Oxford University Press, Ely House, London W. 1

GLASGOW NEW YORK TORONTO MELBOURNE WELLINGTON
CAPE TOWN SALISBURY IBADAN NAIROBI DAR ES SALAAM LUSAKA ADDIS ABABA
BOMBAY CALCUTTA MADRAS KARACHI LAHORE DACCA
KUALA LUMPUR SINGAPORE HONG KONG TOKYO

*Printed in Great Britain by Richard Clay (The Chaucer Press), Ltd.,
Bungay, Suffolk*

Acknowledgements

THANKS are due to the following publishers for permission to reproduce passages from works under copyright: to Éditions du Mercure de France ('Odelette' from H. de Régnier, *Jeux rustiques et divins*); Librairie Hachette, éditeur (extract from Colette, *La Maison de Claudine*); Librairie Gallimard (extract from Proust, *A la recherche du temps perdu*); and Éditions Bernard Grasset (extract from Mauriac, *Thérèse Desqueyroux*).

Contents

Introduction

A. *AIMS*

'Nous ne croyons pas, nous, qu'on
puisse compromettre le génie en
l'expliquant.' BAUDELAIRE

THE critical method known by the name of *explication de texte*, which for nearly a century has occupied such a prominent place in French educational practice—'l'exercice que notre enseignement considère à bon droit son joyau'[1]—, has come in for some sharp attacks lately. For every man of letters today who will say, like Paul Guth:

> Je dois tout à l'Université; je dois plus que tout à l'explication de textes. Mes maîtres m'avaient prouvé qu'elle était la clef qui ouvre l'armoire aux trésors de la littérature... J'ai été si profondément formé par elle qu'elle est devenue ma seconde nature. Je ne peux pas lire une page sans la transformer en explication de texte. Grâce à nos maîtres, chez moi lecture et explication se confondent en un seul et même élan[2]

there must be many who would echo Eugène Vinaver:

> No educated Frenchman of today with a feeling for great poetry and prose would apply to his own reading the method of analysis he once mastered at school. More than that: the process of literary appreciation usually has to wait until the last vestiges of the method have been effaced.[3]

---

[1] A. François-Poncet, in a speech, Paris, 1958, in honour of the centenary of Lanson's birth (quoted in P. Mansell Jones, *The Assault on French Literature and other Essays* (Manchester, 1963), p. 89).

[2] Préface to G. Delaisement, *Les Techniques de l'explication de textes* (Paris, 1968), pp. v–vi.

[3] *Modern Languages*, XLII (1961), p. 4. The whole of Professor Vinaver's article, 'Le chêne et le roseau', from which this passage is taken, is devoted to a searching criticism of traditional *explication de texte*.

Present-day critics of *explication de texte* are condemning a method which played a central part in their own intellectual formation; a method—as they see it—whose rigid formalism and impersonality are fatal to the genuine appreciation of literature, and which has consequently had a pernicious effect on the critical faculties of generations of cultured and well-educated Frenchmen. In this country, a notable broadside was delivered by the late Professor Mansell Jones in his essay 'The Formal Method Arraigned'.[4] For Mansell Jones, *explication de texte* was the essential manifestation of an academic approach to literature which had dominated the Faculties of Letters of French universities, and the literature classes of the French *lycées*, for several generations, to the detriment of the French cultural tradition. Because of the immense influence exercised by Gustave Lanson, both as scholar and teacher and as head of the École Normale Supérieure, it is with his name more than any other that this method is associated; and it has recently been 'elevated' (at least ironically, by its critics) to the status of a doctrinal orthodoxy, with the label 'le lansonisme'. Mansell Jones agrees with Professor Vinaver in acknowledging the virtues of *explication* as training in rational analysis, but endorses Vinaver's indictment that 'the method of *explication* as traditionally conceived is not, and never could be, the proper means of discovering great poetry and prose'.

Mansell Jones's essential criticism of the traditional *explication de texte* is that it sets too much store by the intellectual content of the work being analysed, and that it is therefore totally inadequate as a means of evoking and recording a reader's response to those non-rational elements which are most characteristic of twentieth-century literature; in particular

> the poetry written in France during the period, the whole urge of which tends to get away from anything like imitation, or even recognition, of the rationally-controlled productions of the seventeenth and eighteenth centuries, and to revert to the intuitive sources of primitive impulse, to the rich chaos of unconscious motivation, and above all to fantasy, free association and fresh, spontaneous sensation.[5]

Attacks such as those here quoted are of course aimed at a wider target than *explication de texte*, and they have not been confined to

4 Op. cit., pp. 89–104.   5 Ibid., p. 100.

the post-1945 period; indeed, the most celebrated onslaught that 'le lansonisme' has had to face was that delivered by Charles Péguy, in the form of an attack on the persons of Lanson and Gustave Rudler, in 1911. Péguy goes far beyond a mere criticism of method, and takes up a resolutely anti-academic and anti-critical stance, according to which any practising writer, simply by virtue of being a creative artist, 'quand il ouvre seulement un roman de Flaubert, un roman de Maupassant, y a, y trouve (sans chercher), y reçoit des intelligences instantanées qu'un Rudler ne recevra jamais, qui d'ailleurs ne se trouvent point, ne s'obtiennent point.'[6] Such attacks are of course directed against a convenient Aunt Sally, an abstraction exaggerated for the purpose of polemic, and are consequently highly unjust to Lanson himself and what he stood for; for, if he was capable of writing that 'la littérature est, dans le plus noble sens du mot, une vulgarisation de la philosophie', it should in all fairness be recognized that in *L'Art de la prose* (1909) Lanson also produced one of the first contributions to the modern development of the study of stylistics. Gustave Lanson's own scholarship was far broader and more eclectic than the caricatural stereotype with which his name is nowadays so disparagingly associated.[7]

However, it must be admitted that the history, and the academic origins, of *explication de texte* as a pedagogic exercise do indeed give cause for some suspicion. It came into being three-quarters of the way through the nineteenth century, at a time when an already well-defined analytical and rationalistic tendency in the French national character had acquired considerable authority and influence as a result of the new prestige of the academic profession. The particular form which nineteenth-century positivism conferred on this tendency was the belief that all manifestations of the human intellect were capable of being studied in a methodical, scientific manner by being categorized and classified according to historical principles. It is perhaps natural that, when the study of French literature was encompassed in this development, it should be the historical associations, the philosophical content, and the social relevance of a work, in short those aspects which are more obviously susceptible of objective analysis, that were stressed; the organization of the study

---

[6] *Œuvres en prose, 1909–14* (Paris, 1961), p. 1003.

[7] For a very different assessment of Lanson as a scholar, and a generous appreciation of his influence, see Henri Peyre's Introduction to G. Lanson, *Essais de méthode, de critique et d'histoire littéraire* (Paris, 1965), pp. 9–28, which provides a specific reply to Mansell Jones.

of literature according to positivist principles was regarded as a necessary corrective to the vague impressionism of an undisciplined appreciation. In his *Évolution des genres* (1890), therefore, Ferdinand Brunetière adapted the principles of Darwinism to the study of the way in which literary genres develop; Lanson's *Histoire de la littérature française* (1895) was a monument to the systematic and methodical study of the literature of the past; while in obedience to the same spirit 'l'explication de textes' was proclaimed in A. Gazier's *Traité d'explication française* (1880), and was to be further publicized in various articles and manuals published during the following decades, as the means by which a sound critical method, based on the precise reading and the clear understanding of a text, could be transmitted from one generation to another.

The principles of clarity and precision enunciated by Lanson as the aims of *explication*[8] indicate the firm basis of this exercise in a French intellectual tradition stretching back to Descartes, whose 'méthode' had taught a very similar emphasis. And, indeed, going well back beyond the seventeenth century, there is an obvious affinity to be seen with the scholastic exercise of textual commentary as practised in the universities and seminaries of the Middle Ages:

> . . . a work of subtle analysis, wherein the commentator twisted in every way possible the text to be examined, and, indeed, dissected it. The lecturer . . . commenced by discussing a few general questions, having reference to the treatise which he was called upon to explain, and, in the customary Aristotelian fashion, treated of its material, formal, final and efficient causes. He pointed out the principal divisions; took the first division and subdivided it; divided again the subdivision, and repeated the process until he had subdivided to the first chapter. He then again divided, until he had reached a subdivision which included only a single sentence or complete idea. He finally took this sentence, and expressed it in other terms which might serve to make the conception more clear. He never passed from one part of the work to another, from one chapter to another, or even from one sentence to another, without a minute analysis of the reasons for which each division, chapter or sentence was placed after that by which it was immediately preceded. Each day this painful and

---

[8] Lanson defined the achievement bestowed by the pursuit of this method as 'lire . . . pour acquérir une intelligence claire, précise et distincte des textes' (*Méthodes de l'histoire littéraire* (Paris, 1925), p. 44).

tedious labor was renewed, and it could have no other result but to give the auditors as exact a knowledge as possible of a text indefinitely analysed and paraphrased.[9]

Perhaps we should regard Montaigne, who criticized the scholasticism of the colleges of his day, with their fondness for repetitious commentaries, at second or third hand, on a limited number of authoritative texts ('Nous ne faisons que nous entregloser... tout fourmille de commentaires; d'auteurs il est grand' cherté'),[10] as a precursor of those who criticize the shortcomings of *explication de texte* in our own day. Be that as it may, the method of *praelectio*, or 'lecture expliquée', was taken over by the new humanist colleges in the sixteenth century, and extended from the fields of theology and philosophy to the study of Greek and Latin secular literature; and this was to provide for the next three centuries, in the hands of the Jesuits and other educators, the staple means of teaching the understanding of a classical text:

> Le livre n'a tant d'importance au regard des éducateurs jésuites que parce qu'il est l'instrument par excellence de l'enseignement... Mais il ne suffit pas de le lire pour le comprendre, car on ne lit bien que ce que l'on comprend très bien. Le rôle du maître apparaît dès lors net: il lui faut lire le texte à son disciple, surtout mettre son disciple à même de le bien lire lui-même, en le lui expliquant. Les anciens, de qui les Jésuites tenaient cette idée fort juste, avaient pour désigner l'acte un mot très expressif: *praelegere*... Ils parlaient de la *praelectio*, nous demandons au lecteur la permission d'en conserver la forme francisée *prélection*, dont le sens étymologique est plus expressif que notre mot explication. Si les Jésuites n'ont pas inventé cet exercice, ils l'ont si bien perfectionné qu'il a pu paraître une de leurs créations.[11]

Such appears to be the ancestry of *explication de texte*, as it emerged in the second half of the nineteenth century as a method of studying French literature.[12] In the first place it had been

---

[9] G. Compayré, *Abelard and the Origin and Early History of Universities* (New York, 1893), pp. 184-5.

[10] *Essais*, Bk. III, no. xiii, 'De l'expérience'.

[11] F. de Dainville, S. J., *La Naissance de l'humanisme moderne* (Paris, 1940), I, 98.

[12] Cf. Vinaver: 'The technique and the spirit of the mediaeval grammatical commentary still survive almost intact in the modern *lecture expliquée*, and La Fontaine is read in French secondary schools today very much as Virgil was read in the cathedral schools of mediaeval France' (art. cit., p. 4).

developed as a pedagogic exercise designed to further the accurate reading and clear understanding of a text written in a foreign language; in a dead language, moreover, where the answer to linguistic difficulties was to be found, not in reference to current usage or living tradition, but in systematic comparison with a limited corpus of surviving literary texts. The primary purpose of such an exercise was elucidation; and although Littré does not gloss *explication de texte* as a separate entry, one of the meanings he gives for the word *explication* itself is not without significance in this context: '5°. *Terme de classe*. L'explication, la traduction de vive voix d'un auteur après préparation ou à livre ouvert.'[13]

Essentially, then, the classical exercise of *explication* was a translation (or possibly a paraphrase) of a text, accompanied by such commentary as was necessary to prove one's understanding. The more accomplished the commentator, the more extensive, no doubt, would be the range of comparisons with other texts, drawing where possible on the erudition of German and other scholars, for this was the dawn of the golden age of classical philology. At best, this sort of *explication* would be an exercise in meticulous scholarship; at a humbler and more pedestrian level, a training in accuracy and precision applied to linguistic matters. In any case, the emphasis would be on the lucid restatement of the meaning of the original; so much seems clear from the prescriptions formulated by the eighteenth-century educationalist Rollin in his influential *Traité des études* (published in 1726, and regularly reprinted throughout the eighteenth and nineteenth centuries):

> On peut réduire à cinq ou six articles les remarques qu'on doit faire en expliquant les auteurs: 1° la syntaxe, qui rend raison de la construction des différentes parties du discours; 2° la propriété des mots, c'est-à-dire leur signification propre et naturelle; 3° l'élégance du latin, par où l'on fait connaître ce que cette langue a de plus fin et de plus délicat; 4° l'usage des particules; 5° certaines difficultés particulières plus marquées; 6° la manière de prononcer et écrire le latin, qui n'est pas indifférente même pour l'intelligence des anciens auteurs. Je n'ajoute point ici ce qui regarde les pensées, les figures, la suite et l'économie du discours...[14]

[13] The *Dictionnaire de la langue française* was published 1863-9.
[14] 1883 edition, I, 205.

There seems to be no doubt at all that this is the source of our term *explication de texte*; and it is virtually certain that the theory was taken over, along with the term itself, by its early practitioners. This is the reason for the at first sight rather surprising specification contained in the title of the earliest manual, Gazier's *Traité d'explication française* (1880), one which may also, perhaps, have puzzled readers of Gustave Rudler's *L'Explication française* (1902). 'L'explication *française*' is particularized by these and other authors, not because they were writing for foreign readers but because they were transferring to the study of *French* texts a method hitherto recognized as belonging to the study of the classics. As Gazier himself writes:

> Bien des personnes verront avec étonnement le titre de cet ouvrage, car on n'explique guère les auteurs français dans la plupart des collèges...
>
> L'on passe à un exercice considéré bien autrement important, c'est-à-dire à l'explication des textes anciens. Cependant, les classiques français n'ont pas moins besoin d'être commentés que leurs illustres devanciers, et l'on devrait s'arrêter aussi longtemps sur dix lignes de Bossuet ou de Molière que sur dix vers de Sophocle ou de Virgile. Qu'est-ce en effet qu'une explication, du latin *explicare*, déplier, en sorte que rien ne se cache dans les plis?...
>
> Il faut d'abord lire, comprendre et méditer nos grands auteurs; il faut en un mot les expliquer dans nos classes comme nous expliquons les latins et les grecs.[15]

Though Gazier refers in his Introduction to 'l'excellente méthode que fait suivre à l'École Normale Supérieure un maître incomparable, M. Charles Thurot, membre de l'Institut',[16] he appears here to be claiming for his own book the credit for publicizing this pedagogical innovation; and indeed, to the best of our knowledge, Gazier's was the first manual to be devoted to *explication* in its modern sense (as he calls it in his sub-title, a 'méthode pour expliquer littéralement les auteurs français').

From 1880 through to the 1920s manuals devoted to the techniques of *explication* reflect the emphasis of academic scholarship in general during this period. Ferdinand Brunot in two articles published in the *Revue universitaire* of 1895, Rudler in *L'Explication*

---

[15] Op. cit., 2nd edition (1881), pp. v, viii.
[16] Ibid., p. x. A classical scholar and phonetician, Thurot does not seem to have left any published record of his method for posterity.

française (1902), and M. Roustan in *Précis d'explication française* (1911) all stress the virtues of method, order, clarity, and precision. Roustan, for instance, comments on the educational reforms of 1902 (which had officially introduced *explication de texte* into the teaching of French in the *lycées*), and quotes the following ministerial pronouncement:

> S'il est une caractéristique des réformes de 1902 en ce qui concerne l'enseignement du français, c'est que la lecture expliquée, trop subordonnée à l'histoire littéraire, a passé du second plan au premier et devient de plus en plus, dans sa précision nouvelle, un instrument d'éducation intellectuelle et morale. Bien pratiquée, elle est à la fois un exercice de logique et de composition, puisqu'elle marque et fait trouver aux élèves l'ordre dans lequel les idées se suivent et les liaisons qui les unissent; un exercice de précision, puisqu'elle précise le sens exact des termes essentiels par rapport aux idées qu'ils expriment; un exercice de style, en quelque mesure, puisqu'... elle peut inspirer le sentiment des beautés littéraires.[17]

There is a good deal here, of course, with which any modern exponent of *explication de texte*, however forward-looking, would agree; and indeed Roustan's book provides a sensible exposition of method. However, the phrase 'un instrument d'éducation intellectuelle et morale' is one which might be viewed with some suspicion: while the end-product of any study in the humanities must necessarily be part of one's 'intellectual and moral education' in a wider sense (and we should certainly not wish to deny the value of close and accurate reading in this respect), Roustan's phrase nevertheless suggests a rather old-fashioned sense of priorities, an attitude towards *explication* which tends to regard the study of a literary text as the means to something else rather than as an end in itself; and in such a scheme of things it is not surprising that aesthetic appreciation only gets a mention at the end, as an afterthought.

Gustave Rudler's volume is likely to be the best known, and has probably been the most influential, of all the manuals devoted to *explication de texte*. It can still be read with profit by anyone who is looking for a lucid *exposé* of underlying principles, and for guidance as to orderly method. Those who have called Rudler's approach arid and over-academic cannot have noted the considerable place he

[17] p. v.

gives to the aesthetic taste of the individual reader. If he writes at one point that 'le commentaire historique doit en général avoir le pas sur le commentaire esthétique'; and if his declared aim, to 'replacer le texte dans son milieu et à son moment',[18] seems to contain a warning echo of Taine's celebrated phrase, this is merely a question of procedure: situating the piece historically is for Rudler no more than a preliminary, though a very necessary preliminary, to the ultimate task of *explication* as he sees it, which is aesthetic appreciation of the text concerned: 'Quand on aura vu ce qu'il a de relatif, on en comprendra mieux la valeur, la beauté, la portée absolues.'[19]

For Rudler, the cardinal virtue of *explication* as a critical method is precision; but this is no mechanical concern with detail for its own sake:

A vrai dire la précision est moins en elle-même une qualité qu'une forme commune à toutes les autres. Elle est l'esprit de finesse ou de justesse appliqué aux diverses facultés..., qui les réduit et les plie strictement à la mesure de chaque texte. Tout commentaire qui pourrait, dans ses considérations générales ou dans son détail, servir indistinctement à deux morceaux presque pareils..., est mauvais. Si semblables que paraissent deux idées, elles diffèrent toujours dans leur genèse, dans leur orientation, dans la loi de leur développement, dans leurs rapports à ce qui les entoure... La précision consiste à saisir au plus juste tout ce qui donne à un texte sa physionomie unique, et le distingue de tous les autres. On sera précis quand on aura compris la pensée d'un auteur, et la loi singulière des presque innombrables combinaisons d'idées, de souvenirs, d'associations, d'images, de rythmes, de sons, de couleurs, dans lesquelles elle s'est exprimée et développée.[20]

And any critic who maintains that Rudler, as a faithful exponent of 'le lansonisme', was unable to appreciate those qualities of a work of art which are not open to rational analysis need only re-read his specimen *explications*, for instance the commentary on La Fontaine's 'Le Chat, la belette et le petit lapin', or on Ronsard's 'Comme on voit sur la branche, au mois de mai, la rose...', in order to realize that for Rudler the mystery of artistic creation was a real, and a very precious,

[18] *L'Explication française*, 8th edition (Paris, 1948), p. 45.
[19] Ibid., pp. 45–6.
[20] Ibid., pp. 8–9.

thing. To explore and bring to light as many as possible of the circumstances surrounding the making of a work of art—habits of thought, stylistic conventions, linguistic resources—does not have the effect of belittling or 'explaining away' the genius of the individual artist; on the contrary, as Daniel Mornet says, the methodical study of such attendant circumstances 'permet de tracer avec beaucoup plus de précision le cercle à l'intérieur duquel il faut seulement chercher le secret de son génie'.[21]

The principal feature of Rudler's method that stamps him as somewhat old-fashioned by comparison with the authors of more recent treatises on *explication de texte* is a tendency to be too systematic in certain respects. This finds particular expression in his apparent insistence on the separation of 'le fond' and 'la forme' (or, as he himself calls them, 'la Pensée' and 'l'Art'); we have deliberately called it his 'apparent' insistence, because the impression given by his expository chapter is in fact rather misleading, and Rudler's own practice, as demonstrated by the half-dozen specimen commentaries his volume contains, is a good deal more flexible. However, this is one feature on which later authors have fastened, in order to emphasize their own move away from the excessively systematic approach of the earliest manuals. S. Étienne, for instance, writes in his *Expériences d'analyse textuelle en vue de l'explication littéraire* (1935):

> On habitue aisément les jeunes gens — pas tous, bien entendu — à expliquer un poème par lui-même, à condition de les mettre d'abord en garde contre la distinction fausse entre forme et contenu: ils sont sûrs d'échouer s'ils commencent par travailler à défaire l'unité que le poète a travaillé à faire.[22]

For Étienne, the emphasis of *explication de texte* as a pedagogic exercise should be on the study of the act of creation:

> On leur apprend... qu'un poème — ou toute autre œuvre d'art — n'est pas donné, ne se trouve pas dans la nature; il a dû être construit et il n'a de modèle que lui-même.[23]

[21] 'Méthode d'un cours sur l'histoire de la pensée et du goût en France au xviiᵉ siècle', in *Romanic Review*, XXXIX (1948), p. 205.

[22] p. 9. Étienne quotes the following passage from Valéry in support of his own attitude: 'Distinguer dans les vers le fond et la forme; un sujet et un développement; le son et le sens; considérer la rythmique, la métrique et la prosodie comme naturellement et facilement séparables de l'expression *verbale* même, des *mots* eux-mêmes et de la *syntaxe*; voilà autant de symptômes de non-compréhension ou d'insensibilité en matière poétique.'

[23] Ibid., p. 10.

This approach marks a recognizable move towards that 'objective' or 'phenomenological' criticism which Roland Barthes, as spokesman of the 'nouveaux critiques' of the 1960s, sees as the antithesis of a stereotyped and outmoded 'critique universitaire'. The latter, says Barthes, refuses to accept 'l'analyse immanente' of a work of art:

> Tout [lui] est acceptable pourvu que l'œuvre puisse être mise en rapport avec *autre chose* qu'elle-même, c'est-à-dire autre chose que la littérature: l'histoire (même si elle devient marxiste), la psychologie (même si elle se fait psychanalytique), ces *ailleurs* de l'œuvre seront peu à peu admis; ce qui ne le sera pas, c'est un travail qui s'installe *dans* l'œuvre et qui ne pose son rapport au monde qu'après l'avoir entièrement décrite de l'intérieur, dans ses fonctions, ou comme on dit aujourd'hui, dans sa structure; ce qui est rejeté, c'est donc en gros la critique phénoménologique (qui *explicite* l'œuvre au lieu de l'*expliquer*), la critique thématique (qui reconstitue les métaphores intérieures de l'œuvre) et la critique structurale (qui tient l'œuvre pour un système de fonctions).[24]

We shall return later to a consideration of the relationship between 'la nouvelle critique' and *explication de texte*; let it suffice at this point to note the emphasis placed on the *structure*, or internal organization, of a literary text, in manuals of *explication* produced by authors of an older generation such as Étienne, or by an academic writer such as A. M. Boase, who, although he is critical of some of the features of *explication de texte* as traditionally taught, is certainly not altogether hostile to this sort of exercise, carried out in what he considers a more enlightened way. Those who teach the techniques of *explication*, says Boase, should 'substitute for the key concepts of *explanation* and *analysis* those of "focus" and the discovery of "principles of organisation"': 'All analysis of this kind should be undertaken merely with a view to discerning the *organization* or the *principle of structure* of a poem without which its impact on the mind must remain a mere blur.'[25]

It is, of course, true that Boase and Étienne do not necessarily mean the same thing by the 'structure' of a work as do the 'struc-

---

[24] 'Les deux critiques', in *Modern Language Notes*, LXXVIII (1963), pp. 451–2.
[25] *The Poetry of France*, 2nd edition (London, 1967), III, xiv.

turalist' critics represented by Roland Barthes. What is important, however, is to recognize that such reinterpretation of the aims and methods of *explication* as there has been since the days of Lanson and Rudler has been tending towards, not away from, the sort of critical approach for which Barthes is arguing in the passage quoted above. René Wellek has given an excellent assessment of this new tendency; pointing to the French method of *explication de texte* as one of the significant developments in this field in the twentieth century, alongside German formal analysis based on techniques borrowed from the fine arts, the Russian 'formalist' movement, and the Anglo-American 'new criticism', he continues:

Clearly, the aesthetic effect of a work of art does not reside in what is commonly called its content. There are few works of art which are not ridiculous or meaningless in synopsis (which can only be justified as a pedagogic device). But a distinction between form as the factor aesthetically active and a content aesthetically indifferent meets with insuperable difficulties. At first sight the boundary line may seem fairly definite. If we understand by content the ideas and emotions conveyed in a work of literature, the form would include all linguistic elements by which contents are expressed. But if we examine this distinction more closely, we see that content implies some elements of form: e.g. the events told in a novel are part of the content, while the way in which they are arranged into a 'plot' is part of the form. Dissociated from this way of arrangement they have no artistic effect what-soever. . . . Things become even more disastrous for the tradi-tional concepts when we realize that even in the language, com-monly considered part of the form, it is necessary to distinguish between the words themselves, aesthetically indifferent, and the manner in which individual words make up units of sound and meaning, aesthetically effective. It would be better to rechristen all the aesthetically indifferent elements 'materials', while the manner in which they acquire aesthetic efficiency may be styled 'structure'. This distinction is by no means a simple renaming of the old pair, content and form. It cuts right across the old boundary lines. 'Materials' include elements formerly considered part of the content, and parts formerly considered formal. 'Structure' is a concept including both content and form so far as they are organized for aesthetic purposes. The work of art is, then, considered as a whole system of signs, or structure of signs, serving a specific aesthetic purpose.[26]

That the development here outlined is not only compatible with a redefinition of the exercise of *explication de texte*, but in fact owes a great deal to this critical method, is recognized by H. Roddier, who refers to the 'étude intrinsèque' advocated by Wellek and Warren as 'cette façon de remettre en honneur la vieille explication de textes à la française, vivifiée par le recours aux dernières découvertes de la linguistique'.[27]

*   *   *

We have several times spoken of a 'work of art'; but as Mr. Wellek stresses in the same chapter of *Theory of Literature*, one's view of the proper function of the critic will depend on one's answer to the question: what is a work of art? Reviewing various solutions that have been proposed to this fundamental aesthetic problem, Wellek concludes that the 'poem' (or literary work of art) cannot be regarded as an artefact, or object, as is possible with painting or sculpture (since the poem could still exist even if all copies were destroyed); nor is it the 'reading', or sequence of sounds uttered by the reader (since it exists even when no reading is taking place); it cannot be identified with the experience of the author at the time the poem was written, nor with the individual experience of the reader at the time it is read (since two separate readings, even by the same reader, may give two very different 'experiences'); while to say that the work of art is the sum of the experience of all readers, or the experience common to all readers, either involves a proliferation of individual experiences *ad infinitum*, or else reduces all experience to a shallow common denominator:

An answer to our question in terms of individual or social psychology cannot be found. A poem, we have to conclude, is not an individual experience or sum of experiences, but only a potential cause of experiences. Definition in terms of states of mind fails because it cannot account for the normative character of the genuine poem, for the simple fact that it might be experienced correctly or incorrectly. In every individual experience

[26] R. Wellek and A. Warren, *Theory of Literature* (London, 1949), pp. 140–1. (Chapter XII, 'The Analysis of the Literary Work of Art', is by Professor Wellek.)

[27] 'Principes d'une histoire comparée des littératures européennes', in *Revue de i ttérature comparée*, XXXIX (1965), p. 186.

only a small part can be considered as adequate to the true poem. Thus, the real poem must be considered as a structure of norms, realised only partially in the actual experience of its many readers. Every single experience (reading, reciting, and so forth) is only an attempt—more or less successful and complete—to grasp this set of norms or standards.[28]

While Wellek's conclusion may not be wholly satisfactory (for the concept of a 'structure of norms' would seem to need further definition), his analysis is extremely useful in that it focuses attention on the peculiar character of the critic's task, namely the reconciling of his own individual 'experience' with those 'norms' which he has derived from the recorded experiences of others, and with reactions (his own and those of others) to similar works of art:

If we compare works of art among themselves, similarities or differences between these norms will be ascertained, and from the similarities themselves it ought to be possible to proceed to a classification of works of art according to the type of norms they embody. We may finally arrive at theories of genres and ultimately at theories of literature in general. . . . Assuming that we have to start with the analysis of an individual work of art, we still can scarcely deny that there must be some links, some similarities, some common elements or factors which would approximate two or more given works of art and thus would open the door to a transition from the analysis of one individual work of art to a type such as Greek tragedy and hence to tragedy in general, to literature in general, and finally to some all-inclusive structure common to all arts.[29]

In other words, the critic's function is to blend objective analysis with subjective response. And if the French analytical method of *explication de texte*, as expounded by a Gustave Rudler, may seem to teach the sort of routine mechanical precision that stifles subjective response, we should remember, as English students of French literature, that our own national tradition regarding the art of criticism, as practised by our men of letters and as taught in our schools, has always tended very much towards the other extreme. Although it would be wrong to ignore the pioneer work of such figures as I. A. Richards and William Empson in introducing close

[28] Op cit., p. 151   [29] Ibid.

INTRODUCTION

textual analysis into English studies, and their influence as pre-
cursors of the post-war Anglo-American 'new criticism', the kind of
critical writing more characteristic of the English tradition has
generally been marked by intuitive 'flair' rather than by rigorous
method. At its best, this kind of criticism produces the distinguished
interpretative essay based on a genuine empathy with the subject
under discussion; but at a more pedestrian level, and particularly
in the hands of sixth-formers or undergraduates, it all too often
degenerates into a discursive record of subjective impressions, in
which imagination and enthusiasm are insufficiently controlled by
relevance and precision.

   To quote Henri Peyre: 'Il est plus d'une cellule dans le dortoir, ou
dans le laboratoire, de l'histoire littéraire, et la manière anglaise,
teintée d'urbanité et d'humour, agréablement vieillotte, ne manque
souvent ni de charme ni de style.'[30] But, just as the detached positivist method needs tempering by the influence of an imaginative,
intuitive element, which can help the reader to put himself in the
place of the writer, so the 'impressionistic' approach characteristic
of English criticism—particularly if it is being considered as a model
for students to follow—stands in need of the corrective supplied by a
rigorous method, as nearly scientific as possible, which may prevent
the reader's imagination from 'running away with' the text.[31]

[30] Op. cit., p. 15.
[31] It is instructive to note the comments made by two French university teachers
working in this country, on the critical approach to a literary text characteristic of the
British student:

   (i) I had the impression that the text had been made to prove certain preconceived
or pre-borrowed notions about the author and *not* that the students had grappled with
the passage and founded their opinion upon active meditation and intent searching.
. . . Brilliant variations upon the theme supplied had been indulged in. They made
me realize and respect the student's power of independent thought, they were a
credit to his creative imagination, but they did not bring me any nearer to the author
of the piece. Nothing precise, nothing thorough had been achieved, or indeed
attempted. No logical investigation, no truly critical appreciation had been evolved;
there was no evidence that the text had been met face to face, had been intimately
penetrated and understood. The students had failed to grasp the hidden and sometimes the obvious relationship between contiguous ideas, the interdependence of
paragraphs, the unity of thought and expression. Most of them had indeed found such
difficulty in entering into the author's thoughts that they had too often been content
with merely expressing their own. What could I do but reluctantly admit that . . .
there must have been something wrong with their previous training . . ., that as far
as literature was concerned, their former education had apparently failed to awaken
the enchanted stillness of their minds? (F. Boillot, *The Methodical Study of Literature*,
Paris, 1924, pp. 4–5.)
   (ii) Plusieurs n'avaient pas la première idée de ce qu'on entend par une explication.

When he wrote the well-known phrase 'La critique n'est pas seulement un art de goûter, mais aussi un art de fixer le goût',[32] Thibaudet was thinking, no doubt, in a much wider sense, of the critic's role as a teacher offering guide-lines for others to follow; but the phrase can also be applied, very aptly, to the activity of the critic in a purely individual sense. The critical act consists not only in reading and enjoying, but in relating that enjoyment to certain criteria outside the work itself. Étienne writes of *explication de texte* in this light:

> Le lecteur qui, croyant expliquer un poème, s'attacherait à définir le halo sentimental qui s'en dégage, ferait ainsi un autre poème, qui dériverait du premier, qui lui succéderait et qui finirait par se substituer à lui. Expliquer, ce n'est pas lire, goûter, puis rêver; c'est relire; relire assez fidèlement pour maintenir en nous le poème tel qu'il est écrit... Le poète et celui qui l'explique sont les deux hommes qui ne se contentent pas de ressentir les mouvements d'Othello ou les réactions du spectateur; le premier les construit, l'autre regarde comment le premier les a construits.
>
> L'art nous impose une telle attitude, car si la valeur n'est pas de technique, le mélodrame où Margot a pleuré sera l'œuvre par excellence; l'histoire de l'art sera celle des succès et non plus celle des réussites...[33]

*   *   *

Des pages entières sur la vie de l'auteur et sur toute son œuvre. Effusions vagues sur de nombreux sujets sans le moindre rapport avec le passage à traiter. Idées préconçues qu'on ne s'efforce même pas de mettre à l'épreuve. Sermon laïque qui prend le texte pour point de départ, et puis n'en tient plus compte. Désir de briller et 'd'épater l'examinateur' en citant, par exemple, à propos de La Bruyère, Flaubert, Tolstoï, Cervantès, André Gide, Duhamel. Substitution du *moi* du candidat à celui de l'auteur, psychanalyse du premier, ses goûts, ses préférences, ses 'bêtes noires'. Dissertation générale sans aucun effort pour mettre les points sur les *i*, pour comprendre la matière du morceau, pour formuler ce que l'auteur a en vue et comment il s'y prend pour nous communiquer sa pensée. Absence de toute méthode, ou va-et-vient de l'une à l'autre: le candidat ne sait pas ce qu'il essaie de montrer. Ces défauts sont graves, et jugent la mentalité de l'élève. Certains ne voient rien dans le texte, n'en comprennent pas la portée. Somme toute, ils méritent le reproche de ne pas avoir appris à lire les yeux ouverts. (B. Schlumberger, *L'Explication littéraire*, London, 1951, pp. 35–6.)

[32] *Physiologie de la critique* (Paris, 1962 ed.), p. 145.
[33] Op. cit., pp. 6–7.

One of the purposes of *explication*, then, as we conceive it, is to study the techniques of literary creation, to penetrate as closely as possible into the creative act; to explain, if possible, how a particular text came to be written; why it took the form it did take; what means were at the author's disposal, and what use he made of them; why certain effects were sought, how they were attempted, and how far they were successfully achieved. The problem defined by V. Giraud with regard to literary criticism in general:

> La question essentielle à résoudre est, au fond, toujours la même. Étant donné l'individu Pierre Corneille et l'individu Blaise Pascal, comment ont-ils été amenés à concevoir et à écrire l'un, *Le Cid*, l'autre, *Les Pensées*? A la suite de quelles circonstances d'ordre extérieur ou intime? Quelles transformations éventuelles, au cours de la composition, l'idée première a-t-elle subies? Pour réaliser son rêve, à quelles sources l'écrivain a-t-il puisé? Les matériaux qu'il a empruntés à autrui, comment les utilise-t-il? A quelle loi secrète de sa nature obéit-il pour préserver, en dépit de tous ses emprunts, l'originalité de son génie? Comment, dans quelles conditions, suivant quel rythme son imagination, sa sensibilité, sa pensée tout entière entrent-elles en branle pour élaborer l'œuvre entrevue? Quels sont les procédés de travail du poète dramatique et du penseur chrétien? En un mot, comment est née, comment se développe, comment arrive à la vie, dans le cerveau et dans la conscience de l'écrivain, l'œuvre qu'aujourd'hui nous admirons à si juste titre?[34]

has a particular relevance in connection with *explication de texte*: here, more than in any other critical activity, we are concerned with the moment of creation itself, with all the many factors which come into play, determining the unique character of every text and endowing it, to a greater or a lesser degree, with those qualities we prize.

We have sometimes suggested, as a means of persuading students of the importance of focusing on the moment of creation, that they should try to imagine the author, having written the first ten chapters of his novel, the first three acts of his play, or whatever it might be, with a blank sheet of paper in front of him and his pen poised, ready to start on Chapter XI or Act IV, scene i—and ask themselves: why did the page he wrote take the form it did take, and no other? This is a somewhat naïve approach, of course; we are well aware

[34] *La Critique littéraire, le problème, les théories, les méthodes* (Paris, 1946), pp. 11–12.

that creative writing rarely follows such a neat and orderly pattern as that. But at least it is an approach which helps the student to ask some pertinent questions regarding the character, shape, and tone of the text we are dealing with. If we attempt to go through the creative process with the author himself, there may even be some things that we can account for that the author would not have been able to explain—partly because the critic is more detached than the author could ever be, partly because, with regard to such matters as the selection of vocabulary and the handling of images, modern developments in this field (word-frequency counts, concordances, etc.) can tell us far more about the resources at an author's disposal than he can possibly have known. Such an approach can be very fruitful, on condition that we admit in all humility that there are a great many questions in this matter of literary creation to which we can do no more than suggest a possible answer.

Our inquiry into the author's purpose and motivation, and our exploration of the conditioning factors that determined the shape and character of a text, provide us with one of the essential aims of *explication*. A complementary aim is the appreciation of the way in which the author's intentions have been carried out. Here, the student must blend the subjective quality of passive receptivity with the more active analytical inquiry into the way in which effects are produced on the ordinary, representative reader. The first without the second produces an uninformed, uncritical enthusiasm; the second without the first tends to destroy the effect of the writer's art in the very act of analysing it.

A major problem here, needless to say, is the difference between the effect of a text from a past age on the representative reader of that age, and the effect of the same text on the reader of our own day. No amount of 'homework' on the background to the text will enable a reader of the 1970s entirely to recapture the state of mind of the contemporary reader of, say, *Les Tragiques* or *Jean Barois*, for whom the Wars of Religion, or the *affaire Dreyfus*, were a vital part of everyday life. However, such cases of works written in the heat of battle, and designed to be read by contemporaries who were (or had been) equally involved, perhaps present the least difficulty: it is obvious to the reader that some mental adjustment needs to be attempted, and with a certain amount of good will, and an imagination controlled by a sound historical sense, a modern reader can go a long way towards putting himself in the place of a contemporary of d'Aubigné or of Martin du Gard. Similarly, if we know what adjustment is required of us, it is not impossible for us temporarily to suspend our twentieth-century outlook, and to find Corneille's Horace a figure to be admired, or Shakespeare's Shylock a figure fit for mockery. What is much more difficult, because the need is less obvious, is to make a similar sort of adjustment with regard to 'pure' literature: to get on to the right wavelength, as it were, for Ronsard's —or Baudelaire's—imagery; for on the one hand we have perhaps none of us read enough of an author's contemporaries or predecessors to be able to recognize with certainty the originality, or banality, of a given image in the eyes of the reader of the poet's own day, while on the other hand we have all read too much that has been written since, so that our reaction to a given phrase risks being contaminated by anachronistic associations.

What is certain, however, is that this sort of effort is worth while, and that the critic must undertake the preparatory study, and attempt the mental adjustment, which will enable him as nearly as possible to read the text as it was meant to be read. For no literary work is deliberately written to be considered *sub specie aeternitatis*: it is addressed to a specific public, nearly always—though perhaps not invariably—the public of the author's own day; and it cannot be fully understood, or fairly appreciated, unless a real attempt is made to bridge whatever chronological gap there may be.

This is not to say that we do not, as twentieth-century readers, bring to the interpretation of a work of art from a previous age a specifically twentieth-century point of view, which may have its own value in colouring our critical interpretation; and the duty of every critic writing in the twentieth century is surely to make such a work meaningful to his contemporaries, in terms that they will understand:

Une œuvre d'art se présente à nous sous deux aspects. D'une part, elle appartient à un système d'expression plus ou moins éloigné de nous dans le temps, la géographie, les mœurs, parfois inconnu, impénétrable. D'autre part, elle est présente. Dans notre champ visuel. Immédiate. Nous la rencontrons comme notre contemporaine. Elle agit d'une certaine façon sur nous comme fraîchement créée. Et cette contradiction dans l'aspect se double d'une contradiction différente et plus subtile au niveau de la signification. L'œuvre appartient au fonds commun de notre espèce, au fonds d'aventures exploratoires, d'expériences, à la culture humaine.[35]

In this connection, the contributions of such eminent modern French critics as Bachelard, Béguin, Mauron, Poulet, Raymond, or Sartre, who are sometimes brought together under the umbrella of 'la nouvelle critique',[36] must be recognized. These writers have all introduced into literary criticism important new developments in the fields of philosophy or psychology; and there is no doubt that, for instance, Bachelard's 'phenomenological' criticism, Béguin or Mauron with their investigation of dreams or the subconscious, and Sartre's existentialist interpretations, have each helped to fashion a contemporary critical approach to literature which enables the ordinary reader of the present day to understand the works of the past in a new way.

However, a word of caution is desirable here. A distinction must be made between the critics just referred to—who may more properly be regarded as the *forerunners* of 'la nouvelle critique'— and the self-appointed theorists, together with the more extreme exponents, of 'la nouvelle critique' itself. The position of these latter critics is clearly defined. For them, a modern approach which embodies the latest philosophical or psychological developments is not only capable of providing a valuable adjunct to more traditional methods, it is the only form of criticism that has any validity at all. For such writers, there is an unequivocal choice to be made between contemporary, or 'synchronic', reading of a classical text, and an 'anachronistic' reading:

> La seule clef possible pour un Français de 1968... consiste justement à aborder le texte racinien en établissant la communication par-dessus les trois siècles qui nous en séparent, c'est-à-dire en lisant Racine comme s'il s'agissait d'un texte moderne, en lui appliquant notre grille poétique... La seule lecture valable est la lecture actuelle ou synchronique, si l'on préfère. Cela semble une vérité de La Palisse, et pourtant tout notre enseignement de la littérature vise à imposer contre elle une lecture anachronique, une lecture de Racine comme si nous vivions au temps de Racine.[37]

[35] P. Daix, *Nouvelle critique et art moderne* (Paris, 1968), p. 96.
[36] Cf., for instance, L. Le Sage, *The French New Criticism: An Introduction and a Sampler* (Pennsylvania, 1967).
[37] P. Daix, op. cit., p. 140.

The critic's function is no longer characterized by humility and self-effacement before the work of art, but by a self-confident, highly personal involvement; he becomes the interpreter of a work which, uninterpreted, remains non-existent:

> Le sens du texte de Racine n'est pas 'dans' le texte de Racine: il n'est que la résonance, le prolongement, l'écho infinis, sur tous les plans, du plus immédiat au plus subtil et au plus lointain, de l'expérience humaine qui rayonne à travers un langage. Quoi qu'il fasse, le critique est donc, au sens plein, le révélateur de l'œuvre: il n'y a d'œuvre que par lui... Rien de plus vain que la chimère caressée par les critiques effarouchés de leur ombre, et qui rêvent de 's'effacer devant un texte qui ne les a pas attendus pour exister': cet effacement est, épistémologiquement, une sottise, et, moralement, une lâcheté.[38]

This definition of the critic's role by S. Doubrovsky corresponds closely to that of Barthes:

> Il est à peu près impossible de toucher à la création littéraire sans postuler l'existence d'un rapport entre l'œuvre et autre chose que l'œuvre. Pendant longtemps on a cru que ce rapport était causal, que l'œuvre était un *produit*: d'où les notions critiques de *source*, de *genèse*, de *reflet*, etc. Cette représentation du rapport créateur apparaît de moins en moins soutenable: ou bien l'explication ne touche qu'une partie infime de l'œuvre, elle est dérisoire; ou bien elle propose un rapport massif, dont la grossièreté soulève mille objections... L'idée de produit a donc fait place peu à peu à l'idée de signe: l'œuvre serait le signe d'un au-delà d'elle-même; la critique consiste alors à déchiffrer la signification, à en découvrir les termes, et principalement le terme caché, le signifié... Il s'agit donc d'un mouvement général qui consiste à *ouvrir* l'œuvre, non comme l'effet d'une cause, mais comme le signifiant d'un signifié.[39]

It is true that the systematic search by certain representatives of 'la nouvelle critique'[40] for 'le thème symbolique'—the unconscious obsessions which they see as providing the complete key to all literary creation—seems to lead more readily to arbitrary and fanciful

---

[38] S. Doubrovsky, *Pourquoi la nouvelle critique?* (Paris, 1967), pp. 221–2.

[39] R. Barthes, *Sur Racine* (Paris, 1963), pp. 157–8.

[40] See, e.g., J.-P. Weber, *Genèse de l'œuvre poétique* (Paris, 1960), and *Néo-critique et paléo-critique* (Paris, 1966); Marcelle Blum, *Le Thème symbolique dans le théâtre de Racine* (Paris, 1962).

commentary than do various other forms of 'structuralist' interpretation favoured by some of their colleagues.[41] But such ex-
travagances merely illustrate the dangers inherent in the critical
standpoint of all the more doctrinaire adherents of the new movement, namely the excessive importance given to subjective reactions;
the building of impressive systems on the basis of an *a priori* concept,
supported by a very selective use of evidence from the text; and a
proneness to dogmatism. The critic becomes, in effect, a 'secondary
author', reinterpreting and virtually re-creating the original; taking
his stand on the complete subjectivity of all criticism, and the
consequent impossibility of arriving at any objective truth, he posits
the equal validity of all 'structures' or systems into which the work
can be made to fit. To quote Barthes again: 'On retrouve ici,
transposée à l'échelle du discours, la tâche de la linguistique récente,
qui est de décrire la *grammaticalité* des phrases, non leur signification.
De la même façon, on s'efforcera de décrire l'acceptabilité des
œuvres, non leur sens.'[42] As a recent reviewer has put it, for such a
critic 'the task is not to "explain" the supposed significant content
but to develop his own symbolism in a musical relationship of
harmony with the symbolic system of the original. The critic does
not judge content; he tests the coherence of symbolic systems.'

Perhaps the most serious divergence between the more traditional
form of literary criticism represented by *explication de texte* and the
practice of the more extreme among the 'nouveaux critiques' is the
latter's fragmentation of the critical process, the fact that they tend
to fasten on one aspect of literary creation at the expense of all
others. The features which attract their attention are the symbols
and metaphors which characterize an author's writing, the hidden
thematic links between his different works; and they show little, if
any, concern for such aspects as form, function, organization, or the
interrelation of parts to create a coherent whole.[43] It is precisely

[41] For instance, J.–P. Richard or J. Starobinski.

[42] Quoted by the author of the review article (from which the following quotation is
taken) on Barthes, *Critique et vérité*, Doubrovsky, *Pourquoi la nouvelle critique?*, etc.,
Times Literary Supplement, 23.vi.1966.

[43] Cf. this recent comment on the impact of 'la nouvelle critique' on Racinian studies:
'One basic necessity remains for the critic; that of putting forward a coherent and complete interpretation of a work. This is what the critical studies I have mentioned fail to
do. It is hardly surprising. Dismembering Racinian tragedy, they tend to focus on one
aspect while ignoring the others, and can therefore in no way account for that perfection
and relevance of structure which are the hallmark of any masterpiece . . .' (O. de
Mourgues, *Racine, or The Triumph of Relevance* (Cambridge, 1967), p. 166).

against such distortions of the critical perspective that the techniques of *explication* can, if properly applied, provide a safeguard:

> The thesis that explication is criticism, or is at least immediately and intimately related to criticism, proceeds quite reasonably from any theory of poetry which sees the poem as an organized whole— a wholeness of vision, that is, established through wholeness of diverse, but reconciled, parts. . . . The success of explication in persuading us of literary value is a kind of practical test of how well aesthetic theories of order and wholeness do apply to literary works. More specifically, a practical affinity between 'holism' and explication arises because organization and wholeness are matters of structure and hence also of implication. . . . It is not clear to me, indeed, that Dryden, in [writing] 'The last verse is not yet sufficiently explicated', had in mind more than the explication of the explicit. But the explicator will surely not conceive that he has employed his talent to the full unless he performs not only that service (as in glosses and other linguistic and historical observations) but also the explicitation of the implicit. For poetry is never altogether, or even mainly, 'poetry of statement'. The very difference between those two sides of the explicable, the explicit and the implicit, and the ways in which one may relate to the other are matters with which the explicator will be deeply engaged.[44]

To conclude: even if we agree with Wellek that a literary work has no meaningful objective existence in itself, and only comes to life in the consciousness of the reader, the way in which the critic chooses to bring it to life, and interpret it to others, is not a matter of indifference. There is an informed, and an uninformed, way to read a text; a careful, and a careless, way; a prejudiced, and an unprejudiced, way. A critic with a dominant *idée fixe*, which he imposes systematically on the text he is dealing with, and seeks to impart dogmatically to others, is a less useful critic than one who habitually tests his own subjective reactions against those of the representative reader, whose reading he tries to make better informed and more fully appreciative; one who does not pose as a creative writer, but is content with the role of interpreter.

*   *   *

44 W. K. Wimsatt, *Explication as Criticism* (New York, 1963), pp. 2–3.

It should be evident from the foregoing pages that while we believe wholeheartedly in the value of *explication de texte* as a critical method, the kind of *explication* we favour is something very different from the exercise advocated by the nineteenth-century pedagogues, and lampooned in our own day by Vinaver and others. *Explication* as we understand it is not only concerned with the rational analysis of the explicit 'meaning' of a text; it is just as much concerned—a good deal more, in the case of most texts—with total aesthetic response. The sort of approach we advocate has much in common with the 'practical criticism' of Richards and others, which laid the foundation for post-war Anglo-American 'new criticism'; and in our view, whatever method is chosen by the explicator, it must give a central place to the important developments that this century has seen in the field of stylistics.

Stylistics has been defined as 'the science of literary style';[45] but this is misleading, since style surely contains elements which are not susceptible of scientific study. More properly it may be called the application of the science of linguistics—that is, the objective, dispassionate recording and analysis of features of linguistic usage—to the study of literature. It is true that Bally, the father of modern stylistics,[46] deliberately excluded the literary language from the scope of his investigations, and for him stylistics was merely the study of 'les faits d'expression du langage organisé au point de vue de leur contenu affectif'. Thus defined, it was a science; and the work of certain of his followers, who merely proceeded to apply Bally's descriptive methods to the study of *literary* expression, again going no further than the cataloguing of linguistic features, could also be said to belong to linguistics rather than to literary study. However, once scholars were no longer content with descriptive analysis, but also took into account the aesthetic intentions of the author and the aesthetic effect on the reader—and this is what is meant by stylistics today—they were concerned with something too complex and too intangible to be analysed with scientific precision.

Between the wars, stylistics received a new impetus from the *Stilforschung* of German academics, an influence particularly associated with the name of Leo Spitzer.[47] In Spitzer's work, stylistics

---

[45] *Shorter Oxford Dictionary* (1964 ed.).

[46] See his *Traité de stylistique française*, 3rd edition (Geneva, 1951).

[47] Cf. in particular *Linguistics and Literary History: Essays in Stylistics* (Princeton, 1948); *Stilstudien* (Munich, 1928). For an assessment of the achievements and limitations of Spitzer's method see Wellek and Warren, op. cit., Chapter XIV, 'Style and Stylistics';

represents the marriage of scientific observation of significant detail with the intuitive insight of critical interpretation. What he himself called the 'philological circle' consists in using observed detail as the basis of an intuitive hypothesis about the meaning, or intention, or structure, of the whole work; that hypothesis is then tested by the exploration of further confirmatory detail, until by means of repeated reference backwards and forwards, between particular details and a general consideration of the whole, the critic arrives at an understanding of the 'genetic' principle underlying the work, the relationship between the author's creative imagination and the essential nature of the finished work of art. This critical process, as described by Spitzer, resembles the inductive method of the experimental sciences—though, given the nature of the subject-matter, the confirmation of the critic's hypotheses can never possess the status of scientific 'proof'. The fundamental difference in character between the science of linguistics and the study of literature is admirably expressed by Professor Hough:

> The linguist aims to describe the object of his investigation as fully and explicitly as possible, without any ambiguity or appeal to intuition. The literary student finds complete description superfluous or stultifying, often values the suggestive rather than the explicit, and is tolerant of diverse interpretations. For the linguist value resides in the completeness and exactitude of his descriptions; the actual material he works on may be a mere *corpus vile* used for experimental purposes. For the literary student value resides in the work of art under consideration; description and interpretation are ancillary and subservient to a kind of contemplative understanding that is essentially independent of these activities.[48]

To rely overmuch on the purely descriptive techniques proper to linguistics would be to subject *explication de texte* to a new kind of positivism, and this is a danger of which we should be well aware. But as Spitzer's own commentaries show, the precise and accurate perception of linguistic features provides the surest basis for the informed, penetrating comprehension that should be the object of all *explications*.

B. Gray, 'The Lesson of Leo Spitzer', in *Modern Language Review*, LXI (1966), pp. 547–55; and G. Hough, *Style and Stylistics* (London, 1969), pp. 59 ff.

[48] Op. cit., pp. 108–9.

B. *METHOD*

> 'On s'inquiète de ce que j'ai
> voulu *dire*, c'est ce que j'ai
> voulu *faire* qui importe.'
> VALÉRY

A FUNDAMENTAL evolution in the attitude of the explicator necessitates a thorough reappraisal of method. Rudler's method, as we have seen, has generally been found too rigid; and even that of Helmut Hatzfeld, of all our predecessors in the field of *explication* perhaps the one who has shown himself the most responsive to recent developments in stylistics,[49] may be criticized as being insufficiently flexible, with the result that his own illustrative commentaries tend to appear a shade mechanical.[50] We believe it is important to preserve the greatest possible flexibility of method: there is no one formula which can be applied automatically to passages of widely differing character.

First of all, it is necessary to distinguish between various types of exercise, all covered by the term *explication de texte*. To begin with, there is the prepared *explication* on a familiar text, undertaken with the aid of whatever reference works may be available; on the other hand, the exercise is frequently carried out unprepared, as an examination test, on a passage chosen from a prepared, or familiar, work; while another common form of examination test is the commentary on an unseen and completely unfamiliar passage. Whatever the value of the 'unseen' exercise as a test of a student's critical ability and method, the possibilities of this form of *explication* must inevitably be limited by the degree of a candidate's familiarity with the kind of writing represented by the text chosen, his acquaintance with the literature of the period concerned, and the extent of his knowledge of any relevant background. In particular, the kind of assignment favoured by some examiners, which invites candidates to ascribe a date (and sometimes even an author's name) to an unidentified passage, although it may test some of the attributes of the explicator, makes use of these for a sort of detective work based on inductive reasoning in order to arrive at an answer which (even if

---

[49] In his *Initiation à l'explication de textes français* (Munich, 1957). The Introduction to this (the second) edition was rewritten in order to take account of advances in 'les investigations stylistiques, sur lesquelles doit être basée l'explication de texte'.

[50] He recommends the following stages in the preparation of an *explication de texte*: (i) 'localisation du texte'; (ii) 'compréhension générale'; (iii) 'sources'; (iv) 'forme structurelle'; (v) 'analyse stylistique'; (vi) 'critique'.

correct) should always be one of the basic *données* of the genuine *explication*.

In any case, even if there is a place for such a test in the examining systems of our schools and universities, the best training in the critical techniques involved is surely the sustained practice of *explication de texte* as a prepared exercise. It is therefore with this form of *explication* that we are concerned, and our remarks about method are based on the assumption that the texts on which it will be practised will be texts currently being studied, or at any rate texts with which the student will be familiar; the commentary may then be either the individual work of a single student, or, as a very useful alternative to this, the joint product of a group studying the text together. For this reason—because we believe that a passage from a text currently being studied will give rise to the most effective and profitable analysis—we have not, unlike the authors of some other manuals on *explication*, accompanied our own specimen commentaries with a selection of texts suitable for analysis by students; in fact, it is our sincere belief that once the student has learned the techniques of *explication*, these can be practised with profit on virtually any literary text. The illustrative commentaries that we offer here are nearly all taken from works we have been familiar with, and worked on, for some considerable time; in all cases, their composition was preceded by the same sort of preparatory study that we here recommend.

The starting-point for this preparatory study should be the choice of an edition to work from. This need not be an elaborate critical edition, but it must be an edition which presents an accurate text. This cannot by any means always be taken for granted; and when one is dealing with a work that has been much reproduced by modern publishers, it is always worth comparing available texts as a check on reliability, so that one can start by being as nearly certain as possible that one is dealing with the chosen passage in the form in which the author wrote it and wished it to be read. Genuinely debated readings, such as Classical scholarship must necessarily contend with all the time, are rare in post-medieval works, for the obvious reason that they are normally the result of mistakes on the part of the copyist of a manuscript; however, there are important exceptions, notably cases in which a work was only published posthumously (e.g. Pascal's *Pensées*, Molière's *Dom Juan*, or Chénier's poems), and where, consequently, no edition has the authority of the author's approval. In such cases it is important to ascertain the authority for a given reading on the editor's part, and the explicator will no doubt consider whether it is necessary to discuss the merits of alternatives in the course of his commentary.

It goes without saying that the reading of the passage must not be casual, but careful and scholarly. That is to say, the student will make use of whatever reference works can assist him to an accurate reading of his text: the more he brings to it in this and every other way, the more he will get from it, and by 'reading' the text, in connection with the preparation of an *explication*, we mean reading, meditating, and re-reading it; if it is possible to read it, sleep on it, and re-read it the next day, so much the better. This process should include, wherever possible, reading aloud: essential in the case of dramatic texts, and with all poetry, this is also highly desirable in the case of any prose passage of an oratorical or rhetorical nature. Where a recording of the work is available, it too can be of great help to the reader, and any assistance of this sort should be welcomed.

Throughout this first reading, or series of readings, the explicator should have certain objectives in mind. First, the initial reading will help him to arrive at a provisional formulation of the central theme of the piece: an approximation which may be modified in the course of subsequent investigation, and which will not necessarily appear in this form in the final commentary, but which provides him with a working hypothesis. Similarly, he will be able to frame a first approximation to the definition of the structure of the passage—again, subject to modification as a result of more detailed analysis. Assuming that he is already familiar with the context of the passage, he will be on the look-out for ways in which the latter fits into the larger unit of the whole work: echoes, explicit references, implicit allusions; this is necessary not only in the more obvious sense of 'context' in the case of a dramatic or narrative work, but also with regard to the links which relate a poem, for instance, to the *recueil* from which it is taken, and, beyond this, to the author's whole *œuvre*, to his 'univers imaginaire'. The preparatory reading will also be the occasion for noting what research is necessary for a complete comprehension of the text: the elucidation of any references it contains; the investigation of sources; the following-up of any thematic links in the author's own work, and a comparison with relevant parallels in other authors. At this point, too, any variant readings should be considered: not only the kind already referred to, but also manuscript readings of earlier drafts of the text which may have been rejected by the author before publication; or (where the text chosen represents the original edition of the work concerned) any emendations contained in subsequent editions.

It is these four elements (outline of theme; outline of structure; relation between the passage itself and the work to which it belongs; and, more generally, relation to the world outside) which, when one comes to write the commentary, will go together to form the introduction to the detailed analysis that constitutes the heart of the *explication*. They are interrelated, and need not be treated formally under separate heads; it is not possible to prescribe any order of priorities or of importance, for these will vary from one text to another. The assembling of this introductory material does, however, present a particular problem in the case of any passage taken from a longer work. Even if it is legitimate to assume that the reader to whom the commentary is addressed will either himself already be familiar with the work in question, or can take steps to make himself acquainted with it, there remains a difficult decision to take with regard to theme, for instance: how much should be included of what could more properly be called general comment on the work as a whole rather than specific comment on the passage under consideration? This calls for a nice exercise of judgement; and there is a sense in which a complete *explication de texte* is possible only in the case of a text which itself forms a complete unit. It is certain that a self-contained sonnet or similar short poem is much the most satisfactory subject for an *explication*, since problems of context and cross-reference do not arise in the same way.

We now come to the detailed analysis which constitutes the main body of the commentary. This should proceed, via a division into the more obvious sections (the stanza, the paragraph), towards a breakdown into the appropriate component units: metrical in the case of a verse text—the line, the hemistich—and syntactical in the case of prose. As one considers the interrelation between these component parts, it can be seen how on the one hand the author has developed his argument, message, or theme, while on the other hand creating the formal structure of the passage. Once again, let us stress that the two things go hand in hand, and that the formal analysis can seldom be satisfactorily separated from the analysis of theme or argument. If we say that a passage is 'dialectical' in character, for instance, we are saying something about the way in which the ideas are developed, by the contrasting of opposed statements, and at the same time, inevitably, something about the formal structure of the piece; if we describe an author's manner as 'expository', meaning that it proceeds by elucidation and amplification of an initial statement, then again this has implications for the structure of the passage concerned as well as characterizing the presentation of the argument or theme.

Next, within these metrical or grammatical units, the line or the sentence, we must be ready to carry out a further breakdown, to analyse the composition of, and relationship between, phrases, and to take a close look at individual words. Our purpose will be to analyse first the selection, and then the arrangement, of the author's 'raw material': to try to appreciate the sort of choice that he has made from the linguistic resources at his disposal, and the creative use he has made of this material. The first and most elementary consideration is meaning; we shall naturally be on the look-out for any lexical changes that may have occurred between the time at which the text was written and our own day, so as to establish 'period usage' with regard to a given word or phrase (e.g. changes since the seventeenth century with regard to *admirer*, *honnête*, *vertu*), and within the general context of period usage we must be ready to register any cases in which our author's personal vocabulary marks an idiosyncratic departure from the norm (e.g. a word like *généreux* in the case of Corneille, or *ennui* in the case of Baudelaire). Similarly, we should note any words used with particular frequency, either in the passage under discussion or in the author's writings generally: in extreme cases it is even possible to talk of a genuine obsession,[51] but any predilection of this sort may be significant.[52] Archaisms, neologisms, technical terms, foreign words or phrases, popular speech, dialectal forms, will all be noted; and it should nearly always be possible to suggest the reason for the choice of such terms. More generally, we should observe the overall character of the vocabulary of the passage, and any contrasts in this respect between different sections: whether it is predominantly concrete or abstract;

[51] Though one should beware of the excesses committed by certain kinds of critic in their zealous search for this sort of 'obsession'.

[52] See, for instance, Spitzer's analysis of the use of *à cause de* and other causal prepositions and conjunctions by the novelist Charles-Louis Philippe (*Linguistics and Literary History*, pp. 11 ff.).

the 'particularity' or 'generality' that it reveals; the extent to which it may convey colour, or movement of any sort; any instances of onomatopoeia, or other cases in which a word has obviously been chosen because the sound matches the sense. Finally, we should note the degree of literalness of the vocabulary: the extent to which the author may have selected words for their figurative, rather than their literal, meaning; and in those cases in which he has committed himself to figures of rhetoric such as personification, or metonymy, or more generally to metaphor rather than to direct statement, the degree of clarity or ambiguity of the figure chosen should be assessed.[53]

This review of the vocabulary of the passage should not be a mere record of archaisms, metaphors, etc., but should help us to look beyond the text itself to the creative process, and enable us to see why the author has introduced these particular features. When we have identified the overall character or tone of the vocabulary, we should be in a position to attempt a provisional definition of the function of the passage: to say whether it is descriptive, narrative, lyric, heroic, comic, satiric, etc.—remembering that such a definition does not by any means always conform to the obvious *formal* characteristics associated with a given genre (e.g. a dramatic work may obviously contain a passage whose function is narrative, or whose tone is lyrical; an epic poem may contain passages satirical in tone and function, etc.).

It would be misleading to suggest that 'selection' of vocabulary by an author is likely to be a static process, carried out as an isolated part of the activity of writing; it is, of course, normally accompanied by a simultaneous consideration on the author's part of the way in which the words are to be arranged. However, it is helpful for the purposes of critical analysis to distinguish between the inert properties that a word possesses on its own (its lexical meaning, its semantic associations, its tone) and the qualities that it acquires

---

[53] One does not have to be a committed partisan of *la nouvelle critique* in order to recognize that each reader's reaction to an author's imagery is largely coloured by his own subjective experience; to quote Philip Toynbee:

By the time a man has acquired his maximum power over language, there is hardly a word left which hasn't acquired a whole complex of transparent meanings which are inextricably bound to its literal sense. . . Every word is a private possession of each speaker, as well as a means of communication: a great writer can somehow make others half-hear these private reverberations of his; and the 'effect' of a word is that of two echo-systems meeting and reverberating together (Review of G. Wagner, *The Wisdom of Words* in *The Observer*, 1.vi.1969).

through its dynamic association with other words—even if this distinction is not necessarily always formally adhered to when we come to write our *explication*.[54]

When we turn to the way in which our author has disposed the various elements of his vocabulary, the main lines of the construction of the passage—length of paragraph, of sentence; arrangement of clauses within the sentence—should offer an immediate clue to the author's intention in writing it. The desire to persuade will be indicated by the adoption of an orator's carefully constructed periods, while a less controlled lyrical *élan* will suggest enthusiasm, and the desire to rouse or uplift the reader; a well-articulated style, with much subordination, will reflect the desire to convince the reader by logically satisfying argument, while a disjointed, staccato style will convey emotional stress and an appeal to the reader's sympathy. These first impressions may be modified, or diversified, as we examine in detail syntactical features such as the prominence given to noun, verb, or adjective by the use of particular types of construction; or examples of apostrophe, ejaculation, or the rhetorical question, which may all suggest an appeal to the sensibility of the reader rather than to his intellect. If the writer brings himself and his opinions into the passage, it will be instructive to note how this is done; the choice of pronoun: *je, nous*, or *on*, can be very revealing, as regards both an author's attitude to his subject and his relationship with his reader. With regard to word-order, we shall note cases where a special emphasis is given to a word or phrase by a departure from normal usage, and in particular any instances of the use of adjectives in the affective, instead of the logical, position.

In the case of a verse passage, we shall have the metrical pattern, rhyme-scheme, etc., to guide our detailed analysis of the structure, and in many ways this makes stylistic analysis of verse easier than is the case with prose, where no such guide-lines exist, and the explicator has to create his own. Here, more than anywhere, pure descriptive cataloguing (of formal characteristics such as *rime riche*, *enjambement*, or *vers ternaires*) as a self-contained exercise should be avoided: such features are only of interest if they can be related to the author's presumed intention, or to their effect on the reader. In the case both of syntax and of versification (and the same is true

---

[54] 'Once the architecture of the work of art has been laid bare, the scaffolding, which the critic had to erect provisionally for this purpose, can be scrapped. Stylistics, as I conceive it, is an exclusively auxiliary science' (Spitzer, op. cit., p. 218).

of prose rhythm too), while the alert reader should be able to analyse and take stock of all details, it is not necessary to record in detail everything so noted: the scansion of a line, like the parsing of a sentence, is the essential starting-point, but only such features as seem to make a telling contribution to the total effect need be recorded in the finished commentary. As with syntactical structure, so too the verse-structure can provide a clear guide to the poet's purpose; and it is perhaps the relationship between the sentence, or grammatical unit, on the one hand and the metrical unit of the line on the other that provides the most fruitful area of investigation. (For instance, if we take Corneille at his most dialectical, the very high degree of coincidence that is to be observed between the grammatical and the metrical units forms an obvious contrast with Racine's remarkable flexibility in this respect, which naturally suggests a much greater range of poetic effect.)

The analysis of prose rhythms is certainly a more tricky business: not only are these almost entirely governed by the syntactical divisions of the sentence, so that it is often not possible to speak of any 'rhythm' other than that provided by the punctuation (whereas verse offers a second kind of articulation of its own, which can, as we have seen, be quite independent of the sentence-structure), but even when a long sentence or clause needs breaking up into the breath-groups which may be considered the rough equivalents of the Alexandrine line or hemistich, there is not always agreement among readers as to where these 'natural' divisions occur. However, it is quite indisputable that, in some cases, the deliberate arrangement of phrases in a prose passage—ternary grouping, for instance, with 'ascending' or 'falling' cadence—can be just as effective, in the reinforcement it brings to the expressivity of the linguistic elements concerned, as the corresponding features of a passage of verse.[55]

-More strictly rhetorical arrangement of words and phrases—balance, antithesis, anaphora or repetition, and similar features—is easier to deal with. Too often, however, one is presented in a commentary with a mechanical record, without interpretative comment—whereas the perceptive critic should ask: what effect was the author trying to achieve by this example of chiasmus, or by that

[55] There have been a number of perceptive studies of this aspect of stylistics recently, to which the student will find it helpful to refer. See Bibliography, entries under Cherel, Deloffre, Krafft, Sayce.

oxymoron? and measure the intention against the effect produced on himself as a reader.

It is when we turn from the more straightforward formal patterns and relationships so far dealt with to the consideration of purely phonetic phenomena, as adjuncts to the logical meaning or (more frequently) to the affective force of a passage, that we are faced with the most difficult part of our stylistic analysis. 'La phonostylistique', or the study of the relationship between sound and sense, is an extremely delicate and controversial topic—and one, moreover, which seems to exercise a fatal fascination for the novice. Genuine onomatopoeia is easy enough to recognize (though it is not nearly so common as some readers seem to think); and similarly the 'harmonie imitative' of a line like Racine's 'Pour qui sont ces serpents qui sifflent sur vos têtes?' is hardly to be disputed—though in this case only the one word *siffler* is properly speaking onomatopoeic. However, when we turn from such obviously imitative alliteration to the analysis of vowel-sounds, and of the combination of vowels and consonants, the task ceases to be such an easy one; to take another well-known example from Racine, while most readers would no doubt agree that the fourfold repetition of the vowel (i) in the line 'Tout m'afflige et me nuit et conspire à me nuire' makes a significant contribution to the total effect of the line as an expression of Phèdre's anguish, the precise means by which this effect is produced is not at all easy to determine. Indeed, this is an area in which scientific precision is impossible: clearly, a great deal depends on subjective reactions on the part of the reader, and any critical observations that are made must be put forward tentatively, as being no more than speculations based on subjective response.

There have, of course, been theorists who have gone a good deal further than this, and who have seen fit to draw up a systematic classification, identifying a given sound or combination of sounds with a fixed range of emotional responses. The notion has a long and reputable ancestry—it can be taken back, indeed, to the discussion of the origin of language in Plato's *Cratylus*—but its development in connection with modern stylistics is particularly associated, in the field of French studies at any rate, with the name of Maurice Grammont, whose classification of vowels into 'aiguës', 'claires', 'éclatantes', 'sombres', and 'nasales', and of consonants into 'momentanées' and 'continues', is followed by a schematic exposition of the expressive capacity associated with each group. It is true that

Grammont concedes that 'les phonèmes ne deviennent expressifs que si l'idée qu'ils recouvrent s'y prête'[56]—but when he proceeds to criticize writers for their inappropriate use of certain vowels (as in the case of Hugo's line 'Un enfant sans couleur, sans regard et sans voix', of which he says: 'Ce vers bourré d'éclatantes, pour peindre un être frêle et débile, fait contresens',[57] this betrays the arbitrary and *a priori* nature of any such classification.[58]

The subject has been approached with scholarly caution and admirable good sense by Paul Delbouille in his *Poésie et sonorités*. In this substantial and well-documented study of modern theories and their practical application M. Delbouille insists on the subjectivity of all 'systems' based on the notion that expressivity of this sort is inherent in sounds themselves; and prudently concludes that 'l'analyse des effets sonores, là où ils existent, n'est ni impossible ni interdite dès l'instant où l'on sait s'astreindre à ne la mener qu'en fonction du sens'.[59] A similar point of view is developed by J.-G. Cahen:

> Il convient de noter que les sons ne portent pas en eux le pouvoir d'évoquer nécessairement certaines images. Considérés comme sons, et non comme mots, ils ne sont pas les signes obligatoires de certaines idées ou de certains sentiments. Mais quand ils sont rapprochés d'une manière qui flatte l'oreille, l'esprit se trouve comme invité, par l'intermédiaire des sons, à éprouver plus vivement l'émotion poétique.
>
> Par exemple, il serait absurde de prétendre que la voyelle *i* suivie de -*ss* évoque une idée de violence et de rapt; mais dans les vers d'*Iphigénie*:
>
> > ...Et jamais dans Larisse un lâche ravisseur
> > Me vint-il enlever ma jeunesse et ma sœur?
>
> l'harmonieuse répétition du son -*iss* produit à l'oreille une impression agréable qui, aussitôt, met l'esprit lui-même, grâce à

---

[56] *Le Vers français* (Paris, 1947 edn.), p. 241.

[57] Ibid., p. 253.

[58] More recent critics who have adopted a point of view similar to Grammont's include G. Michaud (see *L'Œuvre et ses techniques* (Paris, 1957)) and H. Morier (see *La Psychologie des styles* (Geneva, 1959) and *Dictionnaire de poétique et de rhétorique* (Paris, 1961)).

[59] *Poésie et sonorités* (Paris, 1961), p. 221. See also pp. 214 ff., in which three analytical commentaries on the same poem (Verlaine, 'Il pleut dans mon cœur...') by Grammont, Michaud, and Delbouille himself are compared.

la brève euphorie dans laquelle il se trouve plongé, en un état particulièrement propice à la réceptivité poétique.

Cette explication est celle qui convient dans la plupart des cas. Elle est moins séduisante peut-être que celle qui confère à chaque son une valeur particulière et définie, mais elle est plus conforme à la vérité... Les sons ne jouissent d'un pouvoir de suggestion que dans la mesure où les mots qui les contiennent ont été préalablement interprétés comme signes.[60]

Let the student by all means not neglect the investigation of 'l'harmonie expressive' as a factor which may have contributed to the affective force of the text he is studying. But it is essential that such considerations should rest on the firm basis of a precise and accurate knowledge of phonetics; that any conclusions arrived at should be determined by the reader's own empirical response to the text, not by the mechanical application, on an *a priori* basis, of someone else's systematic classification; and that the student should always bear in mind that he is concerned not with sounds in the raw, but with meaningful words. To quote Delbouille again:

Le lecteur, quoi qu'on fasse, lit des mots constitués en phrases, non des suites de lettres ou de sons; ce que le critique doit faire, n'est-ce pas précisément essayer d'expliquer le texte en tenant compte du mécanisme de cette lecture?[61]

Finally, it is important that, in the course of this detailed stylistic analysis, the explicator should not develop a myopic disregard for the shape and character of the whole, and be unable to 'see the wood for the trees'. The careful study of detail can provide essential clues for the understanding and appreciation of the whole, but by the same token, it is only by reference to the place they occupy in the larger unit of the whole text that the details can be accurately interpreted; the constant reference backwards and forwards of which Spitzer speaks is the only safeguard against arbitrary misinterpretation. For this reason, again, the ideal text for the purposes of *explication* is one which is as nearly as possible complete and self-contained; and any passage chosen must be full enough to provide a satisfactory 'whole' to which the parts can be related in this way. For it is from our

[60]*Le Vocabulaire de Racine* (Paris, 1946), p. 233. See also I. A. Richards, *Practical Criticism* (London, 1964 edn.), pp. 227–34.

[61] Op cit., p. 174.

'two-way' apprehension of the relationship between the parts and the whole that the qualities of coherence, consistency, and clarity on the one hand, and variety, ambiguity, and suggestiveness on the other, may be said to emerge—qualities which, for all their elusiveness and resistance to clear-cut objective definition, are of vital importance to the aesthetic appreciation of a work of art.

Once the stylistic analysis is completed, and once these subtle relationships between the parts and the whole have been explored, it only remains to conclude. We are now in a position to confirm or modify our provisional assessment of the mood, tone, or feeling of the piece, our estimate of the author's purpose in writing it and of the effect with which this has been carried out. There are those who would eschew all value-judgements in the name of scientific detachment; but the object of reading is the appreciation and enjoyment of literature, and the object of *explication de texte* is to provide the soundest possible basis for our appreciation and enjoyment. So there is certainly room for—indeed, it would be wrong to omit—an informed critical assessment of the piece as a whole: if the author has succeeded in moving us, or rousing us, or appealing to our sense of humour, our appreciation of his art will not be lessened because we have tried to understand how it is done.

This may appear to carry the implication, with regard to the selection of texts for critical commentaries, that only passages of distinct literary merit should be regarded as suitable. If the object is to produce well-informed appreciation based on meticulous reading, this will obviously be the more rewarding, the more outstanding is the quality of the passage chosen; and it may well be thought that the application of this critical technique to a work of mediocre quality is hardly worth while. However, even if the final judgement on a certain passage may be unfavourable, it seems better that such a judgement should be arrived at on the basis of the same thorough, careful reading that one would give to a passage of outstanding merit. And in any case, to regard *explication de texte* purely as a means of studying examples of great literature is surely to run the risk of losing sight of the real purpose of this exercise. For, as we understand it, the end-product is not merely to have written a formal study of a work of art whose intrinsic merit may have made the effort worth while: much more important is it that, as a result of the training in method inculcated by the practice of *explication*, one's reading of any text will henceforward be enriched, since the process of reading will have become more accurate and more perceptive.[62]

It is true that some distinguished examples of *explication* have taken their place as major contributions to literary criticism, and possess permanent value as part of the essential critical literature of the subject: one thinks of Gustave Cohen on Valéry's 'Cimetière marin',[63] or Spitzer on the 'récit de Théramène' from *Phèdre*;[64] while, in a rather more specialized field, the exegeses of various Mallarmé scholars have won a significant place in the critical writing devoted to that author. But the great majority of published *explications de texte* are interesting and instructive primarily as examples of method, and do not pretend to be definitive contributions to the critical literature on the author with whom they are concerned. The best *explications* offer a valuable insight into the way in which the critic's mind works, and in this respect they might be said to be like the writing-up of a scientific experiment. This analogy cannot be taken too far, however, for the intuitive element in literary criticism is just as important as the rationalistic, and, in a sense, the 'experiment' only holds good for the particular reader who has conducted it. So that while it is possible to speak of a 'definitive' biography or a 'definitive' critical edition of a text, the notion of a definitive *explication de texte* is quite inconceivable, for this kind of critical activity makes use of the tools of objective scholarship to fashion a product whose distinguishing feature must in the final analysis be its subjective character. What Rudler writes about the relationship between the objective techniques of positivist scholarship and 'la critique':

Ces techniques, si pénétrées qu'elles soient d'esprit critique, ne sont pas exactement la critique. Elles lui préparent les voies, lui déblaient le terrain, l'aiguisent, l'assurent, mais elles ne dispensent pas du corps-à-corps avec la pensée et la forme des œuvres, dont l'intelligence et l'appréciation constituent proprement la critique. Les qualités qui y sont nécessaires, tout en pouvant se développer jusqu'à un certain point par un entraînement méthodique, ne se réduisent guère en corps de méthode;

---

[62] Cf. F. R. Leavis's definition: 'Analysis . . . is the process by which we seek to attain a complete reading of a poem—a reading that approaches as nearly as possible to the perfect reading' (quoted by D. H. Rawlinson, *The Practice of Criticism* (Cambridge, 1968), p. 3).

[63] In the *Nouvelle Revue Française*, 1.ii.1929.

[64] In *Linguistics and Literary History*, pp. 87–134.

elles sont un don de nature, et relèvent de la formation générale de l'esprit[65]

can be applied very aptly to the relationship between the objective and subjective elements in *explication de texte*.

To conclude: *explication de texte* is not something which eliminates the need for other, more traditional critical approaches to literature. Rather, it assimilates them; and the student must be prepared to call on his knowledge of all the related branches of his subject, linguistic as well as literary. Those of us who teach a modern language at sixth-form or university level are well aware of the latent tension that exists between the two halves of our discipline, 'language' and 'literature'. Traditionally, these two branches have been taught as distinct and separate elements: all too often, they are rivals competing for time-table space and for priority in matters of syllabus and examinations. Not the least recommendation in favour of the exercise of *explication de texte* as we have defined it, based squarely on stylistic analysis—the study of the way in which linguistic phenomena combine to produce literary effect—is that it seems to us to provide an excellent means of reconciling two branches of study which have too long been separated, of bridging the gap between them, and of doing away with divisive tensions.[66]

[65] *Les Techniques de la critique* (Oxford, 1923), p. 204.
[66] Cf. this similar conclusion by Professor Hough: 'It is not likely that the stylistic study of literature will ever become a science, but there is no need for it to be a riot of subjective fancy. Professional linguists are apt to say that their science has literary bearings to which students of literature pay insufficient attention. I think it is obvious that *most* of what the science of linguistics now does cannot be usefully related to literature at all; but there are bridges to be built, and it is in the area of stylistics that the opportunities for doing this are greatest' (op. cit., p. 19).

1 Rabelais

Je diray plus. Icelle herbe moyenante, les substances invisibles visiblement sont arrestées, prinses, detenues et comme en prison mises; à leur prinse et arrest sont les grosses et pesantes moles tournées agillement à insigne profict de la vie humaine. Et m'esbahys comment l'invention de tel usaige a esté par tant de siecles celé aux antiques Philosophes, veue l'utilité impreciable qui en provient, veu le labeur intolerable que sans elle ilz supportoient en leurs pistrines.

Icelle moyenant, par la retention des flotz aërez sont les grosses orchades, les amples thalameges, les fors guallions, les naufz chiliandres et myriandres de leurs stations enlevées et poussées à l'arbitre de leurs gouverneurs.

Icelle moyenant, sont les nations que Nature sembloit tenir absconses, impermeables et incongneues à nous venues, nous à elles: chose que ne feroient les oyseaulx, quelque legiereté de pennaige qu'ilz ayent et quelque liberté de nager en l'aër que leurs soit baillée par Nature. Taprobrana a veu Lappia; Java a veu les mons Riphées; Phebol voyra Theleme; les Islandoys et Engronelands boyront Euphrates; par elle Boreas a veu le manoir de Auster, Eurus a visité Zephire. De mode que les Intelligences celestes, les Dieux, tant marins que terrestres, en ont esté tous effrayez, voyans par l'usaige de cestuy benedict Pantagruelion les peuples Arcticques en plein aspect des Antarctiques franchir la mer Athlanticque, passer les deux Tropicques, volter sous la Zone torride, mesurer tout le Zodiacque, s'esbatre soubs l'Æquinoctial, avoir l'un et l'autre Pole en veue à fleur de leur orizon.

Les Dieux Olympicques ont en pareil effroy dict: 'Pantagruel nous a mis en pensement nouveau et tedieux, plus que oncques ne feirent les Aloïdes, par l'usaige et vertus de son herbe. Il sera de brief marié, de sa femme aura enfans. A ceste destinée ne povons nous contrevenir, car elle est passée par les mains et fuseaulx des sœurs

fatales, filles de Necessité. Par ses enfans (peut estre) sera inventée
herbe de semblable energie, moyenant laquelle pourront les humains
visiter les sources des gresles, les bondes des pluyes et l'officine des
35 fouldres, pourront envahir les regions de la Lune, entrer le teritoire
des signes celestes et là prendre logis, les uns à l'Aigle d'or, les
aultres au Mouton, les aultres à la Couronne, les aultres à la Herpe,
les aultres au Lion d'argent, s'asseoir à table avecques nous, et nos
déesses prendre à femmes, qui sont les seulx moyens d'estre deifiez.
40 En fin ont mis le remede de y obvier en deliberation et au conseil.

RABELAIS, *Le Tiers Livre*
Date of first publication: 1546
Ed. M. A. Screech (Geneva: Droz,
1964), pp. 344–7

THE closing chapters of Rabelais's *Tiers Livre* are devoted to preparations for a voyage which Pantagruel, Panurge, and their party are
about to undertake. The linking motif of the Third Book has been
provided by Panurge's attempts to obtain advice on the question
whether he should marry; having consulted theological, legal,
medical, and philosophical opinion—in chapters which allow
Rabelais full scope for his satire on prevailing intellectual fashions—
he finally approaches the court jester Triboulet, and as a result of
his interpretation of the latter's enigmatic pronouncement, resolves
to set off on a voyage in order to consult the Oracle of La Dive
Bouteille. Chapter XLIX begins to recount the preparations for the
voyage, but after a brief introductory passage, a quite disproportionate amount of space—the remainder of this chapter and the
three which follow—is devoted to the description of the herb
'pantagruelion', of which the strange cargo seems largely to consist:

> Nauchiers, pilotz, hespaliers, truschemens, artisans, gens de
> guerre, vivres, artillerie, munitions, robbes, deniers et aultres
> hardes print et chargea, comme estoit besoing pour long et
> hasardeux voyage. Entre aultres choses, je veids qu'il feist charger
> grande foison de son herbe Pantagruelion, tant verde et crude que
> conficte et præparée.

'Pantagruelion', although the treatment accorded to it is highly
imaginative, is not by any means a wholly imaginary substance. The

initial description of its physical appearance and natural properties makes it clear that what Rabelais had in mind corresponds closely to the plant usually known by the name of hemp (*cannabis*); indeed, a large part of this material is modelled on a similar account in Book XIX of the *Natural History* of Pliny the Elder. In this extensive passage Pliny, like many Renaissance writers who followed him, treats of hemp and flax as a single plant: a plant endowed with so many remarkable properties that its description constitutes a real *tour de force*, and presents a challenge to any writer like Rabelais, who had a voracious appetite for miscellaneous erudition of all sorts. Thus, after a long excursus on the naming of plants in general, with digressions into other botanical fields, the plant pantagruelion is enthusiastically praised in Chapter LI for its varied and important medicinal uses; for the range of services which products derived from it—ropes, cords, sailcloth, canvas, and other cloths—perform in various aspects of human life; and in Chapter LII (again following an error of Pliny's) for its marvellous scientific properties in the shape of asbestos.

Rabelais's whole treatment of this subject remains somewhat enigmatic. Whereas Pliny, as a natural historian, had written a factual account of flax/hemp, as part of an encyclopedic scientific treatise, Rabelais has chosen to incorporate the passage into a framework of narrative fiction, and to disguise the identity of the plant by inventing a name for it which links it with his principal hero. The name is justified, the author tells us, because Pantagruel was the inventor of some of its uses, and also 'par ses vertus et singularitez':

> Comme Pantagruel a esté l'Idée et exemplaire de toute joyeuse perfection... aussi en Pantagruelion je recongnoys tant de vertus, tant d'energie, tant de perfection, tant d'effectz admirables, que, si elle eust esté en ses qualitez congneue lors que les arbres... feirent election d'un Roy de boys pour les regir et dominer, elle sans doubte eust emporté la pluralité des voix et suffrages.

Since Pantagruel has been gradually presented as the embodiment of that ideal philosophy of life which Rabelais himself terms 'pantagruélisme', it would seem that we are hereby invited to identify his allegorical plant with the same concept, and this is indeed one key to the enigma that has frequently been proposed. Another interpretation is stressed by the most recent editor of

Le Tiers Livre, for whom these closing chapters devoted to the allegory are above all the culmination of the dominant theme of the volume, which is a satirical attack on certain kinds of empty rhetoric:

> La rhétorique peut être un moyen de faire passer l'erreur pour la vérité... L'épisode du pantagruélion est un exercice de rhétorique, destinée à montrer combien il est facile de faire du diable un ange... Cachez le nom de cette humble plante, dit Rabelais, et vous verrez comment la rhétorique vous fera croire qu'il s'agit de quelque chose de miraculeux.[1]

This emphasis is useful in putting the 'éloge du pantagruélion' as a whole into the right perspective; but it will be seen that it is of much less relevance in connection with the passage under consideration than with the rest of the episode.

The paragraphs selected for commentary form the conclusion to Chapter LI. Although Pliny forms the *point de départ*, Rabelais here shows most fully the originality of his reinterpretation of his source. Not only are the geographical references brought up to date to take account of the recent expansion of world horizons, but also the tone of Pliny's paragraph, pessimistic and cautious:

> No curse is too strong to pronounce on that early inventor who, not content to see man end his days on dry land, enabled him to perish, without a burial-place, at sea . . .

gives way to a confident and enthusiastic tribute to man's achievements in the field of exploration and travel. Professor Screech comments:

> (Pline) va jusqu'à faire du chanvre le symbole de l'extrême ingéniosité de l'homme. Rabelais, lui, trouve plaisant de développer cette idée, abstraction faite du pessimisme de Pline[2]

—but this hardly does justice to the tone of the particular passage we are concerned with, in which Rabelais is no longer content merely to produce an imaginative *tour de force*. In this passage, at least, the 'symbole de l'extrême ingéniosité de l'homme' deserves to be taken seriously, for the author seems to have been so carried away by his enthusiasm for his subject that it is no longer erudition for its

---

[1] *Le Tiers Livre*, ed. M. A. Screech, p. xxii.
[2] Ibid., p. xxiii.

own sake, or a satirical purpose, which provides the keynote, but a genuine idealism and crusading zeal.

The previous paragraph has listed a variety of uses of hemp: sacks, ropes, clothes of all sorts, shrouds. Up to this point, if somewhat long-winded and laborious, Rabelais's treatment of the herb pantagruelion has at least been realistic, and there has been little that would suggest a purpose other than the exhaustive cataloguing of the properties of an actual botanical species. The beginning of our passage (para. 1) may be regarded as transitional in subject-matter: hemp, as canvas, enables man to harness the winds, by providing sails for windmills. From this point onwards we pass to the subject which inspires the remainder of the passage: the use of canvas in sailing-ships is another means of harnessing the winds (para. 2); thus travel and exploration have become possible on a scale hitherto unknown (para. 3), so that the gods, alarmed at this challenge from man, consult as to how to meet it (paras. 4 and 5). The first paragraph is 'original', in the sense that Rabelais adds windmills to the list of illustrations derived from Pliny—for the good reason that windmills were unknown to the Ancients; but the rest of the passage reveals a much more fundamental kind of originality, in spite of textual reminiscences of the Latin model. For in para. 4 (and even in the middle of para. 3, since the theme is adumbrated in ll. 20–2), the recital of man's achievements in the field of geographical expansion gives way to an assessment of man's potential as an explorer and inventor, and to a prophetic forecast of future achievements (*sera inventée... pourront les humains...*, *pourront envahir...*). Not only is Pliny's pessimism rejected, but also Rabelais's passage takes on the optimistic fervour of a humanist's statement of faith in human progress.

To turn to a systematic analysis: the first paragraph contains various features characteristic of Rabelais's style:[3] the juxtaposition

---

[3] Any 16th-C. text naturally presents linguistic difficulties not found in texts of a later period. We shall assume access to an edition containing a glossary, or preferably to a specialist dictionary of 16th-C. French. As regards morphology, we shall not comment on normal archaic forms such as *icelle* (l. 1) or *voyra* (l. 18); nor, where syntax is concerned, on features which, though different from modern usage (e.g. omission of pronoun subject in *m'esbahys* (l. 4), agreement of *voyans* (l. 21)), represent the normal usage of Rabelais's own time. *Icelle herbe moyenante* (l. 1) does, however, require comment: this would appear to be, not a participial construction with the verb *moyenner*, but an example of the participle used, quite normally, as a preposition (= 'moyennant cette herbe'; cf. ll. 9, 13), though with the feminine form used irregularly instead of the masculine.

of *invisibles* and *visiblement*, opposed in a construction not unlike that of chiasmus, and forming a strong contrast, similar to that obtained by oxymoron; the enumeration of virtual synonyms in *arrestées, prinses, detenues et comme en prison mises*, which is saved from being pointlessly repetitious by the pleasing contrast between the three abstract terms and the strikingly concrete *en prison mises*; and the rather elliptical latinized construction of *à leur prinse et arrest* (= 'by apprehending and arresting them'). This latter phrase takes up the participles *arrestées, prinses*, lending a shape and co-herence to the whole sentence. *Impreciable* is an example of a sixteenth-century neologism, typical of the heavy borrowing from Latin sources to enrich the capacity of the language for abstract expression; and *pistrines*, formed from the Latin term *pistrinum* ('mill'), is presumably preferred to *moulins* as a slightly pedantic touch of local colour—possibly, too, because the Latin term had a secondary meaning of 'drudgery', so that the knowledgeable reader might recognize an echo of the *labeur intolerable* of the previous line. In the sentence beginning *à leur prinse et arrest*, the force of the particular statement which serves as an illustration of the general-ized abstraction that precedes it is enhanced by the rhythm of the words: the group containing long vowels (*grosses et pesantes moles : mole* = mod. Fr. 'meule') gives way to a group whose quicker rhythm again matches the sense (*tournées agillement*), while in the remainder of the sentence (*à insigne profict de la vie humaine*) the quick tempo of the phrase again reinforces the idea of bustling activity.

The next paragraph is more explicit: whereas it is left to the reader to identify the *substances invisibles* (the winds) in line 1, and the whole of the first paragraph is similarly allusive, Rabelais now clearly refers to the *flotz aërez* whose 'capture', by a comparable process, facilitates the mariner's task; though it will be noted that this phrase still avoids the direct and prosaic 'vent', and that *la retention des flotz aërez* is an instance of poetic suggestion rather than straightforward statement. This sentence offers another example of Rabelais's characteristic enumeration, again far from lifeless: even though pedantic erudition may have played its part in the choice of the terms *orchades, thalameges, chiliandres* and *myrian-dres*, these seem, to a modern reader at any rate, to possess a most pleasing lyrical quality, due partly to their exotic flavour, which fits in so well with the theme of geographical exploration, and partly to the felicitous rhyme of *chiliandres* and *myriandres*. We may guess that the words possessed something of the same remote and esoteric charm for Rabelais's contemporaries as well, for all four are neologisms of his own coining from the Greek (*orchade* = 'transport vessel'; *thalamege* = 'Egyptian gondola fitted out with suites of rooms'; *chiliandre* = 'carrying a thousand men'; *myriandre* = 'carrying ten thousand men'). Even with *nauf* he avoids the ordinary term 'nef', and adopts the much rarer form based on the Provençal—no doubt for the very reasons which might lead a modern writer in search of atmosphere to choose, instead of 'navire', the now obsolete *nef*!

Full advantage is here taken of the flexibility allowed by sixteenth-century usage with regard to word-order. The effect is on the one hand to throw into prominence the adverbial phrase *par la retention des flotz aërez*, and on the other hand, by a process not unlike the inversion we find practised in the classical Alexandrine, to accentuate a 'couple tonique'[4] (the two terms *de leurs stations* and *enlevées*)—whereas normal prose word-order would subordinate the latter to the former, the word-order here adopted picks out both of them and gives them prominence. This striking care for the arranging of words, together with the inventive forging of new words and the imaginative use of periphrasis, are all examples of a truly poetic attitude towards language.

Paragraph 3 examines the results of the use of hemp for purposes of navigation and travel: in the first sentence in quite general terms, followed by the specific instances listed in the next. The third sentence introduces what is to provide the main theme of para. 4—the alarm felt by the gods—but the emphasis is here still on the achievements that have occasioned that alarm. In the first sentence are to be noted the following features of construction: the rhetorical repetition of a trio of near-synonyms in *absconses, impermeables et incongneues*; the reinforcing of the point by the chiasmus of *les nations... à nous venues, nous à elles*; and the parallel clauses *quelque legiereté...* and *quelque liberté...*, the second amplifying the first. The end of this sentence, *...baillée par Nature*, links up with the beginning, *...que Nature sembloit tenir...*, and thus, by a means loosely comparable again to that of chiasmus, gives an effective coherence to the argument: in his voyages, man is overcoming the limitations imposed by Nature, and creating for himself, to this end, the sort of adjunct with which Nature has chosen to endow

[4] Cf. our commentary on the Molière passage, p. 66 and note 8.

certain other creatures. The phrase *nager en l'air*, a further example of poetic periphrasis, also links the notion of the bird's travels in the air with a suggestion of man's journeys through the sea.

The second sentence of this paragraph might easily have been an unartistic catalogue; it is saved from this by the variety in the verbs used, and in the tenses of these verbs (perfect and future), as well as in the kinds of proper noun used. Thus *Taprobrana* (Ceylon), *Lappia* (Lapland), *Java*, *les mons Riphées* (mountains in Scythia), and *Phebol* (an island in the Arabian Sea) are real place-names, while *Theleme* is imaginary: it is the name of Rabelais's own ideal community, described in the closing chapters of *Gargantua*; with *Islandoys* and *Engronelands* we pass to the *inhabitants* of Iceland and Greenland, while the last four terms are, of course, the names of winds in Latin, and represent the four quarters of the globe. Rabelais proceeds from the simple statement *Taprobrana a veu Lappia* (an example of metonymy: the names of the countries stand for the inhabitants of those countries) to another similar statement, where again *Java* must represent 'les Javanais', and yet a further statement of the same kind, this time with the verb in the future. This is followed by an example which is much more dynamic, because of the unexpected verb: *les Islandoys et Engronelands boyront Euphrates*, in which the names, as well as illustrating the meeting of East and West, also suggest a link between modern geographical discovery and ancient civilization. And finally, in the most poetic and evocative of all these references, we have a sort of double metonymy (the four winds represent in the first place the four quarters of the globe, and in the second the *inhabitants* of these parts of the world), and in a vivid image the Southern Hemisphere becomes the homely *manoir de Auster*. Thus distances are annihilated, and the whole globe is brought, by means of sailing-ships dependent on the canvas of their sails, within the compass of man's curiosity and ingenuity.

The last sentence of this paragraph does perhaps at first sight appear to have something of the catalogue about it, with less variety in the construction (all the verbs are infinitives depending on *voyans*), and what might seem a rather jarring rhyme in *Arcticques . . . Antarcticques . . . Athlanticque . . . Tropicques*. The geographical terms, too, are on the whole less varied and evocative, belonging to the new technical vocabulary of the Renaissance. The two passages of enumeration in lines 17-20 and 22 ff. are, however, separated by the main clause of this third sentence, which makes the first statement of the principal theme of the passage. The way in which this idea is presented stresses its importance: the simple subject *les Dieux* is elaborated by the oratorical device of threefold repetition, in the synecdoche of *les Intelligences celestes* and the antithetical figure of *...tant marins que terrestres*. The reaction of the gods is a human one: they are *tous effrayez*, and before we come to the enumeration of the subjects of their apprehension, pride of place is given to the root cause: *cestuy benedict Pantagruelion*. The use of the Christian term *benedict* (mod. Fr. 'béni') may be fortuitous: at any rate it strengthens the contrast between man, fortified by the virtues of the herb, and the pagan divinities.

When we come to the geographical terms themselves, the association of noun and verb in each case does produce considerable variety, as we graduate from the simple *franchir* and *passer* to the figurative *volter* (='voleter') which, together with its accompanying phrase *sous la Zone torride*, turns geographical abstraction into a vivid picture of the excitements and the hardships of voyages of discovery; *mesurer tout le Zodiacque* sketches the breadth of the astronomer's knowledge; and *s'esbatre sous l'Æquinoctial* suggests relief from hardship in a friendly climate of which man is now the master. The sentence concludes with a magnificent metaphor as its climax, the concrete *avoir en veue* and *à fleur de leur orizon*, as well as expressing an intuition of the physical appearance of the Earth as seen by a navigator in outer space, also standing figuratively for the immense broadening of the intellectual horizons of Renaissance Man.

Taking the gods' alarm as his starting-point, Rabelais uses the rest of the passage to develop the idea of man's progress as a challenge to the gods themselves. These are *les Dieux Olympicques*, the inhabitants of the Greek pantheon: not the omnipotent embodiment of a divine Providence, but a community of beings themselves subject, in spite of their supernatural attributes, to the limitations of a superior destiny (*Necessité*). Classical references here become, not laboured proof of erudition, but the raw material for a highly imaginative piece of writing. The example of the *Aloïdes* (giants who tried to attack the gods, piling Pelion on Ossa) is invoked as a contrast to that of Pantagruel, the modern giant (symbolizing human knowledge and wisdom), whose challenge will be more successful: inevitably so, because the Fates (*les mains et fuseaulx des sœurs fatales*) have decreed that the advance of the human race cannot be checked. In the next sentence the reference to *human* progress becomes quite direct, and from this point onwards Rabelais dispenses with the allegorical cover provided by his giant-protagonist: Pantagruel and his prospective descendants give way to *les humains*, and the hypothetical achievements of *ses enfans* are quite clearly those of the human race as a whole. The full measure of man's audacious challenge is conveyed most effectively by discreet mythological reference, coupled with a very satisfying example of ternary phrasing: *les sources des gresles, les bondes des pluyes et l'officine des fouldres*—richly poetic, because it is suggestive rather than explicit. The threefold image does not refer to specific activities associated with Mount Olympus (even if the third term does, no doubt, remind the reader of Vulcan's forge), but yet evokes imaginatively the mystery and power always attributed by the simple mind to the heavens, which man is now seen as capable of invading. The rest of this sentence both restates this idea (*envahir les regions de la Lune, entrer le teritoire des signes celestes*) and also, by a complementary process, renders the gods themselves less remote, more familiar, and therefore more vulnerable. The constellations, for instance, sometimes represented by the Ancients as the dwellings of the gods, are here imaginatively, and humorously, treated as inn-signs; and the gods are seen to be looking on men as their own rivals for bed and board. Thus Rabelais's flights of prophetic fancy are given vivid concrete form by his imaginative handling of mythological references, and this very personal profession of faith in men's capabilities is much more eloquent than any abstract statement. Though nothing specific is predicted, the passage stands as a remarkable forecast of ever wider-ranging achievements, as not only the earth but the whole universe is brought under man's domination and, in the closing phrase, man attains equality with the gods.

In conclusion, what is the scope of the ideas contained in a passage such as this? In the Prologue to *Gargantua* Rabelais advises the reader in search of the hidden meaning of his work to 'rompre l'os et sugcer la substantificque mouelle'. Inevitably, readers will differ as to the 'marrow' they find. For some, it will be tempting to interpret this climax of the 'pantagruelion' allegory as a humanist profession of faith, and to see implied in it, beneath the assertion that the gods of classical mythology have been outgrown and discarded, the hidden suggestion that Christianity will also one day be declared redundant; to read it not only as a tribute to man's capabilities but as a declaration of belief in his self-sufficiency. Whether or not one chooses to attribute this particular veiled meaning to Rabelais must depend on one's considered assessment of his religious standpoint as a whole, and of the position of the writer in general in the intellectual climate of sixteenth-century France: in short, the extent to which one thinks that a humanist's confidence in man's capabilities was compatible with orthodox Christian faith.

Opinion among the scholars has of course varied greatly on the subject of Rabelais's religious views, but it must be said that the most recent Rabelais scholarship would not support the view that the author of *Le Tiers Livre* had consciously thought out such a conclusion, or that he wrote this passage with the intention that his allegory should be taken in such a far-reaching sense.[5] For many modern readers, however, an extension of Rabelais's meaning along these lines must be implicit, even if they accept it as most likely that he himself stopped short without making the (to them) obvious application. At the very least, the passage expresses a challenging and stimulating declaration of the author's belief in man's self-reliance, a glorification of his past achievements and a forecast of future accomplishments. It would, perhaps, not be prudent to venture a dogmatic opinion on how far the author may have gone in thinking out the implications of such a belief in religious terms.

While these more far-reaching implications, if they exist at all, certainly remain hidden beneath the surface of the text, there can be no doubt about the way in which Rabelais's creative imagination responded to the stimulus of the more obvious themes of travel, discovery, and triumphant conquest. Whereas the rest of the pantagruelion episode exemplifies the burlesque, parodistic side of his imagination, as he pours out a spate of erudition and mock-erudition on an incongruously insignificant subject, in this passage he suddenly—and unexpectedly—finds the inspiration for a truly poetic flight of fancy. The treatment of the plant, which has up to

---

[5] See, for instance, M. A. Screech, *L'Évangélisme de Rabelais* (Geneva, 1959); and A. J. Krailsheimer, *Rabelais* ('Les Écrivains devant Dieu', Paris, 1967), for whom Rabelais's religious beliefs represent a synthesis: 'Humanisme pratique et vertueux, christianisme humble et énergique' (p. 83).

now been half literal, half metaphorical, all at once assumes the quality of a powerful symbol, and the closing paragraphs stand as a magnificent evocation of the spirit of the Renaissance.[6] The richness of his verbal invention, the range of his poetic fantasy, and the suggestive touches of his comic vision (in the brief sketch of the all-too-human gods) combine to give a characteristically exuberant expression to the spirit of adventure and exploration; so that even across four centuries today's blasé readers in an age of space travel can feel on reading these lines something of the buoyant optimism and intellectual excitement that inspired them.

[6] A. Glauser (*Rabelais créateur* (Paris, 1966), pp. 227–8) compares the climax of this passage with Hugo's 'Plein Ciel' as a similar 'chant de triomphe' on the theme of man's conquest of the universe. Indeed, there is also a striking affinity here with 'Le Satyre', another poem from *La Légende des siècles*, in which Hugo, like Rabelais, makes creative use of an original myth, in order to portray the overthrow of the pagan gods by the new spirit of the Renaissance.

2 Ronsard

Ode a Cassandre

Mignonne, allon voir si la rose
Qui ce matin auoit declose
Sa robe de pourpre, au soleil,
A point perdu cette vesprée,
Les plis de sa robe pourprée,   5
Et son teint au vostre pareil.
  Las, voiés comme en peu d'espace,
Mignonne, elle a dessus la place,
Las, las, ses beautés laissé cheoir!
O vraiment maratre Nature,   10
Puis qu'une telle fleur ne dure
Que du matin iusques au soir.
  Donc, si vous me croiés, mignonne:
Tandis que vôtre age fleuronne
En sa plus verte nouveauté: 15
Cueillés, cueillés vôtre ieunesse,
Comme a cette fleur, la vieillesse
Fera ternir vôtre beauté.

RONSARD, *Les Amours*
Date of first publication: 1553
(in 2nd (enlarged) edition, p. 266)
Text of first published version

RONSARD'S famous evening-song to Cassandre was first placed at
the end of *Les Amours*, then included in the *Odes* (1555), and finally
incorporated in the *Œuvres* (seven editions from 1560 to 1587). In
the case of a poet dedicated to the pursuit of formal perfection by
means of incessant self-correction it is significant that despite its

13

many re-editions this poem is one of the relatively few compositions which Ronsard deemed it unnecessary to alter except for minor changes of spelling and punctuation. It is also significant that the date of its first publication (May 1553) coincides with a turning-point in Ronsard's poetry—the evolution between 1553 and 1556 towards simplicity, lightness and economy, the achievement of an apparently effortless, natural grace and ease, the alliance of a sense of measure and moderation with a style equally averse to excess ('Ny trop haut, ny trop bas, c'est le souverain style'). The delightful ode to Cassandre is an early, but consummate model of Ronsard's new 'style moyen', and, as such, it was readily accessible to all readers and enjoyed an immense contemporary and posthumous success. From the start this little masterpiece was universally known, imitated in France and elsewhere, and set to music between 1567 and 1597 by no less than six composers, notably by Guillaume Costeley. It was on the lips of the sixteenth-century courtiers who laughed at Ronsard's long, erudite Pindarics, and the Duc de Guise himself is said to have been humming it in 1588 when he left his mistress to walk across the courtyard of the Château de Blois before entering the room where his assassins were lying in ambush. During Ronsard's long eclipse the poem lived on not only in the song-books, but also in Fontenelle's *Recueil des plus belles pièces des poètes français* (1690) and in the eighteenth-century *Encyclopédie* (Marmontel's article on *Anacréon*). Even today it is probably the best known of Ronsard's poems. It is doubtless regrettable that many of those familiar with this charming *odelette* are often ignorant of the wider scope of Ronsard's varied achievement. It remains true, however, that the three brief stanzas of *Mignonne, allon voir...* have probably contributed more to Ronsard's popular renown than all the rest of his work.

It comes from the long series of poems connected with the Cassandre episode (1545–55). The first Muse of Ronsard's love poetry, Cassandre occupies a place of honour in the gallery of the poet's mistresses, and her fresh, primal image, so redolent of youthfulness and spring roses, was never to fade entirely from his memory. It was during the royal festivities at the Château de Blois (21–23 April 1545) that the twenty-year-old Ronsard first saw 'une beauté de quinze ans enfantine'. It was Cassandre Salviati, half Florentine and half French, who in 1546 was to marry a local seigneur. As Mlle de Pray she remained a barren field for the poet; but as

Baudelaire puts it, 'la femme dont on ne jouit pas est celle qu'on aime... Ce que la femme perd en jouissances sensuelles, elle le gagne en adoration.' Ronsard has described her 'grace enfantine', the contrast of golden hair with her dark, Southern looks, her 'douce faconde', the enchantment of her singing and her skill on the lute, the proud, inexorable virtue which made her proof against the lure of roses and the promise of poetic immortality. Clearly there was an insuperable barrier between the Dame de Pray and the tonsured clerk with his 'bonnet rond'; but even if Cassandre represented no more than the name of a girl briefly glimpsed at a Court ball it was a Classical name (rare in France, but more common in Italy) which appealed to a humanist like Ronsard, and his youthful dreams crystallized around it. The creature of flesh and blood seems to have rapidly become an 'idée' enriched by Ronsard's perfervid imagination and by his plundering of classical and modern poetry. His love for Cassandre is no doubt sincere; but it is the love of a Renaissance artist, and in her name he has composed a series of hymns to Beauty—beauty of woman, beauty of nature, beauty of poetry. They are not so much fragments of a great confession as works of imagination, notable primarily for Ronsard's poetic sense and technique. The poet's own emotions keep breaking in; but his passion is mainly cerebral, and his memories serve largely as the pretext for the creation of 'un profond rêve d'amour sensuel'. In Ronsard's wishful dreams erotic fantasy, literary convention and imitation, even technical virtuosity bulk larger than personal experience, and as regards the 'Ode a Cassandre' in particular Raymond Lebègue is of the opinion that 'cette célèbre piécette est beaucoup moins le récit d'un fait vécu qu'un exercice littéraire et rythmique, dans lequel le poète a harmonieusement mêlé une imitation d'Ausone et une de Pontano'.[1]

The poem is addressed to Cassandre; but its theme has a wider, universal application which transcends Ronsard's 'partenaire-prétexte'. The theme is indeed an eternal commonplace: time is fleeting; life is short; beauty flowers briefly; youth must be gathered before the onset of old age and death. The moral is *Carpe diem* or rather *Carpe florem*, for the commonplace is illustrated by the allegory of the rose. The poem is essentially a flower-piece with the rose-maiden motif. The rose symbolizes at once beauty and transience, and the delight which it excites is tinged with melancholy.

---

[1] *Mélanges Jamati* (Paris, 1956), p. 170.

It is an emblem of mutability; but paradoxically the frail beauty of the rose is a symbol which never dies. Ronsard's ode represents in this sense the culmination of a long tradition stretching from Classical Antiquity through the Middle Ages to the neo-Latin, Italian, and French poets of the fifteenth and sixteenth centuries. The rose-image lingers on in the neo-classical poetry of the seventeenth and eighteenth centuries; but the motif is specially common in Renaissance poetry, inasmuch as it expresses the Renaissance cult of beauty together with the neo-pagan sense of the transitoriness of life; and of all the Renaissance poets none was more obsessed with the rose-symbol than Ronsard, who returns to it no less than thirty times in his poetry—without, however, surpassing the unique perfection of the 'Ode a Cassandre'. The poem goes back, through the innumerable Renaissance variations on the theme, to Pontano (*Amores*, I, iv: 'Puella molli delicatior rosa...') and to its primary source, Ausonius' idyll ('De rosis nascentibus'). Itself inspired by Ausonius, Pontano's ode 'Ad Fanniam' is, like Ronsard's poem, a composite of elegy and mild invective, and has the same *Carpe florem* conclusion. It is notable for its light, conversational tone, its rich sensuousness, and its somewhat modern creation of mood; but excessive frills make it twice as long as Ronsard's *odelette*, and its vivacity is marred by a certain effeminate 'mignardise' as well as by the abuse of Italianate diminutives. Ausonius' poem, which had such a great influence upon the Renaissance lyric generally, supplied the theme, development, and moral of Ronsard's ode, as well as the apostrophe to Nature; but it is far lengthier (fifty lines), with a lush profusion of descriptive detail and an excessive wealth of over-elaborated, recherché imagery. Ausonius does not concentrate upon a single rose—he presents a whole garden, with herbs and cabbages as well as roses! The Alexandrian artifice of his style contrasts with the simplicity of Ronsard.

There is hardly any detail in Ronsard's ode which cannot be paralleled elsewhere; but the poem is in no sense a stale, slavish copy. It is an imitation which surpasses its models, and the selection and rearrangement of the material, the novelty of treatment, and the superiority of execution make it a new artistic whole. He has renewed a trite theme and extracted from it an apparently spontaneous poem of exquisite freshness, grace, and charm. The turn of mind and phrase are authentically French, and the logic, clarity, and delicacy also betray the Gallic touch. Concision and brevity have been achieved by the elimination of fussy, precious minutiae in the evocation of the rose-image. Ronsard's masterstroke, however, was to introduce the girl so that she can see for herself her beauty and her destiny mirrored in the flower. The assimilation is natural and discreet, with a progression from the girl to the rose and from the rose back to the girl. The flower is described in terms applicable to a girl, and the girl in terms suggestive of a flower, so that finally they become one. Ronsard himself also takes the stage and puts his own stamp on the poem by his personal involvement. The rose itself is not just a banal literary image, but a familiar, fondly described flower from the gardens of the Vendômois, and the borrowed theme harmonizes so intimately with Ronsard's own attitude to life that an unmistakably subjective note is struck. The poem is suffused with lyrical emotion, and Ronsard displays here greater empathy with the theme than any of his predecessors. His ode also possesses far more immediacy than its sources: the past tense is replaced by the present; the narration becomes a conversation; the poem turns into a little drama with a mounting pathos which is peculiarly Ronsard's invention.

The ode was for the Pléiade the lyric poem *par excellence*. Ronsard, the 'prince des Odes', cultivated Pindarics, Horatians, and Anacreontics, and also invented the *odelette*, a very brief, light ode with seven- or eight-syllable lines organized in couplets, quatrains, or sixains. From 1554 he designated certain poems as *odelettes*; but some earlier odes might equally have been so called. Like the ode, the *odelette* was designed to be sung to musical accompaniment; but unlike the ode, which was a song in the antique manner, the *odelette* represents in effect a conscious or unconscious revival of the French medieval *chanson* under a new name. From 1552 Ronsard actually entitled certain light odes *chansons*. Like many such poems, the 'Ode a Cassandre' could equally well be styled an *odelette* or a *chanson*, for it constitutes a perfect marriage of the classical ode technique with the traditions of the old French *chanson*. The brief, slim strophes are made up of eighteen octosyllabic lines and consist almost exclusively of short monosyllabic or disyllabic words. The three sixains are all 'measured to the lyre': the number and length of the lines, the rhyme-scheme, the alternation of masculine and feminine rhymes, are maintained throughout the poem, so that each stanza is adapted to the same succession of musical notes. The *octosyllabe* itself is one of those short lines which Ronsard calls 'merveilleusement propres pour la musique, la lyre et autres instruments'. Here it supplies a series of easy-flowing lines with rhymes which follow close and which slightly slow down the poetic tempo. Their lightness is in perfect accord with the delicacy of the rose-theme, and their suppleness lends itself to the expression of lyric emotion. Their rhythm is not mechanical or monotonous. A *césure médiane* is to be found in lines 4, 12, 15, and 18; but the majority of the lines do not conform to this rigid, symmetrical pattern (4 + 4), and some have more than one *coupe*: lines 2 (1 + 3 + 4), 7 (1 + 2 + 5), 8 (2 + 2 + 4), 9 (1 + 1 + 6), and 13 (1 + 5 + 2). The variable *coupes* closely follow the subtle shifts of thought and mood. Together with the rhymes they throw into relief the essential words and deftly stress the parallelisms and antitheses. The meaning often carries over the end of the lines, suggesting a swift expansive movement (the flowering of Beauty's rose in ll. 2–3 and 14–15), or a flowing and especially a descending movement (the fall of the petals in ll. 8–9, and transience in ll. 11–12 and 17–18). The isometric sixains with their identical rhyme-scheme (AABCCB) consist in effect of a couplet followed by *rimes embrassées*, and since the A and C rhymes are feminine there is a marked predominance of soft feminine rhymes. Their languid, delicate mute *e*'s combine with the dozen unelided final *e*'s within the body of the lines to enhance the slow, quiet, slightly sad cadence of the poem. Ronsard tends to reserve the privileged place at the rhyme for his key-words; but he is more concerned with the meaning and the general harmony of his poem than with the quality of his rhyming. In the case of *soleil-pareil*, for example, he tolerates a *rime faible*, and he retains a *rime banale* like *ieunesse-vieillesse*—doubtless because these two 'mots ennemis' form one of those temporal antitheses so characteristic of his outlook and manner. There is certainly no superstitious straining for rare, rich rhymes: three (*vesprée-pourprée*, *cheoir-soir*, *nouveauté-beauté*) are *rimes riches*, but the rest are simply *suffisantes*.

The language itself is sensuous and picturesque. It possesses the youthfulness and freshness of the sixteenth-century period style. The quaint archaism of the spelling, grammar, and syntax has for the modern reader a special savour: *a* for 'à' (title and l. 17); *allon* for 'allons'; *auoit* for 'avait'; *declose* for 'déclose' (=opened, un-folded), a past participle agreeing with the following direct object (an optional Old French concord; cf. *perdu*) so as to rhyme with

18

rose; the omission of 'ne' (l. 4); *vesprée* for 'vêprée' (=evening); *pourprée* for 'empourprée'; *vostre* for 'vôtre' (l. 6), and *vôtre* for 'votre' (ll. 14, 16, 18); *las* for 'hélas'; *-iés* for '-yez' (ll. 7, 13) and *-és* for '-ez' (l. 16); *espace* used in a temporal sense; *dessus* employed as a preposition; *cheoir* for 'choir' (=fall); *maratre* for 'marâtre'; *puis que* for 'puisque'; *iusques au* for 'jusqu'au'; *age* for 'âge' (=life); *fleuronne* for 'fleurit'; *ieunesse* for 'jeunesse'. The old-fashioned punctuation also calls for brief comment: commas stressing the previous word (ll. 4, 5, 17); comma for exclamation-mark (ll. 7, 9) and exclamation-mark for full stop (l. 9); full stop for exclamation-mark (l. 12); colon (ll. 13, 15) and comma (l. 16) emended to a comma and a colon respectively in the 1584 and 1587 editions of Ronsard's *Œuvres*.

A conspicuous feature of the ode is its colour and light: *Sa robe de pourpre, au soleil; Les plis de sa robe pourprée; vôtre age fleuronne En sa plus verte nouveauté*. The colours are bold and vivid—glowing flesh tints (*pourpre, pourprée*), and the poet's obsessional green, which he so often associates with freshness, youth, and spring—and they are lit up by the bright radiance of the Renaissance sun. Ronsard often dwells upon 'la plaisante lumière de notre beau soleil'; but the sunlight is flecked with shadow: 'Un Soleil voit naistre et mourir la rose...' The sun illumines the colourful beauty of the rose; but the duration of its brief flowering is inexorably fixed by the sun's gradual, stealthy advance *du matin iusques au soir*.

Not the least charm of the poem is the conversational tone— friendly and intimate, yet at the same time courtly. It is the gentle urbanity of a sixteenth-century nobleman who is expressing melancholy resignation and epicurean fatalism rather than a violent Romantic rebellion against Nature.

Stanza I has most *élan*, with its brilliant opening that plunges straight *in medias res*; but all the strophes begin in fact with a lively, attention-catching attack: *Mignonne... Las... Donc...*, and through- out the ode the numerous interpellations, exclamations, and im- peratives contribute to the vivacity and movement of the poem. The couple stroll to the rose; but this movement in space is only suggested (*allon voir... Las, voiés...*). The real movement here is that of the poetic rhythm itself. This rhythmic movement is en- hanced sometimes by the exact repetition of sounds, sometimes by echoes with slight variations. There is the subtle interplay of assonance and alliteration: the liquid *l* and *r* (ll. 1–6); the delicate *b* and *p* (*p* by itself or in combination with *r* or *l*) in lines 3–6; the plaintive *u* (Stanza 2); the sighing *s* (ll. 7–9); the faintly rasping *r* (ll. 10–12); the hard [k] sounds (ll. 11–12); the soft, velvety *v* and *f* (Stanza 3). There is a similar, songlike repetition or echoing of words, often for special effects: the insistence on the girl/rose assimilation (*robe de pourpre/robe pourprée; fleur/fleuronne/fleur; beautés/beauté*); the underscoring of the basic temporal antithesis (*matin-vesprée* and *matin-soir*); the accentuation of disappointment and regret (*Las... Las, las*); the constant reminder of the girl's presence (*mignonne*). Of all these verbal repetitions, however, the most successful is that of *mignonne*. This graceful term, suggestive of dainty, delicate charm and equally applicable to the girl and the rose, introduces a tender, personal note. It recurs three times in all, once in each stanza, in a varying, but always prominent, position (opening of poem, beginning of l. 8, and rhyme of l. 13) and every time with a subtle change of tone—gay (Stanza 1), sad (Stanza 2), and admonitory (Stanza 3).

Composition is not generally the strong point of Ronsard, who is more inclined to the loose, open, complex structure of baroque art than to the tight, closed, clearly articulated classical form. Here, however, he observes a strictly logical, linear order of presentation. There is a beginning, middle, and end, and the poem as a whole is organized around the central rose-motif which colours and unifies the parts. Structurally, it falls into three sections of equal length exactly corresponding to the three self-contained, endstopped strophes: the invitation to see the rose; the lament over the catastrophe; the moral. The tripartite structure has been likened to the panels of a triptych; but it has been more frequently and more pertinently compared to a playlet in three scenes.

The first stanza is full of vernal freshness, colour, and sunlight. Ronsard is talking to Cassandre; but she is not directly named except in the title, nor does she ever speak herself. Her silence suggests a modest, chaste reserve. Despite the familiarity of the word *Mignonne* Ronsard does not at first go beyond the limits of sixteenth-century *honneste amour*, and always addresses her respectfully as *vous*. The opening invitation (*Mignonne, allon voir...*) is light, gay, and dashing, and we mentally picture the handsome couple in their period costume strolling down the path of one of those *jardins à l'italienne* outside some Renaissance château not far from the silver Loire. The identification of the girl and the rose is already adumbrated in the two most prominent words of the first line: *Mignonne... rose*. The rose is recalled blooming in all its colourful splendour; but its beauty is evoked in the past tense which lends it a frail poignancy. It is now evening, and the sun is declining. The faint melancholy of *vesprée* contrasts with the lightness and brightness of *matin*. The symbolic meaning of the rose-image is already prepared here by the application to the flower of terms suggestive of a girl. The refined, slightly precious periphrasis, *robe de pourpre*, likens the sheath of velvet petals to a crimson gown. *Les plis de sa robe pourprée* is a richer, more precise elaboration of the previous image. The furled array of petals is now compared to the folds of a robe. *Pourprée* represents an intensification of *pourpre* by implying that the rose has by now turned a deeper shade of crimson. There is a slight pause after line 5, and the final line of the stanza introduces a deft, smiling compliment by pointing out the analogy between the colour of the flower and Cassandre's complexion. The use of the word *teint* again suggests a person rather than a flower and rounds off the rose/girl assimilation.

By line 7 Ronsard and Cassandre have already reached the rose in the garden. The poet's painful disappointment makes this stanza the most melancholy of the three. The disaster which has overtaken the rose confronts the optimistic Renaissance cult of beauty with the implacable order of nature. The ravages of time are sharply brought home to Ronsard, who realizes with a sudden disquiet how soon (*comme en peu d'espace*) the rose has faded. The abrupt change of mood is indicated by the sigh (*Las*) which opens the stanza, and which is first echoed in the rhymes of lines 7–8, then repeated twice in rapid succession in line 9. The sad rhyme sounds of this strophe contrast with the bright rhymes of Stanza 1, and there is a certain insistence on the final syllables of lines 9–12. The poet's emotion also betrays itself in the jerky rhythm produced by the multiple *coupes* of lines 7–9. The rose petals strewn over the ground (*dessus la place*) form a pathetic image of the decay of earthly beauty. Ronsard feels a sense of desolation and waste. This rose has not been plucked. Solitary and unloved, it has simply withered and died by the inevitable process of time. The use of the abstract word *beautés* (another periphrasis for petals) again extends the reference beyond the flower. Ronsard is mentally comparing the rose to the girl, and *Mignonne* here takes on a wryly compassionate, insinuating tone. The inversion of lines 8–9 has the effect of throwing into relief the verb *cheoir*. The marked descending movement also brings with it a melancholy suggestion of decline which offsets the gracious associations of *beautés*. Ronsard seems to be succumbing to despair; but a sharp break occurs between lines 9 and 10, and elegiac lament gives way almost to invective as the poet turns from this sad phenomenon of nature to address an indignant protest to Nature herself. Ronsard holds the Renaissance view of Nature as the vital, all-controlling force behind the ceaseless generation and mutation of forms in the sublunar world, and he often personifies her as 'notre mère Nature'. She is sometimes presented as 'Nature bonne mère'; but since she needs a constant flow of matter in order to create new forms she can take on the appearance of 'l'avaricieuse Nature'. Ronsard's apostrophe to beldame Nature in line 10 takes the form of an elliptical construction: 'O Nature (whom I truly call) harsh step-mother since . . .' Nature creates beauty, but she does not love or watch over it. She callously allows it to perish. However, Ronsard's outburst rapidly subsides. Lines 11–12 have a continuous flow and trickle away in a dying fall. There is a final impression of mournful resignation and fatalism.

In the last stanza the example-image swiftly becomes a 'moyen de parvenir', for this *memento mori* seems only to sharpen Ronsard's amorous ardour, and adopting a playfully warning tone he offers some worldly and not entirely disinterested advice. Line 13 reverts to the light, colloquial style of line 1, and the mood suddenly becomes gay again; but this is accompanied here by a new, eager desire to persuade. The exhortation opens with a forceful *Donc* which surprisingly and somewhat disingenuously attempts to invest an 'invitation galante' with the outward form of a scholastic syllogism. But Ronsard is a 'clerc dispos' and he uses this term of logic to announce his familiar *argumentum ad feminam*:

> Le temps s'en va, le temps s'en va, ma Dame,
>> Las! le temps non, mais nous nous en allons,
>> Et tôt serons étendus sous la lame...
>> Pour-ce, aimez-moi, ce-pendant qu'êtes belle.

He also assumes an air of superior experience in the presence of the young girl (*si vous me croiés*). The poet's chief stratagem, however, is his reversal of the initial rose/girl assimilation. Previously the rose had been evoked in terms suggestive of a person; Cassandre is now described in terms suggestive of a flower. There is, for example, the carefully selected verb *fleuronne*, an archaism which derives from 'fleuron' (a diminutive of 'fleur') and which, while more or less synonymous with 'fleurit', has a softer, more delicate sound. Then again, *En sa plus verte nouveauté* resembles superficially 'en ta première et jeune nouveauté' (sonnet on the death of Marie); but in addition to this general sense of youthful freshness[2] *verte nouveauté* also seems to suggest here the outer cover of green leaves surrounding a rose-bud. The girl/rose image is prolonged in the insistent repetition of the verb *Cueillés, cueillés...* which evokes not a brutal snatching, but rather a delicate, gentle action. It is a virtuoso variation on Ausonius' *Carpe florem* moral ('collige, virgo, rosas, dum flos novus et nova pubes'). The latter is taken over by Ronsard in the sonnet for Hélène ('Cueillez dés aujourd'huy les roses de la vie'); but here he substitutes *ieunesse* for 'roses', an original touch which completes the fusion of the girl and the rose. The essential meaning of lines 16–18 (youth must be gathered before old age dims its beauty) is concentrated in the last three rhymes (*ieunesse-vieillesse-beauté*), which echo Ronsard's constant refrain:

> Tu es encore jeune en la fleur de tes ans,
> Use donq de l'amour et de ses dons plaisans,
> Et ne souffre qu'en vain l'Avril de ta jeunesse
> Au milieu de son cours se ride de vieillesse.

Ronsard is here preaching the pleasures of the flesh in accordance with the Renaissance gospel of nature. However discreetly and poetically expressed, this neo-pagan moral is based on the vulgar epicureanism which appealed to the poet's sensual temperament. He was, however, a sad voluptuary, forever haunted by the thought of old age, the forerunner of death. *La vieillesse* here casts its shadow on Ronsard's hedonistic philosophy. The last two lines with their descending movement have a melancholy tonality, and this lends a special poignancy to the concluding word *beauté*, which sticks in the memory and leaves the final, lingering impression.

[2] Speaking of the 'beautés qu'il voudrait en s'Amie', Ronsard declares:

> L'âge non mûr, mais verdelet encore,
> C'est celui seul qui me dévore
> Le cœur...

Cassandre is only a passing incarnation of feminine beauty; but the poem has captured and fixed for ever her frail, transient loveliness. The final rhyme sums up in one word the whole content of the ode, and prolongs Ronsard's dream beyond the formal conclusion of his poem.

3 Du Bellay

Heureux qui, comme Ulysse, a fait un beau voyage,
  Ou comme cestuy la qui conquit la toison,
  Et puis est retourné, plein d'usage & raison,
  Vivre entre ses parents le reste de son aage!
Quand revoiray-je, helas, de mon petit village   5
  Fumer la cheminee, & en quelle saison,
  Revoiray-je le clos de ma pauvre maison,
  Qui m'est une province, & beaucoup d'avantage?
Plus me plaist le sejour qu'ont basty mes ayeux,
  Que des palais Romains le front audacieux,   10
  Plus que le marbre dur me plaist l'ardoise fine:
Plus mon Loyre Gaulois, que le Tybre Latin,
  Plus mon petit Lyré, que le mont Palatin,
  Et plus que l'air marin la doulceur Angevine.

DU BELLAY, *Les Regrets*, XXXI
Date of first publication: 1558
Ed. J. Jolliffe and M. A. Screech
(Geneva: Droz, 1966), p. 98

ONE of the best-known poems of the Pléiade and a glory of all the anthologies, Du Bellay's little masterpiece represents a summit of French poetry. This legendary poem, engraved in slate on the façade of the humble *mairie* of the poet's provincial hamlet, strikes a characteristic note of personal disquiet and nostalgia; but at the same time the 'sonnet du petit Liré' expresses a broadly human, universal theme, for in rendering his own homesickness Du Bellay has captured the very essence of an emotion experienced by most men at some time or other in their lives.

Among Du Bellay's *Poëmata* (1558) there is a long Latin elegy in the Ovidian manner which reveals close correspondences with this sonnet ('Patriae desiderium',[1] ll. 45–6 and 49–56). There is no certainty that the Latin poem was composed before the French text; but it seems probable that the elegy contains the first sketch of the theme, while the sonnet represents the definitive version. Like the sonnet the elegy expresses a mood of profound nostalgia: *Ipsa mihi patriae toties occurrit imago*. It fondly recalls the fertile fields of Anjou, the banks of the Loire, the poet's native village and his beloved home. There is an allusion to Ulysses in lines 41–6, though none to Jason's quest for the Golden Fleece. There is the same opposition between lines 45–6 and 49–50 as between the two quatrains of the sonnet; but the antithetical parallelisms in the sestet are missing from the elegy, for the evocation of Rome (ll. 51–6) is not set off against the poignant images of home. Some touches of local colour are already present: *notae fumantia culmina villae/de mon petit village Fumer la cheminee* and *regni iugera parua mei/le clos de ma pauvre maison, Qui m'est une province*; but there is no *ardoise fine*, no *air marin*, no *doulceur Angevine*. Compared with the more conventional manner of the elegy the sonnet has a richer, more personal savour with its intimate lyricism and its wealth of precise, evocative details. A greater density of style results from the constraints of the more concentrated sonnet form; the contrasts have been sharpened; a subtler musical harmony has been achieved. There can be no doubt that Du Bellay has improved on himself in the French version. As Sainte-Beuve remarks, a poet can only be wholly himself in his own language: 'On n'atteint que là à ce qui est proprement la signature du poète, la particularité de l'expression'.[2]

The sonnet comes from Du Bellay's most original and popular work, *Les Regrets* (composed 1555–7, published 1558). It consists of 191 sonnets, some elegiac, some satirical, but all equally personal and intimate. Sonnet XXXI belongs to the elegiac section (VI–XLIX). *Les Regrets*, a title suggested by Ovid's *Tristia*, indicates the basic note of the poetry which springs from the deep, bitter experience which was the main event of Du Bellay's life. It is a kind of poetic journal covering not only his sojourn in Rome, but also his journey there and back (1553–7). He notes down 'simplement' and 'naïvement' the impressions of his long odyssey together with his personal tribulations—the frustrated hopes of honour and

[1] Du Bellay, *Poésies françaises et latines*, ed. E. Courbet (Paris, 1918), I, 445–7.
[2] *Nouveaux Lundis* (Paris, 1863–72), XIII, 343.

26

fortune, the irksome bondage of his post as 'intendant-secrétaire' to Cardinal Jean Du Bellay, his isolation from the French Court, his friends and fellow-poets, his failing health and the approach of premature old age. This sense of failure and decline is accompanied by a growing disenchantment with the ostentation, hypocrisy, and intrigue of the corrupt Roman milieu ('Rome n'est plus Rome...', CXXXI) which forms the background to his personal ordeal and offers a broad target for caustic satire (LXXVII–CXXVII). Though Du Bellay seems to blame Rome for all his disappointments his Italian journey marks in fact a decisive turning-point in his literary career, enlarging his horizons, deepening his sensibility, and bringing out his full originality. The four works (*Regrets, Jeux rustiques, Antiquitez de Rome, Poëmata*) which appeared almost simultaneously in France in 1558 had been largely composed in Italy, and his most significant poetry of this period displays a new, subtle blend of primitive, Gallic spirit and mellow *romanitas*. 'Là donq', Françoys', he had called in the *Deffence*, 'marchez couraigeusement vers cete superbe cité romaine: et des serves depouilles d'elle (comme vous avez fait plus d'une fois) ornez voz temples et autelz'; and it was in this spirit of high endeavour that he had set out for the Mecca of Renaissance humanism (XXXII). He proclaims in the *Antiquitez* that 'Rome fut tout le monde, & tout le monde est Rome' (XXVI), and he boasts of having 'chanté, le premier des François, L'antique honneur du peuple à longue robbe' (XXXII). But having sung the grandeur that was Rome and meditated upon the poetry of its ruins he seems to have gradually wearied of Imperial Rome and Papal Rome alike. The arrogance of 'la Rome neuve' reminds him of the *hubris* which destroyed 'la vieille Rome' just as it did the legendary Giants who rebelled against heaven. Cut off from his motherland, he feels a sense of physical privation 'comme un aigneau qui sa nourrice appelle' (IX). He curses the day when he abandoned 'la France, & mon Anjou dont le desir me poingt' (XXV). 'Ainsi qu'un Promethé, cloué sur l'Aventin' (X), he can see no end to his torment (XL). It is the exact reverse of Ovid's plight: the Latin poet, banished among the barbarous Scythians at Tomi on the Black Sea, longs for the pleasures and excitements of Rome; the 'Ovide françois', exiled in Rome, yearns to return to the peace and calm of his *petit Lyré*. Enhanced by distance and intimately bound up with the nostalgia for lost youth, home is always best. Small, humble, and obscure, Liré appeals to the poet's heart more than the spectacular surroundings of Rome. The humanist gives way here to the man, and his thoughts hark back to his own country, his own village, his own home. Seen through the halo of memory, 'le plaisant sejour de [sa] terre Angevine' becomes a dream landscape with its woods, its 'champs blondissans', its vineyards, its gardens '& les prez verdissans, Que [son] fleuve traverse' (XIX); but amid this idyllic setting the poet's eye singles out a little village beside a modest manor with a grey, pointed roof of *ardoise fine*. The fire in the hearth is for Northern man the domestic symbol *par excellence*, and Du Bellay pictures himself here as the returning exile who glimpses from afar the smoke curling up from the familiar chimney. A poignant but evanescent vision, it briefly hovers before the mind's eye only to dissolve again with the thin wisps of smoke which scatter and vanish. At once the source of nostalgia and the frail hope of return, it represents the fundamental image of *Les Regrets*. Absent and yet omnipresent, Home is explicitly or implicitly the central theme around which the architecture of the work is organized.

Seen within the context of *Les Regrets*, the 'sonnet du petit Liré' clearly expresses in quintessential form the *idée fixe* of the whole work. At the same time it constitutes a subtly harmonized synthesis of the various elements which make up Du Bellay's poetic genius, for he has distilled the whole of his mind and art into this short, moving poem which illustrates Boileau's dictum: 'Un sonnet sans défaut vaut seul un long poème.'

The mythological similes of lines 1–2 (the comparison of the poet's odyssey to the fabulous voyages of Ulysses and Jason)[3] may strike us today as disproportionate and artificial; but as a humanist Du Bellay chose these archetypal *exempla* because they were part of the common classical culture of his age, and the sixteenth-century public would have regarded these brief reminiscences as familiar, natural character-images. By adding a classical dimension they ennoble prosaic reality, universalize the theme and lend the opening of the poem a certain epic quality. This heroic element,

---

[3] For the possibility of topical allusions attaching here to Ulysses, Jason, and the Golden Fleece, see *Les Regrets*, ed. Jolliffe and Screech, pp. 99 and 242. Cf. also *Poëmata*, 'Ad milites Gallos':

> Qualeis Troia viros genuit, qualeis tulit Argo,
> Vos modo, vos tellus Gallica protulerat

and Jodelle's Argonautic mascarade for the royal banquet at the Hôtel de Ville in Paris in February 1558.

however, is played down and deftly subordinated to the general tonality of the sonnet by the wry envy of the initial formula (*Heureux qui...*). There is no direct satire of Rome here, just a few touches of faint aversion in the sestet; but Du Bellay's mixed feelings give the poem a certain bitter-sweet flavour. The dominant note, however, is elegiac. 'Tendre de nature' (XL), the poet almost seems to take a languorous pleasure in intoning in dolorous accents his plaintive lament. There is, however, no mistaking the genuineness of his 'mal du pays'. Personal and direct, he speaks from the heart and takes the reader into his confidence. It is 'poésie intime', a penetrating expression of the poet's deepest feelings. True, he always remains a humanist and draws upon the traditional repertory for myths, images, and certain picturesque details;[4] but whether these reminiscences are a result of imitation or 'innutrition' they are all smoothly integrated into the poetic texture and perfectly fused with 'la réalité vécue'. Du Bellay always remains himself because even when he borrows it is because of a deeply felt affinity or self-identification. The poem remains rooted in direct observation and experience. The throbbing emotion, the distinctive 'goût du terroir', and the obsessional image of home lend it the accent of sincerity and truth.

The poem is a regular sonnet with its fourteen lines distributed in two quatrains followed by two tercets; but whereas the end-stopped quatrains consist of one sentence each the tercets are bound together by the long final sentence. In the quatrains there is the usual repetition of *rimes embrassées* (ABBA ABBA). Two types of rhyme-scheme were regularly employed in the sestet of the sixteenth-century sonnet: CCD EDE, the form invented by Peletier, and CCD EED, the only arrangement practised by Marot. As in most of the sonnets of the *Regrets* Du Bellay uses here 'les tercets marotiques'; but since the tercets are linked they really approximate to a traditional sixain—*rimes plates* followed by *rimes embrassées*. In

---

[4] *plein d'usage & raison* is a Homeric touch (*Od.*, I, 3; cf. 'Patriae desiderium', l. 45); the smoke rising from the ancestral hearth is a detail from the Ulysses legend which had become proverbial (Homer, *Od.*, I, 57–9; Ovid, *Pont.*, I, iii, 33–4; Erasmus, *Adagia*, I, ii, 16; Marot, 'A la Royne de Navarre', l. 162); *des palais Romains le front audacieux* and *marbre dur* are the very phrases used in Du Bellay's version of the *Aeneid* to render Virgil's *minaeque murorum ingentes* (iv. 88–9) and *solido de marmore* (vi. 69); the contrast of home and the metropolis in the sestet perhaps owes something to Cicero's preference for his native Arpinum (*De legibus*, II, i. 1–3, ii. 4–5); the final line may also distantly recall 'the mild death off the sea' which Teiresias prophesies for Ulysses in *Od.*, XI.

accordance with the rules of the genre the last line rounds off the sonnet with its striking 'trait final' and leaves behind an indelible impression of *la douceur Angevine*. Like all the poems of the *Regrets* the sonnet is written in Alexandrines. The classical Alexandrine is notable for its weighty gravity and formal majesty; but the sixteenth-century Alexandrine is lighter, freer, more flexible. Certainly Du Bellay's Alexandrines here are not rigid or mechanical. The caesura is never absent, but it varies in force and is occasionally no more than vestigial (ll. 2, 7, 9, 10). The subtle changes of rhythm resulting therefrom are enhanced by the discreet use of enjambment with the *rejet* or *contre-rejet* taking up a whole hemistich (ll. 5–6, 6–7). A master of varied accentuation, Du Bellay gives full relief to the inflexions of sense and mood by deft stresses and expressive pauses, especially at the hemistich (ll. 1, 3, 5, 6, 8, 12, 13) and at the rhyme (ll. 5, 6, 7, 8, 9, 10, 11, 14). As in most of the poems of the *Regrets* he strictly observes the law of the 'alternance des rimes' with masculine rhymes predominating over feminine. All the rhymes, however, are soft or muted (the masculine ones are mostly nasal, with hardly any harsh consonants), and the sonnet ends with the exquisitely soft feminine rhyme *fine-Angevine*. As regards the quality of his rhyming Du Bellay admits 'de [ses] vers la ryme si facile' and roundly declares:

> Quant à moy, je ne veulx...
> ...pour polir ma ryme,
> Me consumer l'esprit d'une songneuse lime,
> Frapper dessus la table, ou mes ongles ronger (II).

All his rhymes here are at least adequate, and three are rich (*toison-*[5] *raison, saison-maison, Latin-Palatin*); but the search for rare, rich rhymes counts for less with Du Bellay than the interior rhythm of the line and the general harmony of the poem: 'Regarde principalement qu'en ton vers n'y ait rien dur, hyulque' (*Deffence*). Here there is just one case of mild hiatus (*et‿en quelle saison*), and in the sestet the antithesis of home and the metropolis is reinforced by the contrast between the caressing softness of the images of Anjou and the faint asperity of the terms evoking the various aspects of Rome; but in general the poetry has a smooth, harmonious flow. Du Bellay's 'chant mélodieux' arises principally from the subtle interplay of assonance and alliteration: *i* (17 times), *u* (10), [ã] (6), [ɛ̃] (6), [ɔ̃] (12),

5 Pronounced [twɛzɔ̃] in the 16th C.

unelided final e (15), l (31), m (17), [s] (18), f (4), v (9), [ʒ] (9). The suave melody with its occasional plaintive, piercing notes is an admirable example of Du Bellay's musical virtuosity, and like those other poet-musicians Lamartine and Verlaine he exploits the music of his verse in order to express indirectly an 'état d'âme'.

The images too serve as an oblique expression of mood. They are sometimes derivative; but since they are primarily elementary signs of profound affection or aversion they are all enhanced by the intensity of the lyrical feeling. The poetic atmosphere of the sestet, in particular, arises less from the quality of the isolated image than from the rapid, dreamlike succession of parallel images with their accompanying antithetical shades of emotion. The repetition of the verb *revoiray* underlines the visual character of the imagery which conveys the impression of direct, personal experience. Subtle touches of local colour are introduced by a few deft strokes which reveal the artist's eye for the telling detail, and the brief, precise notations result in an exquisite purity and density of imagery. Some of the details have a homely simplicity, but all are endowed with poetical delicacy and charm. There is no minute or lush description, for the main point here is not the form or colour of things, but the emotions which they stir. Enhanced by contrast with uncongenial surroundings, the familiar, beloved objects are evoked by nostalgic reverie to produce a perfect fusion of image and sentiment.

The archaic language, spelling, and punctuation do not present serious difficulties for the comprehension of the poem and may be briefly glossed here:

beau = 'grand', 'héroïque'; *cestuy la*, alternative form of 'celui-là'; *plein d'usage* (= 'd'expérience') *& raison* (= 'et de savoir-vivre'); *entre* = 'parmi', 'au milieu de'; *aage* for 'âge' (= 'vie'); *revoiray* for 'reverrai'; *helas, cheminee, sejour* (omission of acute accent); *saison* = 'temps'; *clos* = 'enclos', 'jardin fermé'; *m'est* = 'est pour moi l'équivalent de'; *d'avantage* for 'davantage'; *Plus me plaist le sejour* (bold archaic inversion); *plaist* for 'plaît'; *basty* for 'bâti'; *ayeux* for 'aïeux'; *Romains, Gaulois, Latin, Angevine* (capital for small letter); *front* = 'fronton', 'partie supérieure d'une haute façade'; *Loyre, Tybre, Lyré* (*y* for *i*); *Loyre*, fem. in mod. French, but masc. in 16th. C. (cf. Latin *Liger*, m.); *doulceur* for 'douceur'; commas emphasizing previous word (*saison, province, ayeux, Gaulois, Lyré*); comma for exclamation-mark (after *helas*); colon for comma in line 11 (it accentuates *ardoise fine* more strongly than a comma, but at the same time links the two tercets).

The sonnet is essentially an attempt by Du Bellay to assuage his suffering by poetic utterance, and its basic elegiac tonality is established, on the one hand, by its all-pervasive sweet *tendresse* and, on the other, by the lassitude and faint monotony of the softly sighing, musical verse. However, Du Bellay's 'vers doucereux' avoids mushy sentimentality thanks to the measure and moderation of his temperate style. The style is notable for its purity, grace, and charm, its clarity and suppleness, its suggestive conciseness, the dainty nicety of detail coupled with the perfect finish of the whole; but the two outstanding qualities are, first, the personal intimacy, and, second, the modest simplicity which makes the sonnet as readily accessible as a popular *chanson*. The facility and simplicity are not, however, entirely artless. Du Bellay is never more calculating than when he seems most spontaneous, and though there is no vain arti-fice here the poem is enhanced by the schematization and styliza-tion of consummate artistry. Nothing, for example, could be more artistically premeditated than Du Bellay's selection of 'epithetes significatifs': some are at once apt and evocative (*beau*,[6] *audacieux, dur, fine*); some form neatly contrasting pairs (*dur*/*fine; Gaulois*/ *Latin; marin*/*Angevine*); even those which are commonplace (*petit, pauvre*) are charged with tender emotion and point the comparison between the humble modesty of home and the proud grandeur of Rome. The poet also has judicious recourse to expres-sive inversion (ll. 5–6, 9, 10, 11, 14) as well as to those 'figures et ornemens, sans les quelz tout oraison et poëme sont nudz, manques et debiles' (*Deffence*). The figures include metaphor (l. 10), simile (ll. 1, 2, 8), periphrasis (ll. 2, 9), synecdoche (*cheminee*) and ellipsis (ll. 12–14); but the most striking rhetorical devices here are repeti-tion, enumeration, and antithesis. The discreet or marked repetition of the same word or formula, sometimes with slight variations (*comme; quand*/*en quelle saison; revoiray-je; mon petit village*/*mon petit Lyré; plus que; me plaist*), produces the effect of a fixed obsession or a monotonous lament. The numerous parallelisms of

---

[6] The archaic meaning of the epithet lifts the phrase *un beau voyage* above the insipid banality of its modern touristic associations.

lines 9–14, reinforced by anaphora, enumerate Du Bellay's preferences in a manner reminiscent of the Provençal and Italian *Plazer*.[7] The basic aesthetic principle informing the poetic structure, however, is antithesis. It takes various forms: far-ranging adventure/ domestic felicity (ll. 1–2, 3–4); the destiny of the legendary hero/ the plight of the poet (ll. 1–4, 5–8); Roman majesty/*la doulceur Angevine* (ll. 9–14). The greater is systematically set off against the lesser; but the latter is always dearer to the poet. The contrasts are not only spatial (Rome/Anjou), but also temporal (the idealized past/the uncongenial present and the uncertain future). The fundamental opposition, however, is that between the place of Du Bellay's exile and the place where his heart lies, and this finds its most powerful expression in the long final series of parallelisms which build up to the essential contrast of line 14. Antithesis is often merely an artificial, ingenious device; but it is here the basic structural principle because it partakes of the very nature of nostalgia and exactly conveys the poet's psychological and emotional condition.

The development of the sonnet is simple and natural; but it is underpinned by the firm, coherent structure of classical art. The keynote of each stanza is struck by the initial attack: *Heureux qui... Quand revoiray-je, helas... Plus me plaist... Plus...* The quatrains stand in a relationship of discreet antithesis—an exclamation of envy followed by an anxious question and a deep sigh. The linked tercets are an emphatic, reiterated assertion of the poet's preference for home. The last line rounds off the sonnet by connecting its end (*l'air marin*) with its beginning (ll. 1–2) and evocatively summing up the essential theme of homesickness (*la doulceur Angevine*). The individual stanzas are unified by the nostalgic mood—oblique in the first quatrain; direct and personal, but still slightly muted, in the second; sharply insistent in the sestet.

The heartfelt *Heureux qui* with which the poem opens is an exclamation of envy in the antique manner (cf. 'Patriae desiderium', l. 45: 'Felix qui') and a favourite formula of Du Bellay (XCIV). The loose syntax of lines 1–2 must be construed: 'Heureux qui comme Ulysse, ou comme cestuy la qui..., a fait...'; but the order of line 1, reinforced by the strong accentuation, throws the proper name (*Ulysse*) into sharp relief, while the absence of a secondary

---

[7] See R. T. Hill, 'The Influence of the Noie on the poetry of J. Du Bellay', in *Essays in honor of A. Feuillerat* (New Haven, Conn., 1943), pp. 85–92.

coupe in the first hemistich of line 2 coupled with the attenuation of the caesura lends the line a broad epic sweep appropriate to the fabulous feat evoked. *Et puis* is a free, colloquial transition which omits the normal repetition of the relative pronoun and swiftly passes from the heroic adventures of lines 1–2 to the homecoming of lines 3–4. The stanza expresses the two successive, contrasting aspirations of human nature (the wanderlust of youth and the final urge to return to one's roots); but the accent here is not so much on the *beau voyage* as on the homecoming. The double reminiscence (Homer's *Odyssey* and Apollonius' *Argonautica*) commingles the myths of the two legendary travellers—Ulysses and his cousin Jason. Ulysses exemplifies the much-suffering wanderer who after a long, heroic voyage returns home mellowed by his experience of men and cities. No attempt is made here to single out any of the strangely varied exploits of the Odyssean hero who is simply referred to by his name; but the Ulysses theme is a leitmotif of the *Regrets* ('A Monsieur d'Avanson', XXVI, XL, LXXXVIII, CXXX), and the mere mention of his name is evocative enough. The *Odyssey* with its centripetal, homeward movement is the great poem of return, and its hero represents for Du Bellay, as he did for Ovid, the reluctant wanderer who yearns for his remote, undistinguished little kingdom and who after twenty years' absence returns at last to the rugged, barren island of Ithaca to live in peace and contentment reunited with the faithful Penelope and his son Telemachus. Jason, on the other hand, is a simpler, more straightforward character than the complex, ambiguous Ulysses and less resourceful than the 'man of many turns'. He does not outshine his distinguished companions on the *Argo* and is something of a backseat hero. That is perhaps why he is not directly named in line 2, but merely designated periphrastically by his one great feat which here serves as an illustration of the fabulous poetry of 'les voyages merveilleux'. Together with the fifty Argonauts he had sailed to Colchis at the easternmost end of the Black Sea and carried off the Golden Fleece which hung from an oak in a sacred grove and was guarded by an unsleeping dragon. But Jason's deed was accomplished only with the aid of Medea's magical arts, and to judge by his subsequent fate the Fleece seems hardly to have been worth the trouble which it cost him to procure it. Having lost the favour of the gods by breaking faith with Medea he wandered homeless from city to city, hated of men, and returning finally to Corinth he was about to hang himself from the prow of the *Argo* when the ship toppled forward and killed him. Clearly Jason's story does not correspond with lines 3–4 of the sonnet, which refer only to the homecoming of Homer's wanderer-hero and which form the transition to lines 5–6 with the reminiscence of Ulysses' famous yearning to see again the smoke rising from his ancestral hearth.

The first stanza has the outward appearance of a general, sententious reflection on the nature of travel. Du Bellay does not speak directly in his own name; but though he is writing of Ulysses and Jason he is also thinking of his own melancholy situation which he is mentally comparing to that of the legendary heroes. No conquering hero, he envies not so much their adventurous exploits as their successful return home. The stanza is not an 'invitation au voyage', but rather fits into the general, obsessive preoccupation with the homeward journey in the *Regrets*. A mediocre, unheroic traveller, Du Bellay prefers the joyous return (XXXVI, CXXIX) to the inauspicious departure (XXV) and the perilous voyage (XXVI, XXXIV). Unlike Ulysses who returns *plein d'usage & raison* the poet 's'acquiert en voyageant un sçavoir malheureux' (XXIX). Jason at least carries off the Golden Fleece; but Du Bellay will bring back a less radiant prize:

> ...je suis venu si loing,
> Pour m'enrichir d'ennuy, de vieillesse, & de soing,
> Et perdre en voyageant le meilleur de mon aage.
> Ainsi le marinier souvent pour tout trésor
> Rapporte des harencs en lieu de lingots d'or,
> Aiant fait, comme moy, un malheureux voyage (XXXII).

Weary and disappointed, he has abandoned his former hopes of honour and fortune. All that he can look forward to is to return home and *vivre entre ses parents le reste de son aage*; but even the word *parents* has a sad resonance here for those who recall Du Bellay's other melancholy lines:

> Qu'ay-je depuis mon enfance
> Sinon toute injuste offence
> Senty de mes plus prochains ? ('Complainte du Desesperé')

'Les affaires domestiques' with their burdens, difficulties, and acrimonious dissensions were the bane of Du Bellay's existence, and his return home was to be ironically that of a disappointed Ulysses:

Et je pensois aussi ce que pensoit Ulysse,
   Qu'il n'estoit rien plus doulx que voir encor' un jour
   Fumer sa cheminee...
Las mais apres l'ennuy de si longue saison,
   Mille souciz mordants je trouve en ma maison,
   Qui me rongent le cœur sans espoir d'allegence.
Adieu donques (Dorat) je suis encor' Romain... (CXXX)

In the second stanza the poet expresses his nostalgic feelings no longer obliquely, but directly and personally. There is a discreet antithesis between the successful return of Stanza 1 and the more problematic return of Stanza 2. The exclamation of envy is followed by the insistent repetition of the anxious question: *Quand revoiray-je... en quelle saison, Revoiray-je...* The stanza conveys with touching simplicity and heartfelt sincerity a mood of profound homesickness; but the idea of return arouses melancholy rather than joy. It is relegated to a remote, indeterminate future, and the sorrowful sigh of line 5 (*helas*), heavily stressed by the caesura, suggests a deep-seated fear that Du Bellay's failing health ('J'ay le corps maladif', XXXIX) may prevent the realization of his dream ('Je ne suis asseuré de retourner en France', XL). He already feels 'en [sa] vieille saison', 'en l'hyver de [sa] vie' (XXXVII), and his untimely death was indeed to take place only two years after his return to France. The melancholy mood heightens the poignancy of the visual imagery, and the enjambment of lines 5–6 and 6–7 strengthens the impression of distance in space and time. From afar the exile pictures the simple, homely sights which would catch the eye of the returning wanderer. There is, first, the general impression of the village[8] where Du Bellay was born and bred; then, picked out by the inversion, the familiar chimney is more closely focused; finally, the poet's eye alights on the walls enclosing his family home. The accent here is on the smallness of the country hamlet; but though it may be little and obscure the poet belongs here, and his warm sense of attachment is emphasized from here on by the insistent repetition of the possessive adjective: *mon petit village, ma pauvre maison, mes ayeux, mon Loyre Gaulois, mon petit Lyré*. The chimney is an image of home, and its soft, grey smoke blots out any lingering memory of the radiance of the Golden Fleece. The village, however tiny, would have

---

[8] Liré (Maine-et-Loire), situated on the left bank of the Loire facing Ancenis, half-way between Angers and Nantes.

more than one fire burning; but the poet has eyes only for one chimney, that of his own home. *Maison* is for Du Bellay an almost magic word, the symbol of cosy immobility as opposed to the restless, violent imagery of sea and ship. Enclosed by its protective walls, home is a haven of peace and security. Du Bellay speaks here of his *pauvre maison*, and the epithet reinforces the impression of humble modesty already associated with his *petit village*. The sonnet acquires thereby a wide appeal and permits readers from the lowliest homes to identify with the poet. The description may well seem a poetic exaggeration; for his home was in fact the Château de la Turmelière, and the still remaining ruins suggest that this feudal castle must once have been impressive in its way. But its architecture was medieval; it was built in stone, not marble; and to an Italian eye it would have seemed 'poor' beside the *palazzi* of Renaissance Rome. Its very modesty, however, endears it to Du Bellay. His home may not be grandiose; but it stands for personal freedom and independence. 'Monsieur de Lyré' is his own man; he is 'sa court, son roy, sa faveur, & son maistre' (XXXVIII). His estate is small ('trente-deux septerées de terre, en un tenant'); but the real value of things is dependent on the heart, and for Du Bellay his little demesne means as much as a vast Roman province *& beaucoup d'avantage* (the world-wide Empire of which a province was only a territorial division?). Line 8 supplies in this sense a smooth, natural transition to the theme of the sestet.

The comparison of Anjou and Rome, hitherto only implied, is explicitly elaborated in the long parallel of lines 9–14 which vigorously assert over and over again the poet's warm preference for home. His preference is not rational or objective but emotional, and his excitement betrays itself in the quicker, livelier rhythm of the short stanzas which contrasts with the slow, ample movement of the quatrains. The sestet consists of an accumulation of brief, antithetical images which evoke precise, characteristic features of Anjou and Rome. The double series is introduced by the bold inversion *Plus me plaist... Que...* (ll. 9–10), a formula which is insistently repeated as in a kind of litany, but with slight variations so as to avoid excessive monotony: *Plus que... me plaist...* (l. 11); *Plus... que...* (ll. 12, 13); *Et plus que...* (l. 14).[9] The basic symmetry is also varied by certain dissymmetries: the first parallelism extends over two lines, with one image to each line; the remainder take up

[9] The verb *plaist* is understood in the last three lines.

only one line, with one image to each hemistich. Similarly the Roman image sometimes suggests the corresponding image of Anjou (ll. 11 and 14); but more often the process is reversed (ll. 9–10, 12, 13). The enumeration builds up to the final line which impressively completes the series.

The parallel begins with the comparison between Du Bellay's home and the palaces of Rome, and the caressing softness of line 9 by its contrast with the harsher sonority of line 10 seems already to indicate in itself a marked preference. *Sejour*, used here in a material rather than its usual temporal sense, belongs to the category of 'langage élevé', and Du Bellay's *pauvre maison* is thus restored by the ennobling periphrasis to its proper distinction as an abode rich in ancestral traditions and associations (*le sejour qu'ont basty mes ayeux*). The natural family pride which inspired the epitaph composed by the poet for his own tomb:

> Clara progenie et domo vetusta
> Natus...
> Sum Bellaius, et poëta...

contrasts with the arrogance of the patricians and cardinals who built the huge, sumptuous palaces of Rome. The inversion of line 10 throws into relief *le front audacieux*, i.e. the lofty, imposing façades of these palaces (cf. the Palazzo Farnese). The personification (*front* for 'fronton') suggests the pretentious ambitions of their owners. The proud-fronted palaces match the 'front audacieux des sept costaux Romains' (*Ant.*, XII) and the 'front audacieux' of the members of the papal entourage (CXVIII). They seem to embody the grandiose arrogance of modern Rome, itself a resurgence of the *superbia* of ancient Rome.

The parallel continues in line 11 with the contrast between the *marbre dur* and the *ardoise fine*. The profusion of hard, massive marble confers upon Rome the appearance of a city built for eternity; but the epithet also hints perhaps at the hardness of its citizens. Certainly its cold whiteness contrasts with the soft, melancholy greyness of the *ardoise fine* which evokes not only fragile delicacy, but also the discreet tints and subtle shades wrought by time and climate. The finest French slate is found in Anjou, especially at Trélazé, and the slate roofs of the province would strike a traveller returning from the South where red Roman tiles predominate. It is a picturesque touch of local colour which produces a penetrating poetic effect here.

In line 12 Du Bellay juxtaposes the two rivers which form an integral part of their respective landscapes. Rivers are an image at once of transience and permanence: their waters flow away, but they themselves remain (*Ant.*, III). Of all the aspects of Rome Father Tiber ('Dieu tortueux', *Ant.*, XIII) is treated with most respect. 'Le fleuve Thusque au superbe rivage' (X) is rich in historical associations; but it remains none the less *le Tybre Latin*, i.e. a foreign river, the river of Rome. The poet makes no attempt here to contrast the yellowish, muddy Tiber with the clear, pale waters of the Loire. His preference for his *Loyre Gaulois* is based simply on his patriotic pride, which is an extension of his family pride. The 'Fleuve paternel' beside which he asked to be buried has a name which rhymes easily with 'gloire' and is a leitmotif of his poetry. The cradle of the French Renaissance and, in the sixteenth century, the French river *par excellence*, the 'Loyre fameux' is here a concrete symbol and virtually a synonym of France itself.

Line 13 mentions for the first time the name of the poet's native village which owes the whole of its modest fame to Du Bellay himself. He insists once again on its smallness, and the phrase *mon petit Lyré* is charged with warm affection. It is perched on top of a hill overlooking the wide valley of the Loire, and the 'coteau lyréen' clearly means more to Du Bellay than *le mont Palatin* with its commanding view of all Rome from the Lateran to the Janiculum. The very symbol of Rome, the Palatine Hill is by tradition the original nucleus around which the city grew, and on its slopes were built the mansions of the leading citizens of the Republic and the palaces of the Caesars. But by the sixteenth century they were no more than romantic ruins overgrown with luxuriant vegetation, and like all the seven hills —'ces monts, ces sept monts qui sont ore Tumbeaux de la grandeur qui le ciel menassoit' (*Ant.*, IV)—the Palatine seems to Du Bellay to symbolize the fallen pride of ancient Rome.

The 'chute' of the sonnet (line 14) is appropriately the most striking and the most richly evocative line in the poem. The *air marin* seems to evoke not only the Roman climate with its fresh, cool sea breezes (e.g. the *ponentino*) which were probably unfavourable to the poet's delicate health, but also, in a broader sense, the call to adventurous sea-voyages and maritime conquest (cf.

ll. 1–2). Du Bellay, however, shares Ovid's aversion for the sea which he always regards as a menacing, hostile force:

> ...ceste mer Romaine
> De dangereux escueils & de bancs toute pleine
> Cache mille perils... (XXVI).

Certainly the faintly rasping *r*'s of *air marin* contrast with the melodious softness of the second hemistich. It is clear that Du Bellay prefers the softer, balmier air of Anjou which has a continental climate, with no hint of the sea. However, *la doulceur Angevine* refers not only to the mild, temperate climate of Anjou, but also to its soft, gently undulating countryside and to the friendly, easygoing character of its inhabitants (*Andegavi molles*, as they seemed to their Roman conquerors). Anjou has often been called the most 'French' of all the provinces of France, and it is not surprising that Du Bellay has compressed into the phrase *la doulceur Angevine* all his nostalgic yearning for his native land.

A true son of his province, 'le doux Bellay' was in the habit of signing his works with the initials I.D.B.A. (Joachim Du Bellay, Angevin). The final rhyme of this sonnet seems to imprint his hallmark on the poem.

4 Montaigne

Trois d'entre eux, ignorans combien coutera un jour à leur repos et à leur bon heur la connoissance des corruptions de deçà, et que de ce commerce naistra leur ruyne, comme je presuppose qu'elle soit desjà avancée, bien miserables de s'estre laissez piper au desir de la nouvelleté, et avoir quitté la douceur de leur ciel pour 5 venir voir le nostre, furent à Roüan, du temps que le feu Roy Charles neufiesme y estoit. Le Roy parla à eux long temps; on leur fit voir nostre façon, nostre pompe, la forme d'une belle ville. Apres cela quelqu'un en demanda leur advis, et voulut sçavoir d'eux ce qu'ils y avoient trouvé de plus admirable: ils respondirent trois 10 choses, d'où j'ay perdu la troisiesme, et en suis bien marry; mais j'en ay encore deux en memoire. Ils dirent qu'ils trouvoient en premier lieu fort estrange que tant de grands hommes, portans barbe, forts et armez, qui estoient autour du Roy (il est vray-semblable que ils parloient des Suisses de sa garde), se soubs- 15 missent à obeyr à un enfant, et qu'on ne choisissoit plus tost quelqu'un d'entr'eux pour commander; secondement (ils ont une façon de leur langage telle, qu'ils nomment les hommes moitié les uns des autres) qu'ils avoyent aperçeu qu'il y avoit parmy nous des hommes pleins et gorgez de toutes sortes de commoditez, et que 20 leurs moitiez estoient mendians à leurs portes, décharnez de faim et de pauvreté; et trouvoient estrange comme ces moitiez icy necessiteuses pouvoient souffrir une telle injustice, qu'ils ne prinsent les autres à la gorge, ou missent le feu à leurs maisons.

Je parlay à l'un d'eux fort long temps; mais j'avois un truchement 25 qui me suyvoit si mal, et qui estoit si empesché à recevoir mes imaginations par sa bestise, que je n'en peus tirer guiere de plaisir. Sur ce que je luy demanday quel fruit il recevoit de la superiorité qu'il avoit parmy les siens (car c'estoit un Capitaine, et nos matelots le nommoient Roy), il me dict que c'estoit marcher le premier à 30 la guerre; de combien d'hommes il estoit suyvy, il me montra une¹ espace de lieu, pour signifier que c'estoit autant qu'il en pourroit en une telle espace, ce pouvoit estre quatre ou cinq mille hommes; si, hors la guerre, toute son authorité estoit expirée, il dict qu'il luy en restoit cela que, quand il visitoit les vilages qui dépendoient de luy, on luy dressoit des sentiers au travers des hayes de leurs bois, par où il peut² passer bien à l'aise.

Tout cela ne va pas trop mal: mais quoy, ils ne portent point de haut de chausses.

MONTAIGNE, *Essais*, Bk. I, xxxi
Date of first publication: 1580
Ed. P. Villey (Paris: Alcan, 1922),
I, 276–7

THIS passage comprises the last three paragraphs of the essay 'Des Cannibales', published in 1580 in Book I of the *Essais*, and probably composed, according to Pierre Villey's dating, in 1579.

The essay is noteworthy as an early statement of the author's faith in 'nostre grande et puissante mere nature', and of his critical attitude towards the customs and usages of conventional society; it is an interesting contribution to the literary tradition of the 'noble savage', which is often thought of as an eighteenth-century invention, but which can be traced back to Tacitus, and was revived by sixteenth-century voyages of discovery before becoming a commonplace in the philosophical writings of the eighteenth century. Although travellers' accounts had been published dealing with the tribes of the Brazilian coast, where Villegagnon's expedition had landed in 1557, Montaigne professes his distrust for the tendentious writings of the 'cosmographes', and prefers to rely on his own conversations with natives and with the less sophisticated kind of traveller. As regards its form, 'Des Cannibales' lies somewhere between the style of the very earliest essays, which consist of a perfunctory, and rather formal, treatment of a single moral theme, and the characteristic quality of the 'personal essay' as shown in Book III: the spontaneity and conversational flavour are already there, but there is rather more regard for relevance than in the typical

¹ The gender of *espace* was still variable in the sixteenth century.
² The orthography is misleading here: this is the imperfect subjunctive of *pouvoir*, just as in l. 27 *peus* is past historic.

discursive essay of the maturer Montaigne. Thus the whole of this brief composition is devoted to a single theme, with hardly any real digression; and although the theme is treated somewhat haphazardly, by accumulation of anecdotes, rather than by carefully constructed dialectical argument, the essay presents a sustained case for the belief in primitive virtue and in the soundness of natural law unspoiled by civilization.

In the preceding pages of the essay, Montaigne has praised the naturalness of the cannibals' way of life, and shown them as being ignorant of the moral depravity, as of the physical infirmity, that are common in European societies; he has described the simplicity of their social organization, and of their natural religion; he has defended their cannibalism (only practised on defeated enemies, and a consequence of their fanatical attitude towards war) in contrast with the inhuman brutalities of the French Wars of Religion; he has written in favourable terms of their system of polygamy; and he has given a sample of their lyric poetry, to show the quality of the imagination of these so-called 'savages'. The final page of the essay, therefore, is not linked to the rest by continuous argument, and the anecdote with which he has chosen to end the essay does not provide any positive conclusion; as is so often the case with Montaigne, the order of the contents could well have been changed, and additions or deletions could have been made, without essentially altering the nature of the essay as a whole.[3] The reader is made to feel that it is the haphazard reminiscing of the anecdotal conversationalist, and not the conscious art of the man of letters, that is responsible for the composition of the essay.

Syntactically, too, the link is a weak one: though the sense is quite clear, the reader would search in vain for a precise grammatical antecedent for the *eux* of line 1; this is another illustration of the author's casual, conversational style. On the other hand, the construction of the first sentence of the passage is far from casual: it is highly literary, and suggests the concision and economy of a complex Latin sentence. In particular, it exemplifies a stylistic feature frequently found in the *Essais*: the main clause *Trois d'entre eux... furent à Roüan* is filled out with two groups of clauses qualifying the subject, though in each case the principal unit is an adjectival phrase without a finite verb:

[3] On this essentially 'baroque' feature of Montaigne's style, see R. A. Sayce, 'Baroque Elements in Montaigne', *French Studies*, VIII (1954), pp. 1-16.

Trois d'entre eux, ⸜*ignorans...,*
⸝*bien miserables..., furent à Roüan...*

This use of participles or adjectives provides the writer with a very economical means of presenting different time-perspectives in the same sentence by simple juxtaposition, without explanatory linking words.[4] Here, the group depending on *ignorans*[5] looks forward to the future, whereas the group depending on *bien miserables* looks back to the past; while the main verb *furent* fixes the whole at a precise moment in time. One could imagine the same ideas being expressed more conventionally in this way: 'Trois d'entre eux furent à Rouen...; ils ne savaient pas encore..., mais ils étaient déjà bien misérables...' There is a most agreeable balance within this sentence: the two clauses (*combien... et que...*) of the first half are matched by a similar pair in the second half (*de s'estre laissez piper... et avoir quitté...*); and the terms used in the second part correspond reasonably well to those of the first, though they substitute more vivid concrete expressions for the abstractions of the clauses depending on *ignorans* (*connoissance, corruptions, commerce, ruyne*; compare *s'estre laissez piper, la douceur de leur ciel, venir voir le nostre*). The effect of contrast obtained by this sort of juxtaposition of abstract and concrete is one of the most characteristic (and one of the most pleasing) features of Montaigne's style; in this case *se laisser piper*, although it is by no means a fresh metaphor, retains enough of the flavour of the primary meaning of the verb ('to cheep', hence 'to lure birds by imitating their call') to provide a homely restatement of the ideas implied in the earlier part of the sentence (*la connoissance des corruptions; de ce commerce naistra leur ruyne*). This opening sentence is for the most part devoted to providing an objective setting for the anecdote that is to follow; though there is a characteristic intrusion by the author himself, in the cynical aside of lines 3-4, which breaks up the temporal framework as analysed above in order to suggest that the harm predicted

---

[4] Cf. F. Gray, *Le Style de Montaigne* (Paris, 1958), p. 55.

[5] It was normal 16th-C. usage for the present participle to agree, whether it was used 'adjectivally' or 'verbally'; cf. *portans barbe* (l. 13). Other instances of 16th-C. usage as regards syntax and accidence are: *soit* (l. 4), an example of the more flexible use of the subjunctive in noun clauses after verbs of saying, thinking, etc.; *s'estre laissez piper* (l. 4): agreement of participle; *neufiesme* (l. 7) for modern 'neuf'; *en suis bien marry* (l. 11): omission of pronoun-subject; *qu'on ne choisissoit* (l. 16): omission of *pas* in a negative construction; *comme* (l. 22) for 'comment'; *ces moitiez icy* (l. 22) for 'ces moitiés-ci'; and *c'estoit marcher* (l. 30) for 'c'était de marcher'.

for the future is already being anticipated (as is indicated in the precise and literal use of *presuppose*) by the impatient march of time.

The long opening sentence having narrowed down the perspective to a particular moment with *du temps que le feu Roy Charles neufiesme y estoit* (that is, in 1562), the narrative continues with *Le Roy parla...* We should note *parla à eux* for modern 'leur parla', as an example of the greater freedom of sixteenth-century syntax, and appreciate the variety of construction that results from this: *Le Roy parla à eux... on leur fit voir...* This sentence, by means of its brevity, provides an effective contrast to the long opening sentence; a contrast pointed by the rhetorical phrasing of the ternary *nostre façon, nostre pompe, la forme d'une belle ville.* Further verbs in the past historic now follow: *demanda..., voulut sçavoir...,*[6] *respondirent*; and then Montaigne very typically interrupts the narrative with another characteristic 'aside' to the reader: the use of the first person, the verbs in the present tense (*en suis bien marry... j'en ay encore deux...*), as well as the gratuitous nature of this characteristically self-deprecatory confidence, combine to produce the desired effect of intimacy with the writer in the act of writing.

The impression given by the passage *ils respondirent... deux en memoire* is one of complete sincerity on the author's part: by this apparently ingenuous confession he persuades us of his lack of artifice as regards his manner, and this in turn helps to lend conviction with regard to the subject-matter. Whether or not Montaigne is faithfully reproducing an actual interview, or whether he is putting imaginary comments into the mouths of his interlocutors, is quite irrelevant: in fact, the remarks made by his naïve observers tally with the sort of criticism of organized European society that he often advances elsewhere on his own account, and the reader should bear in mind, as an indication of the way in which these comments by the 'savages' are to be taken, an earlier passage from the same essay:

> Je trouve... qu'il n'y a rien de barbare et de sauvage en cette nation, à ce qu'on m'en a rapporté, sinon que chacun appelle barbarie ce qui n'est pas de son usage... Ils sont sauvages, de mesmes que nous appellons sauvages les fruicts que nature, de soy et de son progrez ordinaire, a produicts: là où, à la verité, ce

---

[6] *Admirable* is here much nearer to its Latin source than to the modern meaning: 'worthy of note, of wonder' rather than 'admirable'.

sont ceux que nous avons alterez par nostre artifice et detournez de l'ordre commun, que nous devrions appeller plutost sauvages.

Here, he is concerned to make two simple points: firstly, the absurdity, in a hereditary monarchy, of the succession passing to an heir too young to exercise effective control—a practice which, in Montaigne's own time (the cases of François II and Charles IX) had been one of the principal causes of the Wars of Religion; and secondly, the monstrous injustice of the contrast between ostentatious wealth and extreme poverty—a contrast exacerbated by the same wars. The simple outsiders present themselves (or are conveniently supposed to have presented themselves) as ideal commentators, with a fresh, unprejudiced viewpoint; and the fact that Montaigne does not explicitly identify himself with their point of view, but maintains his separateness with the faintly patronizing remarks in parenthesis (*il est vray-semblable que...*, *ils ont une façon...*) must not be taken to mean that he rejects their observations as too naïve to be valid. Rather, he is deliberately using the 'savages' as spokesmen for his own criticisms of society: the technique of ironical detachment in presenting the opinions of naïve outsiders is one that was to be thoroughly exploited by the eighteenth-century *philosophes*.[7] It is surely for this reason, as well as to convey the impression of the genuine interview, that Montaigne pretends to have to 'interpret' the savages' comments (*il est vray-semblable qu'ils parloient des Suisses...*). The point made is so naïve and unsophisticated—moreover, it is one which surely could have been made with equal justice as a criticism of many 'primitive' societies, in which hereditary rule by a minor was not unknown—as to suggest that Montaigne's interlocutors are not so much real savages, viewing European customs from the standpoint of a different culture, as artificial embodiments of abstract Reason, created with a view to demonstrating the absurdity and irrationality of all human institutions.

Not that Montaigne is advocating the abolition of hereditary monarchy; still less that the poor should rise up and slaughter the rich. The purpose of such a passage, as indeed it is a major aim of

---

[7] For instance, Montesquieu's Persians (*Lettres persanes*), and Voltaire's Quaker (*Lettres philosophiques*) or Huron Indian (*L'Ingénu*). Cf. the latter author's comment on his Quaker: 'Voilà comme mon saint homme abusait assez spécieusement de trois ou quatre passages de la Sainte Écriture qui semblaient favoriser sa secte...' (*Lettres philosophiques*, no. 1).

the whole essay, is to present a critique of civilized society considered as a product of human intelligence: far from being based on rational principles, the social system fails to satisfy even the most elementary requirements of simple reason. The essay 'Les Cannibales' is a product of the same 'crise pyrrhonienne' as gave rise to the 'Apologie de Raymond Sebond'; it reflects a similar mood of scepticism with regard to the effectiveness of human reason, and was written, in part at least, with the same aim, of illustrating the unreliability of man's rational processes. It is to this end that Montaigne adopts the term *moitié*, together with the interpretation of it which introduces the second observation: although this produces a rather cumbersome construction, it is justified in that the argument—that the natural equality of men is violated by the distribution of wealth in organized society—is thereby put across more effectively. This is not, however, a point on which Montaigne chooses to dwell: the contrast between rich and poor was an inescapable part of life, and is here treated not as a subject for sentimentalizing, but as an example of the bizarre absurdities inherent in all human institutions, when these are judged by the standards of pure reason. The descriptive precision of *mendians à leurs portes, décharnez de faim* is not designed, therefore, to make an effective appeal to the reader's sensibility, but to lend force to the cannibals' protestations of surprise at their discovery.

The next paragraph seems to make the point, somewhat wordily, and with another characteristically gratuitous 'conversational' reminiscence (*mais j'avois un truchement... guiere de plaisir*)[8] that the values of a primitive way of life are just as much to be esteemed as the more showy and superficial ceremonial by which rank is honoured in European societies. But we must note that Montaigne himself makes no such comment, and that this concluding part of the anecdote is narrated completely objectively: it is left to the reader to draw his own conclusions in the light of what has already been said about the cannibals and their way of life. If there is any comment, it is to be found in the brief and enigmatic final paragraph, in so far as this may be taken as relating in particular to what immediately precedes it—for it naturally also provides a general conclusion to the essay as a whole.

Enigmatic though it may appear if taken on its own, this concluding paragraph is quite clear if it is looked at in relation to all that

[8] *Imaginations* here = 'idées'.

precedes it, and it is a brilliant example of that ironical detachment that has already been referred to. On the face of it, Montaigne appears to be saying: 'That is all very well as far as it goes, but of course we cannot expect very much of savages who do not even know how to dress'—dismissing all that may have been said or implied in favour of the cannibals' way of life in deference to conventional prejudice against a nation lacking the most rudimentary attributes of 'civilization'. However, the ironical intention is clear enough: the fact that he has chosen, as a symbol of 'civilized' living, such a specific feature of contemporary fashion—the word *haut-de-chausses* is only attested from the middle of the sixteenth century—may perhaps be seen as a pointer; and the real effect of this closing sentence is surely to challenge the conventional values of a civilization which sets great store by outward signs such as fashion, and to sum up, in a neat and memorable phrase, the 'message' of the whole essay.

In its general character, the style of this passage is not that which we associate most readily with Montaigne: what Professor Huntington Brown calls the 'prophetic' style of the discursive essay, full of aphoristic statements with an energetic personal flavour.[9] The reason is, of course, that the whole of this passage is narrative in function: Montaigne is relating an interview, and the critical observations which provide the purpose of the piece are not delivered by the author himself in his own person but indirectly, through the medium of reported speech. Thus the structure of the passage depends to a large extent on the framework of the interview: *Quelqu'un en demanda leur advis, et voulut sçavoir...; ils respondirent...; Ils dirent qu'ils trouvoient... estrange que..., et qu'...; secondement... qu'ils avoyent aperçeu qu'..., et que...; et trouvoient estrange comme..., qu'ils..., ou...; Sur ce que je luy demanday quel..., il me dict que...; de combien..., il me montra...; si..., il dict que...* Inevitably, then, the sentences composing the passage contain a large number of subordinate clauses, and a relatively high proportion of purely 'functional' elements such as the repeated conjunction *que*, and the interrogatives *combien, quel, si*, all of which are necessitated by the question-and-answer pattern of the interview. It is interesting to note how in the second paragraph Montaigne adopts a paratactic construction, suppressing the linking words that would normally be used to introduce the second and third

9 In *Prose Style: Five Primary Types* (Minneapolis, Minn., 1966).

clauses dependent on *Sur ce que je luy demanday…*; it is difficult to say whether this heightens or attenuates the effect of complexity in the sentence-structure, but it certainly produces an impression of economical, unadorned writing, in which elegance is sacrificed to concision. It can be seen, perhaps, as an example of what Brown calls the 'inventory style' associated with legal documents, and it is possibly legitimate to wonder whether this may not have been a case of Montaigne's early familiarity with such texts influencing his manner as an essayist. If the effect achieved here seems excessively functional, as the noun-clauses dependent on *je luy demanday…* are 'ticked off' or itemized, and if in general the style of this extract has less of his characteristic personal flavour than we expect of Montaigne at his best, there are nevertheless touches which give the passage an idiosyncratic stamp: the 'confessional' parenthesis of lines 11–22, the subjective reminiscing at the beginning of the second paragraph, and above all the last sentence, which has all the flavour of a spontaneous spoken comment, and yet which, managing to say a great deal in a little space, brings the essay to such an effective conclusion. These are examples of Montaigne at his most familiar; and the constant contrast between these familiar touches and a more formal rhetorical or 'prophetic' manner—a contrast that is brought out not only by sentence-structure and arrangement of phrases, but also by choice of vocabulary, learned or popular to match the overall style—is what creates the charm of Montaigne's writing.

5 Corneille

Pauline: Que de soucis flottants, que de confus nuages
    Présentent à mes yeux d'inconstantes images!
    Douce tranquillité, que je n'ose espérer,
    Que ton divin rayon tarde à les éclairer!
5   Mille pensers divers, que mes troubles produisent,
    Dans mon cœur incertain à l'envi se détruisent:
    Nul espoir ne me flatte où j'ose persister;
    Nulle peur ne m'effraye où j'ose m'arrêter.
    Mon esprit, embrassant tout ce qu'il s'imagine,
10   Veut tantôt mon bonheur, et tantôt ma ruine,
    L'un et l'autre le frappe avec si peu d'effet,
    Qu'il ne peut espérer ni craindre tout à fait.
    Sévère incessamment brouille ma fantaisie;
    J'espère en sa vertu, je crains sa jalousie;
15   Et je n'ose penser que d'un œil bien égal
    Polyeucte en ces lieux puisse voir son rival.
    Comme entre deux rivaux la haine est naturelle,
    L'entrevue aisément se termine en querelle:
    L'un voit aux mains d'autrui ce qu'il croit mériter,
20   L'autre un désespéré qui le lui veut ôter.
    Quelque haute raison qui règle leur courage,
    L'un conçoit de l'envie, et l'autre de l'ombrage:
    La honte d'un affront, que chacun d'eux croit voir,
    Ou de nouveau reçue, ou prête à recevoir,
25   Consumant dès l'abord toute leur patience,
    Forme de la colère et de la défiance,
    Et saisissant ensemble et l'époux et l'amant,
    En dépit d'eux les livre à leur ressentiment.
    Mais que je me figure une étrange chimère,
30   Et que je traite mal Polyeucte et Sévère!
    Comme si la vertu de ces fameux rivaux

Ne pouvait s'affranchir de ces communs défauts!
Leurs âmes à tous deux, d'elles-mêmes maîtresses,
Sont d'un ordre trop haut pour de telles bassesses.   35
Ils se verront au temple en hommes généreux;
Mais, las! ils se verront, et c'est beaucoup pour eux.
Que sert à mon époux d'être dans Mélitène,
Si contre lui Sévère arme l'aigle romaine,
Si mon père y commande, et craint ce favori,   40
Et se repent déjà du choix de mon mari?
Si peu que j'ai d'espoir ne luit qu'avec contrainte,
En naissant il avorte, et fait place à la crainte;
Ce qui doit l'affermir sert à le dissiper.
Dieux! faites que ma peur puisse enfin se tromper!

P. CORNEILLE, *Polyeucte*, Act III,
sc. i
Date of first performance: 1641–2
Text of first edition (1643)

THIS soliloquy, spoken by Pauline at the beginning of Act III of
Polyeucte, marks a pause in the action before the developments
which will lead to the crisis and the denouement. Pauline, daughter
of Félix the Roman governor of Armenia, and recently married to
Polyeucte, an Armenian nobleman, has had a dream in which
Sévère, whom she had formerly loved but rejected on her father's
orders, and whom she thought to have since died in battle, has
appeared and foretold her husband's death; as she tells her con-
fidant in Act I, scene iii, her father seemed to threaten Polyeucte,
and the latter's death was then brought about by Félix and Sévère,
together with a troop of Christians. Sévère in fact arrives, and in
an interview with Pauline in Act II, in which he is informed of her
marriage to Polyeucte, the two lovers bid each other farewell. We
have also learned in Act I of Polyeucte's baptism as a Christian (of
which his wife as yet knows nothing), and seen his departure at the
end of Act II, full of new-found zeal, to destroy the idols at the
pagan ceremony for which Sévère has ostensibly come to Mélitènco.
The premonitory dream, which has already begun to be fulfilled
in that Sévère has returned from the dead, thus provides the
essential basis of the fears expressed in the soliloquy. However, the

situation is strongly marked by dramatic irony, since the danger Polyeucte is deliberately courting comes from a very different source from that apprehended by his wife; and the spectator, already aware of the hero's conversion, is able to put quite another interpretation on the dream from the one Pauline herself has given to it.

The commonest purpose of the long soliloquy in the Classical theatre is to show a character in a state of hesitation, either torn between conflicting courses of action, or (in the case of the more passive characters) undecided in his reactions to the situation confronting him; particularly in Corneille's theatre, such a soliloquy is frequently the occasion for a dialectical set-piece, in which alternatives are debated in a formal, logical manner, and a solution arrived at. In the present instance, the structure does not quite conform to the traditional dialectical pattern: thesis followed by antithesis, leading to synthesis; though a formal division of the speech along not too dissimilar lines can be observed, as follows:

> *lines 1–12*: introductory statement of Pauline's mental confusion; hope conflicting with apprehension.
> *lines 13–28*: theme of apprehension and alarm.
> *lines 29–35*: theme of consolation and hope.
> *lines 36–end*: conclusion on a note of uncertainty, but with apprehension predominating over hope.

Nor does the structure of the speech give such a rigid impression of a series of independent four-line stanzas, as is conveyed by many of Corneille's soliloquies.[1] While the first two major divisions do occur at the end of four-line groups, and while the first half of the speech possesses a very distinct stanzaic pattern, this dominant pattern becomes blurred at line 24, where there is no grammatical break, and the sentence runs on to fill the whole of a longer, eight-line 'stanza'; and again at lines 35–6, where the grammatical break is anticipated by a break in the sense, the last line of this group performing a transitional function as far as sense is concerned. Similarly, the inconclusive character of the soliloquy, with the closing lines taking up the same position as the beginning, also helps to attenuate the effect of an over-formal, almost mechanical exercise in logic such as is produced by the monologues of some of

---

[1] Cf. J. Scherer, *La Dramaturgie classique en France* (Paris, 1950), pp. 297–8: 'l'élément le plus caractéristique des passages lyriques visant à la pompe est le quatrain.' Examples are *Pompée*, V, i; *Rodogune*, II, i.

Corneille's characters, and to give a slightly more spontaneous, reflective impression.

Although, as has been said, the dream recounted in Act I lies behind this speech of Pauline's, there is no explicit reference to it here, and it is her present, waking state of mind that is being analysed at this point. However, the opening lines do introduce vocabulary already used to refer to the dream itself: cf. 'un amas confus des vapeurs de la nuit' (l. 7 of the play), which is taken up in the *confus nuages* of line 1 of the passage; and 'ma douleur trop forte a brouillé ces images' (l. 241), echoed in *images* of line 2 and in *brouille ma fantaisie* of line 13. The visual image of clouds representing a confused mental state is prolonged through the first 'stanza' with *à mes yeux, inconstantes images, rayon* and *éclairer*. The chiasmus of line 1 (noun: adjective . . . adjective: noun), the transfer of epithets (*flottants* logically belongs with the concrete *nuages*, and *confus* with the abstract *soucis*), the personification of the abstraction *tranquillité* as a being with godly attributes (*divin rayon*), all help to create a high degree of stylization; one has only to compare the much more immediate pictorial effect that 'nuages flottants' would have, to appreciate the intellectualizing tendency of this manner of writing.

In the second 'stanza' the same theme is repeated, but this time shorn of the imagery of the first four lines: the *confus nuages* have now become *mes troubles,* and instead of *images* they produce *mille pensers divers.* Lines 7–8 take the examination one stage further, identifying the emotions *espoir* and *peur,* and opposing them in a couplet whose high degree of isometry, or phonetic identity between the two lines[2]—only the contrasting terms *espoir* and *peur,* the verb accompanying each of these nouns, and the first two syllables of the rhyming word, are different—makes it thoroughly characteristic of Corneille's dialectical style.[3]

The opposition between the two central terms *espoir* and *peur* having been established, the next group of four lines develops it by means of antithetical formulae common to all oratorical writing, and much used by Corneille in his introspective or analytical soliloquies:

[2] To use the term in the same sense as J.-G. Cahen (*Le Vocabulaire de Racine,* pp. 168–9).
[3] It is interesting to note that a variant reading from later editions of the play gives even greater emphasis to this feature by increasing the visual similarity of the lines:

> Aucun espoir n'y coule où j'ose persister;
> Aucun effroi n'y règne où j'ose m'arrêter.

tantôt... tantôt..., *l'un et l'autre*; the contrast between *bonheur* and *ruine* repeats by implication the conflict between 'hope' and 'fear', and these two original terms themselves are restated, this time in verbal form, in line 12. *Embrassant* is used in the sense of 'accepting', 'believing'; and in line 10 the meaning of *veut* is perhaps rather unusual: it is presumably 'my mind . . . *pursues* now my happiness, now my downfall'; in any case the reading *voit* of later editions seems preferable to *veut*. Again, as a result of its antithetical construction, and of the 'echoes' of *bonheur*, *ruine* in *espérer* and *craindre*, this group of four lines possesses a striking coherence and density of expression.

The second part of the monologue, beginning at line 13, develops the interpretation which Pauline's apprehensions suggest to her. The first four-line unit specifies the cause of these fears in simple terms, which are then elaborated in the rest of this section. Sévère is named first, as it is his arrival which is the occasion of her alarm (*brouille ma fantaisie* = 'trouble mon imagination'); but Polyeucte is immediately afterwards introduced in very similar terms, and his jealousy, as well as Sévère's, is seen as a potential source of danger. Line 14, it is true, repeats the hope-fear balance of the previous stanza (and takes up the antithetical terms from lines 7–8 and 12) in a line sharply divided at the caesura, with paratactic construction aiding the force of the antithesis; but line 15 (*d'un œil bien égal* = 'indifferently') brings the balance down on the side of fear, and in this couplet (ll. 15–16) the antagonism between husband and lover, reinforced by the emphatic positioning of *Polyeucte* and *son rival*, asserts the menace of this opposition.

Lines 17–20 develop the ideas of 13–16, but it is as if Pauline, having named her husband and her former lover as the source of her fears, now calls on a stock of 'idées reçues' in order to predict, not how Polyeucte and Sévère as individuals will behave, but how 'a lover' and 'a husband' are likely to behave in such circumstances. The result is a series of generalizations (ll. 17–28) not far removed from the impersonal style of the moral *sentences* found throughout Corneille's theatre: *Polyeucte* and *son rival* of line 16 are translated into the generalized abstraction *deux rivaux* of line 17, and it is only the strong definite article at the beginning of the following line (*L'entrevue* = 'cette entrevue'), perhaps aided by the semantic connection between *l'entrevue* and *voir son rival*, that ensures the link with the particular examples which concern the speaker.

In this central section of the soliloquy, antithesis is used for a different purpose, to characterize the behaviour of the hypothetical 'husband' and 'lover': for example, in lines 19–20, quite remarkable in the degree of detachment with which they sum up the situation, with *l'un* and *l'autre* representing the *deux rivaux*, and Pauline herself reduced to the status of the neuter *ce qu'il croit mériter*. As has been indicated, from line 21 onwards the four-line 'stanzas' give way to an eight-line unit. While this may be fortuitous, it is at least possible that the running-on of the sentence at lines 24–5, together with the enjambment of lines 23–4, is intended by the poet to provide a fitting vehicle for the ideas at this point. These lines successfully express the mounting tension of the imagined quarrel, rising to a climax at line 28, with antithesis helping to point the stages in the action. To whatever extent their emotions (*courage* = 'cœur') are controlled by reason, one lover will be susceptible to jealousy, the other will be quick to take offence: the antithetical opposition of *l'un... l'autre* is again brought into use, this time within a single line, as the pace quickens. One rival imagines he has already received an insult, the other thinks he is about to be insulted: *chacun d'eux* is used this time instead of *l'un... l'autre*, but the effect is similar, since the enjambment carries it forward to the next line, and links it equally with *Ou... reçue* and *ou... à recevoir* (this rather cryptic expression means 'ou près d'être reçue': the seventeenth century did not distinguish between *prêt à* and *près de*). One of them feels anger, the other suspicion (l. 26); and finally both (*et l'époux et l'amant*) become victims of their feelings. *Ressentiment*, in Corneille's time, normally meant 'la peine profonde, sans cesse renouvelée, que l'on éprouve à la suite d'un malheur dont on a été vivement touché' (Cayrou—cf. *Cinna*, lines 1651–2); here, however, it appears to have the more restricted modern meaning of 'hostilité envers quelqu'un qui nous a causé un mal; rancune'. The change of rhythm of the sentence beginning at line 23 helps to build up the climax of the imagined quarrel: the vigorous verbal structure, and in particular the parallelism of lines 25–6 and 27–8, with the gerundive construction in each case followed by a main verb (*Consumant... Forme... Et saisissant... les livre...*) help to bestow a sense of movement and urgency on the otherwise rather lifeless abstractions represented by *affront... patience... colère... défiance... ressentiment*.

At line 29 the stanza-pattern is resumed, and the contrary theme is now developed, as Pauline attempts to subdue her fears and to assert an optimistic view of the situation. Once more the grammatical unit becomes identified with the single line (ll. 29, 30) or the couplet (ll. 31–2); and there is a certain weak parallelism in the two exclamations of lines 29 and 30. The latter line provides an instance of the 'anticipatory rhyme' frequently found in the Classical theatre, especially when a proper name appears at the rhyming position. Here, with the first line of the couplet ending in ...*chimère*, the beginning of the next line *Et que je traite mal Polyeucte et...* makes it absolutely clear that the rhyming word will be ...*Sévère*; the effect is to give a particular prominence to the second hemistich, and in this context the use of a strong anticipatory rhyme perhaps serves to emphasise the change of mood.

For Polyeucte and Sévère are not ordinary rivals: they are *ces fameux rivaux*; and we now see that the 'idées reçues' to which the present situation has been related in the previous section of the soliloquy were misleading, and that Pauline's husband and lover may be expected to rise above the behaviour of ordinary men. Lines 31–5 are typically Cornelian in spirit, embodying as they do the notion of a moral élite, whose members are enabled by their *vertu* (a term which has a particular Cornelian resonance: 'force, vigueur, tant du corps que de l'âme'—Furetière, *Dictionnaire universel*, 1690) to overcome the temptations of the baser passions. The placing of the adjective in the affective position in lines 31 and 32 brings it into prominence: Polyeucte and Sévère are still *rivaux*, but it is now regarded as more important that they are *fameux* (i.e. that they have already gained a well-deserved reputation as members of this élite); similarly the *défauts* of line 32 may be human weaknesses, but it is more important that they are *communs* (i.e. typical of ordinary men, but not shared by this superior élite); the affective position of the adjective conveys on the one hand admiration, on the other hand scorn. The next couplet reiterates this distinction, now asserting it confidently in a positive form: the two heroes (throughout this section they are considered together, no longer separated by such formulae as *l'un... l'autre...*) are endowed with the supreme attribute of self-mastery (the second half of l. 33 cannot fail to recall to any reader of Corneille the climactic line of the previous play, *Cinna*: 'Je suis maître de moi comme de l'univers'), and are thus incapable of behaving ignobly—the point is made by the simple, but forceful, antithesis between *haut* and *bassesses*. Finally, making the particular application to the event she has been fearing, Pauline is able to declare that even when they meet at the ceremony in the temple they will behave not as the *deux rivaux* of lines 17–18, but *en hommes généreux* (*généreux* at this time still retained a close connection with Latin *generosus*: 'qui a l'âme grande et noble, et qui préfère l'honneur à tout autre intérêt'—Furetière).

However, by a very abrupt transition—the break occurs not at the end of a 'stanza', nor even at the end of a couplet, but at the end of an odd line—this confidence is immediately replaced by a more realistic doubt, the simple language of line 36 reminding us that even though Pauline can appreciate the motivation of the heroic élite, she is not herself one of them and is consequently a prey to more normal 'human' reactions. The next four lines develop her fears afresh, this time in a much more specific manner, related to the particular situation. For the first time in this speech Pauline adopts a point of view which identifies her sympathies with Polyeucte, not only by the obvious intimacy of the possessive adjective: *mon époux* (l. 37), *mon mari* (l. 40), compared with the detachment of *ce favori* (l. 39), but also by the construction of the four-line group as a whole, which starts from *mon époux* and moves through *Sévère* to *mon père*, then returns through *ce favori* to *mon mari*.

Finally, after a long middle section almost without imagery (except for the striking metonymy of l. 38: *arme l'aigle romaine*, for 'puts the Roman army into the field'), the closing group of four lines reverts to the metaphor of the beginning of the passage. The sequence *luit... avec contrainte*, *affermir*, *dissiper* takes up the image of light trying to pierce through the clouds, though the subsidiary images in *En naissant il avorte* provide a rather awkward mixture of metaphors. The speech ends on an apostrophe to the gods, appealing for a favourable outcome to the situation: the plural *Dieux* provides an ironical reminder that Pauline's apprehensions are based on a misinterpretation of appearances, and that if danger threatens at the ceremony whose outcome she now awaits, it is not from the rivalry of Polyeucte and Sévère but from the former's new religion. The next scene brings the news that the pagan gods have been destroyed; this brief pause is over, and in the meantime the action has taken an irrevocable step towards its climax.

From the point of view of dramatic action, Act III, scene i, contributes nothing to the play. Corneille's purpose was presumably to reinforce the spectator's sympathetic interest in his heroine, by dwelling on her predicament; and the soliloquy reminds us of his *tour de force* in combining in one play an uplifting tragedy of martyrdom with the psychological interest of a drama based on the most 'worldly' of all problems: the conflict between love and society. Up to this point, the former element has been confined to two scenes between Polyeucte and Néarque, while the remaining scenes have developed the relationships between Pauline and her husband, lover, and father. This soliloquy presents a final analysis of the situation from Pauline's point of view, before the two themes are forcefully brought together in Act III, scene ii.

We can guess that her anguish is about to be increased by the disclosure of what is now happening offstage; and we appreciate the dramatic irony of the situation which makes her apprehensive of an imaginary danger, while being unaware of the real crisis that is about to break. At the same time, there is some justification in Voltaire's criticism (in his *Commentaires sur Corneille*) that 'Ce monologue, qui n'est qu'une répétition de ses terreurs, et même des terreurs qu'elle ne peut avoir qu'en vertu de son rêve, languit un peu à la représentation... Le grand défaut de Corneille est de faire des raisonnements quand il faut du sentiment.' Although here, as Voltaire goes on to say, 'cette faute est un peu couverte par l'intérêt qu'on prend au rôle si neuf et si singulier de Pauline', the reader may perhaps agree that the heroine's examination of her situation is a trifle long-drawn-out, at a moment when we are keyed up by the knowledge that Polyeucte is engaged in smashing the idols; and we may be tempted to feel, with Voltaire, that a less formal, less intellectualized—and perhaps shorter—expression of her reactions to the situation would have been more effective. However, for playgoers of Corneille's own generation, it seems—to judge from the comments of Mme de Sévigné, for instance—to have been Pauline and her predicament that constituted the principal appeal of the play. Rational analysis of an emotional dilemma was very much to the taste of the audiences and readers to whom the play was addressed, and this soliloquy is a masterly illustration of the way in which the emotional possibilities of an extraordinary situation can be explored so as to provide keen intellectual pleasure.

6 Molière

Orgon :   Alte-là, mon beau-frère :
  Vous ne connaissez pas celui dont vous parlez.
Cléante : Je ne le connais pas, puisque vous le voulez ;
  Mais enfin, pour savoir quel homme ce peut être...
Orgon : Mon frère, vous seriez charmé de le connaître,   5
  Et vos ravissements ne prendraient point de fin.
  C'est un homme... qui... ha !... un homme... un homme enfin.
  Qui suit bien ses leçons goûte une paix profonde,
  Et comme du fumier regarde tout le monde.
  Oui, je deviens tout autre avec son entretien ;   10
  Il m'enseigne à n'avoir affection pour rien,
  De toutes amitiés il détache mon âme ;
  Et je verrais mourir frère, enfants, mère et femme,
  Que je m'en soucierais autant que de cela.
Cléante : Les sentiments humains, mon frère, que voilà !   15
Orgon : Ha ! si vous aviez vu comme j'en fis rencontre,
  Vous auriez pris pour lui l'amitié que je montre.
  Chaque jour à l'église il venait, d'un air doux,
  Tout vis-à-vis de moi se mettre à deux genoux.
  Il attirait les yeux de l'assemblée entière   20
  Par l'ardeur dont au Ciel il poussait sa prière ;
  Il faisait des soupirs, de grands élancements,
  Et baisait humblement la terre à tous moments ;
  Et, lorsque je sortais, il me devançait vite,
  Pour m'aller à la porte offrir de l'eau bénite.   25
  Instruit par son garçon, qui dans tout l'imitait,
  Et de son indigence, et de ce qu'il était,
  Je lui faisais des dons ; mais avec modestie
  Il me voulait toujours en rendre une partie.
  'C'est trop, me disait-il, c'est trop de la moitié ;   30
  Je ne mérite pas de vous faire pitié' ;

Et, quand je refusais de le vouloir reprendre,
Aux pauvres, à mes yeux, il allait le répandre.
Enfin le Ciel chez moi me le fit retirer,
35   Et, depuis ce temps-là, tout semble y prospérer.
Je vois qu'il reprend tout, et qu'à ma femme même
Il prend, pour mon honneur, un intérêt extrême ;
Il m'avertit des gens qui lui font les yeux doux,
Et plus que moi six fois il s'en montre jaloux.
40   Mais vous ne croiriez point jusqu'où monte son zèle :
Il s'impute à péché la moindre bagatelle ;
Un rien presque suffit pour le scandaliser ;
Jusque-là qu'il se vint l'autre jour accuser
D'avoir pris une puce, en faisant sa prière,
45   Et de l'avoir tuée avec trop de colère.

MOLIÈRE, *Tartuffe*, Act I, sc. v
Date of first performance: 1669
Text of first edition (1669)

MOLIÈRE'S *Tartuffe* is a play which has always been praised for its masterly exposition. The author himself claims: 'j'ai employé... deux actes entiers à préparer la venue de mon scélérat', and indeed, before his appearance in Act III, scene ii, Tartuffe has been portrayed at second hand, discussed and analysed almost continuously throughout the first two acts of the play. However, such an approach can easily lead the reader to overlook the fact that it is not Tartuffe but Orgon who is the central character: Orgon, the role played by Molière himself, which fits into a whole series of similar comic characters running through his theatre. It has been well said that if Tartuffe himself did not appear (or if his role was much reduced in importance), the presence of Orgon as the 'père ridicule' would be enough to preserve the resemblance to Molière's other great comic plays, whereas without Orgon, *Tartuffe* would be a sombre melodrama totally unlike anything else in Molière's theatre. However, even if we bear this undoubtedly correct perspective in mind, the exposition is still unusually protracted, and our introduction to Orgon himself is more gradual than is normally the case with Molière's central characters. The playwright has chosen to open this play with a gallery of secondary characters, constituting the household of the *père de famille* who is later to assume the central role: his mother, his wife, his brother-in-law, his son and daughter, and his servant; and the first scene shows them all discussing Tartuffe, the intruder, and the impression he makes on the family. The hold that this *faux dévot* has on Madame Pernelle, Orgon's mother—the only other member of the family, besides her son, to be taken in by him—is shown to us directly, whereas to begin with we are only given an indirect view of the effect on Orgon. After Madame Pernelle's departure we learn from Dorine, in reply to Cléante's exclamation of surprise at the old lady's infatuation with Tartuffe, that

> tout cela n'est rien au prix du fils,
> Et si vous l'aviez vu, vous diriez: C'est bien pis!

and in the thirty lines which follow this couplet (ll. 181–210) the servant gives a portrait of the relationship between her master and Tartuffe, which is to be fully confirmed on the arrival of her master himself. The latter enters in Act I, scene iv, and is mocked by Dorine, as he betrays the full extent of his idolatry in the celebrated 'Et Tartuffe?... Le pauvre homme!' sequence.

As Orgon and his brother-in-law are left alone in Act I, scene v, Cléante at once expresses his amazement that any man should be able to exert such an influence over another:

> Et se peut-il qu'un homme ait un charme[1] aujourd'hui
> A vous faire oublier toutes choses pour lui,
> Qu'après avoir chez vous réparé sa misère,
> Vous en veniez au point...?

He is interrupted by Orgon with the words which open the passage under consideration. Orgon cuts him short, for to him the matter admits of no discussion: it is not a question of generalizations ('se peut-il qu'*un homme...*?'), but of a particular instance, of which Cléante is not in a position to speak: 'Vous ne connaissez pas *celui dont vous parlez.*' Cléante's reply is conciliatory, though it is not clear what form his uncompleted sentence would have taken: presumably either 'in order to be able to judge at first hand what kind of man he is, (I should need to have the opportunity of meeting him)' or '(... is it necessary to know him at first hand?)'; or else—taking *pour* + infinitive in its common seventeenth-century

---

[1] *Charme* has the strong 17th-C. sense of 'sortilège, puissance magique'.

sense as a causal construction (cf. *Tartuffe*, l. 966)—'the fact that you are in a position to judge at first hand (does not prevent you from error)'. It would appear as though Molière has deliberately left the uncompleted sentence ambiguous, and that while the second alternative is much more likely to represent Cléante's meaning, the ambiguity enables Orgon to interpret the phrase in the other sense, and to interrupt accordingly.

The latter readily accepts what he takes to be an invitation to describe Tartuffe, to endow the general 'un homme', 'quel homme ce peut être', with the particular attributes of the individual he knows; but first, the opening couplet of this speech, expressing his conviction that Cléante's reactions would inevitably be the same as his own, contains an involuntary revelation, for although *charmé* is here used in something like its attenuated modern sense, the semantic connection with *charme* as used by Cléante seven lines earlier is still apparent; and both this term and *ravissements* (*ravissement*: literally 'ce qui nous ravit à nous-mêmes') can be seen as unconscious admissions that there is some truth in Cléante's charge, and that Orgon is 'under the spell' of Tartuffe. The description of Orgon's idol starts confidently, hesitates uncertainly, and comes to an ignominious end, all in the space of a single line; the attempt to convince Cléante falls back lamely on the very generalization: 'un homme' which Orgon has found unsatisfactory in Cléante's original question: a brilliant expression in a nutshell of the absurdity of Orgon's infatuation. The Grands Écrivains editors put forward, apparently as worthy of consideration (although they do finally reject it) an interpretation of this line which is surely not to be entertained for a moment: 'On est tenté d'accentuer ces mots: 'un homme enfin', ce qui signifierait un homme ayant toute sa virilité morale, une énergie stoïque.'[2] However, the contemporary *Lettre sur la comédie de l'Imposteur* (based on the version of the play performed in 1667) appears to confirm, if confirmation were necessary, the reading of this line as a comic expression of Orgon's fatuity:

> (Orgon) commence à dire que *c'est un homme*, de sorte qu'il semble qu'il aille faire un long dénombrement de ses bonnes qualités; et tout cela se réduit pourtant à dire encore une ou deux fois *mais un homme, un homme*, et à conclure, *un homme enfin*, ce

---

[2] *Œuvres*, ed. Despois and Mesnard (Paris, 1873–93), IV, 416.

qui veut dire plusieurs choses admirables: l'une que les bigots n'ont, pour l'ordinaire, aucune bonne qualité et n'ont pour tout mérite que leur bigoterie, ce qui paraît en ce que l'homme même qui est infatué de celui-ci ne sait que dire pour le louer; l'autre est un beau jeu du sens de ces mots: *C'est un homme*, qui concluent très-véritablement que Panulphe [the name given to the character in the 1667 version] est extrêmement un homme, c'est-à-dire un fourbe, un méchant, un traître et un animal très-pervers, dans le langage de l'ancienne comédie.[3]

In the following couplet Orgon tries to recover face: instead of relying on his own inspiration, which has failed him so signally, he uses a borrowed jargon. The devotional terminology (*...goûte une paix profonde*), the echoes of Biblical phraseology in *comme du fumier regarde tout le monde* (cf. Phil. 3:8: 'Christ Jesus my Lord, for whom I suffered the loss of all things, and do count them but dung'), and the aphoristic style of the couplet, all suggest that this is a manner of speaking that he has learned from Tartuffe. However, he is incapable of reproducing it without bringing in a comic ambiguity, for line 9, as well as meaning 'considers the world as nothing but dung' (*tout le monde* here = 'le monde entier'), can also be taken to mean 'contemplates the world from the top of his dung-hill' (cf. the proverbial 'hardi comme un coq sur son fumier', 'être comme Job sur son fumier'). We have already had from Dorine in scene ii a description of the way in which Orgon has become *tout autre* as a result of his *entretien* with Tartuffe, and we can judge—Dorine, like Cléante, having established herself as a sympathetic character and a reliable witness—that he has little cause for complacent self-congratulation on this score. It should be noted that *entretien* here means more than 'conversation'; it has mystical connotations which might easily escape a modern reader or spectator: 'Il se dit, dans le langage mystique, des muettes communications avec la Divinité.'[4]

The remainder of this speech contains what must surely rank as

---

[3] *Œuvres*, ed. Despois and Mesnard (Paris, 1873–93), IV, 536–7.
[4] Littré, s.v. 'Entretien', where the following example is quoted:

> Quelles grâces, Seigneur, ne dois-je pas te rendre,
> A toi, ma seule gloire et mon unique bien?
> Mais qui suis-je pour entreprendre
> D'élever mon esprit jusqu'à ton entretien?

> (Corneille, *Imitation de Jésus-Christ*.)

the most provocative lines of this highly provocative play. For when Tartuffe bends the language of *dévotion* to serve his own ends, Molière is careful to make it clear (in the stage-direction to l. 1487) that 'c'est un scélérat qui parle'; here, however, we have Orgon, who is not a hypocrite but a sincere believer, expressing an opinion which, for all its revolting inhumanity,[5] is demonstrably close to the letter of an authentic Christian text: 'If any man cometh unto me, and hateth not his own father, and mother, and wife, and children, and brethren, and sisters, yea, and his own life also, he cannot be my disciple' (Luke 14:26). It is true that, in his obsessive self-centredness, Orgon leaves out the phrase 'yea, and his own life also', which gives the Biblical text its full meaning; but even though his own formula may misrepresent in this way the spirit of Christ's teaching, the resemblance to the letter is undeniable. The closeness to Luke's 'If any man hate not . . .' is particularly striking if one compares this text with the much milder version of the same passage given by Matthew: 'He that loveth father or mother more than me is not worthy of me; and he that loveth son or daughter more than me is not worthy of me' (10:37).

Nor does Cléante's rejoinder diminish the boldness of Molière's writing at this point: he does not protest that Orgon's statement is a travesty of *Christian* principles, but of *sentiments humains*. In the immediate context, *humains* refers back to *un homme enfin* of line 7, and beyond that to *quel homme ce peut être* of line 4 and the 'un homme' of Cléante's original question: it gives a striking density and cohesion to this piece of dialogue, and serves as a wry comment on the sort of human being that Orgon has become by following the 'leçons' of his spiritual director. But the implications of Cléante's remark are wider than this: it would no doubt be giving too much explicit meaning to this single line to assert that it is to be taken as a protest in the name of a well-defined philosophy, and that Cléante should be seen as the spokesman for an enlightened humanism against a repressive form of Christian doctrine; but the suggestion is there, and it is at any rate not contradicted by any other passage in the play, and is consistent with a reading of Cléante's own 'profession de foi' of lines 351–407.

---

[5] The *autant que cela* of l. 14 is accompanied by a traditional gesture, and refers to 'l'imperceptible bruit de l'ongle du pouce, un moment appuyé sous l'extrémité des dents d'en haut' (G. É. F. edition, IV, 417). To snap one's fingers would be an equivalent, and more meaningful, gesture to an English audience.

Orgon's long speech consists of two parts: lines 16–33 are a detailed narrative of his first meetings with Tartuffe, and lines 34–45 describe the state of his household, as he sees it, since Tartuffe's arrival. The speech has therefore an expository function, in that it fills in the previous history of the two principal characters before the opening of the play; but it does so from a very subjective point of view, and is therefore more important for what it reveals directly of Orgon's personality. The principal dramatic effect throughout the speech is the irony with which Molière repeatedly puts into his mouth phrases which mean one thing to the speaker himself, and something quite different to Cléante (and to the spectator). This speech for the first time gives prominence to what is to become the principal theme of the play: the conflict between reality and appearance, and the relationship between ocular evidence and judgement.[6] *Ha! si vous aviez vu...*:[7] Orgon uses the same formula as Dorine has used to Cléante in the line already quoted: 'si vous l'aviez vu'; but whereas the opening scene has established that both Cléante and Dorine are sensible characters, and we therefore readily accept the latter's unspoken premise that they would interpret ocular evidence in a similar manner, we have already deduced that there is no such common ground between Cléante and Orgon, and we soon see that in Orgon's case visual evidence is interpreted in the light of an *a priori* obsession.

The verb *voir* itself only occurs twice in this passage, but the phrases *tout vis-à-vis de moi* (l. 19), *il attirait les yeux* (l. 20) and *à mes yeux* (l. 33) are all closely linked semantically, and develop the same notion of reliance on ocular evidence with the same forceful irony. What to Cléante—and to the spectator or reader—is abundant evidence of Tartuffe's purpose, to play on Orgon's pious gullibility, is to Orgon himself, whose narrowness of vision prevents him from distinguishing between appearance and reality, proof of Tartuffe's piety and of his own discernment.

The second couplet of the speech shows how inversion in the

---

[6] This theme remains prominent throughout the play, reaching its climax in Act V, where the now disillusioned Orgon tries to disabuse his mother:

> Je l'ai vu, dis-je, vu, de mes propres yeux vu,
> Ce qu'on appelle vu... (ll. 1676–7).

[7] Line 16 contains the following linguistic features characteristic of 17th-C. usage: *comme* for 'comment'; *en* used with a personal antecedent; *faire rencontre* for mod. Fr. 'faire la rencontre'.

classical Alexandrine can be used constructively to point the articulation of the sentence. Here we have a short sentence consisting of pronoun subject, modal verb, and reflexive infinitive, and no less than five adverbial phrases: a combination which in normal prose order would be impossibly awkward; yet Molière's couplet, by a combination of inversion and the rhythm provided by the caesura and subsidiary *coupes*, not only dispenses with all awkwardness but by emphasizing each adverbial phrase in sequence constructs a graphic narrative in miniature of Tartuffe's entry into the church: (i) *chaque jour*—normal priority given to the adverbial phrase denoting time; (ii) *à l'église* ('where we, the congregation, were already seated'); (iii) (*il venait*) *d'un air doux*—close to the verb to denote the manner of his approach; (iv) *tout vis-à-vis de moi*—picking out his 'victim' and choosing an appropriate position; (v) (*se mettre*) *à deux genoux*—preliminaries successfully completed, the significant posture is assumed. The minute stages in the narrative sequence, itemized in this way, help to suggest not only Orgon's complacent self-congratulation at the 'discovery' of Tartuffe but also the deliberate nature of the latter's calculations. The extravagance of Tartuffe's ostentatious behaviour, which rises to more pronounced heights later in the passage, is already present here in *à deux genoux*, normal genuflexion being a matter of one knee only.

The following couplet exemplifies a rather more conventional use of inversion: to produce the strong 'couple tonique'[8] of *poussait sa prière* at the end of the line, here emphasized by the alliteration (*pousser* here = 'exprimer avec une vivacité passionnée'). Lines 22–3 adopt a straightforward word-order: in the first, the nouns *soupirs* and *élancements* are emphasized, but the second is a rather banal line, in which rhythm seems to cut across logical emphasis —though we should note that the action described is particularly outlandish, smacking of the prostration practised as a form of penance in some religious communities. In the next couplet, inversion lends effective support to the meaning, and again helps to convey the impression of Tartuffe's eager ostentation, as the two swift actions *il me devançait vite* and *Pour... aller à la porte* are inserted by a sort of chiasmus between *lorsque je sortais* and *offrir de l'eau bénite*. The construction in *m'aller à la porte offrir* (as in *me voulait... rendre* of l. 29, *le vouloir reprendre* of l. 32, and *se vint...*

---

[8] 'Deux termes accentués, étroitement unis par le sens' (J. B. Ratermanis, 'L'Inversion et la structure de l'alexandrin', *French Studies*, VI (1952), pp. 58–66).

accuser of l. 43) conforms to the older usage with modal verbs; however, this was already giving way in the seventeenth century to modern practice, and Molière was free to adopt whichever word-order fitted in with metrical requirements: cf. *il allait le répandre* of line 33. Here again, the formal observances practised by Tartuffe are extravagant compared with normal usage: to offer holy water is common enough between relatives or close friends, but not between male strangers!

Line 26 ends with a forceful 'couple tonique' brought about by inversion: *dans tout l'imitait*; but this is matched by a very obvious 'cheville', as the second hemistich of line 27 seems particularly lacking in inspiration. This couplet introduces Laurent, Tartuffe's servant (of whom we have already heard from Dorine, ll. 203 ff.); the irony of *qui dans tout l'imitait* is to be noted: it is another of the phrases with which Orgon reveals how easily he has been duped. By now we are under no illusions about Tartuffe's motives, and whereas Orgon delivers the next couplet as evidence of his hero's indifference to worldly things (*modestie* = 'modération'), we are more likely to be struck by the fact that Tartuffe offered to return merely 'une partie' of Orgon's gifts. Finally, the climax of the narrative—the distribution to the poor of part of what he has been given (the masculine object pronouns of ll. 32 and 33 have no antecedent, but we may suppose that *le reprendre*, logically if not grammatically connected with what has gone before, takes up the idea expressed in *en rendre une partie*)—makes it clearer than ever that Tartuffe is playing a part in front of a credulous spectator: whereas *à mes yeux* again contains a nuance of self-congratulation on the speaker's perspicacity, it is the crowning proof to Cléante and to the reader of Orgon's naïve gullibility.

At line 34, Orgon turns to comment on the effect Tartuffe's arrival has had on the family. We are now in a position to judge that it was not *le Ciel* that inspired Orgon, but that he was the instrument—though perhaps an equally passive one—of Tartuffe's will. We have already learned from Damis and Dorine in scene i of the tiresome consequences of the arrival of Tartuffe, so that the complacent blindness of line 35 seems all the more inappropriate. *Je vois qu'il reprend tout* takes up the phrase used by Madame Pernelle in the opening scene; but whereas her 'il ne reprend rien qui ne soit à reprendre' is a reasonable, if a subjective, view of the situation, Orgon's formulation *Je vois qu'il reprend tout* betrays the extremism of the petty domestic tyrant. For a modern reader or spectator, lines 36–9 are perhaps the most obviously comic of the whole speech: the adverbial phrase *pour mon honneur* is again so placed as to bring out the irony of the situation with maximum effect. Dorine has already hinted at Tartuffe's possible interest in Elmire: 'Je crois que de Madame il est, ma foi, jaloux'; but quite apart from this, the simple, unsuspecting husband thrusting his wife into the arms of a lover is a stock theme of medieval *fabliau* and farce, and Orgon's attitude puts him in the company of the countless cuckolds of a long literary tradition. This traditional reference is 'up-dated', however, and to a contemporary audience these lines would also have a topical satirical bite, for in addition to the comic self-portrayal on Orgon's part, they would almost certainly see in the officious interference ascribed to Tartuffe here an allusion to the Compagnie du Saint-Sacrement, the body of largely lay churchmen whose opposition to the play had been partly responsible for its banning from 1664 to 1669, and whose activities, particularly after the official dissolution of the Company by edict of the Parlement in 1660, were much concerned with private family relationships, which they sought to influence by means which included acting as spies and informers. Whether or not one takes the view that *Tartuffe* as a whole was conceived as an attack on the Compagnie,[9] it seems impossible that Molière could have written these particular lines without having the Compagnie in mind.

The last six lines of the speech provide the ridiculous climax of the portrait. There is a comic contradiction, to begin with, between the idea contained in *jusqu'où monte son zèle* and the *moindre bagatelle* of the following line: in fact even before the example is given, the ambiguity of line 42 (*Un rien...*) enables us to guess that this is another case of irony, and that what is brought forward as proof of Tartuffe's extreme piety will prove in fact to be yet another instance of Orgon's uncritical obsession. The anecdote itself has its origins, according to the Grands Écrivains editors, in the legend of Saint Macarius who, having killed a flea, imposed on himself the penance of living naked in the desert and fasting for six months; though another source, not as close in detail, but less remote in time and therefore possibly equally relevant, is the sixteenth-century Jesuit St. Robert Bellarmine, of whom it is related that he refused to

---

[9] As has been maintained by, e.g., R. Allier, *La Cabale des dévots* (Paris, 1902); A. Baumal, *Molière et les dévots* (Paris, 1919).

disturb the fleas in his clothes because, since they could not look forward to theological bliss, it would be wrong to deprive them of the only nourishment to which they could aspire! Though such anecdotes may help to suggest the background of ideas (devoutness leading to ostentatious asceticism) to which Molière himself probably related the incident, knowledge of possible sources adds little to one's appreciation of this crowning absurdity. It should be stressed, however, that the object of ridicule here is Orgon, not Tartuffe. A genuinely pious man who imitated Saint Macarius in this way might be found ridiculous; but in this case, the ridicule falls on the gullible narrator who is taken in by such behaviour. Throughout the passage, the self-portrait establishes Orgon as a comic character, and arouses our critical laughter. Although, like Cléante, we penetrate the impostor's disguise with every line that Orgon speaks, yet the dramatic context makes us concentrate on Orgon's self-exposure. As long as we are forced to laugh at this ridiculous figure, the moral indignation we should feel against a real-life Tartuffe is inhibited: even if unconsciously, by our laughter we connive at his deception of Orgon and applaud its success.

7 La Fontaine

L'Huître et les plaideurs

Un jour deux pèlerins sur le sable rencontrent
Une huître, que le flot y venait d'apporter:
Ils l'avalent des yeux, du doigt ils se la montrent;
A l'égard de la dent il fallut contester.
5   L'un se baissait déjà pour amasser la proie;
L'autre le pousse, et dit: 'Il est bon de savoir
    Qui de nous en aura la joie.
Celui qui le premier a pu l'apercevoir
En sera le gobeur; l'autre le verra faire.
10   — Si par là l'on juge l'affaire,
Reprit son compagnon, j'ai l'œil bon, Dieu merci.
    — Je ne l'ai pas mauvais aussi,
Dit l'autre; et je l'ai vue avant vous, sur ma vie.
— Eh bien! vous l'avez vue; et moi je l'ai sentie.'
15   Pendant tout ce bel incident,
Perrin Dandin arrive: ils le prennent pour juge.
Perrin, fort gravement, ouvre l'huître, et la gruge,
    Nos deux messieurs le regardant.
Ce repas fait, il dit d'un ton de président:
20   'Tenez, la cour vous donne à chacun une écaille
Sans dépens, et qu'en paix chacun chez soi s'en aille.'

Mettez ce qu'il en coûte à plaider aujourd'hui;
Comptez ce qu'il en reste à beaucoup de familles,
Vous verrez que Perrin tire l'argent à lui,
25   Et ne laisse aux plaideurs que le sac et les quilles.

LA FONTAINE, *Fables*, Bk. IX, ix
Date of first publication: 1671
Ed. R. Radouant (Paris: Hachette,
1929), pp. 354-5

FABLE IX of Book IX was one of a handful first published in 1671 in the *Fables nouvelles et autres poésies*: that is, between the appearance of the *Fables choisies mises en vers*, comprising the contents of the first six Books (1668), and the publication of Books VII to XI in two stages (1678 and 1679). Unlike the great majority of La Fontaine's fables, this poem has no recognized literary source in the works of the classical or oriental fabulists or of Renaissance humanists; however, the anecdote it relates must have been current in some form or other, as is shown by the conclusion to one of the fables of the 1668 collection (I, xxi):

> On fait tant, à la fin, que l'huître est pour le juge,
> > Les écailles pour les plaideurs.

Apart from unrecorded popular tradition, there is almost certainly a much more immediate source, since Boileau had written a fable on the same subject in 1669, publishing it as a tailpiece to his first *Épître* in 1670.[1] This is the text of Boileau's version:

> Un jour, dit un auteur, n'importe en quel chapitre,
> Deux voyageurs à jeun rencontrèrent une huître.
> Tous deux la contestaient, lorsque dans leur chemin
> La Justice passa, la balance à la main.
> Devant elle à grand bruit ils expliquent la chose,   5
> Tous deux avec dépens veulent gagner leur cause.
> La Justice, pesant ce droit litigieux,
> Demande l'huître, l'ouvre, et l'avale à leurs yeux,
> Et par ce bel arrêt terminant la bataille:
> 'Tenez, voilà, dit-elle, à chacun une écaille.   10
> Des sottises d'autrui nous vivons au Palais:
> Messieurs, l'huître était bonne. Adieu. Vivez en paix.'

In spite of his first line, it appears likely that Boileau had no recognized written source, but that he was giving literary form to a popular anecdote. It cannot be proved, of course, that La Fontaine was aware of Boileau's version, though circumstantial evidence is very strong indeed. The two poets had already produced rival versions of Aesop's 'Death and the Old Man' (Boileau in 'Le Bûcheron et la Mort', La Fontaine in 'La Mort et le bûcheron', I, xvi), and

---

[1] In 1672 he removed it from *Épître* I, and in 1674 placed it at the end of the new *Épître* II, written for the purpose; this is where it will be found in modern editions of Boileau.

modern editors are agreed in regarding 'L'Huître et les plaideurs' as the latter's rejoinder to Boileau's 'fable de l'huître' published in the preceding year.

A comparison between the two versions shows certain textual similarities which seem very unlikely to be fortuitous, and which may be taken as corroboration of this view. These may be listed as follows (in the order in which they appear in La Fontaine's poem): *Un jour...* (although this and other adverbs and adverbial phrases denoting time are naturally often to be found in the opening line of La Fontaine's narrative, they very rarely appear as the opening word or phrase, and only two other fables begin with the words 'Un jour...'); *rencontrent Une huître* (cf. other possible verbs: 'trouver', 'voir', 'apercevoir', any of which would surely have been more usual in such a context); *contester; Tenez... à chacun une écaille; Sans dépens* (cf. Boileau's *avec dépens*); *en paix*. While none of these coincidences, by itself, would be conclusive, taken all together they must appear so; and the existence of a common 'canevas' of this sort establishes beyond any reasonable doubt that La Fontaine did deliberately set out to produce a *réplique* to Boileau's version. Assuming that this is the case, it is all the more interesting to compare the two texts in order to see what differences of approach can be discerned.

The outstanding characteristic of Boileau's poem is the concision and economy with which the episode is narrated: the 'entrée en matière' (ll. 2–4), the climax (l. 8), and the succinct expression of the moral of the fable (l. 11) are all equally striking in this respect. The personified abstraction of Justice carrying the scales gives the piece a stylized classical air (there is even something rather incongruous in such a figure actually eating the oyster); and the conventional way in which epithets are used, either in colourless near-clichés (*grand bruit, bel[2] arrêt*), or—where more specific—conveying an abstract notion (*ce droit litigieux*), and the absence of any particularizing detail, also contribute to this effect. The unbroken pattern of Alexandrines also perhaps helps to give a rather pompous tone to Boileau's lines, while the only attempt at a more lighthearted touch, in the second half of line 1, seems somewhat laboured, as *chapitre* is all too obviously introduced in order to provide the rhyme with *huître*. The combination of classical features such as these with the spontaneous conversational tone of the last three lines gives

---

[2] Though this is lent a certain force by the irony of the comment.

Boileau's version of the fable something of a mock-heroic flavour—though it lacks the wit of *Le Lutrin*, his masterpiece in the mock-heroic genre.

The most obvious feature of La Fontaine's fable, compared with Boileau's version, is that the moral has been removed from the narrative itself, and is contained in a four-line tailpiece. More generally, it is noticeable that La Fontaine's version is less concise: it is in fact twice the length of Boileau's. In particular, La Fontaine has chosen to expand the account of the argument between the travellers, and Boileau's single hemistich 'Tous deux la contestaient' provides the basis for lines 3–14 of 'L'Huître et les plaideurs'; however, there is a slighter, albeit significant reduction of Boileau's material at the climax, since four lines of La Fontaine's (ll. 15–18) correspond to lines 3–9 of the former's. The overall result of these changes, of course, is a marked increase in the ratio of dialogue to description and narrative: with La Fontaine, exactly half of the fable proper (excluding the separate moral conclusion) is devoted to dialogue, compared with a quarter in the case of Boileau. To talk of the 'dramatic' nature of La Fontaine's writing is something of a truism: a genre requiring the use of dialogue as well as narrative will inevitably appear to have a certain affinity with dramatic writing, and comparison with other authors—as with Boileau in the present case—suggests that if La Fontaine's style is more 'dramatic', this is only a question of degree.

It is perhaps more instructive to examine the *kind* of dramatic writing with which the style of a given fable invites comparison. In this instance, whereas Boileau evidently saw the subject of the two travellers and the oyster as lending itself to a sort of mock-heroic treatment, La Fontaine seems to have recognized its affinity with a stock theme of medieval farce and *fabliau*—the hoodwinking of the simple dupe by the clever rascal—and to have adopted an appropriate style. The extra prominence given to dialogue; the more colloquial nature of the dialogue itself; the replacing of Justice by the homely figure of Perrin Dandin; the particular character of some of the 'stage-directions': all these features recall the characters and the literary flavour of farce or popular comedy. According to one account, Boileau's source for the anecdote was his father, 'à qui il l'avait ouï conter dans sa jeunesse; elle est tirée d'une ancienne comédie italienne'. Whether this is literally true or not, the *commedia dell'arte*, like the French farce, represents in general the sort of literary antecedent with which the theme of the fable demands to be identified; and of the two poets, it was La Fontaine whose discernment led him to treat it in a style in keeping with its origins.

This approach is apparent from the first line. Although Chauveau's illustration to the original edition shows two figures equipped with the traditional pilgrim's staff, the choice of the term *pèlerins* does not necessarily mean that these characters are any more particularized than in Boileau's text. *Pèlerins* could, of course, mean 'pilgrim', but the word was also widely used in the seventeenth century in the more general sense of 'traveller' which its Latin source would suggest ('qui voyage dans la campagne'—Furetière); it seems very likely indeed that La Fontaine deliberately chose this variation on Boileau's 'voyageurs' as being more familiar in tone; cf. other examples of the use of *pèlerin* in the *Fables*: II, x, line 7; IX, xiv, line 11, etc. (and Molière's *Dom Juan*, I, i, where the term means no more than 'homme rusé, gaillard, drôle').

In the first line, the inversion *sur le sable rencontrent* brings about an effective enjambment: *rencontrent Une huître*, which reinforces the comic incongruity; compare Boileau's much less striking use of the same words. This first couplet also introduces certain details not in Boileau's account: both *sur le sable* and *que le flot...* are presumably intended to indicate the freshness of the oyster; at any rate, they provide a certain picturesque detail—and a precise detail, for *le flot* is not to be taken merely as a poetic equivalent of 'la mer', but as a technical term (= 'la marée montante'). It has been suggested that the rhythm of the last nine syllables of line 2 (3 + 3 + 3) 'concourt merveilleusement à l'expression de l'idée du mouvement régulier des vagues successives'[3]—but most readers may well find this comment too speculative.

Lines 3–6 provide an excellent illustration of the popular, comic character of La Fontaine's version, and we can soon see why he has chosen to devote a dozen lines to the exchanges which Boileau had dismissed in half a line. For in the space of a dozen lines he is able to present these two *pèlerins* as characters of farce, and to sketch a vivid little scene. What makes the sketch live is its dynamic quality, for these characters are endowed with the pronounced gestures, and even with the knockabout antics, of popular comedy. The use of the present tense in *avalent, montrent, pousse* perhaps

---

[3] F. Boillot, *Les Impressions sensorielles chez La Fontaine* (Paris, 1926), p. 63.

helps to give the impression of a sustained piece of miming: we can imagine the two men circling round their find, ogling it (*avaler qch. des yeux* is an expressive phrase fitting this familiar style; in fact, it is La Fontaine's variation on the normal 'dévorer qch. des yeux')[4] and pointing it out to each other; the 'stage-direction' is made more striking by the pleasing chiasmus in line 3. Line 4 interrupts this sequence of verbs in the present tense, and in place of the direct, 'dramatic' presentation of events the author adopts the tense of the more customary narrative in retrospect. The imperfect of the following phrase, *se baissait déjà*, acts as a link between one narrative viewpoint and the other, as line 6 resumes the sequence of presents. The progression *des yeux... du doigt... à l'égard de la dent* is comic because of the neatness of the formula; however, this is a 'literary' joke of the author's, independent of the comic characterization of the two protagonists; as is the use of the incongruous *proie* to refer to the oyster, or indeed, the choice of *dent*: wholly inappropriate if taken literally, it is an example of synecdoche, and the elevated figure of speech contrasts amusingly with the passage in popular style which follows. But with *L'un se baissait...* and *L'autre le pousse...*, the characterization is continued, and in terms very reminiscent of the physical gestures of the comic theatre. There can be little doubt that La Fontaine meant us to take his *pèlerins* in the familiar sense of 'bonshommes', and not as pilgrims.

Like these 'stage-directions' indicating mime and gesture, the dialogue also reproduces features of popular comic style. Vocabulary is unpretentious, and includes such terms as *gobeur* ('*gober*: terme familier. Avaler sans savourer, sans mâcher'—Littré); *l'autre le verra faire* ('façon populaire de dire: s'en priver, s'en passer'—editor's note, Hachette edition); *Dieu merci* and *sur ma vie*: the sort of oath with which La Fontaine frequently gives a familiar flavour to a passage of lively dialogue. The triviality of the argument: *j'ai l'œil bon... — Je ne l'ai pas mauvais aussi[5]... je l'ai vue avant vous...* helps to characterize the speakers as simple-minded, and line 14 rounds off the exchanges with a comic incongruity. The flexibility of both the metrical pattern and the rhyme-scheme is designed, as elsewhere in the *Fables*, to suggest a freer and more spontaneous conversational style, by comparison with the more

---

[4] See J. D. Biard, *The Style of La Fontaine's Fables* (Oxford, 1966), p. 49.
[5] *Aussi* in a negative construction was standard 17th-C. usage, where Mod. Fr. would use 'non plus'.

formal Alexandrine couplets and a regularly alternating rhyme-scheme. Thus, whereas, for instance, the second half of line 9, the second half of line 11, and the two halves of line 14 are all natural conversational phrases which fit without any sense of strain into the metrical unit of the hemistich, the eight-syllable units of lines 7, 10, and 12 can be said to bring variety, and a consequent impression of spontaneity, into the dialogue.

Lines 15–18 illustrate another function of the shorter line. As often in the *Fables*, La Fontaine uses the octosyllable at line 15 to indicate a fresh start: the opening of a new 'paragraph', as it were. Here it is doubly effective, as the brief phrase *Pendant tout ce bel incident* provides a concise and ironical summary of the dispute (it is difficult not to see *ce bel incident* as echoing Boileau's 'ce bel arrêt'; La Fontaine's irony at the expense of his own characters is perhaps flavoured by a hint of parody at Boileau's expense). In lines 16 and 17 the Alexandrine is used for the sake of concentration. All the vital action of the anecdote is compressed into these two lines: two preliminary stages in the balanced hemistiches of line 16 (the terse statement *Perrin Dandin arrive* would not have been nearly so cryptic to La Fontaine's contemporaries as it may appear to a modern reader; this character would be familiar to all readers of Rabelais),[6] and in line 17—closely modelled on Boileau's line 9—the swift, decisive solution to the problem. The two Alexandrines are closely bound together by rhyme—the sort of unexpected rhyme[7] which belongs to the province of burlesque, since it couples the dignity implied in *juge* with the much more earthy associations of the verb *gruger*, a familiar synonym for 'manger'—while line 18 is similarly linked with the other octosyllable, making this a compact and striking group of four lines. It may possibly seem to some readers that to follow the pithy climax of line 17 by an adverbial phrase qualifying *...et la gruge* produces an anti-climax, and weakens the effect. However, we may assume that La Fontaine was well aware of this danger: such a combination of Alexandrine and octosyllable is frequent in the *Fables*, and here the poet's purpose was evidently to emphasize the effect that the new arrival's action has on the other two actors in the story. They are accordingly reintroduced in line 18 (which incidentally expands Boileau's 'à leurs yeux') and referred to with mock-respect as *Nos deux messieurs: monsieur*

---

[6] *Tiers Livre*, ch. xli.

[7] Although the rhyme *gruge-juge* had already occurred in the *Fables* (I, xxi).

was not yet used as a mere civility, but implied consideration and respect, so that applied to the two *pèlerins* of this fable, it would certainly be highly ironical; while the use of the possessive adjective here, as often in La Fontaine, brings the reader in on the author's side, and invites his agreement.

Rabelais's original Perrin Dendin [*sic*] was not a judge, or even a professional lawyer, but a self-styled 'appointeur de procès' or arbitrator whom, in a pleasing flight of fancy, his creator presents as making a good living by settling disputes out of court. The name Dandin given by Racine to the judge in his comedy *Les Plaideurs* (1668) should not mislead us, therefore: La Fontaine deliberately calls his character *Perrin* Dandin (and in the following line Perrin without the surname) in order to indicate that it is Rabelais's unofficial arbitrator, not Racine's judge, that he has in mind. La Fontaine's character, then, is likewise conceived first and foremost, as line 16 suggests, as an amateur playing at being a judge; and the *fort gravement* of line 17 and *d'un ton de président* (line 19) are further 'stage-directions' emphasizing that the character is acting a part: a further affinity, perhaps, with the comic sketches of the *farceurs* and the *commedia dell'arte*.

If this is realized, the comic flavour of lines 19–21 can be appreciated. Quite apart from the obviously humorous touch of *Ce repas* referring to the eating of a single oyster, which again is incidental to the comedy deriving from the characterization, it is amusing to see this 'arbitre de rencontre'[8] borrowing the jargon of the lawcourts—the more so when its formulae are applied to such a trivial issue. Again, we are amused by the incongruity in this setting—a deserted shore—of such terms as *président* and *cour*; the comparison with Boileau's allegorical figure of Justice is very much to La Fontaine's advantage. The exact meaning of the formula *sans dépens* in this context is open to question; does Perrin Dandin mean: 'without (paying) any further costs' or: 'without (the award of) costs', in the sense in which Boileau had written: 'Tous deux avec dépens veulent gagner leur cause'? Perhaps in La Fontaine's text the former is the more likely, though either could equally well be followed by the condescending admonition to keep the peace.

There remain the four lines which point the moral. It is not a question here, as in the conclusion to so many of La Fontaine's

---

[8] *Œuvres de La Fontaine*, ed. H. Regnier (Paris, 1884), II, 406.

fables, of expressing in human terms what has already been suggested as valid in the fanciful context of animal relationships; the story of the travellers and the oyster is equally fanciful, perhaps, but the 'lesson' has emerged clearly enough, and it is not necessary to restate it by means of parallel examples or of moral maxims, as is often the author's practice. For this reason, perhaps, the style of the concluding lines in the present instance is less distinct from that of the body of the fable than is normally the case. The tone remains homely and unpretentious: the reader is himself brought into the picture by the two imperatives and the third verb in the second person; and there is a certain grammatical negligence in line 23, since while *il en coûte* in the preceding line is a self-contained construction, the pronoun *en* in *il en reste...* lacks an antecedent (even if as regards sense the implied antecedent 'de l'argent' is clear enough). *Aujourd'hui* and *beaucoup de familles* are there to remind the reader of the topicality and universality of the lesson to be drawn, in a century in which litigation was unusually widespread; and although *Perrin* maintains a direct link with the narrative section of the poem, it is evident that here the reference is wider: the name now evokes not merely the particular protagonist of the anecdote but behind him, the whole paraphernalia of the legal process.

Up to the last hemistich, the concluding section seems unremarkable, even rather banal, in both thought and expression. However, the last phrase brings an unexpected development: *Et ne laisse aux plaideurs que le sac...* follows on straightforwardly enough, and is self-explanatory in the context (though in addition to the empty money-bag, we may also possibly visualize the bulging brief-case which recurs in the satirical literature of the time), but with *...et les quilles* the phrase is rounded off in quite a different, and in the context surprising, sense. *Ne laisser à quelqu'un que le sac et les quilles* was an established figurative expression, evidently to be explained as originally referring to gambling losses at the game of skittles ('prendre l'argent du jeu et ne laisser aux autres que les quilles et leur sac'—Littré); so that La Fontaine's play on words, which consists in a lighthearted switch from one context to another—from the lesson to be drawn from the fable itself to a popular saying connected with a different (but perhaps not wholly unrelated) field of experience—brings the poem to an end with a touch of inconsequential humour that is completely characteristic. Even if we were tempted to see a slight touch of sententious moralizing in lines 22–3 (the generalizations drawn from popular experience, made more emphatic perhaps by the isometry of the first seven syllables of these two lines), the final couplet quite dispels any such impression, and leaves us with the homely flavour of the proverbial tag.

8 Racine

Dieu des Juifs, tu l'emportes!
Oui, c'est Joas, je cherche en vain à me tromper.
Je reconnais l'endroit où je le fis frapper.
Je vois d'Ochosias et le port et le geste.
5   Tout me retrace enfin un sang que je déteste.
David, David triomphe. Achab seul est détruit.
Impitoyable Dieu, toi seul as tout conduit.
C'est toi qui, me flattant d'une vengeance aisée,
M'as vingt fois en un jour à moi-même opposée,
10   Tantôt pour un enfant excitant mes remords,
Tantôt m'éblouissant de tes riches trésors,
Que j'ai craint de livrer aux flammes, au pillage.
Qu'il règne donc, ce fils, ton soin et ton ouvrage;
Et que pour signaler son empire nouveau,
15   On lui fasse en mon sein enfoncer le couteau.
Voici ce qu'en mourant lui souhaite sa mère.
Que dis-je, souhaiter? je me flatte, j'espère
Qu'indocile à ton joug, fatigué de ta loi,
Fidèle au sang d'Achab, qu'il a reçu de moi,
20   Conforme à son aïeul, à son père semblable,
On verra de David l'héritier détestable
Abolir tes honneurs, profaner ton autel,
Et venger Athalie, Achab et Jézabel.

RACINE, *Athalie*, Act V, sc. vi
Date of first publication: 1691
Ed. P. France (Oxford: O.U.P.,
1966), p. 135

THIS tirade sets Athalie's fate in the perspective of history, and the numerous allusions in the passage require a brief recapitulation of the Old Testament background to Racine's tragedy.

The twelve tribes, formerly united under David, had split in the tenth century B.C. into two kingdoms, Judah and Israel. Judah was still ruled by the Davidic dynasty and its capital was Jerusalem. The crown of Israel passed c. 875 B.C. to Ahab (Achab), son and successor of Omri. Ahab married Jezebel (Jézabel), daughter of the king of Sidon, who introduced the worship of Baal. Their son Jehoram (Joram) succeeded to the throne of Israel, and their daughter Athaliah (Athalie) married the king of Judah, also named Jehoram, and led him into idolatry. Athaliah's husband was followed after a short reign by their equally impious son Ahaziah (Ochosias). Jehu, whom the prophets had anointed king of Israel, put to death the latter, together with his uncle and 'quatre-vingts fils de roi' (l. 714). Jezebel herself was defenestrated and suffered a terrible death:

> Sous les pieds des chevaux cette reine foulée,
> Dans son sang inhumain les chiens désaltérés,
> Et de son corps hideux les membres déchirés (ll. 116-18).

Athaliah retaliated by ordering the massacre of all the descendants of David. She had thus 'rendu meurtre pour meurtre, outrage pour outrage' (l. 720) and 'vengé [ses] parents sur [sa] postérité' (l. 710). She now became queen of Judah, and for the first time a 'femme impie et meurtrière' (l. 747) sat on the throne previously occupied by the legitimate male heirs of David's royal race from which, according to the prophets, the Messiah was to come. However, Jehovah was to 'réparer les ruines De cet arbre séché jusque dans ses racines' (ll. 139-40); for Jehosheba (Josabet), daughter of Jehoram of Judah by another marriage and wife of Jehoiada (Joad) the priest, had rescued from the carnage Joash (Joas), Ahaziah's youngest child, and carried him off 'tout sanglant' (l. 1320) to the Temple. Here the 'précieux reste de la maison de David' was secretly brought up until some seven years later, when he was proclaimed king of Judah and Athaliah was assassinated in a revolt.

The subject of Racine's tragedy is 'Joas reconnu et mis sur le trône'. The passage under consideration which expresses Athalie's reaction to her abrupt reversal of fortune in Act V impressively rounds off the highly dramatic denouement. These are her final words before she is led away to her death. The first section (ll. 1-12)

I

represents Athalie's moment of truth, her bitter admission of defeat; the second section (ll. 13–23), her famous curse and prophecy, predicts the tragedy of Joas himself.

Her last speech is the culminating moment of the play. Athalie's forces have surrounded the Temple; but Joad has no fear:

> Grand Dieu, voici ton heure, on t'amène ta proie...
> L'ange exterminateur est debout avec nous (ll. 1668 and 1698).

Led on by Joad's pious 'équivoque', Athalie forsakes the security of her secular realm and for the second time profanes the 'redoutable sanctuaire' of the living God from which she is excluded at once by her sex and her impiety. With an air of insolent triumph she enters the Temple almost unattended to take Éliacin and the 'trésor de David' which she understands in a material rather than a spiritual sense. A curtain is suddenly drawn back and she is confronted by Joas enthroned. She bids her soldiers rid her of this 'fantôme odieux', but a troop of armed Levites rush in from all sides to defend their king. She has walked into a trap:

> Tes yeux cherchent en vain, tu ne peux échapper,
> Et Dieu de toutes parts a su t'envelopper (ll. 1733–4).

She furiously warns the 'troupe rebelle' that the noise outside is that of her army forcing their way in; but this last illusion is dispelled when Ismaël arrives to announce that her Tyrian mercenaries and Jewish renegades have fled:

> Comme le vent dans l'air dissipe la fumée,
> La voix du Tout-Puissant a chassé cette armée (ll. 1747–8)

and that Baal and his ministers have been overthrown:

> Baal est en horreur dans la sainte cité.
> De son temple profane on a brisé les portes.
> Mathan est égorgé (ll. 1766–8).

Athalie cuts Ismaël's 'récit' in mid-line. Her shrill, despairing cry dramatically sums up the substance of the play: *Dieu des Juifs, tu l'emportes!* Her eyes have at last been opened, and the warning of Jezebel has been confirmed. Dream has become reality:

> Tremble, m'a-t-elle dit, fille digne de moi,
> Le cruel Dieu des Juifs l'emporte aussi sur toi (ll. 497–8).

Ignoring Joad and everybody else she directly apostrophizes the invisible Jehovah whom she identifies as her real adversary and the ultimate cause of her downfall.[1] She has admitted her defeat; but she is not resigned, nor does she show any sign of guilt or remorse. On the contrary, her language is blasphemous in its defiance, for she regards the *Dieu des Juifs* purely as a vengeful tribal deity—mighty perhaps, but not just or fair. She is furious that she has succumbed in this unequal contest with a superhuman foe.

The exclamation of line 1 expresses Athalie's initial shock. The loud cry is followed after a short pause by a series of quieter lines (ll. 2–7), all endstopped and consisting of one short sentence each save for line 6 which has two even shorter sentences corresponding to the antithetical hemistiches. The full stops slow down the movement of the speech which reflects Athalie's gradual recovery of her former clarity of judgement (cf. ll. 871–2).

In line 1 she recognizes the hand of Jehovah; in the following lines she admits the identity of her grandson. All along she has vaguely suspected that Éliacin is really Joas; but she has allowed herself to be deluded: 'Je le veux croire, Abner; je puis m'être trompée' (l. 583). In the previous scene she has still called Joas a 'fantôme' and expressed her incredulity: 'Lui Joas? lui ton roi?' Only now in her final defeat does she see the truth. All futile attempts at self-deception are abandoned, and tragic lucidity takes over in line 2: the strong secondary *coupe* accentuates *Oui, c'est Joas*, while the attenuated caesura throws into relief the despairing *en vain*.

Various unmistakable signs bear witness to Joas' identity. Joad had told her: 'De ton poignard connais du moins ces marques' (l. 1720), thus recalling an earlier image of Athalie:

> De princes égorgés la chambre était remplie.
> Un poignard à la main, l'implacable Athalie
> Au carnage animait ses barbares soldats (ll. 243–5).

At last she recognizes the scar of the wound inflicted at her command. The laconic, callous matter-of-factness of this line (l. 3) contrasts with the greater 'noblesse' of line 4 with its *et... et...* and the inversion of the impressive royal name *Ochosias*. 'Le petit

[1] Throughout the speech Athalie will remain obsessed with the God of the Jews: *tu l'emportes! ; toi seul as tout conduit ; C'est toi ; tes riches trésors; ce fils, ton soin et ton ouvrage ; ton joug ; ta loi ; tes honneurs ; ton autel.*

Joas' sitting majestically on the throne reminds Athalie of her own son. The inversion singles out and throws into prominence the two features which Joas has inherited from his father: *le port* (i.e. 'le port de tête') and *le geste*. He is every inch a king. Athalie can no longer doubt the truth of Joad's proclamation: 'Voilà ton roi, ton fils, le fils d'Ochosias' (l. 1721). 'L'impie Ochosias' (l. 1288) was the son of Athalie; but like Joas he belonged to the house of David. Athalie's hatred for this family seems almost to hiss in the sibilant consonants of line 5: *Tout me retrace*[2] *enfin un sang que je déteste.*[3] *Sang* is an example of metonymy and stands here for the whole family of David. Similarly, *David* and *Achab*, two names which constantly recur in the play, represent their rival houses and add a kind of ancestral dimension to the dynastic conflict whose result is summed up in the despairing line: *David, David triomphe. Achab seul est détruit.* For the followers of Jehovah David is the exemplary monarch ('des grands rois le plus parfait modèle', l. 1286); but Athalie, 'd'Achab la fille sacrilège' (l. 1564), loathes him and his descendants:

> David m'est en horreur; et les fils de ce roi,
> Quoique nés de mon sang, sont étrangers pour moi (ll. 729–30).

All her hatred wells up in the obsessive repetition of the name *David, David.* The verb *triomphe*, stressed by the strong caesura, forms a sharp antithesis with the verb at the rhyme (*détruit*), and there is a marked contrast between the ascending movement of the first hemistich and the descending movement of the second. It is with a bitter sense of injustice that Athalie cries: *Achab seul est détruit*, and once again she turns to accuse the merciless foe of the house of Ahab:[4] *Impitoyable Dieu, toi seul as tout conduit.*[5] *Impitoyable Dieu* fills out a whole hemistich, dominating and overshadowing the preceding names of Joas, Ochosias, David, and Achab. But Athalie, though trapped, remains defiant, and the long adjective in the 'position affective' (*Impitoyable*) is charged with resentment. She sees herself as the victim of a disproportionate contest. She has

---

[2] = 'rappelle'.
[3] A very forceful rhyme. Cf. *détestable* (l. 21).
[4] 'Dieu dont le bras vengeur...
    Sur cette race impie est toujours étendu' (ll. 233–4).
[5] Perhaps the key-line of a play in which the divine omnipotence reigns supreme. Invisible and yet omnipresent, Jehovah directs all the characters either by enlightening them or by blinding them.

been tricked by an external, superior power who all along has been controlling the course of events. As Joad has told her, 'Ce Dieu que tu bravais en nos mains t'a livrée' (l. 1735).

The series of short sentences stops at this point. Now that the full truth has dawned on Athalie her speech becomes freer and more fluent and begins to pick up speed. The first section ends with one long, flowing sentence which runs on from line 8 to line 9 and continues by way of two participial phrases linked by *tantôt... tantôt...* as far as line 12. Looking back on her disquiet, uncertainty, and imprudence, Athalie realizes for the first time that like some mysterious, inward force invading her subconscious mind and undermining her will, Jehovah has deluded her with the hope of *une vengeance aisée*, caused her strange, contradictory conduct (cf. ll. 885-7) and played on her feelings, whether good or bad, in order to destroy her. Earlier she had had Éliacin at her mercy; but she had felt *remords* and spared the child. This upsurge of tender, maternal compassion which is so foreign to her hard, masculine character ('Je serais sensible à la pitié?', l. 654) has led to her downfall no less surely than her cupidity ('pour l'or sa soif insatiable', l. 48). Joas is the only 'trésor de David'; but 'cette reine avare' (l. 1591) has been tempted by the rumour of the *riches trésors* hidden in the Temple, and fearful of losing them in a violent assault she has been lured in virtually unaccompanied and has fallen unsuspecting into the trap. It all seems like a direct fulfilment of Joad's prayer that God should implant in the queen 'cet esprit d'imprudence et d'erreur, De la chute des rois funeste avant-coureur' (ll. 293-4).

At this juncture Athalie rears up and starts to hit back. She is beaten, but she is determined to go down fighting and looks to the future for revenge. This final section contains the most striking and powerful verse in the whole speech—first Athalie's curse on her grandson (ll. 13-16), then her prophecy about his future degeneration (ll. 17-23).

She begins by accepting the inevitability of his advent (*Qu'il règne donc*); but there is no mistaking the distaste conveyed by the demonstrative *ce fils*.[6] She feels no kinship with this descendant of David, the one who got away. Scornfully she tells Jehovah that he is

---

[6] Note the sibilant consonants. The same phenomenon will be very marked in the following lines: *soin, signaler, son, fasse, sein, enfoncer, voici, ce, souhaite, sa, souhaiter, espère, indocile, sang, reçu, son, son, semblable, détestable.*

ton soin[7] *et ton ouvrage*. As such he is disowned by his grandmother who pronounces a curse upon him instead of a last blessing. She wishes that the beginning of his reign may be stained with bloodshed, and though she is referring to her own death she seems to feel an evil glee at the prospect of the dagger-thrust which will repeat that of the dream:

> J'ai senti tout à coup un homicide acier,
> Que le traître en mon sein a plongé tout entier (ll. 513–14).

In line 15 the verb *enfoncer* has a brutal vigour, and the inversion throws into relief the physical detail *en mon sein* as well as the *mot propre* at the rhyme: *couteau*. Athalie is more than once depicted with a dagger in her hand (ll. 244, 1537). This weapon of murder is the legacy which she is bequeathing to Joas, and in a short line of slow, careful deliberation she takes a perverse pleasure in the fact that her assassination will make Joas a parricide like herself: *Voici ce qu'en mourant lui souhaite sa mère.*[8] Joas is Jehovah's *ouvrage*, and his restoration is bright with messianic hope; but he is also the grandson of Athalie, and his *nouveau règne* will mark in part a return to the dark ancestral past. It will gradually dawn on Athalie that she was wrong in saying that *Achab... est détruit*; for the blood of Ahab lives on in Joas, and it is through her grandson that she will be avenged.

Athalie's curse forms, in short, the prelude to her prophecy, and the word which supplies the logical transition is the verb *souhaiter*. Athalie's recovery of her self-possession is reflected in her command of language. She lucidly distinguishes and emphasizes the verbs which follow in an ascending order of confidence and assurance. She rejects *souhaiter* as too weak and inapt; she savours with great relish *je me flatte*; and *j'espère* means here, as it often does in the seventeenth century, 'I confidently expect.' She is carried away by a fierce, vindictive joy in the long, final sentence which overflows from line 17 to line 18 and builds up with increasing momentum and mounting emotion to reach an awesome climax in line 23. In lines 18–20 there is an accumulation of parallel adjectival phrases: *indocile... fatigué... Fidèle...* form a symmetric pattern, and in line 19 monotony is avoided by the insertion of the relative clause with its defiant rhyme *moi*; but the series is resumed and deftly

[7] = 'l'objet de ton soin'.
[8] = 'grand'mère'.

varied by the elegant chiasmus of line 20: *Conforme*[9] *à son aïeul,*[10] *à son père semblable*. All five adjectives are piled up in lyrical apposition to the delayed noun object *héritier* (l. 21) with its forceful epithet *détestable*[11] thrown into prominence at the rhyme by the inversion. But there is barely any pause as Athalie plunges on, panting breathlessly, from *On verra* to the following dependent infinitives, all three of them verbs of mounting violence: *Abolir... profaner... Et venger*[12]... The speech reaches a frenzied crescendo with the alignment of the three baleful, harsh-sounding Biblical names: *Athalie, Achab et Jézabel*. Jezebel, the very symbol of ungodliness in the play, occupies the place of honour in the final line, and her name forms a blasphemous rhyme with *ton autel*. Athalie's fate had been prefigured in the gruesome end of Jezebel, and as in the dream we seem to divine here the strange bond of affection between daughter and mother. *Jézabel*, at any rate, is Athalie's last word before she makes her exit, escorted by the Levites.

But she goes to her death, having exultantly predicted the future falling away of Joas which had already been prophesied by Joad in Act III and which we know will be fulfilled. Joas will remain faithful not to Jehovah but to the *sang d'Achab*, the evil heredity which she delights in having passed on to him. She herself is on the brink of death; but her spirit will live on in Joas who will turn out like his grandfather, 'l'infidèle Joram' (l. 1288), and his father, the 'triste Ochosias' (l. 1311), who both rebelled against Jehovah. David's *héritier détestable* will abolish the worship of the true God, defile the altar with the blood of his friend Zacharie, son and successor of Joad, and thus avenge Athalie and her parents. These closing lines open up and enlarge the perspective to embrace past, present, and future. Calling herself by her own name and associating herself objectively with Ahab, Jezebel, and Joas over against Jehovah, Athalie seems to stand back from the action and—within the limits of her understanding—to contemplate from outside a continuing historical process which involves not only the tragedy of the house of Ahab, but also the ultimate salvation of the human race. That the obstacles lying across the path leading to the In-

---

[9] = 'agissant comme'. Note how *conforme* picks up again the *f* of *fatigué* and *Fidèle*.

[10] = 'grand-père'.

[11] = 'maudit, digne de malédiction'. *De David l'héritier détestable* is one of the many expressive genealogical periphrases in *Athalie*. The loaded epithet stresses here the secret duality of Joas' heredity.

[12] Note the double alliteration: *verra–venger, venger–Jézabel*.

87

carnation should be so mercilessly crushed is a scandal to the un-
believer and a mystery to the believer:

> O promesse! ô menace! ô ténébreux mystère!
> Que de maux, que de biens sont prédits tour à tour!
>   Comment peut-on avec tant de colère
>   Accorder tant d'amour? (ll. 1212–15)

The chorus answers its own question with an act of faith:

> Cessons de nous troubler. Notre Dieu quelque jour
> Dévoilera ce grand mystère (ll. 1226–7).

Athalie's tirade combines with Joad's prophecy to make the play
the Mount Sinai of Racinian drama. The confrontation of 'cette
superbe reine' with the *Deus Absconditus* in his redoubtable Temple
on the day of Pentecost is highly dramatic. The speech itself is a
powerful résumé of the whole action and points prophetically beyond it. Recovering her lucid self-possession and rising to an
almost monumental stature, the old, defeated queen displays to the
end her proud self-assertiveness, her sincere, passionate sense of
injustice, her blasphemous hatred and scornful bravado in face of
the living God. Full of barbarous ferocity and vindictive malice,
she stubbornly refuses to give in. Like a magnificent tigress at bay
she can still show her claws, and though Racine here sides with the
somewhat fearsome lambs in the Temple he has invested his heroine
with a terrible grandeur. Faced with the 'fureurs d'Athalie', we
cannot help wondering with Mauriac whether 'Racine n'a peut-être
pas conscience de son plaisir lorsqu'il souffle à la vieille reine
indomptable cet affreux courage de braver Dieu, le couteau sur la
gorge. Lui qui a choisi de se soumettre, de servir en tremblant, il ne
sait pas qu'une part de lui-même se satisfait de ces blasphèmes et se
grise de cette audace désespérée.'[13]

---

[13] *La Vie de J. Racine* (Paris, 1928), p. 203.

9 Voltaire

Je trouvai le lendemain, dans un café malpropre, mal meublé, mal servi, et mal éclairé, la plupart de ces messieurs, qui la veille étaient si affables et d'une humeur si aimable; aucun d'eux ne me reconnut; je me hasardai d'en attaquer quelques-uns de conversation; je n'en tirai point de réponse, ou tout au plus un oui et un non; 5 je me figurai qu'apparemment je les avais offensés tous la veille. Je m'examinai, et je tâchai de me souvenir si je n'avais pas donné la préférence aux étoffes de Lyon sur les leurs; ou si je n'avais pas dit que les cuisiniers français l'emportaient sur les anglais, que Paris était une ville plus agréable que Londres, qu'on passait le 10 temps plus agréablement à Versailles qu'à Saint-James, ou quelque autre énormité pareille. Ne me sentant coupable de rien, je pris la liberté de demander à l'un d'eux, avec un air de vivacité qui leur parut fort étrange, pourquoi ils étaient tous tristes: mon homme me répondit d'un air renfrogné, qu'il fesait un vent d'Est. Dans 15 le moment arriva un de leurs amis, qui leur dit avec un visage indifférent: Molly s'est coupé la gorge ce matin. Son amant l'a trouvée morte dans sa chambre, avec un rasoir sanglant à côté d'elle. Cette Molly était une fille jeune, belle, et très-riche, qui était prête à se marier avec le même homme qui l'avait trouvée morte. Ces 20 messieurs, qui tous étaient amis de Molly, reçurent la nouvelle sans sourciller. L'un d'eux seulement demanda ce qu'était devenu l'amant; *il a acheté le rasoir*, dit froidement quelqu'un de la compagnie.

Pour moi, effrayé d'une mort si étrange et de l'indifférence de 25 ces messieurs, je ne pus m'empêcher de m'informer quelle raison avait forcé une demoiselle, si heureuse en apparence, à s'arracher la vie si cruellement; on me répondit uniquement qu'il fesait un vent d'Est. Je ne pouvais pas comprendre d'abord ce que le vent d'Est avait de commun avec l'humeur sombre de ces messieurs, et 30 la mort de Molly. Je sortis brusquement du café, et j'allai à la cour,

plein de ce beau préjugé français qu'une cour est toujours gaie. Tout y était triste et morne, jusqu'aux filles d'honneur. On y parlait mélancoliquement du vent d'Est. Je songeai alors à mon
35 Danois de la veille. Je fus tenté de rire à la fausse idée qu'il avait emportée d'Angleterre; mais le climat opérait déjà sur moi, et je m'étonnais de ne pouvoir rire. Un fameux médecin de la cour, à qui je confiai ma surprise, me dit que j'avais tort de m'étonner, que je verrais bien autre chose aux mois de novembre et de mars;
40 qu'alors on se pendait par douzaine; que presque tout le monde était réellement malade dans ces deux saisons, et qu'une mélancolie noire se répandait sur toute la nation: car c'est alors, dit-il, que le vent d'Est souffle le plus constamment. Ce vent est la perte de notre île. Les animaux même en souffrent, et ont tous l'air
45 abattu. Les hommes qui sont assez robustes pour conserver leur santé dans ce maudit vent, perdent au moins leur bonne humeur. Chacun alors a le visage sévère, et l'esprit disposé aux résolutions désespérées. C'était à la lettre par un vent d'Est qu'on coupa la tête à Charles I, et qu'on détrôna Jacques II. Si vous avez quelque
50 grâce à demander à la cour, m'ajouta-t-il à l'oreille, ne vous y prenez jamais que lorsque le vent sera à l'ouest ou au sud.

VOLTAIRE, Letter to M. ***
Date of composition: 1728
Date of first publication: 1784
In *Lettres philosophiques*, ed.
G. Lanson (Paris: Hachette,
1924), II, 261-3

THE letter from which this passage is taken was written in 1728, and was most likely intended by Voltaire to introduce a collection of 'English Letters'. However, the plan was not destined to be carried out as originally intended; when Voltaire's book about England appeared in 1734, its contents were accurately indicated by its title: *Lettres philosophiques*, for it dealt almost exclusively with various aspects of the intellectual life of the country, whereas the letter of 1728 had suggested a volume of quite a different character, something more akin to the descriptive pictures of the English social scene produced by such writers as Muralt or Prévost.

The letter is addressed to an unknown correspondent, and is over 3,000 words long. It begins with a critical reference to a recent work by an Englishman, who had seen fit to dogmatize about the French character on the basis of a fortnight's visit to the country. Voltaire's correspondent had asked him to give his opinion of the English, but this, he says, is even more difficult, since the English are more reserved and less sociable than the French. Ambassadors to London commonly leave at the end of their stay having learned nothing of London and the English; and even 'un particulier qui aurait assez de loisir et d'opiniâtreté pour apprendre à parler la langue anglaise...' (that is to say, Voltaire himself) would inevitably give a misleading impression, if he were to record his first reactions. In order to prove his point, he then proceeds to describe his own experience (whether genuine, or invented for the sake of the opposition between 'true' and 'false' on which his argument depends, it is impossible to say) on first arriving in England. It was a fine spring day, and all the population were on holiday, enjoying a fête and river pageant with races, games, and abundant refreshments, on the occasion of a royal progress down the Thames to Greenwich. This 'spectacle ravissant' suggests to the foreign observer that the English are a vivacious, friendly people, full of *joie de vivre*; but this impression does not last long. That same evening he meets 'quelques dames de la cour' who, far from sharing his enthusiasm, disdainfully dismiss the happy holiday-makers as mere servants and apprentices; and his complete disillusionment comes the following day, in the episode recounted in this passage.

The content of the passage may be summarized as follows. The first paragraph contains the account of a conversation in a coffeehouse in which, after some general remarks on the unsociability of Voltaire's English companions, attention is focused on a particular event, the suicide of a young girl. In the second paragraph, the scene changes to the Court, where a conversation between the narrator and a doctor relates this particular event to a general tendency towards suicide, widespread among the English. The two paragraphs are linked by a common theme, namely that sociological phenomena of this kind are to be explained by features of a country's climate.

The tone of the passage, taken as a whole, is not very serious. Voltaire has chosen to answer his correspondent's question in a

light-hearted manner, and is clearly presenting an exaggerated
view of both the 'false' and the 'true' impressions of the English
character. The theme of climatological influences is also handled
in a humorous way, considerable imaginative play being made with
the phrase *le vent d'Est*; though the underlying idea is of course far
from being merely a product of the author's subjective fancy. This
is only one of several passages in which French writers of this period
dwell on the frequency of suicide in England; Voltaire was not the
first to explain this phenomenon by relating it to the climate of the
country, and the theory of the influence of climate on character,
dear to many thinkers of the Enlightenment, was often interpreted
with extreme literalness. Of travellers who had preceded Voltaire
in England, one Lesage (1715) had attributed this tendency among
the English to their excessive consumption of beef; but this was
countered by La Mottraye (1727), who thought it due to 'la nature
du climat humide et nébuleux'. It was Montesquieu, for whom the
doctrine of climatological influence was to assume a central importance in *De l'esprit des lois* (1748), who was to go most fully into
its application in this particular instance: referring to England as
'une nation à qui une maladie du climat affecte tellement l'âme,
qu'elle pourrait porter le dégoût de toutes choses jusqu'à celui de
la vie', he ascribed this to 'un défaut de filtration du suc nerveux'.[1]
In an earlier text,[2] Montesquieu had been more specific about the
nature of the climatic feature involved: he had compared the influence of the sirocco wind on the Italian temperament with that
of the 'vent d'Est' on the English character. This text was probably
written a few years later than Voltaire's own letter, and in any case,
like the letter, it remained unpublished until much later in the
century; but it seems likely that both Montesquieu and Voltaire
were following the Abbé Dubos, who had written on the same
subject in his *Réflexions critiques* of 1719:

On a observé dans la capitale de ce royaume..., que de soi-
xante personnes qui se défont elles-mêmes dans le cours d'une
année, cinquante se sont portées à cet excès de fureur vers le
commencement ou bien la fin de l'hiver. Il règne alors dans cette
contrée un vent de Nord-Est qui rend le ciel noir, et qui afflige
sensiblement les corps les plus robustes.

---

[1] *De l'esprit des lois*, Bk. XIV, chs. xii-xiii.
[2] *Essai sur les causes qui peuvent affecter les esprits et les caractères.*

It will be seen, therefore, that Voltaire's subject-matter had considerable topicality. He is repeating what must already have seemed to French readers something of a commonplace about the English character; and underlying his not altogether serious treatment of the English penchant for suicide is the theory, already very much 'in the air', of the influence of climate on character.

The features of Voltaire's style which stand out on a first reading of this passage are probably the asyndetic, or 'disjointed', sentence-structure, largely consisting of independent, unlinked propositions; and the apparent prominence of verbs in the constructions used throughout. It is not that the frequency of verbs is unusually high: indeed, the proportion of verbs to other parts of speech (approximately one to 5·75) is slightly smaller than in two other passages by Voltaire chosen at random (one from the *Lettres philosophiques*, one from *Candide*) for purposes of comparison; and, what is perhaps more surprising, it scarcely differs from that in much more abstract passages, by Montesquieu and Rousseau, subjected to a similar analysis. However, in the passage under consideration, the effect of the simple sentence-structure, relying very largely on a series of main clauses, with relatively little subordination, is to produce a very dynamic prose style, in which the verb assumes an unusually prominent role. This is particularly the case in the first part of each paragraph, in which a series of verbs in the first person singular of the past definite provides the dominant narrative thread: *Je trouvai..., je me hasardai..., je n'en tirai point..., je me figurai..., Je m'examinai..., je tâchai; je ne pus..., je sortis..., j'allai..., je songeai..., je fus tenté.*

Even in those parts of the passage in which there is a more highly organized sentence-structure—the sequence of indirect questions in the first paragraph, and the series of indirect statements in the second—the impression of simplicity and rapidity is preserved by the repetition, within the framework of indirect speech, of simple clauses in parallel:

(*a*) ...me souvenir ⎰ si je n'avais pas donné...
⎱ ou si je n'avais pas dit ⎧ que les c.f. l'emportaient...
⎨ que Paris était...
⎩ qu'on passait...

(*b*) ...me dit ⎧ que j'avais tort...
que je verrais...
qu'alors on se pendait...
que presque tout le monde était...
et qu'une mélancolie noire se répandait...

For the rest, such cases of subordination as the passage contains consist almost entirely of relative clauses, and there is a complete lack of logical links of a causal or concessive nature. Even in the sole conditional sentence (ll. 49–51) the fact that the apodosis has its main verb in the imperative mood deprives it of the logical force normally associated with the use of the conditional construction. The overall effect of such an extreme simplicity and directness of style is that on the one hand the narrative progresses in a swift and lively manner, while on the other hand the theme of the passage is developed undogmatically, by suggestion rather than by persuasive argument. The author presents the factual evidence, without himself drawing conclusions from it.

The setting for the disillusioning encounter narrated in the first paragraph is one of the many coffee-houses in which London abounded: there are said to have been five hundred by the reign of Queen Anne, and they filled a very central role in the commercial, as well as the social, life of the capital; in fact, the customers encountered by Voltaire are 'quelques négocians pour qui j'avais des lettres de recommandation', whom he had met by chance on the previous day. The gloomy atmosphere is at once characterized, effectively but without over-emphasis, in the four epithets which contrast forcibly with the 'ciel sans nuages' and the 'sérénité de la nature' which had marked the previous day's proceedings. The four epithets are arranged in a pleasing rhythm, ascending from the two-syllable unit *malpropre* to the five-syllable *et mal éclairé*, so that their arrangement enhances the effect produced by the simple four-fold repetition of *mal*. On the other hand, the rhyming effect produced by the repetition of the suffix *-able* in line 3 is somewhat jarring, and one can judge how the sentence might be improved by substituting, for example, 'si sympathiques et d'une humeur si aimable'. The choice of the phrase *attaquer* (*quelqu'un*) *de conversation* (=‘lui adresser la parole pour l'exciter à parler' — Littré) suggests the extrovert nature of the French visitor, taking the initiative in the conversational exchanges, just as the brisk sequence *aucun d'eux ne me reconnut... je me hasardai...je n'en tirai... je me figurai...* expresses the narrator's quick mind, as well as his self-centredness. The interest is carried forward to the longer phrase which concludes the sentence, containing a hypothesis that the next sentence examines humorously. In a series of balanced propositions, contrasting four pairs of terms and forming four variations on the same theme: *étoffes de Lyon... les leurs; cuisiniers français... (cuisiniers) anglais; Paris... Londres; Versailles... Saint-James*, Voltaire pokes mild fun at the English, as he 'plays up to' the conventional caricature of insular prejudice, rounding the sentence off with the ironical *...ou quelque autre énormité pareille*; though since it soon becomes clear that the caricature only exists in his own imagination, this is really an example of self-critical humour, not of satire directed against an external target. The concluding phrase, *ou quelque... pareille*, exemplifies the 'minor cadence', or closing of a series by the shortest, instead of the longest, term, throwing the attention forward to the next sentence, in which the opposition between *air de vivacité* and *tous tristes* puts in a nutshell the contrast between the lively French temperament and English taciturnity; while the indirect question *...pourquoi ils étaient tous tristes* brings to a head the narrator's curiosity, which the reader by now shares. The answer comes in a brief sentence of ternary form, nicely balanced and decisive: *mon homme me répondit | d'un air renfrogné | qu'il fesait un vent d'Est*—a cryptic and intriguing conclusion to this first part of the passage. *Mon homme*—like *ces messieurs* in line 20—has the effect of emphasizing the gap between the narrator and the rest of the company, of presenting their attitude in a detached, if not a critical, light.

From this point to the end of the paragraph, the narrative appears to go off at a tangent, with the account of an irrelevant *fait divers*. The news of the young girl's suicide is related in the most matter-of-fact way possible: adverbs and adverbial phrases (*avec un visage indifférent, sans sourciller, froidement*) emphasize the complete lack of emotion on the part of the new arrival and his friends, which is suggested clearly enough by the reported conversation; while the details of the manner of the girl's death (*Molly s'est coupé la gorge*[3]..., *avec un rasoir sanglant à côté d'elle*) seem to be given for the sake of

---

[3] A detail possibly taken from Muralt (*Lettres sur les Anglais...*, published in 1725, though written in 1694): 'présentement, la mort qui est le plus en usage, c'est de se couper la gorge'.

precision, not in order to create a sensational effect. The sentence beginning *Cette Molly était...* forms a sort of parenthesis: Voltaire here states the facts (the girl's youth, beauty, wealth, and marriage-prospects) which might form the basis for a 'normal' reaction of horror or shock at such an event, but he is careful not to draw any conclusion, or express any feelings of his own, at this point. The detail conveyed in the final sentence of the paragraph again avoids any suggestion of identification with the bereaved lover: the question denotes mere curiosity, while the laconic answer, revealing a reaction so utterly different from what is conventionally expected in such circumstances as to be quite incongruous, produces a very modern touch of 'humour noir'.

Voltaire's style in reporting the incident of Molly's suicide has so far reproduced the detached, matter-of-fact tone of the dead girl's English friends; even in the explanatory aside of lines 18–20, as we have seen, there is no emotional appeal to the reader, and the event is still treated completely objectively. But at the beginning of the second paragraph the tone changes: the same event is now looked at from the narrator's own point of view, and for the next three and a half lines some appeal is made to the reader's feelings. The author, who has been temporarily absent from the narrative, returns with the emphatic *Pour moi...*; the vocabulary takes on an emotive character with *effrayé...* and *...si cruellement*; and whereas in the previous paragraph the event has been referred to in terms (*...s'est coupé la gorge*) which in no way tone down the brutality of death, now Voltaire has recourse to an emotive abstraction (*s'arracher la vie*). This concession to humane feeling is skilfully placed, however, to lead to another anticlimax, as the mystifying formula *il fesait un vent d'Est* is repeated. The bare, laconic statement contrasts effectively with the rather rhetorical phrasing of lines 25–8 (cf. the ternary grouping of the indirect question) which, together with their more emotive vocabulary, express the foreigner's excitability.

Half a dozen short sentences now follow, providing a transition between the anecdote about Molly and the conversation with the 'fameux médecin de la cour' which concludes the passage. Voltaire seems ready to put himself in the position of the mystified reader: *Je ne pouvais pas comprendre d'abord...*; though by the use of the imperfect and the insertion of the adverb *d'abord* he preserves the advantage of hindsight, and makes it clear to the reader that an answer to the riddle will be forthcoming. The pose of the naïve traveller is sustained in the next sentence, with the *beau préjugé français;* there is a touch of satire here, perhaps, at the expense of the frivolity of the French Court. Once again disillusionment is in store: even the *filles d'honneur,* the English counterpart to the young ladies ('Filles de qualité qui sont auprès des reines, des grandes princesses'—*Dictionnaire de l'Académie* 1694) who enjoyed a lively reputation at Versailles, contribute to the generally melancholy impression; and here too—more or less predictably, for it is now becoming a sort of refrain—the sole topic of conversation is the 'vent d'Est'. At this point Voltaire appears to digress, with the mention of a Danish courier whom he had met on the previous day, and who had left for home without his erroneous view of England being corrected. However, far from being irrelevant to the central theme of the passage, this reference leads back to it with a novel development, for instead of remaining the amused spectator, Voltaire now presents himself as beginning already to be affected by climatic determinism—after a stay of twenty-four hours! This time, for variety's sake, there is no explicit mention of the East wind; in any case, the use of the abstract word *climat* helps to make explicit what had only been implied up to now, by relating the specific instance of the East wind in England to the whole notion of climatic influence in general.

The element of exaggeration and fantasy contained in this last claim runs through the whole of the concluding section of the passage. The medical authority quoted here is either entirely a product of Voltaire's own imagination, or else—if real—one to whom he has chosen to attribute something of his own creative fantasy, embroidering on the accounts of such writers as Dubos. The latter, as has been seen, had provided a likely source for the assertion that this climatic influence reached its peak at the beginning and end of winter, but the phrase *alors on se pendait par douzaine,* even if the numbers involved may conceivably have justified it from a factual point of view, nevertheless contains an element of extravagant fancy in its suggestion of concerted mass action. The next two statements are not so sensational, but it is evidently a gross exaggeration to say that *presque tout le monde* was ill, and that *toute la nation* was afflicted with melancholia—for the term *mélancolie* refers to something much stronger than the modern meaning, 'tristesse vague et douce', would suggest; less specific, perhaps, than the primary meaning of 'excess of black bile' (otherwise *mélancolie noire* would be an obvious pleonasm), it probably corresponds here to Littré's third definition: 'disposition triste provenant d'une cause physique ou morale, dite aussi vulgairement vapeurs du cerveau'.[4]

At this point Voltaire switches to direct speech, and it is appropriate that the first words put into the doctor's mouth should be the by now familiar phrase about the East wind, completing the explanation of the relationship between cause and effect. The rest of the paragraph, leaving the more specific subject of suicide, deals with the wider effects of the East wind on the population at large. The first statement: *Ce vent est la perte de notre île*, is the most sweeping claim of all, unless it is to be taken as a very much watered-down cliché; it is supported, first by an assertion perhaps based on Dubos (who had claimed that climatic influence was to be observed 'même dans les animaux'), but rendered more extravagant by the absolute ...*ont tous l'air abattu*; and then by two sentences which may also be seen as an expanded version of Dubos' statement that the North-East wind 'afflige sensiblement les corps les plus robustes'. The second of these sentences translates the more general *perdent... leur bonne humeur* of the first into more particular effects on the body and the mind, leading up to *résolutions désespérées*. This phrase provides the necessary link with the last two sentences in which Voltaire, speaking through his doctor-character, rounds off the piece in an original and highly imaginative manner. There is a certain looseness in the logical link, however, and the function of *alors* in line 47 is not absolutely satisfactory. This adverb has occurred twice in the preceding lines, referring back clearly enough to ...*aux mois de novembre et de mars*, and although three short sentences have intervened without any temporal qualification, it would be most appropriate to take *Chacun alors a le visage sévère* as referring back to the same phrase; but neither of the historical events cited in the following sentence did in fact take place in November or March, and in view of the link between *résolutions désespérées* and these two events, it is probably more reasonable from the logical point of view, even if grammatically it leaves something to be desired, for *alors* to be understood as referring back to the three intervening sentences, with the sense of 'lorsqu'il souffle un vent d'Est'.

---

[4] Cf. Duclos: 'Une noire mélancolie, causée par le dépit et les remords..., conduisit à la fin Innocent XIII au tombeau' (in Littré, art. *mélancolie*).

There could be no better illustration for a French reader of the time of the 'résolutions désespérées' to which Englishmen were sometimes driven, than the execution of Charles I and the deposition of James II. Charles's widow had taken refuge in her native France, and James and his family had fled to the French Court; and both events had aroused great popular sympathy for the royal victims. At first sight, therefore, one might be tempted to see in the choice of these two examples a reflection of this conventional sympathy, and of the horror felt by the French nation, even though it suggests a somewhat extreme view of the role of chance in determining historical events. However, eighteenth-century opinion, at any rate among enlightened French thinkers, had become much more critical of the theory of the divine right of kings; and the trial and execution of Charles, and more particularly the Bloodless Revolution of 1688, were soon to be hailed as examples of responsible acts on the part of a sovereign people. In the *Lettres philosophiques*, Voltaire himself was to write:

> Ce qu'on reproche le plus en France aux Anglais, c'est le supplice de Charles I, qui fut traité par ses vainqueurs comme il les eût traités s'il eût été heureux.
>
> Après tout, regardez d'un côté Charles I vaincu en bataille rangée, prisonnier, jugé, condamné dans Westminster, et de l'autre l'Empereur Henri VII empoisonné par son chapelain en communiant, Henri III assassiné par un moine ministre de la rage de tout un parti, trente assassinats médités contre Henri IV, plusieurs exécutés, et le dernier privant enfin la France de ce grand roi. Pesez ces attentats, et jugez[5]

—and although even when he was writing seriously as a historian, he was occasionally tempted by the theory which ascribed a considerable importance to chance, it is more than likely that on this occasion he was merely seeking to round the passage off with a striking and provocative sally. This interpretation is surely reinforced by the final sentence, which—in so far as there is a connecting-link provided by the word *cour*—seems to couple the two outstanding events in English political history of the seventeenth century with court-life in its most superficial and trivial aspect; the 'minor cadence' of the penultimate sentence leads in to the phrase *Si vous avez quelque grâce à demander...*, which has the effect of irreverently

[5] Letter VIII, text of 1734.

associating the narrator himself with the two unfortunate monarchs. Stylistically, the final sentence is most pleasing: the doctor's confidential advice brings the narrator back into the picture, from which he has been absent for a dozen lines, and in the final *reprise* of the 'leitmotif', instead of the expected 'lorsque le vent sera à l'est', we have, for variety's sake, ...*que lorsque le vent sera à l'ouest ou au sud.*

The structure of the piece as a whole, the occasional touch of the absurd or of 'humour noir', the repeated insistence on the theme of climatic influence which, if taken literally, would be quite obsessive, the imaginative play on the formula *le vent d'Est*, and the skilful conclusion: all this goes to suggest that it would be wrong to regard this passage as a serious investigation of the influence of climate on character. Much later, Voltaire was to express his scepticism with regard to Montesquieu's theory:

> Les Anglais ont le *spleen* ou la *splin*, et se tuent par humeur. Ils s'en vantent, car quiconque se pend à Londres... est mis dans la gazette... Mais si l'on voulait rabattre cet orgueil, on leur prouverait que dans la seule année 1774, on a compté à Paris plus de cinquante personnes qui se sont donné la mort. On leur dirait que chaque année il y a douze suicides dans Genève qui ne contient que vingt mille âmes, tandis que les gazettes ne comptent pas plus de suicides à Londres, qui renferme environ sept cent mille *spleen* ou *splin.*[6]

It is impossible to say, in the absence of further evidence, how far this scepticism had already been aroused in the 1720s by those publications which had given the theory a preliminary airing. The tone of the two passages is quite different, of course; in the 1728 letter Voltaire does not commit himself to a direct expression of opinion: he reports the opinions of others, and when he does appear to contribute an observation of his own (*le climat opérait déjà sur moi, et je m'étonnais de ne pouvoir rire*), it is so obviously absurd that the extravagance of the idea calls in question his whole attitude. It would perhaps be safest to conclude that Voltaire was very ready to follow other writers in giving an account of a feature of the English character which could be explained in terms of a fashionable theory; but that he accepted this opportunity the more willingly because of the scope it offered for his creative imagination, as an exercise in literary composition controlled by good-humoured,

[6] *Commentaire sur l'Esprit des lois* (1777).

gentle irony.[7] Gustave Lanson, publishing the *Lettre à M.* *** as an appendix to his edition of the *Lettres philosophiques*, refers to it as a 'charmant morceau'; the epithet can certainly be applied without any reservations to this extract from the letter.

[7] 'Voltaire peut bien avoir tout l'esprit du monde; il n'en est pas moins très exactement humoriste à ses heures' (A. Laffay, *Anatomie de l'humour et du nonsense* (Paris, 1970), p. 10). Indeed, if one accepts M. Laffay's definition of that characteristically English phenomenon, *l'humour*, this passage can be seen to be an excellent example of it: '...une manière volontairement impassible et d'une minutie quasi-scientifique, de décrire le bizarre, l'insolite ou le ridicule, avec l'arrière-pensée de faire ainsi accepter son propre particularisme sous l'effet d'une tolérance réciproque' (p. 47).

10 Beaumarchais

LE COMTE

Ta joyeuse colère me réjouit. Mais tu ne me dis pas ce qui t'a fait quitter Madrid.

FIGARO

C'est mon bon ange, Excellence, puisque je suis assez heureux pour retrouver mon ancien maître. Voyant à Madrid que la ré-
5 publique des lettres était celle des loups, toujours armés les uns contre les autres, et que, livrés au mépris où ce risible acharnement les conduit, tous les insectes, les moustiques, les cousins, les critiques, les maringouins, les envieux, les feuillistes, les libraires, les censeurs, et tout ce qui s'attache à la peau des malheureux gens de lettres,
10 achevait de déchiqueter et sucer le peu de substance qui leur restait; fatigué d'écrire, ennuyé de moi, dégoûté des autres, abîmé de dettes et léger d'argent; à la fin convaincu que l'utile revenu du rasoir est préférable aux vains honneurs de la plume, j'ai quitté Madrid; et, mon bagage en sautoir, parcourant philosophiquement les deux
15 Castilles, la Manche, l'Estramadure, la Sierra-Morena, l'Anda-lousie; accueilli dans une ville, emprisonné dans l'autre, et partout supérieur aux événements; loué par ceux-ci, blâmé par ceux-là; aidant au bon temps, supportant le mauvais; me moquant des sots, bravant les méchants, riant de ma misère et faisant la barbe à
20 tout le monde; vous me voyez enfin établi dans Séville, et prêt à servir de nouveau Votre Excellence en tout ce qu'il lui plaira m'ordonner.

LE COMTE

Qui t'a donné une philosophie aussi gaie?

FIGARO

L'habitude du malheur. Je me presse de rire de tout, de peur d'être obligé d'en pleurer.   25

> BEAUMARCHAIS, *Le Barbier de Séville*,
>   Act I, sc. ii
> Date of first publication: 1775
> Ed. E. J. Arnould (Oxford: Blackwell, 1963),
>   pp. 22–3

THE first Act of the play begins at the poetic hour of dawn, and the scene is laid 'à Séville, dans la rue et sous les fenêtres de Rosine'. Count Almaviva is pacing up and down the deserted street. Having glimpsed Rosine in the Prado, he has secretly followed her to Seville. A handsome, wealthy 'grand seigneur libertin', he is tired of easy conquests and has disguised himself as a 'simple bachelier'. 'En grand manteau brun et chapeau rabattu', he is waiting like some romantic 'Espagnol du temps d'Isabelle' for the Beloved to show herself at the bars of her cage. At this moment Figaro, 'en habit de majo espagnol' and with a guitar slung over his shoulder, comes up the street with a sheet of paper and a pencil in his hand, simultaneously composing and singing an epicurean song which sharply contrasts in mood with Almaviva's monologue. The amusing recognition-scene produces another contrast based on a series of comic antitheses reflecting different status and appearance: 'Cet air altier et noble' / 'Cette tournure grotesque'; 'le comte Almaviva' / 'ce coquin de Figaro'; 'monseigneur' / 'maraud'. Having first cursed the intrusion, Almaviva-Lindor sees that Figaro can be a useful ally: 'Deux hommes qui jasent sont moins suspects qu'un seul qui se promène. Ayons l'air de jaser.' Asked what he is doing in Seville, Figaro recounts his career since leaving the Count's service—first as an apothecary in 'les haras d'Andalousie', selling horse medicines for human ailments, writing poetry, and finally dismissed for his attempt to combine 'l'amour des lettres' with 'l'esprit des affaires'; then as a dramatist in Madrid, organizing his own 'claque', but defeated none the less by the 'efforts de la cabale'. He is angry at having been 'sifflé', and if he can ever again confront his enemies in the theatre he vows to avenge himself by mordant satire.

This exchange of short, brisk ripostes leads up to the passage under consideration which includes Figaro's long tirade,[1] a sudden outburst of torrential eloquence which contrasts with the preceding dialogue. This speech is the first sketch of the even longer and more famous tirade in the *Mariage*, V, iii; but his mood is here less sombre, less bitter, less philosophical. Nor is it a monologue, for Figaro has an interlocutor here. True, the Count is watching out for Rosine and is only half listening to Figaro, who has to make an effort to hold his attention ('Que regardez-vous donc toujours de ce côté?'). Almaviva is somewhat distrait; but the Count does in fact here play the part of 'straight man', obligingly feeding his former valet the appropriate questions and providing him with an opportunity for a brilliant résumé of his life and outlook. At the same time the author himself cannot resist the temptation to break the theatrical illusion occasionally and, with a sly wink, to intervene in person. Figaro's tirade is, in fact, to some extent a thinly disguised and highly successful projection of Beaumarchais, a riotous self-vindication addressed not so much to Almaviva as to the audience on the other side of the footlights. Much of this is lost on the modern reader; but for the contemporary public this fluctuating ambiguity of association would have added an extra spice to the comic effect of the tirade.

The verisimilitude of the speech has been sometimes questioned; but Figaro has already captivated the audience, and the Count's distraction makes the tirade plausible enough. It has also been criticized as a dramatic digression, for Figaro seems to step outside the play, take off on a lyrical flight, and then slip back into the action. Strictly speaking, it is extraneous to the plot; but it is not an *hors-d'œuvre*. It is indispensable for the understanding of the deeper meaning of the work, and above all it introduces us to Figaro in his full dimensions. Act I, scene ii marks the advent of Figaro in the French theatre, and in his tirade he presents himself to us in depth as a man with a past, a present, and a future, as well as with a highly individual view of life.

Both the passage as a whole and the tirade itself display a high degree of structural unity and balanced symmetry. The opening sentence of the Count rounds off the preceding dialogue and supplies the transition to the new development, while his following

---

[1] The tirade is somewhat reminiscent of Trivelin's long speech in Marivaux's *La Fausse Suivante* (1724), I, i: 'Depuis quinze ans que je roule...'

question provokes Figaro's tirade. Almaviva's second question elicits the final maxim, which is a restatement and further elaboration of the *joyeuse colère* of the opening sentence. The tirade itself is introduced and concluded with two polite formulae, while the central section consists of two long, symmetrical periods which describe Figaro's two main theatres of action (the Republic of Letters in Madrid and Spain at large), combine his whimsical account of his life with his gay profession of faith, and culminate in both cases in a sudden change of scene (*j'ai quitté Madrid... enfin établi dans Séville...*). Grammatically, the two periods are linked by *et* and form one long sentence. The first half of the sentence is made up of a parallel series of six participles plus one adjective, all construed in a causal sense and all placed in apposition to the subject of the long-delayed main verb (*j'ai quitté*); but the first and last of the participles introduce subordinate clauses (*Voyant* has two object clauses, the second of which contains two relative clauses; *convaincu* has one dependent clause). The second half of the sentence opens with an absolute participial construction with its verb understood (*mon bagage en sautoir*) followed by another string of twelve participles and two adjectives, placed this time in apposition to the object of the other delayed main verb (*vous me voyez*). Apart from the one relative clause in the final 'phrase de politesse' there are no subordinate clauses to slow down the momentum of the second period. Formally, it is a periodic sentence; but it is far from being heavy or cumbersome, for it is broken up not only by the two series of participles and adjectives but also by the occasional use of strong punctuation (semi-colons). There results a final, overall impression not of a periodic sentence, but of a brisk, spritely 'style coupé', especially in the lilting second period which evokes Figaro's nimble, capricious peregrinations through Spain. Any impression of fragmentation, however, is successfully avoided by the fast tempo of the sentence which is so constructed that our attention can never let up or wander from the text. As he sweeps on Figaro communicates a sense of a bustling, almost feverish activity, a restless *perpetuum mobile*. Similarly the contradictions of Figaro's life and character find a kind of stylistic expression in the spate of deftly balanced antitheses: *ennuyé de moi | dégoûté des autres; abîmé de dettes | léger d'argent; l'utile revenu du rasoir | vains honneurs de la plume; accueilli dans une ville | emprisonné dans l'autre; loué par ceux-ci | blâmé par ceux-là; aidant au bon temps | supportant le mauvais; me moquant des sots | bravant les méchants.* Each term contrasts with or contradicts its opposite only to be finally reconciled in the higher synthesis of the gay philosophy which enables its exponent to be *partout supérieur aux événements.* Hence Figaro's intense joy in the present which seems to be reflected in the very use of tenses for the main verbs: *j'ai quitté* (the perfect, i.e. the past tense closest to the present) and *voyez* (present tense). These main verbs combine with the preponderance of participles to produce the effect of a dramatic present, of the past directly impinging on the present, of past and present fusing in a dynamic continuum. The main stylistic basis of the tirade, however, remains the old rhetorical device of enumeration which Beaumarchais borrowed from Rabelais and which he had already used in his *parades.* Enumeration involves the accumulation of a long series of words which gradually gather momentum as they rise to their climax, piling up in a kind of lyrical frenzy and, by their juxtaposition, enormously reinforcing the total comic effect. The device is employed more than once here; but Beaumarchais avoids monotony by skilful variations: he uses common nouns, proper names, present and past participles, often combining them with a view to verbal consonance which in itself creates a kind of rhythm, and, in the case of the participles, varying the grammatical categories of their complements. In this unity in diversity we recognize the characteristic versatility of Figaro and his creator.

The *joyeuse colère* which delights the Count is perhaps the key to Figaro's contradictory, complex character. His alternate or simultaneous expression of indignation and gaiety recalls the peculiar mixed tone of Beaumarchais's *Mémoires.* Figaro is angry; but he is not bitter or disenchanted. He keeps his sense of humour and a cool head. His mood is neither rebellious nor resigned. He is not a revolutionary, but an adventurer, an 'arriviste'. Hence Almaviva's tolerant, amused reaction. He does not take Figaro too seriously. He prides himself, however, on being an 'homme d'esprit', and in addition he needs his ex-servant's help.

Almaviva's second sentence originally ran on: 'et t'a transféré sur le Guadalquivir au midi de l'Espagne', a touch of 'espagnolisme' designed not as authentic local colour but as a prudent cover for political, social, and literary satire, as well as to endow the play with the colourful, picturesque charm of an 'Espagne de fantaisie'. However, Beaumarchais had to shorten the text of his comedy after the first performance, and this detail was suppressed in the edition. In any case it got in the way of the main purpose of the sentence which is to provoke Figaro's tirade. The definitive version is more directly functional.

More polite than in the soliloquy of *Le Mariage*, V, iii, Figaro replies with a compliment which serves as introduction to the long sentence which follows. It is a kind of verbal 'courbette' which recalls the 'orgueilleuse modestie' of Beaumarchais's ironic self-introduction at the beginning of the *Lettre modérée* as 'l'auteur, vêtu modestement et courbé, présentant sa pièce au lecteur'. Although the Count has just asked to be addressed simply as 'Lindor' Figaro here observes the formal, outward marks of respect (*Excellence*). There is, however, a certain camaraderie between master and man. Figaro is genuinely pleased to have come across his old master again because of the prospect of adventure and intrigue. Social position apart the two men have much in common, and Almaviva is here an ally and not yet an adversary. Figaro speaks playfully of his *bon ange* having brought them together again. Pious sentiments are uncommon in Figaro, and we can be fairly sure that what is meant here is really Chance, the controlling force in Beaumarchais's theatre.

When he turns to evoke the prevalent mentality and *mores* of the literary circles in Madrid Figaro's tone at once changes from polite deference to scorn, disgust, indignation. In the Monologue his diatribe will be directed against an apparently universal conspiracy of evil-wishers; but here he confines himself to the literary jungle. *La république des lettres* belongs to the category of 'le style noble'; but its 'noblesse' is at once deflated by the ironic, almost Swiftian reduction of the men of letters to ugly, ferocious beasts (*loups*). For the eighteenth-century *philosophes* the Republic of Letters[2] represented the whole body of European men of letters seen as influential, militant propagandists dedicated to the emancipation of the human mind and to the diffusion of the ideas of the Enlightenment. Beaumarchais himself was after his fashion an heir of the *philosophes;* but his harsh satire here underlines the gap between the ideal and the reality of the Republic of Letters. Figaro speaks

[2] Cf. Voltaire: 'On a vu une république littéraire établie insensiblement dans l'Europe, malgré les guerres et malgré les religions différentes' (*Siècle de Louis XIV*, ch. xxxiv). 'Vous êtes Anglais, mon cher ami, et je suis né en France; mais ceux qui aiment les arts sont tous concitoyens: les honnêtes gens qui pensent ont à peu près les mêmes principes, et ne composent qu'une république' (*Zaïre*, Ép. déd. à Falkener).

only of the literary fauna in Spain; but this is merely a transparent veil for Beaumarchais's own chastening experience of the 'animaux hargneux' of Paris, the very heart of the 'Europe des Lumières'. Far from fostering reason and tolerance, peace and concord, the writers themselves are depicted as engaged in an internecine struggle for existence. The Republic of Letters is here a distinctly Hobbesian world: *homo homini lupus*. Figaro likens it to a pack of wolves, all at one another's throats, and the earliest manuscript version adds: 'à tel point affamés et multipliés dans la capitale qu'ils s'entredévoraient pour y vivre'. Often exploited, slandered, and oppressed, most eighteenth-century writers had a lowly status and led a precarious, dangerous existence; but they also forfeited social esteem and brought themselves frequently into contempt by their mutual hatreds and ridiculous rivalries.

At this point the syntax becomes somewhat free and loose, for *livrés au mépris où*[3]... relates only vaguely to *gens de lettres* several lines further on; but the meaning is clear enough. *Risible* acquires added force from being in the 'position affective', while *acharnement* possesses something of its primary meaning: 'action d'un animal qui s'attache opiniâtrément à la chair qu'il dévore' (Littré). This last word sums up the first scourge of the Republic of Letters. The second is the plague of literary middlemen and hangers-on who batten on the hapless writers. The image of the authors as wolves is appropriately extended by the image of their parasites as a lower, even more repulsive form of animal life. Degraded to a swarm of noxious, stinging insects, the tiny monsters are picked off and neatly crushed like odious vermin by Figaro's deadly irony. The enumeration piles up a long series of skilfully varied, comically pejorative terms. Some express the fanciful insect imagery (*insectes*, *moustiques*, *cousins*,[4] *maringouins*[5]). The others designate professions (*critiques*, *feuillistes*,[6] *libraires*) or carry moral undertones

---

[3] = 'auquel'.

[4] i.e. 'midges', 'gnats'.

[5] = 'moustiques des pays chauds dont la piqûre est désagréable'. The word comes from the Brazilian *marigoui*; but Beaumarchais makes a comic thrust at an enemy by making it seem a derivative of the name of Marin, editor of the *Gazette de France* and a royal censor. Marin had passed the first MS. version of the *Barbier* in 1773, but had subsequently sided with Goëzman against Beaumarchais. The *Mémoires* contain several attacks on 'l'ami Marin' as well as various other puns on his name ('je ne sais quoi de fade, de saumâtre, de mariné', 'goût marin', 'du Marin ordinaire, du Marin superfin').

[6] A neologism coined by Beaumarchais. A pejorative term for journalists and especially newspaper critics.

as well (*envieux*,[7] *censeurs*[8]); but these too are assimilated to the rest by the accumulation so that the men are merged with the insects. The arrangement of the terms is particularly dexterous. In the earlier MSS. the enumeration ran: 'les insectes, les puces, les cousins, les critiques, les feuillistes, les libraires, les censeurs'. But in the last manuscript version Beaumarchais inserted *tous* before *les insectes, les moustiques* before *les cousins* and *les maringouins* after *les critiques*, and in the final printed text he deleted 'les puces' and transferred *les envieux* (added in the last manuscript version before *les libraires*) to before *les feuillistes*. The ingenious reshaping of the original enumeration is a brilliant success. *Tous les insectes*, a generic term embracing all the literal and metaphorical insects which follow, serves as introduction to the series which falls into two equal, symmetrical parts, each with its own climax. The first part consists of four plural nouns linked by comic rhyme or assonance: *moustiques, cousins, critiques, maringouins*. All are accompanied by the definite article and all have two sounded syllables except for *maringouins*, which, as the climax of the first series, stands out in greater comic relief. The second part of the enumeration, which culminates in *les censeurs*, also consists of four plural nouns, all again composed of two sounded syllables and accompanied by the definite article, but this time without any trace of verbal consonance. Finally, the terms are so ordered that the grotesque assimilation proceeds not from the men to the insects, but vice versa. It is as if the insects had taken on human form, and their leech-like, sucking activities, enhanced by the alliteration in [s] and [ʃ], are likewise transferred to a human context: *tout ce qui s'attache à la peau des malheureux gens de lettres, achevait de déchiqueter [9] et sucer le peu de substance qui leur restait.*

[7] Figaro has already described himself as a victim of 'l'Envie aux doigts crochus, au teint pâle et livide' (I, ii), and he will later attribute his literary failure to 'les envieux' (III, v). *Les envieux* was inserted in the tirade in the last MS. version as a substitute for 'hâves et desséchés par l'envie', a phrase placed after *les conduit* in the earlier versions. It is therefore certain that envious men of letters are meant here.

[8] Almost a term of opprobrium in the 18th C. All publications and especially all plays were subject to the approval of the government censorship, which thus controlled and restricted freedom of thought and expression. Beaumarchais's interminable wranglings with the censors are famous; but here he is probably alluding more to unofficial *censeurs* in whom he was tempted to see envious, slanderous enemies and especially 'des grands'. Cf. the rôle of Mme du Barry in the prohibition of the *Barbier* in 1774.

[9] = 'déchiquetait complètement'. The imagery here recalls Beaumarchais's pun on *censeurs/sangsues* in the *Lettre modérée*: 'A peine ils [les ouvrages de théâtre] voient le

Figaro's disgust with the men of letters and their parasites expresses itself in a surging periodic style; but this is succeeded by a kind of contrasting 'style coupé'. There is a series of four past participles plus one adjective; but all are linked by the assonance of their endings (*fatigué, ennuyé, dégoûté, abîmé, léger*), and their complements, which are all introduced by various forms of the preposition *de* and are all composed of two sounded syllables, belong to diverse grammatical categories: *d'écrire, de moi, des autres, de dettes, d'argent*. The overall effect is to create a jerky, staccato rhythm which seems to punch out Figaro's momentary frustration at his defeat. Indeed, this is the section which comes closest to the sombre, world-weary mood of the soliloquy in *Le Mariage*; but his resilient gaiety will reassert itself here more swiftly. *Fatigué d'écrire*: the weariness will soon pass, for no one could be more convinced of the power of the pen than Figaro and his creator. *Ennuyé de moi, dégoûté des autres*: an unusual moroseness, but we may be sure that Figaro will soon recover his extrovert optimism and find a new audience before which to parade his opinions and boost his ego. *Abîmé de dettes et léger d'argent*: the tone is comic, but it seems as if Figaro were here plunged in a veritable abyss of debt which was no doubt Beaumarchais's private conception of Hell.

Like all Beaumarchais's characters Figaro is peculiarly conscious of the power of money,[10] and he has accordingly decided to desert the dramatist's pen for the barber's razor. There is, it is true, no fortune to be made out of the barber's trade even when allied, as it was in the eighteenth century, with that of apothecary and surgeon; but it will provide a modest independence. The earliest manuscript version read: 'j'ai quitté Madrid à la fin, convaincu que l'utile revenu…'; but the revised text is far more effective. It concludes more symmetrically the series of participles (*à la fin convaincu*), ironically affects the 'style noble' with its mocking antithesis and finally builds up to the main clause with its climactic verb (*j'ai quitté Madrid*) which forms the central pivot of the two halves of the long sentence and which, by its shortness and briskness, conveys the impression of a sudden, irrevocable decision.

jour, que, sous prétexte d'enflure, on leur applique les censeurs', and his description of these new plays emerging into circulation 'dépenaillés, défigurés, rongés d'extraits et couverts de critiques' (ibid.).

[10] 'Allons, Figaro, vole à la fortune, mon fils' (I, vi). 'De l'or, mon Dieu, de l'or, c'est le nerf de l'intrigue' (ibid.).

The style of the second period is more 'coupé' than that of the first, for it at once relates and suggests the capricious, spritely meanderings of Figaro wandering about like some picaresque hero all over Spain. He has packed his razor and lancet; but otherwise he travels light and free, with no heavy possessions to weigh him down. He describes himself setting off with his baggage slung over his shoulder, not simply 'traversant' (first MS.), but *parcourant* Spain at large, accepting the vicissitudes of his journey *philosophique-ment*, i.e. without illusions, but also without bitterness or rancour. His itinerary supplies a splash of local colour. Carried away by his *élan*, he gaily reels off the exotic names of the provinces through which he has passed in his progress from North to South—New Castile, Old Castile, Estremadura, La Mancha, Sierra Morena, and Andalusia.

This accumulation of place names fits into a larger enumeration beginning with *parcourant* and culminating triumphantly in *et faisant la barbe à tout le monde*. There is a long series of participles and adjectives, all placed in apposition to the object of the delayed second main verb and consisting for the most part of a succession of antitheses often rhythmically linked by the assonance of the participial endings. But Beaumarchais avoids monotony by combining unity and variety. There is, for example, no verbal consonance in the first antithesis (*accueilli | emprisonné*) or between the antithesis and its appendage (*supérieur*); but this is followed by two past participles ending in *é* and three pairs of present participles ending in *-ant*. The first antithesis which recounts Figaro's contrasting receptions in the towns which he visits is reminiscent of Beaumarchais's own imprisonment in Vienna and his triumphant return to Paris in 1774. The ironic 'style noble' of *et partout supérieur aux événements* expresses Figaro's gay philosophy, the engaging, optimistic outlook of a resilient 'life-man'. He regards everything as a kind of game, takes his ups and downs with cool good humour, and is resigned to the fact that he will be *loué par ceux-ci, blâmé par ceux-là*. This last phrase is the second of the series of antitheses whose binary rhythm seems to reinforce the barber's combative spirit. It was added in the last manuscript version, but omitted in the first two editions and restored only in the Nouvelle Édition. It is a direct allusion to the 'blâme' inflicted on Beaumarchais during the *affaire Goëzman*. In 1774 he was 'blâmé', i.e. branded as a criminal and deprived of all civic rights; but the very next day he was fêted as a 'grand citoyen' by the Prince de Conti, and wherever he went he was acclaimed as a popular hero by the many enemies of the Parlement Maupeou. In the following series of antitheses Figaro goes on to develop his gay attitude to life. Exploiting good fortune and philosophic in adversity, laughing lightheartedly at human folly, but defiant in face of malice, he keeps a sense of humour in hard times and he never takes anybody too seriously. Laughter, after all, can bring the comforting illusion of a kind of victory over the slings and arrows of outrageous fortune.

In this section of the speech Figaro is unmistakably voicing not only his own outlook but also that of Beaumarchais himself. The identification is virtually complete. At this point, however, Beaumarchais fades away, and Figaro re-emerges in his own right. The transition is supplied by *faisant la barbe à tout le monde*. This phrase can be figuratively applied to Beaumarchais's own universal irreverence as much as to Figaro's habit of cocking a snook at authority; but literally it refers more particularly to the itinerant barber who after his wanderings is at last *établi dans Séville* with his own shop and trade-sign: *Consilio manuque. Figaro*. He is now independent, and there is almost an air of patronage in his offer of service; but once again he observes the outward forms of respect, rounding off his tirade with another 'phrase de politesse': *et prêt à servir de nouveau Votre Excellence en tout ce qu'il lui plaira m'ordonner.*[11] It is a kind of verbal 'révérence' which corresponds symmetrically to the 'courbette' of Figaro's first sentence.

In the first manuscript version the Count's reply took the form of a statement: 'Ta philosophie me paraît assez gaie', which was immediately followed by Figaro's explanation: 'C'est que je me presse de rire...' Almaviva had already defined here the keynote of Figaro's philosophy; but his viewpoint remains somewhat superficial and faintly patronizing. By changing the Count's statement into a question: *Qui*[12] *t'a donné une philosophie aussi gaie?* Beaumarchais was able to work in Figaro's unexpected, paradoxical riposte: *L'habitude du malheur*. By this ironical counterpointing a precarious unity is imposed on apparently incompatible opposites, for these contradictions coexist in the character of Figaro whose outlook is radically antinomian. *Malheur* represents the objective reality; gaiety is the subjective response to that reality. It is the

[11] = 'de m'ordonner'; archaic usage.
[12] = 'What?'; a Classical usage.

reaction of a warm, vital personality; but there remain certain undertones of moroseness and worldweariness (*fatigué, ennuyé, dégoûté, misère, habitude du malheur*) which will find fuller expression in the soliloquy in *Le Mariage*, but which are already present here in the final maxim: *Je me presse de rire de tout, de peur d'être obligé d'en pleurer*.

All in all Figaro's tirade is a remarkable 'tour de force'. The sheer verbal exuberance seems to develop a dynamic of its own, independent of creative intention; but such an impression is disproved by numerous alterations in the manuscripts.[13] The speech is the product of conscious artistry which creates the semblance of spontaneous improvisation. It is not so much a tirade in the traditional sense as a series of fanciful dancing movements; for Beaumarchais's prose here is closer to 'la danse' than to 'la marche', the outward sign of the inward dance of the imagination, the stylistic expression of the gay philosophy which triumphs over the capriciousness of Chance by an instinctive sense of balance and an apparently effortless grace. Figaro here is not unlike the dancer described in the *Lettre modérée*: 'Le voyez-vous s'avancer légèrement à petits bonds, reculer à grands pas, et faire oublier le comble de l'art par la plus ingénieuse négligence?'

[13] See E. J. Arnould's monumental *Genèse du Barbier de Séville* (1965), pp. 154-5.

11 Chénier

Tu gémis sur l'Ida, mourante, échevelée,
O reine, ô de Minos épouse désolée,
Heureuse si jamais, dans ses riches travaux,
Cérès n'eût pour le joug élevé des troupeaux.
5   Certe aux antres d'Amnise assez votre Lucine
Donnait de beaux neveux aux mères de Gortyne,
Certes vous élevez aux gymnases crétois
D'autres jeunes troupeaux plus dignes de ton choix.
Tu voles épier sous quelle yeuse obscure,
10   Tranquille, il ruminait son antique pâture,
Quel lit de fleurs reçut ses membres nonchalants,
Quelle onde a ranimé l'albâtre de ses flancs.
O Nymphes, entourez, fermez, Nymphes de Crète,
De ces vallons, fermez, entourez la retraite,
15   Si peut-être vers lui des vestiges épars
Ne viendront point guider mes pas et mes regards.
Insensée, à travers ronces, forêts, montagnes,
Elle court. O fureur! dans les vertes campagnes,
Une belle génisse à son superbe amant
20   Adressait devant elle un doux mugissement.
La perfide mourra. Jupiter la demande.
Elle-même à son front attache la guirlande,
L'entraîne, et sur l'autel prenant le fer vengeur:
'Sois belle maintenant et plais à mon vainqueur.'
25   Elle frappe et sa haine en la flamme lustrale
Rit de voir palpiter le coeur de sa rivale.

A. CHÉNIER, *Bucoliques*
Date of composition: unknown
Date of first publication (posthumous): 1819
Poems, ed. F. Scarfe (Oxford: Blackwell, 1961),
pp. 15–16

As with virtually the whole of Chénier's *œuvre*, the poems now normally grouped together under the title *Les Bucoliques* remained unpublished at the poet's death, and were first published in 1819. A number of them deal with the related themes of Europa and Pasiphae: legend recounts how Europa, daughter of a King of Tyre, was abducted by Zeus, who, having taken the form of a bull in order to seduce her, swam across the sea to Crete, carrying her on his back; here she bore him children, among them Minos, who was to become the famous law-giver and ruler of Crete; when King Minos refused to sacrifice a bull to Poseidon, this god in revenge made his wife Pasiphae fall in love with the bull, to whom she bore the Minotaur, half bull, half man. Further connected with the legendary stories of Theseus and Heracles (Ariadne, Minos' daughter, helped Theseus to enter the labyrinth and kill the Minotaur), the story of Pasiphae stands at the centre of one of the richest and most fertile of Greek myths; its magic is evoked in the celebrated line in which Racine refers to his heroine Phèdre as 'La fille de Minos et de Pasiphaé'. Such is the mythological background to the episode related here of the summary vengeance carried out by Pasiphae on a rival—a heifer she finds enjoying the favours of her animal lover.

The poem here quoted appears in two forms in Chénier's manuscript, the earlier, rather shorter, version being crossed out and replaced by the second. The text of the earliest editions consisted of a contamination of the two versions, omitting lines 5–8, which only appear in the second, but adopting various emendations of the revised manuscript text; the text here reproduced, however, is that of all reputable modern editions, which follow the revised manuscript text in full.

In general, the *Bucoliques* represent the same sort of stylized pastoral idyll as is to be found in Virgil's *Eclogues* (or *Bucolics*), with a considerable admixture of more pathetic, elegiac material of mythological inspiration. Chénier's principal sources in this particular poem were one passage from the *Eclogues* (VI, 45 ff.) and one from Ovid's *Ars Amatoria* (I, 313 ff.), corresponding respectively to the chief subject-matter of lines 1–18 and 19–26 of our text.

Many passages of verse written in regularly alternating Alexandrine couplets with masculine and feminine rhymes acquire from this very fact a superficial appearance of being composed in stanza-form. In the case of the poem under consideration, however, there is much more tangible evidence for talking of a genuinely 'stanzaic' construction, which is here emphasized not only by the punctuation (all the four-line groups are marked-off by full-stops, while only one other line, apart from the last line of the poem, has this strong punctuation), but also by a change of speaker, or of person addressed, at the beginning of each 'stanza'. Thus, lines 1–4 are addressed by the poet to Pasiphaé (*Tu gémis...*); lines 5–8 to the people of Crete (*assez votre Lucine...*); lines 9–12 again to Pasiphaé (*Tu voles épier...*). Lines 13–16 express the unspoken thoughts of the central figure (*O Nymphes, entourez...*); lines 17–20 contain third-person narrative; lines 21–4 open with a line expressing Pasiphaé's unspoken thoughts, and close with a line of direct speech; and the poem is rounded off with a couplet which again uses third-person narrative (*Elle frappe...*). From the point of view of construction, therefore, the poem may be considered as consisting of six four-line stanzas and a final couplet. As regards narrative technique, the considerable variety achieved by the constantly shifting perspective, as the poet changes from addressing the heroine to expressing her thoughts directly, and alternates expression of her thoughts and speech with objective third-person narration, is matched by a remarkable virtuosity in the use of verbs generally. The basic narrative tense is the present, used for immediacy and vividness of effect; but Chénier twice departs from this: in the sequence of verbs in lines 10–12, and in *adressait* of line 20. The futures used to express quoted thoughts in lines 16 and 21, the imperatives of lines 13–14 and 24, and—as will be noted below—the omission of the verb in the constructions of lines 3–4, 14–15, and 23–4; the constant changes of person; and above all, the almost completely paratactic construction of the whole poem (the only conjunctions linking main verbs are the *et* at l. 23 and again at l. 25): all this goes to create a most vigorous, and highly effective, narrative style.

The first four-line 'stanza' combines a couplet of direct, Racinian simplicity with one embodying a much more complex Latin style. In the first hemistich we are presented with a bare unadorned statement, which is to be expanded and explained in the remainder of this stanza and the following one. Line 2 amplifies the pronoun subject; the verb *gémir* is developed in the second half of line 1 and in lines 3–4; while *sur l'Ida* (which is perhaps intended to convey the notion 'in Crete' rather than any more suggestively pictorial local colour depending on our recognition that this is *Mount Ida*) is taken up, by implication, in the geographical references (*Amnise... Gortyne... gymnases crétois*) of lines 5–8. In a truly Racinian manner, *mourante, échevelée* compresses a physical and moral portrait into a memorable hemistich; and line 2 is also reminiscent of Racine in its use of what has been termed 'genealogical periphrasis'.[1] Pasiphaé is nowhere named in the poem (and even the title has only been supplied by modern editors), but she is identified here, first generally as a 'queen', and then in particular as the unhappy consort of Minos. The proper name is relied on to conjure up the rich mythological background—perhaps even, might one suggest, with Racine's *Phèdre* as a significant intermediary? For it is possible that Racine may have been not merely an example, but also a conscious model, for Chénier: not only is the line already quoted ('La fille de Minos et de Pasiphaé', *Phèdre*, l. 36) a most striking instance of this same practice of 'genealogical periphrasis', but *mourante* and *échevelée* both contain reminders of Phèdre as we see her in Act I of Racine's play, where she is referred to (l. 44) as 'une femme mourante et qui cherche à mourir', and herself exclaims, on her first appearance:

> Que ces vains ornements, que ces voiles me pèsent!
> Quelle importune main, en formant tous ces nœuds,
> A pris soin sur mon front d'assembler mes cheveux?
> Tout m'afflige et me nuit, et conspire à me nuire.

The next couplet is quite different, Virgilian rather than Racinian in inspiration. Its prosaic meaning is: 'You who would have been happy, if only domesticated cattle had never existed'; but this is expressed by means of a highly elliptical construction (*Heureuse si...* = 'Toi qui aurais été heureuse si...'), while the transferred epithet in *dans ses riches travaux* (= 'in her labours to produce abundance') and the mythological personification in line 4, by elevating and 'ennobling' the concept, produce a condensed, cryptic couplet, particularly difficult for the modern reader less aware of the Classical context, and less familiar with the stylistic intricacies of such a latinized kind of French, than were Chénier's contemporaries.

The next four lines are designed to provide further elucidation

---

[1] Cf. M. J. O'Regan, 'Genealogical Periphrasis in Racine', *French Studies*, XVI (1962), pp. 14–23.

of the first couplet, in the form of a reflective comment on Pasiphaé's situation, addressed partly to the Queen herself, but also, as the plural *votre*, *vous* show, to the people of Crete as a whole. However, they are so allusive in their approach, and take so much knowledge for granted, they are so thoroughly Classical in their avoidance of direct statement, that the effect is to reiterate the content of lines 3–4, already cryptic enough, in a form even more enigmatic. It is not only to modern readers that these lines have presented something of a puzzle (indeed, it seems likely that this was the reason for their omission in the first published editions of the text), though it is possible that commentators have made them appear rather more difficult than is necessary. The *antres d'Amnise* refer to a grotto near the river of that name in Crete, sacred to Lucina, goddess of childbirth; while as for *Gortyne*, editors point out that this was where Zeus possessed Europa (the fruit of their union being Minos). Professor Scarfe writes: 'In this couplet the poet very delicately apologizes for Pasiphaé's aberration by alluding to Europa.' Certainly, we must assume that for Chénier himself, and for any reader thoroughly familiar with the topography, as well as the mythology, of ancient Crete, the reference to this background of legend would be present, and would constitute an extra element in the allusive richness of the text. But the primary meaning of the couplet is surely simpler, and the development from lines 3–4 to lines 5–8 may be presented as follows: 'You would have been happier without the fatal encounter with Ceres' herds' (i.e. the bull): 'for them others of Gortyn' (i.e. 'of Crete'; a part standing for the whole, a town for the whole island) 'were able to produce with Lucina's help plenty of fine *human* offspring' (*neveux* in the sense of 'posterity', common in the 'style noble' of poetry). One cannot agree, therefore, with Professor Scarfe when he says that line 5 is 'poorly constructed, with *assez* acting as a "cheville" in the middle'; this word is surely essential to the logical construction of a sentence which in prose word-order would read as follows: 'votre Lucine donnait assez de beaux neveux...' The difficulty arises principally from the need to 'translate' Chénier's latinized word-order into the normal order of prose.

Lines 7–8 provide a parallel to the previous couplet, the repetition of *Certes* (the omission of the final letter in line 5 was of course necessary in order to enable the second syllable of the word to be elided) helping to reproduce the same pattern and hence to re-

inforce the parallel. The idea is repeated in more general, less allusive terms: 'There exist in the academies of Crete' (*gymnase*: 'lieu
où les Grecs s'exerçaient à lutter, à jeter le disque, et autres jeux
de force'—Littré) 'a different kind of herd' (*scil.* 'companies of
human youths') 'who would have been more fitting lovers' (*scil.* 'if
you had to be unfaithful to Minos'). Altogether, the concentration
of this 'stanza' is remarkable, and with features such as ellipsis,
synecdoche, the dislocation of normal word-order, and the indirect,
allusive way in which the ideas are expressed, this group of four
lines is the most thoroughly Latin in character of the whole poem,
even though there appears to be no direct source, and there is certainly no counterpart in either the Virgil or the Ovid passage
referred to above.

In line 9 the narrative is resumed, after four lines of reflective
comment; the style is by contrast extremely simple and direct. The
changes of tense at this point have already been mentioned; the
effect is of a certain ambiguity as regards the time-sequence. After
the narrative present of *Tu voles...*, the imperfect of *ruminait*
should indicate a past action (*scil.* 'il ruminait autrefois'); but the
impression conveyed by the two verbs which follow: *reçut* and *a
ranimé*, is that they denote actions in the same temporal sequence
as *voles*—in other words, in lines 11–12, 'what bed of flowers received
(him), what stream refreshed (him)' (*scil.* 'on his return there after
his adventure with Pasiphaé'). The pronoun *il* of line 10, incidentally, has no grammatical antecedent; and though the sense is
clear enough, even the logical link with what precedes (via the
missing second term in the comparison at the end of line 8) is a
very loose one.

Pasiphaé's motivation here is that of any jealous woman: *Tu
voles épier...* (l. 9), and the whole of lines 11 and 12, could easily
apply to a human lover. However, although *ruminer* does possess a
secondary meaning of 'penser et repenser à une chose' (Littré),
pâture must here be taken in its literal meaning, and this forces the
reader to accept the primary meaning of *ruminer*. The Latin source
is followed closely here: a comparison with Virgil's 'ilice sub nigra'
shows that *obscure* has the sense of 'noire'—yet another example of
an archaic or latinizing tendency. Again, the adjective in *son
antique pâture* expresses (according to the nineteenth-century
editor Becq de Foucquières) merely the notion of 'antériorité' (i.e.
this is the pasture which was formerly his home, or to which he has

now returned); while the use of the adjective *tranquille* in the manner of an adverb also shows the influence of Latin. The two lines 11–12 derive from a single line of Virgil's: *lit de fleurs* comes from the latter's 'molli hyacintho', and *l'albâtre de ses flancs* from 'latus niveum'; in both these cases Chénier is following habits of expression characteristic of all French Classical poets, substituting the general term *fleurs* for the more precise and picturesque Latin word, and in *l'albâtre de ses flancs* adopting the nominal construction with its abstract, intellectualizing effect.

A similar feature is found in the next couplet, in the abstraction of *la retraite de ces vallons*; while the choice of *vestiges* ('terme du style soutenu'—Littré) represents another Classical characteristic; here Chénier is closely imitating the Latin poet's 'vestigia' (='footprints', not 'traces', as with mod. Fr. *vestiges*). The most attractive feature of the group of four lines from lines 13 to 16 is the rhythm and repetitive pattern of the invocation to the nymphs, imitated from a similar passage in Virgil addressed to 'Dictaeae Nymphae' ('Nymphs of Dicte'): line 13, with its striking chiasmus, enclosing the two verbs within a framework provided by the repeated *Nymphes*, is followed by another line of very similar structure; here, in line 14, the chiasmus effect is much reduced, in that the outer terms of the construction are not identical, but it is suggested none the less, by the echo of the same two verbs from the previous line, and pleasingly diversified by their being inverted. This is word-play of a very high order.

The remainder of this 'stanza' seems relatively uninspired, and the last line of the group contains the colourless near-cliché of *guider mes pas et mes regards*. Although this line reads like a *trimètre*, the presence of a caesura, however weak, at the sixth foot shows that Chénier was not departing from accepted practice here, any more than in line 11, where similarly the two subsidiary *coupes* are more prominent than the central break.

In lines 17–20 there is a striking change of style, to match the change of perspective, from Pasiphaé's thoughts (or speech) to direct narrative, the third person being used for a properly narrative function for the first time in the poem. Line 17 is a much looser form of Alexandrine than line 16: the central break is a good deal weaker, and the line is divided into four parts rather than three, with the most satisfactory break for a modern reader being 3 + 4 + 3 + 2 (that is, with an 'enjambement sur la césure'); though no doubt readers of Chénier's time would have regarded this as un-orthodox, the alternative would be to impose a break between the proclitic preposition *à travers* and the noun to which it is attached. This dislocation is followed by an enjambment, designed to bring *Elle court* of line 18 into prominence; and this perhaps indicates a conscious effort on the poet's part to make the rhythm of his verse express the content. Perhaps it is not being too fanciful to suggest that the awkward structure of line 17 helps to give the impression of an impetuous flight, checked by the obstacles of the briars, woods, and mountain paths.

Lines 18–20 show a very characteristic attitude towards noun and epithet: in all four pairs the adjective precedes, and even in the first case, where the adjective is one of colour, the effect is to subordinate adjective to noun, to deprive the former of its literal force, and to reduce it to a conventional abstraction. In the case of *belle génisse* the attempt to elevate and poeticize is evident: *génisse* is used for the 'vacca' of both Virgil and Ovid, and again the colourless epithet is subordinated to the more expressive noun. The tendency is less evident in the case of *superbe amant*: although the adjective is again conventional and abstract, here the 'position affective' does perhaps convey some degree of feeling, since the noun in this instance makes less of a claim on the reader's atten-tion. In the case of the last example, we should remember the tyranny of the hemistich on the Classical poet, for whom, in the commonest grouping (article + adjective + noun), the choice of a four-syllable noun inevitably necessitated the selection of a mono-syllabic adjective, thus tending to produce a trite, cliché-like appen-dage to the more expressive noun.[2] But for all that, there is some-thing impressive about the total effect of lines 19–20; and a situation which could so easily have appeared ludicrous if portrayed in too realistic a manner preserves its human dignity—and even, in the context, a touch of real poignancy—precisely because of the stylized nobility of the diction.

At line 21, for the beginning of the last complete 'stanza', the style of presentation again changes, and with great concision the action leads swiftly to the climax of line 24, which with powerful irony brings together the themes of the legend: jealousy, suffering, and sacrifice. Like lines 13–16, line 21 may represent the heroine's

---

[2] e.g. 'la triste Iphigénie', 'le fier Agamemnon' (and, by a converse process, 'un songe épouvantable'); cf. A. Cahen, *Le Vocabulaire de Racine* (Paris, 1946), pp. 198 ff.

unspoken thoughts, or be a fragment of speech; the absence of any punctuation indicating speech is of course inconclusive, and in fact the inverted commas of line 24, although reproduced in all modern editions, are not to be found in Chénier's manuscript. If, as perhaps seems preferable, we take line 21 as being the expression of her thoughts, it represents a particularly streamlined and highly dramatic narrative technique: the suppression of any linking words introducing the line suggests the comparable device of 'style indirect libre', used with a past narrative tense and characteristic of such writers as La Fontaine and Flaubert.

The use of the name *Jupiter* may perhaps strike English readers, accustomed to draw a distinction between this (Roman) name and its Greek counterpart 'Zeus', as a little incongruous in the context of Cretan topography and in view of the Hellenistic inspiration of the poem as a whole. However, the Latin name has been acclimatized in French literature, whether in a Latin or a Greek context, from the Renaissance onwards, and it is unlikely that any such incongruity would be felt by a French reader.[3] The phrase *Jupiter la demande* serves, of course, to bring together the Europa legend and Pasiphaé's own story, with echoes of the sacrifice which the god Poseidon had similarly 'required': ironically, Pasiphaé offers her rival in tribute to the god who is the cause of her own tragic heredity. Her cry in line 24, however, might be the utterance of a woman driven by her jealousy to kill a human rival, and bidding her with savage irony to be beautiful in the eyes of the man they both love. (Similarly in l. 26, where the Latin text has 'Et tenuit laeta pellicis exta manu' ('joyfully holding in her hand her rival's entrails'), since *exta*, 'bodily organs', carries strong connotations of animal sacrifice, Chénier has preferred to 'humanize' this to *le cœur de sa rivale*.)

Once again, *attache la guirlande* (l. 22) is typically Classical in its effect: the precise term *guirlande* is used not for picturesque evocation of detail, but for its symbolic suggestiveness; this is not a touch of realism, but a stylized gesture important for the meaning behind it. The stanza contains two examples of felicitous inversion—a device not by any means always to be considered as the awkward 'pis aller' of a poet unable to manage without it, but rather a stylistic

---

[3] Cf. Cocteau's footnote to his translation of Sophocles' *Antigone*: 'Je m'appuie sur La Fontaine, Maurras, pour remplacer Zeus par Jupiter. Jupiter se prononce mieux dans notre langue' (*Théâtre* (Paris, 1948), I, 13).

procedure which, properly used, distributes the emphasis where it should be placed:

> ...*à son front* ...*la guirlande*
> ...*sur l'autel* ...*le fer vengeur*

and subordinates the less important elements (here, the colourless verbs *attache* and *prenant*). In line 23, *le fer vengeur* achieves the same effect as the pairs of noun and adjective analysed above, though by a contrary process: here, the concrete noun (which in any case is the highly stylized *fer*) gives way to the abstract epithet *vengeur*; the knife is less important as a material object than as a symbol of the heroine's moral purpose. Finally, the omission of the verb in line 24 (*scil.* 'Elle dit: Sois belle...') is a further imitation of Latin verse style.

The poem concludes with a single couplet, strongly marked off by the transition from speech to narrative; and these last two lines contain the most graphic pictorial writing of the whole poem. Abstractions are still used, rounding off the legendary theme (rivalry, hatred, sacrifice): *lustrale* (= 'purifying, pertaining to sacrifice'; here used by extension from the normal Latin use of 'lustralis'); a thoroughly Classical figure of speech in the personification of *sa haine... rit*; and ...*de sa rivale*. However, none of these is a completely colourless abstraction—*le cœur de sa rivale*, indeed, succinctly combines the physical and emotional meanings of *cœur*—and the construction of the sentence: *sa haine en la flamme... Rit de voir palpiter...* brings these conventional images together into a striking tableau which, far from being intellectualized, conveys a strong sensuous quality of dynamic action. What could easily have been another abstract cliché acquires a vivid quality of precise pictorial evocation; and the poem closes with a memorable couplet, both expressing the theme and embodying it in a picture. This is a feature of Chénier's narrative technique that the Parnassian poets, Heredia in particular, were to be very ready to imitate.

Altogether, the poem is a most felicitous illustration of Chénier's manner in the *Bucoliques*. As elsewhere in this collection, the poet's inspiration seems to have been entirely literary, and the two Latin sources between them go a long way towards providing the narrative substance of this little piece. But it is no slavish copy, and 'Pasiphaé' is an excellent example of that 'creative imitation' which French Classical poetics had early established as the proper attitude towards the literature of antiquity. The French poet readily borrows his theme, and the essential details, from his predecessors, but by informing this material with his own sensibility and taste, he transcends mere imitation and creates a satisfyingly original work of art.

12 Balzac

Comment aucun de nos peintres n'a-t-il pas encore essayé de reproduire la physionomie d'un essaim de Parisiens groupés, par un temps d'orage, sous le porche humide d'une maison? Où rencontrer un plus riche tableau? N'y a-t-il pas d'abord le piéton rêveur ou philosophe qui observe avec plaisir, soit les raies faites par la pluie 5 sur le fond grisâtre de l'atmosphère, espèce de ciselures semblables aux jets capricieux des filets de verre; soit les tourbillons d'eau blanche que le vent roule en poussière lumineuse sur les toits; soit les capricieux dégorgements des tuyaux pétillants, écumeux; enfin mille autres riens admirables, étudiés avec délices par les 10 flâneurs, malgré les coups de balai dont les régale le maître de la loge? Puis il y a le piéton causeur qui se plaint et converse avec la portière, quand elle se pose sur son balai comme un grenadier sur son fusil; le piéton indigent, fantastiquement collé sur le mur, sans nul souci de ses haillons habitués au contact des rues; le piéton 15 savant qui étudie, épèle ou lit les affiches sans les achever; le piéton rieur qui se moque des gens auxquels il arrive malheur dans la rue, qui rit des femmes crottées et fait des mines à ceux ou celles qui sont aux fenêtres; le piéton silencieux qui regarde à toutes les croisées, à tous les étages; le piéton industriel, armé d'une sacoche ou muni 20 d'un paquet, traduisant la pluie par profits et pertes; le piéton aimable, qui arrive comme un obus, en disant: Ah! quel temps, messieurs! et qui salue tout le monde; enfin, le vrai bourgeois de Paris, homme à parapluie, expert en averse, qui l'a prévue, sorti malgré l'avis de sa femme, et qui s'est assis sur la chaise du portier. 25 Selon son caractère, chaque membre de cette société fortuite contemple le ciel, s'en va sautillant pour ne pas se crotter, ou parce qu'il est pressé, ou parce qu'il voit des citoyens marchant malgré vent et marée, ou parce que la cour de la maison étant humide et catarrhalement mortelle, la lisière, dit un proverbe, est pire que le 30 drap. Chacun a ses motifs. Il ne reste que le piéton prudent, l'homme qui, pour se remettre en route, épie quelques espaces bleus à travers les nuages crevassés.

H. DE BALZAC, *Histoire des Treize*
Date of first publication: 1833
Flammarion edition (Paris, 1949),
pp. 35-6

THIS passage is evidently a set-piece, of the kind that Balzac commonly inserts at the beginning of a new episode; it occurs in *Ferragus*, one of the three short novels composing *L'Histoire des Treize* which were written in 1833 and published in the same year in a periodical, in 1834 in book form.

The beginning of *Ferragus* is unusually disjointed, for this is but one of a series of digressions with which Balzac interrupts his narrative in the opening chapters. The opening section itself consists of a sociological-descriptive passage on Paris; then, after a certain amount of narrative, we have the above passage, which is closely followed by a fanciful analysis of various kinds of beggar, and this in turn by a brief *reprise* of the Paris motif. Some light is thrown on this method of composition by the fact that the passage in question was written at an earlier date, and for a different purpose, and was subsequently incorporated wholesale into the novel: Balzac's instructions to his printer show that it was already set up in proof as part of an article 'La Théorie de la démarche'. It belongs in inspiration, then, to a kind of occasional writing, the literary journalism with which Balzac had been much occupied during the 1820s, when he had produced such essays as 'La Physiologie de la toilette', 'Le Traité de la vie élégante', or 'La Physiologie du cigare': that is to say, pieces of pseudo-scientific sociological investigation, some more light-hearted than others, in which men and women are classified socially and morally by an analysis of clothes, gesture, and mannerisms. This obsession was to remain with Balzac throughout the *Comédie humaine*, but here we have an example of it almost in a pure state. It is this preoccupation which determines the outline of the passage, which provides the key-word, so rich in Balzacian associations, of *physionomie* in line 2, and which shows through clearly in *cette société fortuite* (l. 26); the *raison d'être* of the passage is the author's pose as a social historian, which leads him to divide a random group of passers-by, completely arbitrarily, into ten distinct categories (nine *piétons* and the *vrai bourgeois de Paris* of l. 23).

Elsewhere in the novels, the reader may possibly be taken in by Balzac's sociological pretensions, and fail to recognize the gratuitous and subjective nature of his classifications of characters and social types. Here, however, the approach is obviously light-hearted, and the whole passage is an expression of the author's inventiveness. It is a very successful humorous extravaganza, which at the same time incidentally provides a lightning sketch of Parisian *mœurs*.

The analytical, mock-sociological approach accounts for the main framework of the passage, but the detailed pattern is rather more complicated. Having established the outline of his subject in the first sentence (*la physionomie... maison*), with a brief comment in the second, Balzac launches straight into his list of types in sentence no. 3 (*le piéton rêveur ou philosophe*), although the remainder of this longish sentence is devoted to what is really an elaboration of the setting sketched in lines 2–3. The third sentence, therefore, fulfils two purposes: it characterizes the first category of *piéton*, and it provides a continuation of the opening sentences, with a clear link between *peintres* (l. 1), *tableau* (l. 4), and the highly pictorial quality of the description itself: cf. *raies, fond grisâtre, ciselures, poussière lumineuse*, and the vivid (if not equally 'painterly') *pétillants, écumeux*. Structurally, then, there is a distinct overlap between the essentially pictorial opening to the passage and the remainder, which is more analytical in its presentation (*Puis il y a le piéton causeur..., le piéton indigent..., le piéton savant...*). The last element of sentence no. 3 (*enfin...*, ll. 9–12) serves as a sort of transition, since *mille autres riens* is so much less precise than the pictorial *raies, ciselures, tourbillons, dégorgements*; while the adjective applied to these 'riens'—*admirables*—stands in contrast to the vivid *lumineuse, pétillants, écumeux*, and merely indicates the mental attitude of the *piéton philosophe*, instead of continuing the objective pictorial description conveyed in the first part of the sentence.

Turning to the sentence-structure of this first section of the passage, we may analyse the breath-groups forming the sentence as being loosely comparable to three long, irregular lines of verse:

Comment / aucun de nos peintres // n'a-t-il pas encore / essayé de reproduire la physionomie // d'un essaim de Parisiens groupés / par un temps d'orage // sous le porche humide d'une
maison

—the first and third of these having a much more clearly marked central 'caesura' than the middle one, and producing a pleasing variety. The contrast of the second sentence, leading into the longer and more complex one which follows, is clear. This latter sentence exemplifies a kind of structure very typical of Balzac: a series of parallel clauses or phrases. Here, four phrases in parallel provide the object of the verb in the relative clause, introduced by *soit...*, *soit...*, *soit...*, *enfin...*, the first of these prolonged by the phrase in apposition: *espèce de ciselures...* (another type of construction of which Balzac is very fond), and the last one also elongated by a characteristic sort of tailpiece, the ungainly adverbial phrase (*malgré les coups de balai...*) tacked on as if by an afterthought.[1]

Characteristic features of vocabulary and idiom in the first section—apart from *physionomie*, *peintre*, and *tableau* already mentioned—are to be found in this last clause, in the ironical *régaler* (certainly not original, of course: *régaler qn. de coups* is a well-established ironical use of the verb) and *maître de la loge*. The latter term, applied to a concierge, seems more original and striking, and Balzac thereby rejuvenates and reinforces the more familiar expression *régaler de coups*. Such irony is very typical of Balzac's manner in this sort of reflective passage, and it can be linked with the device that occurs at the beginning of the same sentence. *N'y a-t-il pas*, chosen in preference to 'Il y a' represents the familiar Balzacian approach: the author claiming to record what is obvious, establishing a sort of lordly complicity between himself and the reader, which carries with it an attitude to his subject which is sometimes downright patronizing, and is generally marked by ironical detachment; the same attitude is surely reflected in the rhetorical question, and in the somewhat condescending *nos peintres* of the first sentence. The repetition of *capricieux* (ll. 7-9), although it does not seem unduly obtrusive, is an illustration of the author's lack of fastidiousness in his selection of vocabulary.

Examining the syntax of the first section, we note first of all the solecism of the double negative in *aucun de nos peintres n'a-t-il pas...*, which it is perhaps sufficient to record without comment. More interesting is the use of the construction *soit...*, *soit...*, which may

---

[1] Cf. a similar appendage to the sentence in ll. 26-31. This tendency in Balzac's writing has been described as follows: 'One clause gives birth to another and there is no close connection between the end of the sentence and the beginning. The general impression given is of a rambling structure' (R. A. Sayce, *Style in French Prose* (Oxford, 1953), p. 94).

perhaps be criticized as inelegant, and which possibly helps the modern reader to situate the passage from a historical point of view. Balzac is here indulging in a descriptive set-piece, a sort of prose poem (though the term had not yet been invented); but his aim is no longer the Romantic (or more properly Preromantic) type of descriptive passage, seen at its best in the 'paysage sentimental' of a Rousseau or a Chateaubriand. Not that the subject he is dealing with would have lent itself very well to such treatment—but in any case he is not using the Romantic style with its harmonious periods, rhetorical effects and emotive imagery, largely carried on by Hugo and (with some reservations) Flaubert. Balzac's aim in passages like this may be said to approach more nearly to the impressionism of the Goncourt brothers, but he is very much of his time in that he relies overmuch on those purely functional parts of speech— relative pronouns, cumbersome conjunctions, or as here the emphatic 'articulation' of a sentence—whose elimination gives to the Goncourts' descriptive writing its characteristic flavour. We may compare a similar repetition in the case of *ou parce que...*, which recurs three times in lines 27-9, and where again the analytical approach weakens the purely descriptive effect; though in this case such a construction is less objectionable, since from line 12 onwards the analytical approach sets the pattern of the whole piece.

The imagery of this first section is almost non-existent. In the main, Balzac's description is direct and pictorial, with the exception of one metaphor (*poussière lumineuse*, l. 8) and one simile (*semblables aux jets capricieux des filets de verre*, ll. 6-7), neither of which is very remarkable. Indeed, this is so for the passage as a whole: Balzac makes little use of conventional figures of speech. There are two more similes (*comme un grenadier...*, l. 13; *comme un obus*, l. 22), the second of which is very striking, as indeed it needs to be, since it qualifies a colourless verb.

The rest of the passage, from line 12 onwards, is primarily analytical in character; this can be seen very clearly if we examine the construction of the sentence which runs from line 12 to line 25. In spite of its length, this sentence is essentially simple, consisting of the main clause *il y a...* and a series of parallel complements, variety being achieved by the length of the phrases qualifying the complements, and by the grammatical nature of the qualification in each case:

(i) le piéton causeur *qui* (a) *et* (b)
(ii) le piéton indigent, *collé...sans...*
(iii) le piéton savant *qui* (a), (b) *ou* (c)
(iv) le piéton rieur *qui* (a), *qui* (b) *et* (c)
(v) le piéton silencieux *qui* (a)
(vi) le piéton industriel, *armé..., traduisant...*
(vii) le piéton aimable, *qui* (a) *et qui* (b)
(viii) le vrai bourgeois de Paris, *homme..., expert..., qui* (a),
sorti..., et qui (b).

Looking more closely at this structure, we see as well as variety in
the grammatical nature of the qualifying clauses or phrases, variety
in the kind of balance achieved in each, so that the whole, instead of
being a bare, unartistic catalogue, reads in a pleasing, lively manner.
Thus in the first case the two phrases are balanced round a sort of
caesura at *portière*, the pairing of terms within the first half being a
familiar stylistic device. In the next section of the sentence (ll 14-5),
we have a ternary structure, which proceeds satisfyingly from
the shortest to the longest element; in the next, though perhaps
it may be criticized for lack of balance (*sans les achever* seems rather
abrupt as it stands, and seems to need amplification on stylistic
grounds), we can notice the deliberate arrangement of the three
verbs, descending to the monosyllable for the one which precedes
the object. In lines 17-18, the echo of *le piéton rieur...* in *qui rit...*
may be thought unfortunate. This section originally read '...crottées
et des voisins', and this would appear to be preferable to the version
Balzac substituted: the balancing of 'femmes crotteés' and 'voisins'
would have produced a better rhythm than the awkward *ceux ou
celles qui...*; but since there is a similar effect of balance involving
a pair of terms in *à toutes les croisées, à tous les étages*, in *armé d'une
sacoche ou muni d'un paquet* and in *profits et pertes*, Balzac may have
wished to vary the rhythm of the whole. The following section is an
excellent example of the variety achieved, and its rhythm is admirably suited to the mood, since it has a sort of staccato urgency.
Finally, the last item in the list slows down the rhythm again, and is
quite properly the longest. Some of the effects of balance and contrast in this long sentence are very pleasing indeed, and in spite of
the occasional stylistic blemish we have noted, the variety of rhythm
achieved, coupled with the impetus given by the repetition of
piéton, makes it an entertaining piece of writing.

The *société fortuite* has been brought together, to provide a pretext for Balzac's analysis; it is now time for them to disperse. Each member of the group looks at the sky, and, just as his behaviour while sheltering from the downpour has been a key to his character, so too the manner of his departure is *selon son caractère*. Less is made of this, and we are merely given a series of adverbial clauses qualifying *s'en va sautillant...* The repetition *ou parce que... ou parce que... ou parce que...* again emphasizes the analytical character of the writing, but one can still see the author's regard for balance and euphony: *sautillant pour ne pas se crotter* matches *ou parce qu'il est pressé* (with assonance of the final syllable), and there is a similar balance between the longer clauses *ou parce qu'il voit...* and *ou parce que la cour de la maison...* Or rather, to be more precise, these would balance if the latter contained a finite verb (*'est* humide') and the sentence ended at *mortelle*; instead, our expectation is not fulfilled: *étant humide...* gives the sentence a new impetus and leads on to the homely proverb which provides the last of the list of reasons for leaving before the rain has stopped, at the same time rounding the sentence off in a pleasingly positive way. (*'Les lisières sont pires que le drap* se dit à un homme qui, se défendant d'être d'un pays qui a quelque mauvais renom, assure qu'il n'en est que voisin. Dans les campagnes normandes, ce proverbe est: *la lisière est pire que le drap*, et signifie que les domestiques sont plus insolents envers les étrangers que les maîtres'—Littré.)

Just as the reader is assuming that all is over, with the dispersal of the various specimens analysed, the author produces an unexpected twist, stimulating our interest afresh, as we find to our surprise that there is one *piéton* left; and the brief vignette of the *piéton prudent* brings the piece to a thoroughly satisfying conclusion. In line 31, even more clearly than in lines 3-4, a short sentence is used to provide a contrast; this one provides an effective summing-up of the somewhat complicated longer sentence of lines 26–30. But the brief *Chacun a ses motifs* is much too short to provide a conclusion: instead, it creates a sense of anticipation, preparing us for the final sentence, in which we do in fact encounter the last *piéton*.[2]

With regard to the vocabulary of this second half of the passage,

---

[2] A similar effect is produced by 'minor cadence' in the arrangement of clauses or phrases within a sentence; cf. comments on the Flaubert and Goncourt passages, pp. 160 and 201.

we may recognize in *fantastiquement* a word very much in vogue at the time Balzac was writing. Literally it should mean: 'd'une manière fantastique, qui n'a d'existence que dans l'imagination', but Balzac is using the word loosely here to mean 'grotesquely, in a bizarre manner'. In the expression *le piéton industriel*, Balzac is using the adjective in its now archaic sense of 'qui exerce un métier, une profession, un travail'. *Citoyens* in line 28 is used in a familiar sense, found already in Boileau: as one might use *bonshommes*, or *individus*, instead of the neutral *personnes*. Whether the adverb *catarrhalement* is a neologism, as one might well suppose, or not, the expression *catarrhalement mortelle* (l. 30) is an individual and strikingly vivid one. Finally, in the expression *nuages crevassés*, the epithet is imaginatively transferred from its normal range of associations, and we may take this to be an original and effective image. Similarly original is the description of the *vrai bourgeois* in line 24: *homme à parapluie, expert en averse :* two 'made-up' phrases which, taken together, give us a lightning physical and moral portrait of the man. Even though we may have our doubts about the syntax of *qui l'a prévue*, where the pronoun object refers back most irregularly to the indefinite *averse*, the little sketch of this character contained in lines 23–5 bears the mark of the real creative artist.

What, in conclusion, does such an analysis enable us to say about the passage under consideration? Some inelegancies have been noted, but these are more than redeemed by the energy and liveliness of the piece as a whole, particularly the engaging rhythms of the long central sentence. This is an admirable example of Balzac's virtuosity: the theme itself may be fairly trivial, but if the passage is taken on the level of humorous extravaganza rather than as a solemn and pretentious attempt at sociology—and there is little doubt that that is the level at which Balzac was aiming in this instance—then it can stand in its own right as a successful piece of imaginative writing, which achieves the required effect of introducing variety of style and subject-matter into the narrative from which it is taken.

13 Musset

Scène v : la chambre de Lorenzo.

LORENZO, DEUX DOMESTIQUES.

Lorenzo : Quand vous aurez placé ces fleurs sur la table, et celles-ci au pied du lit, vous ferez un bon feu, mais de manière à ce que cette nuit la flamme ne flambe pas, et que les charbons échauffent sans éclairer. Vous me donnerez la clef, et vous irez vous coucher. (*Entre Catherine.*)

Catherine : Notre mère est malade; ne viens-tu pas la voir, Renzo? 5

Lorenzo : Ma mère est malade?

Catherine : Hélas! je ne puis te cacher la vérité. J'ai reçu hier un billet du duc, dans lequel il me disait que tu avais dû me parler d'amour pour lui; cette lecture a fait bien du mal à Marie.

Lorenzo : Cependant, je ne t'avais pas parlé de cela. N'as-tu pas pu 10 lui dire que je n'étais pour rien là-dedans?

Catherine : Je le lui ai dit. Pourquoi ta chambre est-elle aujourd'hui si belle et en si bon état? Je ne croyais pas que l'esprit d'ordre fût ton majordome.

Lorenzo : Le duc t'a donc écrit? Cela est singulier que je ne l'aie 15 point su. Et, dis-moi, que penses-tu de sa lettre?

Catherine : Ce que j'en pense?

Lorenzo : Oui, de la déclaration d'Alexandre. Qu'en pense ce petit cœur innocent?

Catherine : Que veux-tu que j'en pense? 20

Lorenzo : N'as-tu pas été flattée? Un amour qui fait l'envie de tant de femmes! un titre si beau à conquérir, la maîtresse de... Va-t-en, Catherine, va dire à ma mère que je te suis. Sors d'ici. Laisse-moi! (*Catherine sort.*) Par le ciel! quel homme de cire suis-je donc! Le Vice, comme la robe de Déjanire, s'est-il si profondé- 25 ment incorporé à mes fibres, que je ne puisse plus répondre de ma langue, et que l'air qui sort de mes lèvres me fasse ruffian

malgré moi ? J'allais corrompre Catherine. — Je crois que je corromprais ma mère, si mon cerveau le prenait à tâche ; car Dieu
30 sait quelle corde et quel arc les dieux ont tendus dans ma tête, et quelle force ont les flèches qui en partent. Si tous les hommes sont des parcelles d'un foyer immense, assurément l'être inconnu qui m'a pétri a laissé tomber un tison au lieu d'une étincelle, dans ce corps faible et chancelant. Je puis délibérer et
35 choisir, mais non revenir sur mes pas quand j'ai choisi. O Dieu ! les jeunes gens à la mode ne se font-ils pas une gloire d'être vicieux, et les enfants qui sortent du collège ont-ils quelque chose de plus pressé que de se pervertir ? Quel bourbier doit donc être l'espèce humaine, qui se rue ainsi dans les tavernes
40 avec des lèvres affamées de débauche, quand moi, qui n'ai voulu prendre qu'un masque pareil à leurs visages, et qui ai été aux mauvais lieux avec une résolution inébranlable de rester pur sous mes vêtements souillés, je ne puis ni me retrouver moi-même ni laver mes mains, même avec du sang ! Pauvre Catherine ! tu
45 mourrais cependant comme Louise Strozzi, ou tu te laisserais tomber comme tant d'autres dans l'éternel abîme, si je n'étais pas là. O Alexandre ! je ne suis pas dévot, mais je voudrais, en vérité, que tu fisses ta prière avant de venir ce soir dans cette chambre. Catherine n'est-elle pas vertueuse, irréprochable ?
50 Combien faudrait-il pourtant de paroles, pour faire de cette colombe ignorante la proie de ce gladiateur aux poils roux ? Quand je pense que j'ai failli parler ! Que de filles maudites par leurs pères rôdent au coin des bornes, ou regardent leur tête rasée dans le miroir cassé d'une cellule, qui ont valu tout autant
55 que Catherine, et qui ont écouté un ruffian moins habile que moi ! Eh bien ! j'ai commis bien des crimes, et si ma vie est jamais dans la balance d'un juge quelconque, il y aura d'un côté une montagne de sanglots ; mais il y aura peut-être de l'autre une goutte de lait pur tombée du sein de Catherine, et qui aura
60 nourri d'honnêtes enfants. (*Il sort.*)

MUSSET, *Lorenzaccio*, Act IV, sc. v
Date of first publication: 1834
Les Éditions Nationales
(Paris, 1948), pp. 191–2

Lorenzaccio, Musset's most ambitious dramatic work, was published as part of the collection *Un Spectacle dans un fauteuil* in 1834: it was not destined for stage-production, and was long regarded as being unactable. The play treats the predicament of a typical Romantic hero, Lorenzo de Medici (the title of the play represents a pejorative diminutive of the name), idealist and self-appointed assassin of the tyrant of Florence, his kinsman Alexander. In order to gain the Duke's confidence and obtain an opportunity to kill him he has become his companion in debauch, and now finds himself, with the deed still not performed, as odious to the people of Florence as the Duke himself. By the fourth Act, his preparations are complete: he has seized a chance to remove the Duke's coat of mail, so that he will be defenceless, and has deliberately interested him in the person of Catherine, his mother's young half-sister, whom the Duke now proposes to seduce; the assignation is to take place in Lorenzo's own room, and it is here that he intends to ambush the Duke and kill him.

The purpose of Act IV, scene v, then, is firstly, to show Lorenzo's final preparations before the deed that is to justify his long period of waiting and compensate for his moral degradation in his own eyes and those of his fellow-citizens; and secondly, to reveal his state of mind at this stage of the action. The brief instructions to the servants are devoted to the former end—it is these opening lines of the scene that provide the link with the events which form the action of the play—and the exchanges with Catherine, and more particularly the long soliloquy which forms the greater part of the scene, to the latter. It will be seen that as well as exemplifying the completely episodic structure of the play—scenes iv and vi of this Act are taken up with the affairs of two other families, representative of political activities in Florence in general, but without any direct bearing on the central plot dealing with Lorenzo—this scene hardly furthers the action of the play at all: it is principally devoted to a static exploration of the character's state of mind. Perhaps the most striking feature of the construction of *Lorenzaccio* is the contrast between scenes of rapid, even perfunctory, action, in which groups of characters representing various families and political factions in Florence plot, quarrel, and manœuvre, and static scenes with an introspective, philosophical content—either soliloquies by the hero, or dialogue of a reflective nature which serves as a vehicle for the analysis of his character. It is this aspect of the play which has earned for Musset's play the label 'Shakespearean', but it would seem that Musset has gone further than Shakespeare in making such an extreme contrast between these two types of scene. The former type is for the most part fairly closely based on Varchi's *Storia fiorentina*, either with or without the intermediary of George Sand's 'scène historique' *Une Conspiration en 1537*; the second type owes much more to Musset's own imagination, to his very personal interpretation of Lorenzo's attitudes and motives.[1]

Stylistically, too, there is a difference between the two kinds of scene.[2] Those scenes whose function is to further the action are mainly written in a simple, unadorned prose style, and are conversational in tone; while the more reflective scenes are marked by a much greater attention to literary effect: considerable use is made of imagery, and the rhythms, repetitions, and balancing of words and phrases lift the writing well above the level of normal conversational usage. In the scene under consideration, there is a clear change in the character of the writing at line 24, on the exit of Catherine. Up to this point, the dialogue could be said to be purely functional. The instructions to the servants are concerned with material things: the flowers, the fire, the key; and Musset's object is to make it clear to the reader or spectator that Lorenzo is completing the final preparations for his essential action. There is possibly a certain literary affectation in the repetition of *flamme* and *flamber*, and in the opposition of *échauffer* and *éclairer*, but this is not pronounced, and Lorenzo's speech hardly goes beyond the conversational in tone.

In the second section, in which Lorenzo is confronted by Catherine, the conversational 'ordinariness' of the dialogue is even more pronounced. This passage serves to bring the audience up to date, as it were, with regard to the hero's relations with other characters: the further deterioration of his relationship with his mother, and his deception of Catherine herself. The last lines (16–24) of this section bring out a strong contrast between the young woman's innocence and the cynical corruption of Lorenzo, in whom we are to believe that habit is so powerful that he involuntarily reproduces the

[1] See P. Dimoff, *La Genèse de Lorenzaccio* (Paris, 1936), which contains, as well as a critical edition of Musset's play, the text of relevant passages from Varchi and the *Conspiration* in full.

[2] See A. Brun, *Deux Proses de théâtre* (Aix-en-Provence, 1954) for a comparison between Musset's 'style de base, atone et incolore', and that used for the 'passages à grand éclat' in this play.

familiar phrases of temptation even though the woman he is addressing is virtually his own sister. However, this passage is too short for the psychological subtleties of such a situation to be fully developed: in spite of the insidious nature of the interrogatory (conveyed effectively by the repetitive phrasing: *...que penses-tu...? — Ce que j'en pense? — ...Qu'en pense ce petit cœur innocent? — Que veux-tu que j'en pense?*), Lorenzo breaks off his immoral suggestion somewhat abruptly before it has been fully expressed, and this part of the scene has a rather perfunctory character, leaving a good deal to the reader's or spectator's imagination.

This impression is reinforced by a comparison with the remainder of the scene, devoted to Lorenzo's soliloquy, in which the same idea is given a much more extensive, and more elaborate, development. The soliloquy almost immediately makes explicit (*J'allais corrompre Catherine*) what the previous passage had only hinted at; and the remainder of the scene consists of introspective philosophising with this as a starting-point. As has been said, the speech is static in terms of the action of the play; nor does it lead to any new development in terms of the audience's awareness of the hero's character, since the same attitudes tend to be repeated throughout the play, expressed by means of different images. However, the soliloquy is not without its logical progression: if not so clearly as some of the monologues of Corneille's tragedies, for instance, nevertheless this speech does exemplify something like the tripartite structure characteristic of the soliloquy of the Classical theatre, built up on the thesis—antithesis—synthesis pattern. Here, if we reduce the 'content' of the soliloquy to its simplest terms, the thesis (ll. 25–35) might be said to be: 'Vicious habits have become so strong in me that I am no longer able to act in any other way', followed by a secondary development (ll. 35–44): 'But how depraved human nature must be in reality, since I tried merely to imitate the outward signs of Vice'; the antithesis (ll. 44–56): 'Yet my good intentions must still count for something, for I shall have saved Catherine from the hands of the truly vicious'; and finally (ll. 56–60), the synthesis: 'When I come to be judged at the end of my life, this good action will be set off against the harm I have done.' It would be wrong, of course, to give too much importance to the dialectical structure of the soliloquy; this characteristic tends to be obscured by the patterns of imagery running through the speech, so that one is more conscious of a series of imaginative restatements of an attitude in figurative terms, than of the argumentative scheme imposed by the intellectual analysis of that attitude.

Like Musset's other dramatic characters with a strong auto-biographical element in their make-up, Lorenzo is presented as a young man with a poet's imagination, who constantly expresses himself by means of imagery. While some of his images are isolated, superficial, figurative illustrations of a train of thought, others fit into a dominant theme of imagery running through the play, and may have echoes in Musset's writing more generally, or in the works of his contemporaries. Thus it is characteristic that the soliloquy begins with the exclamation *quel homme de cire suis-je donc!*; Musset could just as well have made Lorenzo exclaim 'how weak and easily influenced I am!', but the metaphor, conventional though it may be, gives a more pithy and forceful expression to the idea. The following image does more than merely render an abstraction more forcefully: the notion of vice as a garment expresses figuratively an idea which is central to the author's conception of his character. Lorenzo has already used the same image in the course of an important conversation with the elderly patriot Philippe Strozzi in Act III, scene iii: 'Le vice a été pour moi un vêtement, maintenant il est collé à ma peau'; here, it is elaborated on and developed, by being associated with the classical legend of Dejanira. According to this legend Dejanira, wife of Hercules, was advised by the centaur Nessus as he lay dying, killed by her husband, to keep some of his blood, and if ever she needed to win back Hercules' love, to smear it on his cloak; when later she attempted to do this, the cloak clung to his flesh, causing him terrible suffering from which he was only released by death. Hence the *profondément incorporé à mes fibres* of Musset's image: Lorenzo's addiction to vice is no longer assumed like a cloak, it has become part of his real self (and, we may add, extending the implications of the classical reference, will continue its destructive work until his death).

It should be noted that in describing himself as a *ruffian*, Lorenzo is saying something stronger and more specific than is suggested by the English homonym. The French term means 'pander', 'pimp'; this has been the precise nature of his activities in the Duke's service, and it is by apparently being willing to procure even his own mother's sister that he has reached the depths of moral degradation. Now he is forced to acknowledge that this culminating baseness was on the verge of becoming reality, not pretence, and further (*je corromprais ma mère...*) that there are no limits to which he would not descend at the prompting of a perverted intelligence. The theme of the destructive power of pure intelligence is one frequently found in Romantic literature; here it is expressed by the somewhat unusual, but striking, image of the bow. This is immediately followed, however, by a discordant image, that of the nature of the 'divine fire' or vital 'spark' with which Lorenzo thinks he has been endowed: the only connection between the two being the echo of *les dieux* of line 30 in *l'être inconnu qui m'a pétri* of lines 32-3. The notion of the soul, or intelligence, being a fragment of the universal element of fire is common to several early philosophical systems, occurring notably in that of Heraclitus; *pétrir* is a term frequently used before Musset by writers attempting to clothe the abstract concept of creation in a concrete figurative form; but the substitution of *un tison* for the more normal *étincelle* gives a new, and rather bizarre, twist to a fairly conventional image. The idea expressed in these two sentences is now resumed in abstract, analytical terms: *Je puis délibérer...*: the figurative *revenir sur mes pas* is really a 'dead' metaphor, too much of a lifeless cliché to conflict at all seriously with the two strong images which precede.

The second 'movement' of the soliloquy, beginning at line 35, is marked by a change in style, with the exclamation *O Dieu!* and the rhetorical questions which follow. The subject is now not Lorenzo's own corruption but the depravity of man in more general terms—though paradoxically this passage has more of an autobiographical ring, and carries more conviction as a comment by Musset on his own relationship to the society of his time, than the previous section written in the first person. Imagery is more sparing in these lines, though the metaphor of the world as a *bourbier* echoes a passage from the author's own *On ne badine pas avec l'amour*, published in the same year as *Lorenzaccio*: 'le monde n'est qu'un égout sans fond où les phoques les plus informes rampent et se tordent sur des montagnes de fange' (II, v); while the contrast between *masque* and *visages*, followed by *rester pur sous mes vêtements souillés*, takes up again the image of the *robe de Déjanire*. Finally, the striking conceit *je ne puis... laver mes mains, même avec du sang* suggests a possible literary reminiscence, in Lady Macbeth's vain attempt to wash away her guilt as well as Duncan's blood.

With the following passage, we come to the final section of the soliloquy, and to a more specific comment on Lorenzo's immediate position, as he seeks for justification of his treatment of Catherine in the thought that he is saving her from a fate like that of Louise Strozzi (who has died in Act III, poisoned by Salviati, one of the Duke's companions whose advances she had resisted). The apostrophe to Alexander himself introduces another Shakespearean reference: however different the situation may be, and although here the character's reaction is in fact the opposite—Lorenzo wishes that the Duke might have said his prayers, while Hamlet forbears to kill Claudius precisely because he *is* at prayer—there is a reminder of Act III, scene iii, of Shakespeare's play. Perhaps one might suggest that Musset's creative imagination was fed at this point by reminiscences of the passage from *Hamlet* and also of *Othello*, V, ii, where Othello, about to kill Desdemona, exhorts her: 'If you bethink yourself of any crime Unreconciled as yet to heaven and grace, Solicit for it straight.'

Line 51 seems to offer a further instance of the arbitrary association of two unrelated images: while the *colombe* and the *gladiateur aux poils roux* characterize Catherine and the Duke separately in quite an effective manner, they cannot be said to combine very successfully, and the image of the dove falling prey to the gladiator remains rather forced (even though the figurative use of *colombe* in the sense of 'jeune fille pure et candide' (Littré) was evidently not infrequent from the seventeenth century onwards). The short exclamation *Quand je pense que j'ai failli parler!* refers back to the phrase *J'allais corrompre Catherine* at the beginning of the soliloquy, and serves as a link between *paroles* of line 50 and *écouter* of line 55. Finally, in the sentence which brings this section of the speech to an end, there is a further example of imaginative poetic writing in the way in which the abstract thought, by a kind of metonymy, finds expression in a series of graphic word-pictures, each introduced by a verb: the physical and moral abandonment of the unfortunate girls is expressed by *rôdent au coin des bornes*, the taking of religious vows as a desperate remedy by *regardent leur tête rasée dans le miroir cassé d'une cellule*, and corruption at the hands of an unprincipled pander by *ont écouté un ruffian*.

The last section, as has been said, brings together the two contrasting argumentative developments of the passage, the self-incriminating and the exculpatory, and does this by means of the conventional image of the scales of judgement. Although Musset does not explicitly say that the *goutte de lait* outweighs the *montagne de sanglots*, this is implied; and the notion of a single good action compensating for a life of evil, however sound theologically, puts considerable strain on such a concrete image. The image is in fact a rather superficial Romantic cliché; yet the critical reader should remember that the intellectual quality of the writing cannot be his only criterion in analysing a text of this nature: he must at least make an attempt to imagine, and to appreciate, emotive appeal to an audience. The image of the *goutte de lait* conveys simply and unambiguously the notion of Catherine's purity; it is on his protection of this innocent girl that Lorenzo's principal claim to the sympathy of the reader or spectator is based[3] and the figure of the scales of judgement, trite though it may be, rounds the passage off effectively in terms of this dramatic sympathy.[4]

In conclusion, this is one of the key passages of the play from the point of view of the revelation of the hero's character, and the development of the sympathy that we feel for him as a tragic hero. At the beginning of the play Lorenzo's actions have been presented without commentary: his motives appear as equivocal to the reader as they are shown as being to his fellow-Florentines. Two major scenes are devoted to his self-justification, and to the clarification of the enigma presented by his behaviour: an earlier passage (Lorenzo's confession to Philippe Strozzi in Act III) has shown the nature of his 'tragic flaw', in the idealistic ambition which led to his decision to kill the tyrant; and now the present scene is devoted to establishing our sympathy for a character whose idealistic purpose has led to his moral disintegration. In the earlier scene Lorenzo has been able to use devices of rhetoric and persuasion in order to convince Philippe; but in a soliloquy Musset's resources are necessarily less

---

[3] Though, as H. S. Gochberg reminds us, this is only a secondary reason for the killing of Alexander, and the primary reason remains arbitrary and subjective: 'While he is not acting directly to save his kin from corruption, it is nevertheless the imminence of this corruption which strengthens his resolution' (*Stage of Dreams: the Dramatic Art of Alfred de Musset* (Geneva, 1967), p. 195).

[4] If one is tempted to criticize Musset for lack of subtlety in his choice of such a conventional image, it is worth comparing this passage with one from Hugo's poem 'Sultan Mourad' (*Légende des siècles*, I), in which the same image is handled in an extremely crude and unsubtle way. The tyrant Mourad, at the end of a life full of inhuman atrocities, shows kindness to a dying pig, whereupon his good and evil actions are weighed in the scales of the balance:

> ...Dans un plateau le monde et le pourceau dans l'autre.
> Du côté du pourceau la balance pencha (ll. 238–9).

extensive, and the character must fall back on introspective reflection. As has been shown, the speech has enough logical framework to give it coherence; and Lorenzo's reflections open out from his individual predicament in order to comment on human nature in more general terms. Essentially, however, the purpose of this soliloquy is not moral justification by logical argument, nor yet a rational appeal to the spectator to identify himself with the hero. Rather it is an emotive appeal for sympathetic understanding, from a character conscious of having reached an extreme limit of human experience. Hence the exclamatory nature of the long central section of the speech (*O Dieu!... Quel bourbier doit donc être... Pauvre Catherine!... O Alexandre!... Catherine n'est-elle pas... Combien faudrait-il... Quand je pense... Que de filles...*)—and hence above all the imagery by means of which, in a truly Shakespearean manner, Musset succeeds in elevating the soul-searching of his hero into a poetic appeal to the reader's sensibility.

14 Hugo

Demain, dès l'aube, à l'heure où blanchit la campagne,
Je partirai. Vois-tu, je sais que tu m'attends.
J'irai par la forêt, j'irai par la montagne.
Je ne puis demeurer loin de toi plus longtemps.

Je marcherai les yeux fixés sur mes pensées,   5
Sans rien voir au dehors, sans entendre aucun bruit,
Seul, inconnu, le dos courbé, les mains croisées,
Triste, et le jour pour moi sera comme la nuit.

Je ne regarderai ni l'or du soir qui tombe,
Ni les voiles au loin descendant vers Harfleur,   10
Et quand j'arriverai, je mettrai sur ta tombe
Un bouquet de houx vert et de bruyère en fleur.
                              3 septembre 1847

V. HUGO, *Les Contemplations*, IV, xiv
Date of first publication: 1856
Ed. J. Seebacher (Paris: A. Colin,
1964), II, p. 34

BETWEEN the two parts of *Les Contemplations* — *Autrefois 1830–43*
and *Aujourd'hui 1843–55* — lies 'un abîme', the grave of Léopoldine
Hugo. Livre IV, *Pauca meae*, which opens the second part, was
wholly devoted by Hugo to '[son] deuil, Didine et Dieu'. 'Demain,
dès l'aube...' belongs to this central, pivotal section—the Holy of
Holies of *Les Contemplations*.

Hugo's favourite daughter was drowned on 4 September 1843,
together with her husband Charles Vacquerie, in a boating accident
on the Seine near Villequier; but it was not till six days later that,

returning from a holiday, her father entered a café at Soubise and, with Juliette Drouet beside him, read in *Le Siècle* about the tragedy. His grief at the news that 'la moitié de [sa] vie et de [son] cœur était morte' was accompanied by an uneasy fear that he had brought down divine punishment upon himself ('O mon Dieu, que vous ai-je fait?'). He also experienced a new sense of humility:

> Je suis, lorsque je pense, un poète, un esprit;
> Mais sitôt que je souffre, hélas! je suis un homme...

and felt plunged in spiritual darkness:

> Pourquoi m'as-tu pris la lumière
> Que j'avais parmi les vivants? (*Contemplations*, IV, iii)

Despair, doubt, and revolt eventually gave way if not to resignation, at any rate to submission: 'Et mon cœur est soumis, mais n'est pas résigné' (IV, xv). During this crisis he had recourse to occultism and sensed Léopoldine's presence all around him. It came as a spectacular confirmation when she manifested herself at the first table-turning seance at Marine Terrace in 1853.

Every year on the anniversary of her death he felt bound by an oath of eternal fidelity to take the 'noir chemin' to the 'champ triste à côté de l'église'. He set out at dawn and walked over the hills along the Seine to Villequier:[1]

> Je fuyais, seul, sans voir, sans penser, sans parler...
> Et, comme subissant l'attraction d'un gouffre...
> ...je marchais devant moi, j'arrivais.
> O souvenirs! ô forme horrible des collines!
>   ('A celle qui est restée en France')

A great sorrow of his subsequent exile was the enforced separation from his 'douce endormie':

> ...il est impossible à présent que je jette
> Même un brin de bruyère à sa fosse muette (ibid.).

Pauca meae include a series of anniversary poems, all dated 4 September and covering the period 1844-7. The dates represent not

---

[1] Most editors assume that Hugo set out from Le Havre or Harfleur; but ll. 9-10 of 'Demain, dès l'aube...' would seem to indicate that he is proceeding in a westward direction, from Rouen perhaps rather than Le Havre. See R. Journet and G. Robert, *Notes sur Les Contemplations* (Paris, 1958), p. 125.

the chronological sequence of composition, but rather an artistic and psychological order corresponding to the evolution of the poet's feelings. 'Demain, dès l'aube...' which introduces 'A Ville-quier' (IV, xv; 4 September 1847) is dated 4 October 1847 in the manuscript, but 3 September 1847 in the edition. The manuscript date is probably that of the final, revised version, while the edition may indicate the more crucial date of the inspiration and con-ception—Hugo's mood on the eve of 4 September 1847.

The poem seems to emerge out of the night only to fade away again into the gathering shadows of evening. There are intermittent flashes of brightness (dawn, daylight, sunset, sails), but they are glimpsed fleetingly and are at once blotted out by a dense, opaque gloom. Even the evergreen holly and purple heather, the wreath placed at dusk on the 'noir tombeau' (IV, xvii), seem to take on something of the sombre, funereal tonality of their surroundings. This basic contrast which produces a kind of chiaroscuro effect reflects Hugo's dualistic, almost Manichean vision of the universe with its multiple antitheses (light/darkness, life/death, spirit/matter, faith/doubt, joy/pain, hope/despair, activity/passivity, etc.). Light is ultimately identified with God ('Nomen, numen, lumen', VI, xxv), while darkness ('l'immense ombre athée')[2] represents the absence or negation of God:

> Considérez qu'on doute, ô mon Dieu! quand on souffre,
> Que l'œil qui pleure trop finit par s'aveugler,
> Qu'un être que son deuil plonge au plus noir du gouffre,
> Quand il ne vous voit plus, ne peut vous contempler (IV, xv).

The 'ombres' predominate over the 'rayons' in 'Demain, dès l'aube...' which presents not so much a landscape as a Dark Night of the Soul.

Standing outside himself in a kind of dreamlike *dédoublement*, Hugo is peering into the future. The poem is a pilgrimage of the mind, an anticipation of the real journey on the following day, with the three quatrains marking the three stages of the itinerary (de-parture, walk, arrival). Though self-contained and endstopped, the stanzas are unified by the poet's *idée fixe*—the lonely, melancholy tramp from dawn till sunset. Hugo is 'celui que rien n'arrête, Celui qui va' (VI, ii). A dynamic, compulsive movement (*partirai, irai, irai, marcherai, arriverai*) drives him forward to his destination.

---

[2] 'A celle qui est restée en France'.

His arrival brings a relaxation of strain, and the poem culminates quietly but strikingly in the placing of the rustic wreath. This crowning effect seems almost to have generated the organization of the whole poem, and for the reader it is as though the piece, transposing and condensing the poet's obscure, complex emotions into a simple, concrete image, had suddenly blossomed into a 'sombre fleur de l'abîme' ('A celle qui est restée en France').

The pronoun *je* is repeated nine times in the poem; but Hugo's egotism is here less obtrusive than usual, for this is not a monologue. The tender, whispered confidences are addressed to another person, unnamed and almost unnameable: *tu*. The poem echoes 'le vaste et profond silence de la mort' (IV, xi), for Léopoldine does not reply; but the conversation is not the less dramatic for being one-sided. We share the suspense of an attempted communication with the spirit world. It is almost as if the father were trying to raise his daughter from the dead.

The poem opens with a triple apposition marked by punctuation and stress (2 ‖ 2 ‖ 8). The *coupes* have an anxious insistence, and there is a long pause after the *rejet* (*Je partirai*) which is emphasized by the full stop and the strong stress (4 ‖ 2 + 2 + 4). Hugo is reassuring his daughter that he will keep his promise. *Demain*, a key-word of Hugo, is usually bright with hope. The sun too is often identified with God, and the golden dawn can become a divine revelation. But Hugo's mood has changed 'depuis ce jour triste où pour nous ont pâli Les cieux, les champs, les fleurs, l'étoile, l'aube pure' (V, xii), and he associates Léopoldine's death with the pallor of white: 'Ton linceul toujours flotte entre la vie et moi' ('A celle qui est restée en France'). The attenuated caesura in line I creates a slight *effet d'ampleur*: the countryside lies spread out in the cold, pale shroud of light.

In line 2 Hugo begins to use *tutoiement* and falls into a natural, conversational style appropriate between father and daughter. His certainty (*je sais*) is explained by allusions elsewhere to her calling him and listening for his approaching footsteps (IV, iii, and 'A celle qui est restée en France').

The regular, symmetrical rhythm of line 3 (2 + 4 ‖ 2 + 4) combines with the repetition of *j'irai* to suggest a dogged, mechanical plodding.

There is no Romantic communion with nature here, no lavish, colourful description. The outward scene breaks through only in

vague, indefinite outline: *l'aube, la campagne, la forêt, la montagne.*
Turned in upon himself, the bereaved father is speaking here, not
the visual poet. The steep, wooded hills bordering the Seine are in
fact only 'coteaux'; but they seem gigantic to the lonely, weary
walker and loom menacingly. The use of singular for plural (*forêt,
montagne*) gives the impression that Hugo will be tramping through
a dark, thick forest up some colossal mountain.

The manuscript variant of line 4 ('Car je ne puis rester...') was
probably rejected because 'car' belongs more properly to the language of logic, and 'rester' lacks the melancholy resonance of
demeurer. In the printed text line 4 leaps out like a sudden ejaculation, a despairing *cri du cœur*, and the relative weakness of the
caesura throws into prominence the poignant phrase *loin de toi*.

A striking feature of the stanza is the variety of *coupes*, some
irregular, but all exactly adapted to the shifting nuances of meaning
and mood. The jerky rhythm is an outward sign of inward agitation.
The same broken rhythm continues in the second quatrain which
is one long sentence, and the poem begins to sound like an unending,
stumbling funeral march. There are no *rimes riches*; the rhymes in
both stanzas are merely *suffisantes*; but in the second they take on a
muted, plaintive sadness (*pensées-croisées*) or a piercing anguish
(*bruit-nuit*). Throughout all three quatrains the rhyme-scheme is
that of *rimes croisées*.

The second stanza begins with a Romantic *trimètre* which stresses
marcherai... fixés... pensées. Hugo will tramp on with obsessive
obstinacy, absorbed in dark introspection. Blind and deaf, he
accentuates in line 6 his rejection of the outside world by the
repetition of *sans* reinforced by *rien* and *aucun*. The regular, perfect
symmetry $(3 + 3 \| 3 + 3)$ allied with the repetition produces an
effect of mechanical trudging like that in line 3. Thereafter the
rhythm becomes particularly dislocated and suggests a kind of
physical and moral flagging. In line 7 all the *coupes* are equally
stressed $(1 \| 3 \| 4 \| 4)$, and in line 8 the first *coupe* is very strong
$(1 \| 11)$. The unusual, parallel *coupes* after the first syllables of lines
7 and 8 throw *Seul* and especially the *rejet* (*Triste*) into sharp relief,
and the emotive power of these adjectives colours the last lines of
the stanza with their melancholy. Hugo here describes his outward
and inward attitude. Death is the great leveller, and Hugo becomes
Everyman in his tragic bereavement. The literary leader and public
figure has become a solitary brooder (*Seul*); Ego-Hugo, the 'flam-

beau' of humanity, is *inconnu*; physically strong, immensely self-confident and defiantly erect, he seems suddenly aged (*le dos courbé*) and assumes a posture of fatalistic passivity (*les mains croisées*); the robust optimist is *Triste*. This build-up prepares us for the long-drawn-out sigh of line 8. The identification of light and darkness here suggests that the poet is under the baneful influence of that 'affreux soleil noir d'où rayonne la nuit' (VI, xxvi).

From here on the rhythm becomes calmer, and the Alexandrines with their rich, sonorous rhymes (*tombe-tombe*, *Harfleur-fleur*) acquire a grave, solemn amplitude. Lines 9 and 10 have a broad, panoramic sweep, while the *contre-rejet* of line 11 serves as a springboard for the final image which fills out the whole of the last line. The walker is now within reach of his goal, and his arrival at the little cemetery overlooking the Seine is marked by the only strong caesura in the stanza (l. 11). The descending movement of sun and sails is balanced by the ascending movement of the pilgrim, and it almost seems as if the laying of the floral bouquet harmonized with some mysterious cosmic cycle of death and rebirth.

The last quatrain presents a sunset tableau with an antithesis of light and darkness; but the *or* seems less striking than the *soir qui tombe* which occupies a more prominent position at the end of the line, and the white sails which faintly recall the boat in which Léopoldine met her death must be turning pale and dark as they recede into the distance towards Harfleur[3] and the sea—'cet immense abîme Où l'algue et le nuage et les voiles s'en vont' (V, xxiv). In any case the poet refuses to look at the scene, and the double negative (*ni... ni...*) which recalls that of line 6 suggests a similar mood. Finally, the vague, hazy backcloth gives way to the more precise foreground: the father, his child's grave, the wreath.

The manuscript has two deleted variants for line 12:

Une branche de houx $\left\{ \begin{array}{l} \text{et de la sauge} \\ \text{et de bruyère} \end{array} \right\}$ en fleur.

The poet no doubt preferred to *bouquet* the more Romantic simplicity of 'branche'; but holly and heather could hardly belong to the same 'branche', and so he again emended the line to 'Une branche de houx et de la sauge en fleur'. Here the symmetry is disturbed by the article 'la', and Hugo accordingly reverted to his

---

[3] Harfleur lies lower down the Seine from Villequier, round a bend of the river and out of sight.

first, more harmonious and colourful version: *Un bouquet de houx vert et de bruyère en fleur*. It admirably crowns the whole poem and is charged with an intense poetic suggestiveness.

It evokes a whole cluster of memories and associations: Léopoldine ('Elle aimait Dieu, les fleurs...', IV, v); Hugo gathering wild flowers for her (V, xxiv); the relationship of flowers with the dead ('Les fleurs aiment la mort...');[4] the mysterious correspondence between the infinitely small and the infinitely great:

> L'éternel est écrit dans ce qui dure peu;
> Toute l'immensité, sombre, bleue, étoilée,
> Traverse l'humble fleur, du penseur contemplée (III, viii).

The wreath here seems to reflect the 'immensité sombre', the 'Dieu sombre d'un monde obscur' (IV, iii); for the holly is dark-green, and the purple heather seems to take on a sombre hue from its melancholy setting. On the other hand, it is perhaps significant that, though indifferent to the rest of nature, Hugo has at least gathered along the way this rustic bouquet. In IV, xiii he was no longer 'réjoui par les fleurs'; but this bouquet of IV, xiv may betoken a certain advance towards the attitude of IV, xv:

> Maintenant que je puis, assis au bord des ondes,
> Ému par ce superbe et tranquille horizon,
> Examiner en moi les vérités profondes
> Et regarder les fleurs qui sont dans le gazon.

Hugo sometimes sees in flowers the victory of light over darkness, of life over death. Though the shadow of the tomb falls across the wreath here it is just possible that the *bruyère en fleur* symbolizes the idea of spiritual rebirth. For Hugo death was, after all, an 'épanouissement de l'âme... C'est dans le sépulcre que la fleur de la vie s'ouvre' (*Contemplation suprême*).

'Demain, dès l'aube...' is a 'don mystérieux de l'absent à la morte'[5]—not an ornate floral tribute but a simple bunch of wild flowers. Its simplicity results in part from the virtual elimination of any rhetoric, flamboyant description or virtuoso effects. It is certainly not an artless, unpremeditated simplicity. Always a highly conscious craftsman, Hugo has transmuted raw, inarticulate grief into a work of art. The alliance of sensibility and artistry here

[4] 'A celle qui est restée en France.'
[5] Ibid.

illustrates Hugo's definition of style as 'le mot fait âme'. The unobtrusive technical mastery serves only to enhance the spontaneity of feeling, the sincerity of a sorrow undiminished by the passage of time, the anguished sense of the dark mystery of human mortality.

It is an intimate, highly personal poem; but at the same time Hugo has universalized his particular experience and speaks movingly for all the bereaved: 'Ma vie est la vôtre, votre vie est la mienne... La destinée est une. Prenez donc ce miroir, et regardez-vous-y... Ah! insensé qui crois que je ne suis pas toi.'[6]

[6] Preface to *Les Contemplations*.

15 Flaubert

...Quelques-unes de ses camarades apportaient au couvent les keepsakes qu'elles avaient reçus en étrennes. Il les fallait cacher, c'était une affaire; on les lisait au dortoir. Maniant délicatement leurs belles reliures de satin, Emma fixait ses regards éblouis sur le nom des auteurs inconnus qui avaient signé, le plus souvent, com- 5 tes ou vicomtes, au bas de leurs pièces.

Elle frémissait, en soulevant de son haleine le papier de soie des gravures, qui se levait à demi plié et retombait doucement contre la page. C'était, derrière la balustrade d'un balcon, un jeune homme en court manteau qui serrait dans ses bras une jeune fille en robe 10 blanche, portant une aumônière à sa ceinture; ou bien les portraits anonymes des ladies anglaises à boucles blondes qui, sous leur chapeau de paille rond, vous regardent avec leurs grands yeux clairs. On en voyait d'étalées dans des voitures, glissant au milieu des parcs, où un lévrier sautait devant l'attelage que conduisaient au 15 trot deux petits postillons en culotte blanche. D'autres, rêvant sur des sofas près d'un billet décacheté, contemplaient la lune, par la fenêtre entr'ouverte, à demi drapée d'un rideau noir. Les naïves, une larme sur la joue, becquetaient une tourterelle à travers les barreaux d'une cage gothique, ou, souriant la tête sur l'épaule, 20 effeuillaient une marguerite de leurs doigts pointus, retroussés comme des souliers à la poulaine. Et vous y étiez aussi, sultans à longues pipes, pâmés sous des tonnelles, aux bras des bayadères, djiaours, sabres turcs, bonnets grecs, et vous surtout, paysages blafards des contrées dithyrambiques, qui souvent nous montrez à 25 la fois des palmiers, des sapins, des tigres à droite, un lion à gauche, des minarets tartares à l'horizon, au premier plan des ruines romaines, puis des chameaux accroupis;—le tout encadré d'une forêt vierge bien nettoyée, et avec un grand rayon de soleil perpendiculaire tremblotant dans l'eau, où se détachent en écorchures blanches, 30 sur un fond d'acier gris, de loin en loin, des cygnes qui nagent.

Et l'abat-jour du quinquet, accroché dans la muraille au-dessus de la tête d'Emma, éclairait tous ces tableaux du monde, qui passaient devant elle les uns après les autres, dans le silence du 35 dortoir et au bruit lointain de quelque fiacre attardé qui roulait encore sur les boulevards.

FLAUBERT, *Madame Bovary*
Date of first publication: 1856
Conard edition (Paris, 1930), pp. 52–3.

CHAPTER VI of Part One of *Madame Bovary* relates the heroine's upbringing in a convent. In previous paragraphs, Flaubert has described how the impressionable young girl fell under the spell of Romanticism: the vague religious sentiment of *Le Génie du Christianisme*, the colourful medievalism of Scott's novels, the idealized picture of the world presented by a host of popular romances, have all left their indelible mark on her. Everything was accepted uncritically, as long as it was food for her adolescent imagination; this is the beginning in Emma of that Romantic malady which in real life Jean-Jacques Rousseau had identified in himself as the product of a precocious reading of novels:

> Ces émotions confuses, que j'éprouvai coup sur coup, n'altéraient point la raison que je n'avais point encore; mais elles m'en formèrent une d'une autre trempe, et me donnèrent de la vie humaine des notions bizarres et romanesques, dont l'expérience et la réflexion n'ont jamais bien pu me guérir.[1]

Like Rousseau, Flaubert himself, also in his youth an inveterate reader of Romantic novels, had suffered from that incurable affliction defined by Paul Bourget as 'le mal d'avoir connu l'image de la réalité avant la réalité, l'image des sensations et des sentiments avant les sensations et les sentiments'.[2] Cervantes, one of the authors most admired by Flaubert, had based *Don Quixote* on the same phenomenon: his hero too is unable to reconcile the colourful world of his imagination, fed by the 'romans de chevalerie' of the time, with the prosaic realities of everyday life; and just as the opening

---

[1] *Confessions*, Pt. I, ch. i.
[2] 'Du nihilisme de Gustave Flaubert', in *Essais de psychologie contemporaine* (Paris, 1924 ed.), p. 156.

chapter of that novel shows Don Quixote in his study, his head turned by the romances he has read, so Flaubert, in presenting his heroine for the first time, takes care to evoke in detail the causes of her eventual downfall. First, Romantic literature: the novels and other literary embodiments of Romantic idealism; then, in the passage under consideration, the visual counterparts of this material in what may be called the 'pop art' of the time.

A brief transitional paragraph, containing the opening sentences of the passage chosen for commentary, introduces the subject of engravings with a Romantic inspiration similar to that of the novels already dealt with, found in the *keepsakes* brought into the convent by Emma's friends. (A *keepsake* was a sort of autograph-album containing verses and engravings, which it became fashionable in the 1820s to give as a Christmas or New Year present. The fashion originated in England; hence the English name: 'Livre qui se donne en cadeau, et qui renferme des pièces de vers et des fragments de prose, entremêlés de gravures'—Littré.)[3] The long central paragraph of the passage under discussion forms a pendant to a previous one of roughly the same length, in which Emma's favourite reading material had been surveyed; it was clearly Flaubert's intention here to match the catalogue of fictional clichés given in the former paragraph:

> Ce n'était qu'amours, amants, amantes, dames persécutées s'évanouissant dans des pavillons solitaires, postillons qu'on tue à tous les relais, chevaux qu'on crève à toutes les pages, forêts sombres, troubles du cœur, serments, sanglots, larmes et baisers, nacelles au clair de lune, rossignols dans les bosquets, *messieurs* braves comme des lions, doux comme des agneaux, vertueux comme on ne l'est pas, toujours bien mis, et qui pleurent comme des urnes...

with a similar review of trite Romantic commonplaces expressed in pictorial form. Finally, the short paragraph which follows serves to point the 'escapist' nature of Emma's nightly activity, in which her imagination is stimulated by perusing her friends' albums, by means of the contrast between the exotic, imaginary world of the latter and the real world both inside and outside the convent.

---

[3] Cf. 'La vue de son cousin fit sourdre en son cœur les émotions de fine volupté que causent à un jeune homme les fantastiques figures de femmes dessinées par Westall dans les keepsake anglais' (Balzac, *Eugénie Grandet*).

Reference to the manuscript versions extant[4] suggests that whereas the short passages which 'frame' the central passage of lines 7–31 in the final version were subject to considerable alteration in the process of revision, the principal paragraph itself reached at a much earlier stage a form very similar to that in which it now stands. Thus, in place of lines 1–6 of the passage in its definitive form, the manuscript version has:

> ...elle copia... des morceaux de son goût qu'elle choisissait dans les keepsakes. Deux ou trois de ses camarades, filles d'un banquier, apportaient quelquefois dans leur pupitre les beaux livres dorés sur tranche, qu'on leur avait donnés au Jour de l'An. Emma touchait avec joie aux reliures de soie rose, soufflait les papiers de soie qui cachaient les gravures anglaises et contemplait au bas des pages avec respect les noms des auteurs qui étaient des marquis, des comtes ou des barons.

Similarly, lines 32–6 have no counterpart at all as a separate paragraph, the reference to the outside world being interpolated as follows in the main paragraph:

> ...contre la page. Et l'abat-jour carré du quinquet de ferblanc accroché dans la muraille au-dessus de sa tête, éclairait d'une lumière immobile des scènes différentes, qui se succédaient tour à tour dans le silence de l'étude et au bruit lointain de quelque fiacre attardé, qui roulait encore sur les boulevards. C'était...

From this point onwards, however, the manuscript passage corresponds exactly to lines 9–31 of the definitive version, except for small details of expression of minor importance. There are in fact few pages of this early manuscript which correspond so closely to the final version, even among those passages which may be said to have a similar prominence. For Flaubert frequently seems to suspend his narrative at significant points—as he does here—in order to devote himself to a vivid pictorial evocation of a scene or setting with which, by this means, a particular stage in the evolution of the heroine's emotional state is memorably identified; as examples, we may compare the description of the garden at Yonville on the

[4] Cf. *Madame Bovary, nouvelle version*, ed. J. Pommier and G. Leleu (Paris, 1949), in which a composite text is built up from the author's MSS., representing the novel in an 'état antérieur aux corrections et aux sacrifices auxquels Flaubert a procédé, soit spontanément, soit pour répondre aux conseils de L. Bouilhet ou aux désirs de la Rédaction de la *Revue de Paris*'. Comparison of this early form of the text with the text as published throws valuable light on the author's creative process at work.

occasion of the last rendezvous with Rodolphe, or of Rouen seen from the coach as Emma arrives for her weekly assignation with Léon. It would, of course, be going much too far to suggest that the paragraph in question is the product of a spontaneous inspiration, in the sense in which that term is usually understood, for the manuscript reproduced by M. Pommier and Mlle Leleu represents a fairly advanced stage in Flaubert's painstaking process of composition; but the evidence does seem to indicate that the author reached the final form of the text, in all but a few minor details, at a much earlier point than was usually the case.

The opening lines of the passage afford a useful indication of the sort of factors which guided Flaubert in the process of revision and rewriting: in the first place considerations of economy and relevance, in the second place of euphony. The unnecessary 'filles d'un banquier' and 'dans leur pupitre' disappear; the 'reliures de soie rose' become *belles reliures de satin* in order to avoid the repetition of *soie* which recurs in *papiers de soie*; and *comtes ou vicomtes* is preferred to 'des marquis, des comtes ou des barons', no doubt as being more economical and crisper-sounding. More interesting is the addition of the new sentence *Il les fallait cacher....*: this introduces the note of secret, guilty pleasure lacking in the original draft. The word-order: *Il les fallait cacher* should be noted as a stylistic idiosyncrasy on the author's part, harking back to seventeenth-century usage in preference to modern 'il fallait les cacher'. This sentence possibly also reveals a feature characteristic of Flaubert's narrative manner in the second imperfect, which it is most reasonable to take as an example of what is commonly termed 'le style indirect libre'. In *c'était une affaire*, the verb is different in quality from the two imperfects which precede and follow it: whereas the function of *fallait* and *lisait* is the straightforward one of objective narrative, the middle verb may be taken as fulfilling an *indirect* function, and this phrase as representing a personal reflexion on the situation on the part of Emma and her companions, 'quoted', as it were, in this shorthand manner of which Flaubert was so fond.[5]

The first sentence of the long paragraph brings out the heightened state of receptivity into which Emma is drawn, the sensuous pleasure with which she indulges her taste for this illicit form of

[5] On Flaubert and the 'style indirect libre' see, e.g., A. Thibaudet, *Gustave Flaubert*, revised edition (Paris, 1935), pp. 246 ff.; S. Ullmann, *Style in the French Novel* (Cambridge, 1957), ch. ii.

reading. The verb *frémir* belongs to the kind of vocabulary with which Flaubert habitually records a *physical* reaction on the part of his heroine to those aspects of the world around her which appeal strongly to her imagination; and *soulevant de son haleine* also has the effect of establishing contact of a physical kind between Emma and the volume in front of her. The sentence as a whole is a remarkable example of the suiting of sound to sense: there is a discreet use of sibilants to reinforce the idea expressed,[6] and the rising and falling of the *papier de soie* is matched by the rising cadence to *plié*, followed by the falling-away to the end of the sentence. Emma is still the subject of the main verb in this sentence, but the relative clause transfers the reader's attention to the 'keepsake' itself. With the next sentence, we embark on an inventory of the contents of the volume: though the presentation is a good deal less bare and catalogue-like than is the case of the earlier paragraph dealing with the novels, the terms in which the first item is introduced: *C'était...*, recall the 'Ce n'était que...' of the other passage.

The first example evokes the cult of the Middle Ages which became popular in the early decades of the nineteenth century, and which had already been alluded to in the earlier paragraph, with its references to Scott: 'Avec Walter Scott, plus tard, elle s'éprit de choses historiques, rêva bahuts, salle des gardes et ménestrels...' Here, both the *court manteau* and the *aumônière*, details of medieval costume, invite the reader to visualize the sort of conventional engraving which illustrates the popular conception of the Middle Ages, as well as the ever-present obsession with love in an idealized form. From the Middle Ages we pass to the sentimental stereotypes of the late eighteenth and early nineteenth centuries; and the construction used, with the definite article in *les portraits anonymes des ladies anglaises*, suggests that here we are dealing with something particularly conventional and hackneyed. Again, a parallel can be found in the earlier passage, with the difference that the literary allusions there seem to be primarily to sensational or melodramatic incidents, possibly drawn from the traditional themes of the Gothic novel (*dames persécutées...*, *postillons qu'on tue...*, *chevaux qu'on crève...*, *forêts sombres ...*), whereas the references here are to something more placidly sentimental, the pictorial clichés symbolizing the domestic rather than the Gothic tradition in the English

---

[6] The association between sense and sound was expressed more obviously in the MS. by using the onomatopoeic 'en bruissant'.

novel. The main stereotype of the *ladies anglaises* having been established (note the local colour conveyed by the choice of the English term), these are then subdivided, and three further illustrations are presented, each with its own conventional emblems, as it were, representing a different facet of English life as the popular imagination pictured it. In the first illustration, the carriage, the greyhound, and the postilions suggest the grace and leisure of the upper classes; in the second, the opened letter, the moon, and the black curtain stand for the melancholy and capacity for deep feeling associated with the English temperament in the early nineteenth century; while the third, with the dove and the daisy, presents an idealized picture of the natural simplicity of the young English girl. Subsidiary references (*d'une cage gothique, retroussés comme des souliers à la poulaine*) reintroduce the theme of the modern revival of medieval styles and fashions.

Up to this point, the description of the engravings has been straightforward and objective, and the author's irony, where it appears at all, is restrained: for instance, one might see a suggestion of an affected pose in *la tête sur l'épaule*, or a hint of extravgance in *retroussés comme des souliers à la poulaine*. But from line 22, irony takes over, and beneath the apparent objectivity of the inventory (*sultans..., bayadères..., djiaours..., sabres..., bonnets...*) and the detailed analysis of the *paysages blafards*, there is a clear enough indication that Flaubert finds such unselective exoticism the height of absurdity. The familiarity of *Et vous y étiez aussi...* and *et vous surtout...* almost certainly represents a somewhat ambivalent approach: the patronizing, critical attitude of the mature author does not wholly conceal a certain affectionate nostalgia for these old friends of his own youth; for we must not forget that Flaubert was partly drawing on first-hand memories of his own upbringing in describing this phase of Emma's life. As he confessed to Louise Colet in a letter of 3 March 1852,

> Je viens de relire pour mon roman plusieurs livres d'enfants. Je suis à moitié fou, ce soir, de tout ce qui a passé devant mes yeux, depuis de vieux keepsakes jusqu'à des récits de naufrages et de flibustiers. J'ai retrouvé des vieilles gravures que j'avais coloriées à sept ou huit ans, et que je n'avais pas revues depuis.

The medieval and the contemporary English local colour has its Oriental counterpart here in the use of *djiaour* (or 'giaour': 'mot par lequel les Turcs désignent tous ceux qui ne font pas profession de l'islamisme'—Littré) and *bayadère* ('femme indienne dont la profession est de danser devant les temples ou pagodas'—ibid.); both words had been introduced into the language during the vogue for the Oriental and exotic which had begun in the eighteenth century. *Dithyrambiques* presents more of a problem; Littré gives the following familiar and figurative use: '*Dithyrambe*: Grandes louanges... En ce sens,... a souvent un sens moqueur', and this might well be the sense in which it is used here; L. Bopp suggests 'exagérément vantées'.[7] However, the adjective is used by Flaubert elsewhere, in his correspondence, apparently without a critical nuance, and it may be that its choice here is another instance of ambiguous feelings towards his subject-matter.

The final tableau, in which the most impossibly incongruous items are found side by side, is surely a caricature, and seems more likely to derive from the author's imagination than from the observation of any one model—though we should almost certainly be justified in assuming, with the above-quoted remark to Louise Colet in mind, that it is in the main a composite picture of elements taken from various different engravings. The critical intention at last comes through quite unmistakably: *une forêt vierge bien nettoyée* is such a preposterous contradiction in terms that it must be taken as a deliberate intervention on the author's part, designed to cast ridicule on the whole composition. A similar intervention can surely be seen in the phrase 'vertueux comme on ne l'est pas' which likewise appears at the end of the 'Ce n'était qu'amours, amants, amantes...' passage; and here, at least, there would seem to be two instances of Flaubert the satirist prevailing over Flaubert the detached, objective writer: two cases in which, in spite of his much-advertised precept 'ne jamais conclure', he has been unable to prevent himself from pointedly 'directing' the reader to adopt a critical attitude towards his subject-matter.

The closing phrases of the paragraph remind us very strongly of what we should have been conscious of all through this description: that we are dealing with a collection of engravings, and that this whole paragraph is an example of what, in referring to the late-Romantic school of 'L'Art pour l'art', it is customary to call a 'transposition d'art'; that is, the exercise which consists in taking a work created in one medium and 'translating' it into another, re-

---

[7] *Commentaire sur Madame Bovary* (Neuchâtel, 1951), p. 73.

producing as closely as possible the same effects. Thus Flaubert's paragraph contains no colour at all: everything is black and white, like the models he is copying. In the first half of the paragraph, the black-and-white tonality is rendered with considerable detail (*robe blanche... boucles blondes... chapeau de paille... grands yeux clairs... postillons en culotte blanche... billet décacheté... la lune... rideau noir... une tourterelle... une marguerite... leurs doigts pointus*). From line 22 onwards the approach becomes analytical rather than directly descriptive—though *paysages blafards* maintains the same tonality—until the closing lines, in which not only is the black-and-white effect carried on with *rayon de soleil, écorchures blanches, acier gris, des cygnes*, but Flaubert also goes much further in attempting to reproduce the technical effects of the engraver's art: the ray of sunshine which is *tremblotant*, the *écorchures* and the *fond d'acier gris* combine to produce a particularly vivid 'transposition' of the original medium.

Stylistic changes between the Pommier-Leleu manuscript version and the final text can be dealt with briefly. Some adverbs and adverbial phrases disappear in the interests of economy: 'C'était *souvent*, à la balustrade...' (l. 9); 'yeux clairs *comme l'eau des lacs*' (l. 14); 'de *tout* étalées' (l. 14); 'souriant *de côté* la tête...' (l. 20); 'retroussés *par le bout* comme...' (l. 22); the extra adjective 'calmes', which followed *yeux* (l. 13), and the conjunction in 'des palmiers *et* des sapins' (l. 26) have also been eliminated for the same reason. Other changes perhaps reflect a search for greater expressivity: *qui serrait* for 'qui tenait' (l. 10), *contemplaient* for 'regardaient' (l. 17). *contrées* for 'pays' (l. 25), and *chameaux accroupis* for 'chameaux, çà et là' (l. 28), while two changes in the order of noun and adjective are no doubt dictated by the author's sensitive regard for rhythms rather than by any subtle distinction in meaning: *court manteau* (l. 10) was originally 'manteau court', and *paysages blafards* (l. 24) replaces 'blafards paysages'. Finally, there are two changes of a kind which recur throughout the author's writing; he was particularly sensitive to a tendency to overwork the relative construction, and in this passage the original '*qui portait* une aumônière' (l. 11)—particularly obtrusive after the relative of the preceding phrase—and '*qui se promenaient* dans des parcs' (l. 14) are both replaced by gerundive constructions. [8]

[8] 'Les pronoms relatifs ont été le cauchemar de Flaubert, et il pourchasse leur répétition comme une servante hollandaise les araignées' (Thibaudet, op. cit., p. 244).

The concluding phrases of the last sentence of this paragraph provide a good example of what has been called a 'minor cadence': that is, they are arranged in a decreasing, rather than an ascending order. Whereas the contrary arrangement, leading from shorter to longer phrases, gives the effect of the completion or rounding-off of a passage, the 'minor cadence' construction produces an inconclusive or incomplete effect; so that here, we are led to anticipate the next paragraph, which itself provides the necessary rounding-off of the whole passage. This regard for the rhythms of a prose sentence, which we may certainly take to be conscious on Flaubert's part, can in the present instance be linked with a device to which Thibaudet has drawn attention: Flaubert's dynamic use of the conjunction 'et'. Related to the Biblical or Homeric use of the conjunction, this feature of Flaubert's prose, says Thibaudet, is used strikingly 'à la fin d'un paragraphe de description énumérative où il introduit et porte soit le détail final, soit le tableau final.'[9] Here we have a strong example: *Et* in line 32 might well be replaced by 'Cependant', or by an adverbial phrase; in the full context of the passage, and taken in conjunction with the structure of the previous lines, it provides a compelling link between the two paragraphs, so that the reader is forced, as it were, to discard the imaginary creations of the 'keepsakes' in favour of the more substantial presence of the real world. It is possible that Flaubert has deliberately introduced the *fiacre attardé* (l. 35) as a humdrum reminder of reality in contrast to the leisurely elegance of the *voitures* mentioned in line 14; but the connection is rather remote, and any such comment must remain a tentative one.[10] As regards its construction, this final

---

[9] Thibaudet, p. 267.

[10] This passage may perhaps serve to illustrate a pitfall in commentary writing into which students sometimes fall. It is possible to see counterparts or parallels to various elements of this description in later episodes of *Madame Bovary*, and the assiduous commentator may be led to enumerate such 'echoes' as illustrations of the unity and rich texture of the novel. He may even be cautious enough to say, not that 'A reminds us of B' (for instance the *lévrier* of this passage and the 'levrette, Djali' which Emma acquires later on), but that 'A *prefigures*, or *prepares us for*, B': all the same, it is asking a great deal of the reader to carry images and passing references in his mind throughout a novel as long as *Madame Bovary*. It should be a principle of *explication* that only those analogies are regarded as valid that the reader would normally notice in reading the work in the form in which it is presented by the author, and that one should not assume, on the basis of a previous reading, knowledge of what comes later. M. Bopp is surely guilty of this, even though he is careful to talk of 'prérésonance', in his comments on the above passage:

Comme par un nouvel effet de prérésonance ou d'écho, on voit paraître ou reparaître

sentence is well organized and observes the need for a substantial clause to end with: the second relative (*qui roulait...*) is in fact much weaker than the first (*qui passaient...*); its verb is purely descriptive in its function, and there is virtually no break at all from the comma after *les autres* to the end of the sentence. So that although it is still the images of the 'keepsake' with which we are concerned in the main clause (*l'abat-jour... éclairait tous ces tableaux du monde*), the structure of the sentence ensures that the passage closes with a solid reminder of reality.

---

dans ces gravures: le balcon pour des amoureux (il y aura la fenêtre-balcon des comices!), des femmes étalées dans des voitures (il y aura non seulement le boc de Charles, mais le fiacre avec Léon!), puis un lévrier (qui semble annoncer la levrette Djali), puis des postillons (plus élégants que le pauvre Hivert), puis des femmes qui rêvent au clair de lune, sur des sofas, près d'un billet décacheté (on assistera à quelque chose d'analogue au château de Vaubyessard — sans parler du billet de rupture de Rodolphe), puis d'autres femmes qui effeuillent une marguerite (Rodolphe proposera à Emma d'en cueillir)...' (op. cit., p. 73).

It would seem to be more prudent to say that the images which make their appearance here represent the *type* of illusion on which Emma feeds, and the later episodes the *type* of disillusionment continually inflicted by reality.

16 Baudelaire

La Cloche fêlée

Il est amer et doux, pendant les nuits d'hiver,
D'écouter, près du feu qui palpite et qui fume,
Les souvenirs lointains lentement s'élever
Au bruit des carillons qui chantent dans la brume.

5   Bienheureuse la cloche au gosier vigoureux
Qui, malgré sa vieillesse, alerte et bien portante,
Jette fidèlement son cri religieux,
Ainsi qu'un vieux soldat qui veille sous la tente!

Moi, mon âme est fêlée, et lorsqu'en ses ennuis
10   Elle veut de ses chants peupler l'air froid des nuits,
Il arrive souvent que sa voix affaiblie

Semble le râle épais d'un blessé qu'on oublie
Au bord d'un lac de sang, sous un grand tas de morts,
Et qui meurt, sans bouger, dans d'immenses efforts.

BAUDELAIRE, *Les Fleurs du Mal*, LXXIV
Text of second edition (1861)
Ed. J. Crépet and G. Blin (Paris: Corti, 1942), p. 78

THIS poem was published under three successive titles: 'Le Spleen' (*Messager de l'Assemblée*, 1851), 'La Cloche' (*Revue des Deux Mondes*, 1855), and 'La Cloche fêlée' (*Fleurs du Mal*, 1st edition (1857), LVIII). Baudelaire identified the piece first with the mood of Spleen and then with the image of the bell whose chimes sing of the Ideal. Finally he hit upon the definitive title which evokes the essential bi-polarity Spleen/Ideal underlying the poem.

It belongs to the first and longest section of *Les Fleurs du Mal* ('Spleen et Idéal'). This section falls into three groups of poems: the first two Cycles of Art and Love ('Idéal') and the last Cycle ('Spleen'). The central core of the last Cycle (LXXIV–LXXVIII) forms a logically and artistically coherent whole. 'La Cloche fêlée' introduces this series of variations on Spleen which explore the dark, vertiginous depths of the 'gouffre baudelairien'. Viewed as part of the 'secret architecture' of *Les Fleurs du Mal*, the sonnet might well be described as the entrance to Baudelaire's Inferno, the Hell of Spleen.

The poem takes on its full resonance only within the context of the whole work; for *Les Fleurs du Mal* possesses a profound, mysterious unity, and the individual poems themselves are 'comme de longs échos qui de loin se confondent' (IV). 'La Cloche fêlée' has, therefore, to be considered not only in itself, but also as a reflection of the world of Baudelaire's imagination.

Within Baudelaire's profoundly ambiguous and ultimately unresolved dialectic Ideal and Spleen are the twin poles between which his imagination perpetually oscillates. The Ideal seems to be now 'Des Cieux Spirituels l'inaccessible azur' (XLVI), now the lost paradise of childhood. At times it becomes 'un Infini que j'aime et n'ai jamais connu' (XXI), and when religion, art, and love fail the poet there is the recourse to 'les paradis artificiels'. Here and there Baudelaire describes the rare visitations of Grace which momentarily light up his mental gloom; but the radiant vision soon fades like a mirage. The struggle to reach out for the Ideal collapses, and Baudelaire's intense, violent malaise comes flooding back with all its familiar symptoms: nervous depression accompanied by lassitude and *taedium vitae*; an obsession with darkness and winter, old age and death; an anguished sense of a metaphysical Void alternating with a perverse 'goût du néant' (LXXX); terrified, yet fascinated plunges into the dark, yawning 'gouffre intérieur', the abode of Satan, the spirit of negation and the supreme incarnation of Spleen; a tragic feeling of dereliction combined with a sense of irreparable guilt and inescapable damnation; claustrophobic images of confinement; a mysterious disease of the will, a physical and creative powerlessness culminating in a sensation of paralysis, an agony of petrifaction or suffocation.

'La Cloche fêlée' conforms in general terms to this dialectical movement—the aspiration towards the Ideal followed by the relapse into Spleen. One of the most painful elements of Baudelaire's malady is described here in the slow asphyxiation and the violent immobility of the last stanza.

Two sources have been proposed for the sonnet. The opening stanza has been compared with Vigny's lines:

> Qu'il est doux, qu'il est doux d'écouter des histoires,
> Des histoires du passé,
> Quand les branches d'arbre sont noires,
> Quand la neige est épaisse et charge un sol glacé!
> ('La Neige', *Poèmes antiques et modernes*)

Similarly Gautier's description of a return from a visit to a cemetery may have suggested Baudelaire's title and other elements[1] of his poem:

> ...Et, me suivant partout, mille cloches fêlées,
> Comme des voix de mort, me jetaient par volées
> Les râlements du glas (*La Comédie de la mort*, II)

These sources are purely hypothetical, and leaving aside the possibility of mere coincidence the differences are as striking as any resemblances. Baudelaire's bitter-sweet mood is more complex than that of Vigny; he is listening not to 'des histoires du passé', but to more intimate *souvenirs lointains*; and his poem evokes a winter of the soul quite as much as a wintry landscape. In the case of Gautier the verbal analogies are closer and more precise; but the context is objectively presented, whereas Baudelaire's poem is strongly interiorized: it betrays a sharper anguish, a more concentrated intensity. What strikes us here is not literary echoes, but rather that bold, electrifying novelty—the 'frisson nouveau' which startled Hugo in *Les Fleurs du Mal*. Any borrowed details of theme or expression have been transubstantiated by the poet's alchemy into something wholly other, and imperceptibly assimilated into the texture of an authentically Baudelairean poem.

Like almost half of Baudelaire's poems 'La Cloche fêlée' is a sonnet, and its general characteristics suggest some of the reasons for his preference for this form. First, its shortness; for like Poe he thought that a 'long poem' was a contradiction in terms. The brevity is here exploited to produce a concentrated, highly evocative density of implication and association not only in the general design,

---

[1] Cf. the 1855 variant of Baudelaire's l. 12: 'Ressemble aux râlemens...' This somewhat rare noun was dropped in the subsequent versions.

but also in the individual stanzas, lines, words. The sheer difficulty of the sonnet clearly tempts Baudelaire, and he manipulates the formal constraints and limitations in order to heighten the dramatic effect. Only four of his sonnets conform to the traditional rhyme-scheme: ABBA ABBA CCD EDE. The majority are *sonnets libertins* with their rhymes arranged in all possible combinations. 'La Cloche fêlée' is one of these irregular sonnets with its seven different rhymes organized in the rare combination: ABAB CDCD EEF FGG. The quatrains consist of *rimes croisées* with a more rapid, lively rhythm than the slow, monotonous cadence of the couplets which make up the tercets. As for the quality of the rhymes, *vigoureux-religieux* is merely assonant (*rime pauvre*). There is also what seems to be a *rime normande* (*hiver-s'élever*); but the case is unique in Baudelaire's poetry, and even here the false sound should perhaps be attenuated by making the liaison of the final consonant of line 3 with the initial vowel of line 4. Of the remaining rhymes two are *suffisantes* (*fume-brume*, *morts-efforts*), and three are *riches* (*portante-tente*, *ennuis-nuits*, *affaiblie-oublie*). As for the piercing masculine and feminine rhymes of lines 9–12 they have such a close affinity of sound that they resemble *rimes redoublées*. Like most of Baudelaire's sonnets this piece is written in Alexandrines, which lend heroic nobility and solemnity to the tragic theme. The lines are all binary; but liberties are taken with the strict rules of the Classical Alexandrine. The caesura, for example, is sometimes offset by a *coupe* of equal or greater strength (ll. 2, 6, 9, 14). A further element of irregularity is the frequent use of enjambment: the sense overruns the caesura, the rhyme, even the stanza. Both quatrains consist of one sentence, and each is a self-contained, endstopped unit. By contrast the tercets are linked by sentence, rhyme, and enjambment, and this stanza-linking produces a marked descending movement, an almost alarming sensation of sagging or collapse.

Structurally the sonnet splits into two sharply contrasting sections (ll. 1–8 and 9–14) which mirror a mind torn between Ideal and Spleen. The two sections are unified by the repetition and variation of two complementary, superimposed images. The one image (the bell) is auditive, and the other (the soldier) is visual, this second image deriving by analogy from the first. The double image, escorted by supporting imagery, appears in both sections; but in the second there takes place an abrupt reversal of mood. There is an unexpected transition from *la cloche au gosier vigoureux* to the poet's *âme fêlée* with its *voix affaiblie*, and from the *vieux soldat qui veille sous la tente* to the *blessé qu'on oublie*. The scene has switched from the outer world to a Baudelairean soulscape; but outer and inner worlds remain interrelated through the return in modified form of the same double image.

The opening is deceptively gentle. The tone is hushed and confiding; the tableau is cosy and homely; a drowsy, nostalgic reverie is stirred by the chimes. It looks at first sight like a typical piece of 'intimiste' poetry. There are, it is true, certain faintly discordant undertones: the harsh echo *amer-hiver*; the melancholy rhyme *fume-brume*; the series of slightly disturbing contrasts: *amer/doux; nuits d'hiver/feu; feu/fume; carillons/brume*. On the whole, however, the fireside scene is not unpleasant or sinister; it evokes an atmosphere of warm, snug intimacy. This impression is strengthened by the background of soft, soothing sounds. There are contrasting sound effects like the crackling of the fire *qui palpite et qui fume*; but the most striking feature of the 'poésie sonore' here is the predominance of soft *f* and *v*, languid *l* and muted nasals. There is discreet use of alliteration: e.g. the soft, muffled 'tintement' of the distant bell (*lointains lentement*); but alliteration and assonance are most subtly combined in line 4 where the hard consonants seem to register the vigorous striking of the bell, the bright, sharp vowels appear to echo the joyous notes of the carillons, and the nasals suggest the muffling effect of the fog: *Au bruit des carillons qui chantent dans la brume*.

Outwardly Baudelaire is presenting a familiar everyday scene in the form of a general meditation couched in impersonal terms (*Il est... pendant les nuits d'hiver*); but there is a strange ambiguity about the unidentified occupant of the room. Behind Everyman we sense the lurking presence of Baudelaire himself. The scene recalls Courbet's famous portrait of Baudelaire and the poet's many descriptions of himself sitting alone at home, meditating in a corner of the firelit room, with the inhospitable world shut out by curtains and shutters. The room is the typical Baudelairean 'intérieur', at once a warm reassuring refuge and a claustrophobic, solitary cell: the world is shut out, but Baudelaire is shut in. It reminds us especially of the high, remote *mansarde* of 'Paysage':

Je veux...
Coucher auprès du ciel...
Et, voisin des clochers, écouter en rêvant
Leurs hymnes solennels emportés par le vent.

It is a room made in Baudelaire's own image, adapted to spiritual concentration and conducive to poetic reverie. It is a 'chambre tiède' (CX), with the fire, the habitual companion of Baudelaire's winter evenings, burning in the hearth and producing a chiaroscuro effect through the contrast between its warm, protective glow and the cold darkness outside. Always sensitive to the cold, Baudelaire is probably huddling over the fire and staring dreamily into the flickering flames. Their dancing light supplies a kind of animate element in the room; indeed, the fire seems to symbolize the warmth of life. It is not, however, a clear, bright, steady glow: the fire is smoking as if it were not drawing well in the foggy atmosphere. There seems to be a subtle correspondence not only between the throbbing of the fire and that of the bell, but also between the smoke and the fog. Just as the chimes are muffled by the fog, so too the smoking fire seems to suggest that the Ideal is always in danger of being smothered by Spleen.

The wider setting remains for the most part unlocalized. The world outside the room makes its presence felt solely through the sound of the bell and the dark, cold, foggy atmosphere of winter. Winter is an implacable season with its intimations of old age, sterility, and death; night is the sign of Ennui; fog symbolizes 'l'existence brumeuse' (III) of Spleen. No doubt, these elements are held at bay here; but their latent implications lurk in the background. There remains the vague possibility of a sudden, brutal invasion of Baudelaire's inmost being by the hostile forces from without. These harsh elements are lightly sketched in here and seem to represent merely a potential threat temporarily exorcized by poetic reverie; for the outside world reflects Baudelaire's essential duality: its climate is that of Spleen, but the sounds which break into the room are the chimes which sing of the Ideal.

Lines 1–2 consist largely of realistic description; but in lines 3–4 common, everyday reality is raised to a higher level of visionary intensity by Baudelaire's 'sorcellerie évocatoire'. This is plainly one of the poet's 'admirables heures, véritables fêtes du cerveau où les sens plus attentifs perçoivent des sensations plus retentissantes'

(*Curiosités esthétiques*). The poetic reverie is triggered off here by an auditory sensation. The notes of the bell reverberate in space and in time, for the poet describes himself as *hearing*[2] the memories which are summoned up.

In 'Spleen' I 'le bourdon se lamente', and in 'Spleen' IV 'Des cloches tout à coup sautent avec furie Et lancent vers le ciel un affreux hurlement'; but here the sound of the bell is more cheering and suggests the joyous message of the Angelus. The religious memories recalled by the bell merge with those of Baudelaire himself. Like the muffled chimes the *souvenirs lointains* come from afar, and their distance in time deepens the nostalgia of their recall. The memories seem to rise like familiar wraiths, ghostly resurrections of the past. Like the 'défuntes Années' of 'Recueillement' the *souvenirs* resemble personified abstractions and might well have been raised to allegorical status by the use of a capital S,[3] for they here come alive and take wing. The poet's mixed feelings in the face of their return are indicated by the coupling of the antithetical adjectives *amer et doux*. The bitter-sweet mood arises from the ambivalence of memory. The sweetness resides in its idealizing, transfiguring power: 'Charme profond, magique, dont nous grise Dans le présent le passé restauré!' (XXXVIII, ii). The bitterness derives from the cruel contrast between past and present, from the poignant nostalgia for the idyllic, radiant childhood world, from the painful sense of exile, loss, guilt, remorse.

The complexity of mood is reflected to some extent in the syntax. Two parenthetical phrases (*pendant les nuits d'hiver* and *près du feu qui palpite et qui fume*) separate the main verb (*Il est*) from its dependent infinitive (*D'écouter*) and the infinitive itself from its object (*Les souvenirs*). The effect is to create a certain curiosity and suspense by entangling and retarding the development of the theme. In line 3 the object arrives at last, and from here on there is a clear, uninterrupted progression slowed down only by the long, heavy adverb *lentement*. Line 3 forms a kind of *vers-tremplin* which initiates a slow ascending movement. Inside, the smoking flames are curling up the chimney; outside, the notes are floating up through the mist; in the poet's mind the memories are drifting up from the deep well

---

[2] Cf. the 1851 variant: 'De sentir...' This vaguer, more general verb of perception was dropped in the subsequent versions.

[3] Cf. Time's 'démoniaque cortège de Souvenirs' ('La Chambre double'). For Baudelaire's erratic use of capitals in allegory see J. Pommier, *La Mystique de Baudelaire* (Paris, 1932), pp. 124–7.

of the Unconscious. As they slowly rise up together the visual, auditory, and mental images subtly and inextricably merge 'dans une ténébreuse et profonde unité' (IV).

The vague chimes are identified in Stanza 2 with those of a *church bell* (*Bienheureuse, cri religieux*). Here attention is wholly focused upon the old bell which is a picture of rude health and robust strength. The heroic note is struck at once by this 'voix d'airain' with its grave sonority. Its energetic tolling is evoked by the final exclamation mark and by the hard consonants (*b*, [k], *d*, *g*, *p*, *t*) which punch out the lusty, confident peals. The multiple alliteration of line 8 is particularly vigorous: *Ainsi qu'un vieux soldat qui veille sous la tente!* The marked symmetries of the *coupes* also seem to echo metrically the limited, slightly monotonous range of harmonies. There is an exact symmetry in the measure of the two hemistiches of line 5 (3 + 3) and in that of the second hemistiches of lines 6, 7, and 8 (2 + 4), while in line 8 there is a neat inversion (4 + 2 + 2 + 4). Similarly, the first hemistich of line 7 is an identical echo of that of line 6 (1 + 5).

With the initial apostrophe the bell takes on human personality. It is endowed with powerful lungs, and the somewhat barrack-room vulgarity of *gosier*[4] prepares us for the later military simile of line 8. It is an old bell; but the two strong *coupes* of line 6 emphasize that *malgré sa vieillesse* it is still hale and hearty. Symbol of the Faith in a wintry age, the bell still summons men to their religious duties. Amid the darkness and the cold indifference of the world the bell faithfully proclaims its message.

The personification is founded on two analogies. The first analogy resides in the auditory correspondence between the sound of the bell and the human voice. The second analogy takes the form of a typically Baudelairean simile introduced by *Ainsi que*. The bell is likened to *un vieux soldat qui veille sous la tente*. There is a distant affinity between the *cri* of the bell and that of a sentry demanding the password; but the analogy is primarily visual: the old age of the bell and the soldier, and the conical shape of belfry and bell-tent. The image of the soldier[5] completes the personification of the bell.

---

[4] Cf. M. Ruff's remark about 'l'application de la trivialité à la haute poésie, pour produire un éclat soudain, comme un coup de gong' (*Baudelaire* (Paris, 1957), p. 134).

[5] 'Il n'y a de grands parmi les hommes que le poète, le prêtre et le soldat. L'homme qui chante, l'homme qui bénit, l'homme qui sacrifie et se sacrifie' (*Mon Cœur mis à nu*).

He represents the Church Militant, and his alert vigilance is distinctly 'Constantinian'. The tableau of line 8 is, in fact, strangely reminiscent of Piero della Francesca's famous *nocturne*, 'The Dream of Constantine'. Baudelaire's *vieux soldat* is not unlike Piero's bearded Roman veteran standing on guard at the foot of the tall bell-tent, with his back turned and watching over the sleeping Emperor who on the eve of battle is visited by an angel who shows him the sign of the cross: *In hoc signo vinces*. Such triumphalism contrasts with Baudelaire's final dereliction and defeat.

In the first tercet the image of the bell is further developed by the implied comparison with the poet himself, and in the second tercet it is again associated with the image of the soldier by the explicit comparison with *un blessé qu'on oublie*. The second image is once more derived by analogy from the first; but this time the assimilation contrasts tragically with that of the quatrains. The sound, old bell had been likened to a vigilant sentry; but here the poet's *voix affaiblie* is compared to the *râle épais* of a wounded soldier. The voice of Life has become a death-rattle. The supporting imagery also tends to interiorize, intensify, or darken that of the quatrains (*ennuis/ brume ; air froid des nuits/nuits d'hiver ; lac de sang/feu ; tas de morts/ souvenirs*) and culminates in the kinaesthetic horror of the last line.

In the quatrains Baudelaire's approach was outwardly objective and impersonal. In the tercets he turns in upon himself. The poem contracts from the cosy, firelit room to the cold, dark solitude of Baudelaire's *âme*. With this growing inwardness comes a shift of tone, a reversal of mood, a sudden irruption of dark, daemonic emotions. The vigorous confidence of the second quatrain is abruptly succeeded by doubt, discouragement, a chronic, sterile impotence leading via asphyxia to the final death-agony. The reverie turns into a nightmare, and the bitter-sweetness of line 1 becomes unrelieved bitterness. The mood is summed up by the Baudelairean key-word *ennuis* (l. 9), a term virtually synonymous with 'Spleen'. 'Fruit de la morne incuriosité', it can assume 'les proportions de l'immortalité' (LXXVI) and reduce the world to a flat, desolate wasteland—the 'plaines de l'Ennui, profondes et désertes' (CIX). It encourages its victims to acquiesce in defeatism and leads to oppressive melancholia: 'les ennuis et les vastes chagrins Qui chargent de leur poids l'existence brumeuse' (III). The last sense of the word seems to point forward to the second hemistich of line 13; but its other meaning of sluggish inertia is very appropriate to the creative impotence of the first tercet. *En ses ennuis* evokes the prisoner of the dark 'Gouffre de l'Ennui' (XXXVII), and what could be a more apt rhyme for *nuits* (l. 10) than *ennuis*, elsewhere characterized as 'les noirs ennuis' (VIII)?

The tercets disclose an habitual state of mind (*Il arrive souvent*; *l'air froid des nuits*); but the general meditation of the quatrains becomes here an interior monologue. The identity of the mysterious inhabitant is at last revealed, and the metrically isolated *Moi* is a sharp assertion of difference, separateness, solitude. This sudden intrusion of Baudelaire's lonely, unhappy self lends emotional force to the poem and communicates his anguish directly to the reader. *Moi, mon âme est fêlée* rings out like a despairing cry in the night. This bold metaphor explains the title and the basic meaning of the poem. The implied assimilation between the bell and the poet seems to be reinforced by the unusual *coupe* (1 + 5) which exactly repeats that of the first hemistiches of lines 6 and 7. It is as if the sound of the carillons were echoing in the tortured soul of the poet.[6] From this point there is a clear run of one and a half lines. There is a suggestion of a feeble, hopeless attempt to break free from the *stasis* of Spleen and to take flight for the Ideal; but the poet remains earthbound. *Veut* defines the specific character of Baudelaire's 'art volontaire';[7] but here the poet's will is helplessly weak. He yearns to establish poetic communication; but unlike the bell he cannot *peupler* the cold, dark solitude with memories.[8] The chill breath of the night air freezes his inspiration and reduces him to sterile 'impuissance'. There is a pathetic contrast between his *voix affaiblie* and the *gosier vigoureux* of the bell, and compared with its joyous, confident *cri religieux* Baudelaire's *chants* sound like thin, plaintive whimperings. The sharp *i* of the rhymes of lines 9–12 stabs out the poet's wincing pain, and the dirge-like monotony of these wailing vowels seems to catch the agonizing monotony of Spleen itself. Enfeebled by the cold, foggy atmosphere, Baudelaire's voice can only muster a weak, tremulous sound which echoes in the alliteration of lines 11–12: *sa voix affaiblie Semble le râle épais d'un blessé qu'on oublie...*

---

[6] Cf. the analogous phenomenon in 'Chant d'automne', where 'J'écoute en frémissant' (l. 9) echoes 'le bois retentissant' (l. 4).

[7] 'Je veux' is one of the *mots-thèmes* of *Les Fleurs du Mal*. Cf. 'A une Madone', l.1; 'Le Beau Navire', ll. 1, 3, 13, 15; 'Paysage', ll. 1 and 24.

[8] 'Extase! Pour peupler ce soir l'alcôve obscure
   Des souvenirs...' (XXIII).

After this long-drawn-out moan the flagging rhythm is slowed right down by the two strong pauses after *sang* and *morts* before it is finally reduced to rigid immobility by the heavy stops after *meurt*, *bouger*, and *efforts*. There is a progression of lurid shock-images: the death-rattle, the lake of blood, the huge pile of corpses, and finally the dying man. This is not, however, mere sensationalism. There is no mistaking the accent of genuine horror, which recalls the conclusion of 'Un Voyage à Cythère':

> Pour moi tout était noir et sanglant désormais,
> Hélas! et j'avais, comme en un suaire épais,
> Le cœur enseveli dans cette allégorie.

This brutal scene is probably a summit of Baudelaire's sado-masochistic self-laceration; but the acrid relish of suffering is mingled with a tortured spiritual idealism. Baudelaire's Passion recalls his conception of David's painting of the martyrdom of Marat: 'Ceci est le pain des forts et le triomphe du spiritualisme; cruel comme la nature, ce tableau a tout le parfum de l'idéal' (*Curiosités esthétiques*).

Baudelaire's inner world has finally become a bloody battlefield. The reassuring security of the room has vanished together with the protective tent and the vigilant sentry. The poet is like a mortally wounded soldier, exposed in the open and abandoned for dead. He is dying; but nobody knows or cares. He is forgotten. His lonely *râle* is a futile attempt to draw attention to himself, a despairing cry for help which remains unanswered. Just as earlier his voice was enfeebled by the cold, foggy atmosphere, so here his *râle épais*[9] is 'comme un sanglot coupé par un sang écumeux' (CIII). The scene is a kind of continuation and culmination of 'La Fontaine de sang': the blood flowing from the poet's secret wound seems to have coagu-lated with that of all his dead to form a thick, dark-red *lac de sang*. Stagnant lakes remind Baudelaire of 'l'immobilité dans le déses-poir' (*Salon de 1859*), and a lake of blood is what he associates above all with the paintings of Delacroix: 'Delacroix, lac de sang...' (VI). The poem does indeed suggest a kind of poetic emulation of Delacroix's art: the mingling of 'le sang, la lumière et les ténèbres' (*Salon de 1859*); the expressive use of 'rouge sombre' to convey dark, terrible pain; the melancholy poetry of human suffering

---

[9] This striking epithet was introduced after the rejection of the two previous variants: 'Ressemble aux hurlements...' (1851) and 'Ressemble aux râlemens...' (1855).

concentrated upon a noble, central figure threatened with violent death—'une figure plus désolée, plus affaissée que les autres, en qui se résument toutes les douleurs environnantes' (*Salon de 1846*).

The manner of the soldier's death is peculiarly horrid. Like the 'soldat brisé', the 'mourant qu'écrasent les blessés' in 'L'Irréparable' he is being slowly suffocated *sous un grand tas de morts*. The epithet *grand* adds to the intense, obsessional power of the image.

Who are these *morts*? Are they simply the host of anonymous dead who have fallen with Baudelaire in the battle of life? It would seem more probable that they symbolize the victims of the poet's creative sterility. Baudelaire has become a 'vieux corps sans âme et mort parmi les morts' (LXXII). For Baudelaire artistic creation is essentially the imaginative recall which reanimates and resuscitates the past;[10] conversely, artistic 'impuissance' consigns such memories to oblivion. His agony here appears to be primarily the death of his creative power, and the *morts* seem to represent the buried memories which have not been resurrected. Liberated, such memories resemble

> ...chrysalides funèbres,
> Frémissant doucement dans les lourdes ténèbres,
> Qui dégagent leur aile et prennent leur essor,
> Teintés d'azur, glacés de rose, lamés d'or (XLVIII).

The poet's soul, however, has become a melancholy cemetery full of dead, decomposing memories:

> J'ai plus de souvenirs que si j'avais mille ans...
> ...mon triste cerveau
> ...est une pyramide, un immense caveau,
> Qui contient plus de morts que la fosse commune.
> —Je suis un cimetière abhorré de la lune,
> Où comme des remords se traînent de longs vers
> Qui s'acharnent toujours sur mes morts les plus chers
> (LXXVI).

The *souvenirs lointains* conjured up by the chimes are no longer audible and seem to have reverted into this silent *tas de morts* which bears down upon the poet like the dead weight of the indestructible past. 'Plus lourds que des rocs' (LXXXIX), they are pressing down on him like heavy corpses and slowly suffocating him. This stifling

---

[10] 'Mémoire résurrectionniste, évocatrice, une mémoire qui dit à chaque chose: "Lazare, lève-toi!"' (*Le Peintre de la vie moderne.*)

sensation which contrasts with the vigorous 'souffle' of Stanza 2 culminates in the masterly line 14 which seems to catch the last gasp of the dying man. The *m* (especially the double *m*) and double *f*, the final *r*'s and the *s* before the mute *e* impede the flow of the line and produce the effect of a desperate struggle for breath which dies away in the final word *efforts*. The death agony is also accompanied by vowels and nasals with long, deep sounds: [œ],[ã],[u],[ã],[ã],[ɔ:]. The structure of this last line is particularly striking: the laconic brutality of *Et qui meurt*, the physical paralysis (*sans bouger*) highlighted by the strong *coupes*, the contrast by juxtaposition of the mental violence (*dans d'immenses efforts*). This horrifying climax conveys the physical sensation of Spleen and sums up the desolate conclusion of the sonnet.

The fluid imagery of the poem leads us from a cosy fireside tableau down into the dark Hell of Spleen. There is an atmosphere of mystery; nothing is explicit; the sonnet is all suggestion. It ends in a mood of depression and doom. Baudelaire is apparently defeated. From his agony, however, has sprung a 'fleur du mal', a sonnet which powerfully expresses the poetry of human suffering. There is no sentimentality; no moral is drawn. It is a stark, sombre vision.

17 Sully-Prudhomme

Le Vase brisé

Le vase où meurt cette verveine
D'un coup d'éventail fut fêlé;
Le coup dut effleurer à peine:
Aucun bruit ne l'a révélé.

Mais la légère meurtrissure,   5
Mordant le cristal chaque jour,
D'une marche invisible et sûre
En a fait lentement le tour.

Son eau fraîche a fui goutte à goutte,
Le suc des fleurs s'est épuisé;   10
Personne encore ne s'en doute;
N'y touchez pas: il est brisé.

Souvent aussi la main qu'on aime,
Effleurant le cœur, le meurtrit;
Puis le cœur se fend de lui-même,   15
La fleur de son amour périt;

Toujours intact aux yeux du monde,
Il sent croître et pleurer tout bas
Sa blessure fine et profonde;
Il est brisé: n'y touchez pas.   20

SULLY-PRUDHOMME, *Stances et poèmes*
Date of first publication: 1865
Œuvres (Paris: Lemerre, 1883–1904), I, 11–12.

THIS poem comes from Sully-Prudhomme's first collection of poetry, *Stances et poèmes* (1865). Quoted in full by Sainte-Beuve in the *Nouveaux Lundis*, it rapidly became an anthology piece and was set to music by Gounod. No poem was ever more popular or won its author more fame. Admiring salon hostesses asked him so often to recite the elegy that he came to regard his 'pot cassé' as a 'véritable scie' ('Qu'il se brise sur leur nez, ce vase!') In Parnassian circles Louis Ratisbonne composed the mock epitaph:

> Sur ce tertre où Sully-Prudhomme est remisé
> On distingue un vase brisé.

The poet was later to renounce 'la poésie personnelle'; but to his annoyance he was to remain for his contemporaries the author of 'Le Vase brisé'. Today the poem tends to be referred to with ironical condescension, and it may be questioned whether it is nowadays any more generally known than the rest of Sully-Prudhomme's poetry, which has fallen into neglect. If he has any chance of survival at all, however, it is not for his long philosophic and scientific poems, but for certain short elegies like 'Le Vase brisé'. His contemporaries were perhaps not entirely mistaken about this little love-poem, which strikes the personal, original note characteristic of his poetic temperament and fairly illustrates his delicate, but essentially minor talent.

Sully-Prudhomme has here embalmed *la fleur de son amour*, the love which life denied him; and the vase with its *blessure fine et profonde* symbolizes his own broken heart.

It had been a childhood romance: 'Je suis né, je l'ai vue, et déjà je l'aimais' (*Épaves*).[1] From the age of twelve he had loved 'chère L...', a blue-eyed, golden-haired cousin scarcely older than himself. He has described her frail beauty and her soft caress: 'Cette main-là, pas de lèvres au monde En douceur ne l'égaleront' ('Jours lointains', *Stances et poèmes*). A young, heartless coquette, L... does not seem to have returned his love, and in 1861 she married someone richer than Sully-Prudhomme: 'Ce trésor que j'avais répandu sur tes pas pour voir si tu oserais marcher dessus, tu l'as, non pas foulé aux pieds, mais écarté légèrement, discrètement, du bout de ton petit soulier, pour te faire de la place et t'échapper. Voilà, fille bien élevée, fille raisonnable et dure, ce que tu as fait' (*Journal intime*, 7 February 1864). He felt 'ni joie ni peine, état de

[1] (Paris, 1908), p. 19.

mort' (ibid., 21 October 1862). The cruel blow had 'brisé la fleur de [sa] jeunesse' ('Le Pardon', *Épaves*), and with the death of his youth *la fleur de son amour périt*. Assuming a mask of indifference, he hid his private sorrow. His only confidants were his diary and his poetry; he expected neither pity nor consolation from others: 'Que peuvent nos amis, ceux que l'orgie entraîne, De nos soupirs cachés insouciants moqueurs?' ('Les Jeunes Gens', *Stances et poèmes*). It was a quiet, unspectacular, but irremediable tragedy. He was never to marry, and happiness was to elude him all his life:

> Mû de pitié plus que d'envie,
> Sur votre tombeau nuptial
> Je prendrai pour toute ma vie
> Le deuil de mon jeune idéal. ('Deuil de cœur', *Épaves*.)

The poet's unhappy love-affair is discreetly enveloped in the allegory of the broken vase. Though he did not cultivate a Parnassian impassibility[2], he was not an exhibitionist either. He does not flaunt his private life here; he makes no direct, personal allusions. Stripping away the particular, circumstantial details, he shyly discloses only the poetic essence of the experience.[3]

'Le Vase brisé' displays the dominant characteristics of Sully-Prudhomme's poetic temperament and manner—a refined, faintly feminine delicacy; a gentle sensitive 'tendresse Où tremblent toutes les douleurs' ('Rosées', *Stances et poèmes*); a lonely, introspective diffidence; a sincere modesty and a discreet reserve; a quiet sobriety, moderation, and restraint.[4] This elegiac love-poem belongs appropriately to the section of *Stances et poèmes* which is entitled 'La Vie intérieure'. Sully-Prudhomme reveals himself here a delicate analyst of the suffering heart; but the psychology is truthful

---

[2] 'Ne croyez pas... que le poète, pour être un bon ouvrier, doive être impassible' (*Testament poétique* (Paris, 1901), p. 26).

[3] 'J'aime bien mieux prendre l'essence d'une passion, d'une douleur, indépendamment de toute aventure, et chercher la cadence, le rythme qui en est l'éternel et nécessaire accompagnement. Le *contingent* m'est odieux... Les *faits* ne m'intéressent pas; ils ne sont que la floraison des causes, seules essentielles' (*Journal*, 17 June 1868).

[4] 'J'aime à donner un mouvement continu à l'émotion; la compression me semble plus élevée, plus digne que l'expansion. Réprimer l'élan du cœur, c'est mieux compter ses battements, la douleur pesée est plus noble que la douleur criée. J'aime à dire simplement: j'étouffe l'exclamation pour en faire un soupir, j'arrête les pleurs pour les faire retomber sur le cœur; c'est ma manière, ou plutôt, c'est mon idéal' (*Journal*, 26 June 1868).

without being complicated or tortuous.[5] The style is economic, sober, even a little dull and grey, blending harmoniously with the gentle murmur of the *moderato cantabile*. Here and there we note the subtle touches for which Sully-Prudhomme is noted; but in the main the simple clarity conveys 'l'honnête expression des sentiments vrais' (*Lettres à une amie*). Carefully avoiding exaggeration, affectation, or surprise effects, the poet shows a precise, meticulous exactitude in his search for 'la note juste' (*Journal*, 26 June 1868). Perfect appropriateness is for Sully-Prudhomme the supreme elegance: 'Ne cherchons pas l'élégance ailleurs que dans la justesse' (ibid., 28 January 1864). He did not, however, achieve the 'justesse parfaite' of this poem without a painful labour of love:

> Je songe à l'état où j'étais en composant Le *Vase brisé*, l'une des premières pièces dont j'aie travaillé les vers avec une complaisante rigueur. Je ne l'ai pas improvisée: la feuille où je l'ai écrite était couverte de ratures; et pourtant il n'en est peut-être aucune qui m'ait été suggérée par un sentiment plus triste: c'est la sincérité même de ma tristesse qui m'obligeait à des corrections répétées pour en atteindre l'expression exacte: la difficulté de rencontrer le mot absolument juste me faisait sentir les moindres nuances qui distinguent les termes, et par conséquent les intimes caractères du chagrin dont je souffrais.[6]

Easy to remember and too short to cloy, the poem seems to end almost before it has begun. It consists of just five octosyllabic quatrains with *rimes croisées*. Apart from the simple assonance of *bas-pas* (*rime pauvre*), which was no doubt forced upon the poet by his desire to reverse in line 20 the two hemistiches of line 12, all the rhymes are careful and exact, and a couple are *riches* (*meurtrissure-sûre*, *épuisé-brisé*). The *octosyllabe*—'le vers qui soupire'—was an excellent choice for an elegy, for this freest and most flexible of lyric metres with its *coupes mobiles* and frequent enjambment can contract or expand with the ebb and flow of emotion. There are only twenty of these short octosyllabic lines; but with them Sully-Prudhomme has succeeded in capturing an exquisite agony in miniature.

The effect of diminution is enhanced by the close, almost micro-

---

[5] 'Je m'attache aux sentiments les plus simples, à l'expression la moins tourmentée' (letter to Coppée, 2 December 1866).

[6] *Testament poétique*, pp. 26–7.

scopic focus of vision. The brief notation of tiny details builds up a slight, impressionistic sketch rather than an exhaustive tableau. There is a total absence of adjectives of colour, and the background is bathed in a vague 'grisaille' as if veiled by a mist of sunless introspection. Sully-Prudhomme is 'un homme pour qui le monde intérieur existe', and the description here serves primarily as an oblique expression of the poet's inward emotions. The whole poem is organized around the image of the vase, and the concentration upon this one apt, simple image results in a strong unity of effect.[7] The sense of the poem is elaborated by the assimilation of the broken vase and the broken heart. A Symbolist poet would probably have ended the poem at line 12; but Sully-Prudhomme, who specialized in 'le symbole expliqué', develops his symbol in the first three stanzas and then explicitly spells out its meaning in the last two.

The sensitive heart, lightly bruised by *la main qu'on aime*, often *se fend de lui-même*. Though *toujours intact aux yeux du monde*, the broken heart with *sa blessure fine et profonde* is silently weeping, and slowly *la fleur de son amour périt*. The theme is illustrated by the initial image of the vase. *Aucun bruit ne l'a révélé*; but it has been cracked by a *coup d'éventail*, and the delicate *verveine* is dying. The *légère meurtrissure* has produced an invisible crack which has slowly crept round the whole vase. The *eau fraîche* has drained away *goutte à goutte*, and the sap of the flowers *s'est épuisé*. No one yet suspects that the vase is broken; but at a mere touch it would fall to pieces.

The two sections of the poem are linked by numerous parallelisms of word, phrase, or idea: *Le vase/le cœur; cette verveine/la fleur de son amour; un coup d'éventail/la main qu'on aime; effleurer/effleurant; meurtrissure/meurtrit; Personne encore ne s'en doute/Toujours intact aux yeux du monde*; and, perhaps most effective of all these parallelisms,

> Son eau fraîche a fui goutte à goutte...
> Il sent... pleurer tout bas
> Sa blessure fine et profonde.

[7] 'La composition est une, ou plus simplement il y a composition quand tout dans l'œuvre concourt à un effet unique par la justesse parfaite des comparaisons et leur sobriété. Certaines comparaisons sont plus riches qu'on ne voudrait et introduisent des vues nouvelles qui apportent des distractions à l'esprit en détruisant l'unité d'effet; donc, simplicité extrême de la comparaison, et ce n'est pas pauvreté, c'est force et vérité' (*Journal*, 28 January 1864).

The assimilation is rounded off by the final lines of each section with their reversed hemistiches: *N'y touchez pas: il est brisé... Il est brisé: n'y touchez pas.* These parallelisms establish the correspondences between outer and inner world, and some faintly echo one another like sad refrains.

All the stanzas are composed with equal skill, and almost every word in them tells.

The first line flows over into the whole of line 2 like a long-drawn-out melancholy sigh and culminates in the plaintive *fut fêlé* which is thrown into prominence at the rhyme by the inversion. The light blow of the fan seems to be echoed by a few hard consonants in the stanza (*coup d'éventail, coup, dut, aucun bruit*); but the predominance of *f* and *v* creates a general impression of gentle softness appropriate to the elegiac tone of the piece. A tragic note is struck almost immediately by the verb *meurt*, and the dying *verveine*, it should be remembered, is the flower sacred to Venus, the goddess of love. *Coup d'éventail* evokes feminine vanity and flirtatious frivolity, the slight, trivial cause of a major calamity. The vase itself is if not yet *brisé*, at any rate *fêlé*. The lightness of the blow is suggested by the softness of the verb *effleurer*, accentuated by *à peine* and by the absence of an explicit object. The suddenness of the disaster is rendered by the rapidity of the short, endstopped *octosyllabe. Aucun bruit ne l'a révélé* seems to hint, beyond its literal meaning, that the poet has made no recriminations, but concealed his pain behind a discreet *veil.*[8]

Stanza 2 consists of one long, sinuous sentence. After the pauses at the end of lines 5 and 6 it winds on from line 7 to line 8 in slow, serpentine fashion as if imitating the remorseless advance of the invisible crack biting into the crystal and slowly, but surely, encircling the whole vase. Echoing *meurt* and anticipating *meurtrit*, the stanza is notable for its four incisive initial *m*'s (*Mais, meurtrissure, Mordant, marche*) and for the 'grincement' effect of its ten *r*'s. *Mordant*, a strong, expressive verb, dominates the whole stanza. The light glancing blow of the fan makes a *légère meurtrissure*; but the figurative meaning is uppermost here—a vase can hardly be bruised, but a heart can. *Cristal*: it is a fragile, precious vase symbolizing a noble, sensitive heart. *Marche invisible et sûre*: the progress not only of the crack, but also of the secret, inward sickness is evoked here. The long, heavy adverb *lentement* effectively slows

[8] 'Révéler. Tirer comme de dessous un voile' (Littré).

down the *marche* of the short monosyllabic words escorting it in line 8.

Stanza 3 rounds off the allegory. It is all over: the vase is broken. The succession of short, endstopped *octosyllabes* ending in line 12 which is virtually split in two by its strong caesura produces an impression of weakness and exhaustion. There is a lack of 'souffle', and the lines seem to trickle away in a dying fall. *Son eau fraîche* hints at the poet's youthful vitality which has ebbed away *goutte à goutte*. *Le suc* is the vital element which has dried up for lack of nourishment, and the *fleurs* point forward to line 16. *Personne encore ne s'en doute*: a simple, superficially prosaic line, but charged here with the silent, hidden sorrow of the stricken heart. *N'y touchez pas*: the poet adopts an admonitory, almost entreating tone as if he were addressing some well-meaning but clumsy friend. The stanza concludes with the bald, stark phrase: *il est brisé*. No one can help. It is an irreparable disaster.

The image makes way for the explanation in Stanza 4. *La main qu'on aime* is an example of synecdoche. The hand, the part of the body symbolizing the action, stands for the agent; but the lady involved remains unidentified and otherwise unseen. It is a touch of discreet, almost Classical *pudeur*. The poet's own feelings are likewise veiled behind generalized terms (*on, le cœur*). *Effleurant* and *meurtrit* are deliberate verbal echoes of Stanzas 1 and 2. *Se fend* is a strong, almost brutal, verb occupying a central position in the stanza. The assimilation of the broken vase and the broken heart is now explicit, and the last line of the quatrain likewise associates the wilting flower with a dying love.

The first line of Stanza 5 reformulates the idea of line 11; but the most poetic echo of all occurs in lines 18–19 which condense and transpose the essence of Stanzas 2 and 3. *Croître et pleurer* is a particularly bold, striking association. The invisible crack is likened to a *blessure* which is *fine* and yet *profonde*, while the broken vase with its water leaking away *goutte à goutte* suggests the idea of the wound weeping *tout bas*. The sensation conveyed by the verb *croître* is admirably rendered by the enjambment of lines 18–19. In the last line the assimilation is neatly completed by the reversal of the hemistiches of line 12.

Allegory is distinctly unfashionable today, and the logical clarity of the symbolism of 'Le Vase brisé' will strike most modern readers as too explicit and obvious. The poem, however, possesses real, if minor merits. It is brief, slight, and tenuous; but its delicacy and finesse make it a kind of exquisite miniature. The tender, discreet melancholy of the 'amant brisé' set against the elegant background of vases, flowers, and fans has a very uncontemporaneous sentimentality; but it retains a sociological and historical interest as witnessing to a certain aspect of middle-class sensibility in the Second Empire. 'Le Vase brisé' possesses something of the faded charm of a flower pressed between the leaves of a book or album of the period.

18 Verlaine

A Clymène

Mystiques barcarolles,
Romances sans paroles,
Chère, puisque tes yeux,
  Couleur des cieux,

Puisque ta voix, étrange   5
Vision qui dérange
Et trouble l'horizon
  De ma raison,

Puisque l'arome insigne
De ta pâleur de cygne,   10
Et puisque la candeur
  De ton odeur,

Ah! puisque tout ton être,
Musique qui pénètre,
Nimbes d'anges défunts,   15
  Tons et parfums,

A, sur d'almes cadences,
En ses correspondances
Induit mon cœur subtil,
  Ainsi soit-il!   20

VERLAINE, *Fêtes galantes*
Date of first publication
(in periodical *L'Artiste*): 1868
Selected Poems, ed. R. C. D. Perman
(Oxford: O.U.P., 1965), pp. 42–3

VERLAINE'S second published collection of poems, *Fêtes galantes*, appeared in 1869. Its predominant inspiration was the recent revival of interest in eighteenth-century painting, stimulated by the Goncourt brothers' *L'Art du xviiiᵉ siècle*, which had begun to appear in 1859, and in eighteenth-century civilization generally. A particular source for Verlaine's inspiration is Charles Blanc's *Les Peintres des fêtes galantes* (1854), and the subject-matter of the poems composing this collection is drawn for the most part from the elegant, stylized *galanteries* of the social life of the earlier period, as reproduced by Watteau, Lancret, or Fragonard. There are occasional more specific references to the atmosphere of the eighteenth-century theatre—scenes from the *commedia dell'arte*, also treated by Watteau—but elsewhere the eighteenth-century atmosphere is one of vague suggestion rather than of precise description: it is conveyed by such features as the statues in the formal gardens, musical entertainments, or the costumes and other fashions of the previous century; and by the choice of proper names belonging to an indeterminate literary convention with pastoral associations, still affected in the eighteenth century: Atys, Chloris, Églé, Tircis, Aminte, Clitandre. The name Clymène, which provides the title of the poem under discussion, had already appeared in 'Dans la grotte' in the same collection (a poem which in manuscript bore the identical title, 'A Clymène', though there is no other apparent connection between them).

The title, then, suggests the subject: a stylized gallant address to an imaginary woman (cf. the following poem 'Lettre', addressed to an anonymous 'Madame'). This indicates that the poem should be regarded as a somewhat conventional exercise, whose inspiration is to be found in the current literary and artistic interests of the poet, rather than in his personal feelings. In fact, the twenty-five-year-old poet was at this date still living a respectable life as a clerk at the Hôtel de Ville, and his artistic stimulus came from the literary and cultural life of the capital, rather than from the intense personal feelings which lend a different flavour to his later *recueils*. However, if the inspiration of *Fêtes galantes* as a whole looks back to the artificial 'pastoral' atmosphere of leisured eighteenth-century society, this only provides part of the background to 'A Clymène', and there are two respects in which this poem is noticeably more modern than most of the poems of *Fêtes galantes*.

In the first place, as regards the construction of the poem, Verlaine here departs more strikingly than in any other poem of this early collection from that 'rhetorical' manner, characterized by a very close relationship between the sentence-structure and the rhythms of the verse-form, which had hitherto been common to all French poets; a manner that he was to condemn in his own 'Art poétique', and which was to be largely discarded by symbolist and post-symbolist writers. Even such nineteenth-century poets as Hugo and Musset, despite the effective or amusing results they achieved by a much bolder use of enjambment, respected an over-all metrical scheme which retained a close logical connection with the grammatical structure. Here, it is not the fact that Verlaine uses a shorter line that makes the poem much more forward-looking in this respect, for stanzas composed of various arrange-ments of shorter lines had always remained popular with lyric poets (cf. especially Hugo in the nineteenth century) as an alterna-tive to the more stately Alexandrine; but if we look at the poem as a whole, we can see that the metrical system is imposed quite arbitrarily on a single sentence whose grammatical structure is to say the least unusual. An essential first step in reading this poem, therefore, is to analyse its grammatical construction: to rearrange in one's mind the order of the phrases in the first stanza, to pick out the verb common to the series of chief subordinate clauses (the auxiliary in l. 17, followed by the past participle in l. 19), and finally to make sense of the whole by identifying the main clause in the final line of the poem. Not that this exercise is exceptionally difficult: it is obviously not of the same order of difficulty as the task of construing some of Mallarmé's poems, and indeed the alert reader may well be able to take this in his stride even at a first reading. But it should be emphasized that Verlaine is here obliging his reader to approach the formal structure of the poem in an analytical manner that had been quite unnecessary in the case of nearly all French verse since the time of Malherbe.

Secondly, the poem is even more of its time as regards its imagery, for it is a sustained exercise in the realm of synaesthesia, the expres-sion of one sense-impression in terms of images derived from another of the senses. Set out most explicitly in his sonnet 'Corres-pondances':

> ...Comme de longs échos qui de loin se confondent
> Dans une ténébreuse et profonde unité,

Vaste comme la nuit et comme la clarté,
Les parfums, les couleurs et les sons se répondent.

Il est des parfums frais comme des chairs d'enfants,
Doux comme les hautbois, verts comme les prairies...

by Baudelaire (who, however, makes sparing use of it in his own poems), the notion of 'correspondance' was not a nineteenth-century discovery, but it did commend itself very strongly to the sensibility and the imagination of writers in the second half of the century, and in this respect Verlaine shows himself in 'A Clymène', despite the eighteenth-century context to which the poem is apparently assigned, to be very much a man of his time.

The grammatical structure of the single sentence which composes the poem, analysed in detail, is as follows: an apostrophe, followed by a very short main clause (*Chère, ...Ainsi soit-il!*), into which are inserted a series of five parallel subordinate clauses, the first four incomplete (*puisque tes yeux..., Puisque ta voix..., Puisque l'arome..., Et puisque la candeur...*), and the fifth resuming the subjects of the first four in a new subject (*Ah! puisque tout ton être...*), and then providing the verb and complement which complete all five (*A... En ses correspondances Induit mon cœur...*) together with a qualifying adverbial phrase (*sur d'almes cadences*). The subject of each of these subordinate clauses is qualified, in the following manner: (i) by a series of phrases in apposition (*Couleur des cieux*; and also, less obviously, *Mystiques barcarolles, Romances sans paroles*, the two latter phrases being placed irregularly, not only before the noun they qualify but outside the subordinate clause itself); (ii) by a noun in apposition, itself qualified by a relative clause (*étrange Vision qui dérange...*), (iii) and (iv) by the adjectival phrases of lines 10 and 12 respectively; and (v) by three terms of apposition, one of which (*Musique qui pénètre*) contains a brief relative clause. The combination of the very unusual anteposition of the phrases in apposition in the first stanza, together with the series of unfinished subordinate clauses, the plurals of lines 15–16 in apposition to the singular subject of line 13, and the highly contrived structure of the final stanza, containing subordinate verb and main clause, may have the effect of making the whole seem more complex grammatically than it really is; in any case, the impression the poem makes on the reader is of a pleasingly ingenious *tour de force*.

The effect of surprise created by the unusual features of the syntax of the poem is heightened by the impact of its imagery. We should, perhaps, be more readily disposed to take the phrases of the first two lines as being in apposition to the subject of the first subordinate clause, if this did not entail the association of *yeux* with two auditory images (*barcarolles* and *romances*). The apposition produces the closest possible association, moreover, between the terms involved: the eyes 'are' the *barcarolles* and the *romances* just as much as they 'are' sky-blue—a quite normal, unexceptionable sense-impression. *Barcarolles* is perhaps the only term in the whole poem with a specifically eighteenth-century connotation: these vocal or instrumental pieces whose rhythm was modelled on a gondolier's song became popular towards the end of the century. *Romances sans paroles*, on the other hand, seems to echo a later fashion, the Romantic 'song without words' (though the normal French term is *chanson sans paroles*); it also looks forward, of course, to the title of Verlaine's fourth *recueil*, to be published in 1874. Together, these two terms suggest from the beginning of the poem the 'musicality' which was Verlaine's constant preoccupation as a poet (it receives pride of place in the recommendations put forward in his 'Art poétique'), and predispose the reader to attune his ear to the delicate rhythms which follow. For instance, the role of the feminine *-e* in this first stanza is particularly to be noted.

Stanza 2, containing the second subordinate clause, repeats the process of association, by means of an inverse 'correspondence': *Voix* is coupled with *vision*, and also with the essentially visual concept of *l'horizon de ma raison*. What is expressed in this stanza is hardly original: the notion that the presence of the beloved disturbs the poet's peace of mind; but the bringing together of the senses of sight and hearing gives a real originality to this banal idea. The image which follows (*qui dérange Et trouble l'horizon...*) suggests the blurred, hazy contours of some of Verlaine's early nature descriptions, for instance:

> La lune est rouge au brumeux horizon;
> Dans un brouillard qui danse, la prairie
> S'endort fumeuse...
> ('L'Heure du berger', *Poèmes saturniens*);

and it is perhaps not too fanciful to suggest that this impression is enhanced by the double enjambment:

étrange
Vision qui dérange
Et trouble...

which blurs the metrical 'contours' of the stanza.

The third stanza introduces olfactory impressions, and these are closely associated with the visual sense by means of a striking two-way correspondence: we have not only *l'arome*... *de ta pâleur*, but also, reversing the process, *la candeur de ton odeur*, for although the meaning of *candeur* is restricted in normal usage to the abstract moral sense, there can be little doubt that Verlaine has in mind here the meaning of its Latin counterpart *candor* ('whiteness'), taking up the reference to the colour of the swan in the previous line, so that this stanza as a whole forms a sort of chiasmus (*arome — pâleur — candeur — odeur*).

Stanzas 4 and 5 are closely joined by sense as well as by syntax; in *tout ton être*, which provides the subject of the final adverbial clause, are brought together the various sense-impressions: the visual (*Nimbes d'anges défunts*) and those of sound and smell. These combine to form the *correspondances* (l. 18) into which, so the poet tells his mistress, his impressionable heart has been drawn. *Mon cœur subtil*, by a kind of intellectual conceit, takes up the *musique qui pénètre* of line 14: the poet is at once 'penetrated' by the music of his beloved, and at the same time, under the effect of her *almes cadences*, is willingly drawn, or made to 'penetrate' (*subtil*: 'qui est de nature à pénétrer, à s'insinuer promptement'—Littré) into her being. The adverbial phrase *sur d'almes cadences* reinforces the musical suggestions of *barcarolles* and *romances* at the beginning of the poem, as well as of *musique* (l. 14); the cadences, or rhythms, of all these impressions are lifegiving: *almes* represents, like *candeur*, a deliberate archaism on Verlaine's part, for although strictly speaking this seems to be a neologism, it is formed on the model of the Latin *almus* ('nourishing, beneficent').

The last line of the poem not only, as has been said, provides the key to the enigma posed by the unusual syntax; it also gives coherence to the poem in another sense, enabling us to interpret the otherwise rather arbitrary epithet in *mystiques barcarolles*, and to gather up the occasional subtle half-hint—*Couleur des cieux, Vision qui...*, *Nimbes d'anges défunts*—which combine to give an impression of vaguely religious undertones to the poem. The con-

cluding phrase (*ainsi soit-il*: 'formule elliptique... qui termine certaines prières'—Littré) gives a meaning to these suggestive hints,
and we can now account for the form of the poem: it is in fact a
sort of religious invocation, a litany, by which the poet expresses
adoration of, and desire for communication with, his mistress.
Verlaine's prayer, or hymn, is inspired by the 'mystical' (l. 1)
quality of Baudelairean 'correspondences'; and it seems possible
that he has not only borrowed from his predecessor the idea of
synaesthesia, or 'horizontal' correspondence (i.e. between our
various senses, on a purely human level), but that there is also
implicit in this poem the notion of 'vertical' correspondence as
well (i.e. the relationship between the things of this world and an
ideal world above, hidden from our senses), to which the first
four lines of Baudelaire's famous sonnet are devoted.[1] The form
of the invocation, the vague but definite impression of a religious
undertone, might well be taken to suggest—even if only half
seriously, as a lover's conceit—that the poet's love for his mistress
offers him in some mysterious way access to the *cieux* of which
her eyes are an earthly reflection.

How far Verlaine wanted his reader to go in relating the straightforward sensory correspondence which forms the more obvious
theme of this little poem to the idea of transcendental links with an
ideal world, must remain a matter for conjecture. While there is
nothing in the text of 'A Clymène' which obliges the reader to look
beyond what is stated explicitly, and to consider the poet's invocation to his mistress in this light, there is equally nothing that rules
out such an interpretation. If the poem is interpreted on a purely
explicit level, we may well feel that there is something too neat and
almost mechanical about such a deliberate application of the
principle of synaesthesia, and that despite its compelling interest
as a sustained example of this attitude towards imagery, perhaps
the poem does illustrate the limitations, as well as the positive
possibilities, of such a systematic approach. For this reason, it is
tempting to see Verlaine as at any rate suggesting an extra dimen-

[1]   La Nature est un temple où de vivants piliers
       Laissent parfois sortir de confuses paroles;
       L'homme y passe à travers des forêts de symboles
       Qui l'observent avec des regards familiers.

Cf. also: 'C'est cet admirable, cet immortel instinct du Beau qui nous fait considérer
la Terre et ses spectacles comme un aperçu, une correspondance du Ciel' (Baudelaire,
L'Art romantique, ed. E. Raynaud (Paris, 1931), p. 131).

sion, which would anticipate his own later recommendation that the poet should eschew the explicit, in favour of the 'chanson grise Où l'Indécis au Précis se joint'.

What is quite certain is that already at this early date Verlaine's ideal was a verse form with the rhythmical harmony of music; so that whatever metaphysical significance the *almes cadences* may possibly have had for him, the phrase is surely a clear pointer to another important aspect of the poem. The simple rhythm of the short $6 + 6 + 6 + 4$ stanzas, with the lines marked off by predominantly rich rhymes, could easily have produced an over-emphatic rhythm, lacking in subtlety and variety. A very delicate, subtle rhythm has in fact been created, largely by the effective positioning of the many examples of the feminine -*e*: apart from the four-syllable 'refrain' to each verse, there is only one line (l. 19, which leads in to the concluding formula) without a feminine -*e* either at the rhyme (feminine rhymes are always notably less emphatic than masculine) or at a point at which it can damp down and render less obtrusive a subsidiary tonic accent. The result is a delicately lilting musical effect, not with a predictable, obvious rhythm but subtle and varied—the harmonious cadences suggested by the *barcarolles* and *romances* of the first stanza.

Together with the choice of vocabulary, which tends towards vaguely impressionistic imagery rather than descriptive precision, this admirably fulfils the poet's purpose, to reintroduce music into French poetry which had become, in his view, too pompous and rhetorical.[2] The result is a poem of considerable charm, which combines ingenuity of composition with gracefulness of form, like the best of the later *Romances sans paroles*—but which, unlike Verlaine's characteristic 'romances', offers the additional bonus of a challenging application, in highly condensed form, of a significant aesthetic doctrine.

[2] The poem 'Art poétique', which explicitly sets out this attitude to poetry, was written in 1874.

19 Goncourt

Seule à être droite devant la statue, elle se mit à regarder machinalement autour d'elle, dans l'obscurité pieuse, des agenouillements de
femmes, leur châle sur la tête, et qui, pliées comme un paquet, se
cognaient le front contre le bois d'un banc; des vautrements de
paysans enfonçant de leurs coudes la paille des chaises, ne montrant 5
que leurs yeux sauvages où flambait la réverbération des cierges, et
l'énorme cloutis des semelles de leurs souliers; un prosternement
général, incessant, se disputant les dalles; des gens de toutes les
espèces, de toutes les classes, de toutes les figures, des prêtres à
fin profil, le menton appuyé sur leurs mains jointes et leurs doigts 10
noués avec le mouvement des donataires au bas d'un vitrail; des
prières rampantes de jupes de soie et de jupes d'indienne côte à
côte, couchant presque leurs génuflexions par terre; des prières de
désespoir qui viennent de quitter le lit d'un mourant où elles ne
veulent pas qu'il y ait un mort, des prières enragées de mères qui se 15
cramponnent à un miracle!
   A tout moment la porte battante laissait entrer, avec un peu de
jour derrière lui, quelqu'un, un venant du dehors qui, à peine
entré, devenait une ombre, prenait de l'eau bénite au bénitier noir
tenu par un ange blanc, tombait à genoux d'un seul coup, les jambes 20
cassées, se relevait, marchait droit au pied de la Vierge, déposait
dessus un baiser, posait une seconde son front sur l'orteil qu'il
rebaisait ensuite, trempait le doigt à l'huile d'une lampe, s'en
touchait le front. Et rien que cela, et toujours, au milieu des adorations balbutiantes, des contemplations extatiques, des attitudes 25
fascinées, des immobilités mortes coupées de signes de croix, au
bas de cette Vierge qui, de seconde en seconde, entend le bruit
d'un baiser sur son pied, le pied le plus adoré du monde, et dont
l'idolâtrie des bouches ne décolle jamais!
   Émouvant et troublant sanctuaire que ce coin de Sant-Agostino, 30
cette chapelle d'ombre ardente, de nuit et d'or, l'apparence de ce

grand marbre ranci, l'affadissante odeur des cierges et de l'huile
des veilleuses, ce qui reste dans l'air d'une éternité de prières, les
souvenirs des murs, les images parlantes des victoires sur la mort,
35 ce silence chargé d'élans étouffés, la respiration pressée de tous
les cœurs, un marmottage de foi amoureuse, suppliante, invocante,
ce qu'on sent flotter partout de toutes les douleurs des entrailles
de la femme apportées là! Lieu de vertige et de mystère, un de ces
antres de superstition marqués toujours fatalement sur un coin de
40 terre, dans un temple, dans une église, où l'Humanité va, sous les
coups qui brisent sa raison, à la religion d'une statue, à une pierre,
à quelque chose qui l'écoute quelque part dans le monde avec
l'oreille du Ciel!

Les deux Romaines, qui avaient fini leurs dévotions, attendaient
45 à la porte. Madame Gervaisais était toujours plantée debout, le
visage muet et fermé, lorsqu'une mère portant un petit fiévreux
d'enfant lui pencha la tête sur le pied de la Vierge où le pauvre
petit laissa tomber un baiser endormi. Soudain, mue comme par
un ressort, bousculant, sans les voir, les chaises et les gens, l'autre
50 mère marcha droit au piédestal, se jeta follement sur le pied baisé,
mit sa bouche, colla son front au froid de l'or: une prière de son
enfance, remontée à ses lèvres se brisa sous ses sanglots.

Dehors les femmes étaient derrière elle: elle les avait oubliées, ne
leur parla pas.

E. and J. DE GONCOURT, *Madame Gervaisais*
Date of first publication: 1869
Fasquelle-Flammarion edition (Paris, n.d.),
pp. 125-8

Madame Gervaisais, the last of the six novels produced by the
collaboration of the two Goncourt brothers before the early death
of Jules, the younger, in 1870, presents, like all their other novels,
the 'case-history' of the physical and moral decline of a central
character in a particular, well-defined milieu. The eponymous
heroine is a wealthy, free-thinking French widow who takes up
residence in Rome; she finds Italian Catholicism particularly anti-
pathetic, but gradually the atmosphere of the city, with all the
external manifestations of religion, exerts an insidious effect on the
nervous system of this highly-strung woman of delicate health,
excessively susceptible, like all the Goncourts' main characters, to
this sort of environmental influence. The serious illness of her back-

ward child with meningitis brings about a first crisis in her emotional and intellectual development, when she reluctantly agrees to accompany the two Italian women at whose house she lodges, in their visit to the church of Sant'Agostino to pray for the child's recovery. This passage concludes the account of the visit.

The unexpected action with which the passage closes, as Madame Gervaisais joins the other worshippers in kissing the foot of the statue of the Madonna del Parto (to whom are attributed miraculous healing powers in the case of children) is presented as an impulsive, quite unpremeditated act, undertaken in response to a variety of sensory impressions—just as her definitive conversion, later in the novel, is very largely brought about by the cumulative effect of similar influences throughout her residence in Rome. For this reason the passage is very much a 'set-piece', carefully written with an eye to impressionistic effect, in an attempt to re-create for the reader by linguistic means the visual and other sensory impressions which we are to believe work so powerfully on Madame Gervaisais. The whole episode is treated at some considerable length: the extract chosen for commentary contains the last five of the eight paragraphs devoted to it. The first three of these present Madame Gervaisais's initial impressions of the dark interior of the church, with the lamps and candles at the shrine lighting up the gold and precious stones of the statue behind the altar; the second paragraph is particularly interesting for a striking, if somewhat unsubtle, attempt to convey the cumulative effect of rich visual impressions:

Et madame Gervaisais finit par distinguer une belle Vierge du Sansovino, sa belle main longue et ses doigts en fuseau avançant de ce corps enfumé, incertain et douteux, assombri par le caparaçonnement des joyaux, les rangs de perles des colliers, l'écrasante couronne d'un dôme d'or, les diamants des oreilles, le gorgerin de pierreries de la poitrine, les bracelets d'or des poignets, le barbare resplendissement d'une impératrice cuirassée d'orfévrerie byzantine, auquel s'ajoutait encore l'éblouissement du petit Jésus que sa mère portait sur elle, couronné d'or, bardé d'or, le bras enroulé d'une cape de chapelets d'or, de médaillons d'or, de chaînes d'or, le ventre sanglé d'or, une jambe dans un jambard d'émeraudes...

The first paragraph of the passage under consideration carries on the description from an explicitly visual point of view (*elle se mit à regarder...*), and the second continues to record what we may take to be a succession of visual impressions apprehended by Madame Gervaisais herself, though this is no longer explicitly stated. In the third paragraph, a greater variety of sensory impressions is introduced (*l'affadissante odeur...*, *la respiration pressée ...*, *un marmottage de foi...*), and in addition the effect of all these influences on a susceptible nervous system (*sous les coups qui brisent la raison*) is suggested by means of analytical comment (*Émouvant et troublant sanctuaire... Lieu de vertige et de mystère...*). In the last two paragraphs, the perspective of the narrative has clearly changed. Up to this point the reader has been led to see the scene through the eyes of Madame Gervaisais, and to share her impressions (*...madame Gervaisais vit... Et madame Gervaisais finit par distinguer... Il y avait... des images qui... étonnèrent l'œil de madame Gervaisais* in the paragraphs preceding this passage, and in the passage under consideration *elle se mit à regarder...*, all combine to produce this effect); but in the paragraph beginning at line 44 the heroine herself, just as much as *les deux Romaines*, is presented objectively with the conventional detachment of the third-person narrative.

This change in perspective is matched by a very marked difference in style between the two sections of the passage. Whereas the last two paragraphs adopt an unadorned, economical style, and the narrative is presented simply, with little use of distinctive features of either vocabulary or syntax, the earlier part of the extract, and in particular the first two paragraphs, is written in a highly idiosyncratic manner—that impressionistic style to which Edmond de Goncourt himself gave the label 'écriture artiste'.[1]

The adverb *machinalement* (l. 1) has some importance in providing a justification for the impressionistic treatment of this description: we have already been told, when Madame Gervaisais is on her way to the church, that 'elle allait, sans se rendre compte de rien, obéissant à un mouvement mécanique qui la poussait en avant', and the reference back to this earlier sentence, and the repetition (*mécanique/machinalement*) of the idea contained in it, reminds us that the heroine is in a purely passive state of recep-

---

[1] In the Preface to *Les Frères Zemganno* (1879). For a critical analysis of the Goncourts' style, see P. Sabatier, *L'Esthétique des Goncourt* (Paris, 1920), especially pp. 400–26; and S. Ullmann, *Style in the French Novel* (Cambridge, 1957), especially ch. iii, 'New Patterns of Sentence-Structure in the Goncourts'.

tivity to the impressions provided by her senses, and that these are random impressions, neither provoked by her conscious curiosity, nor classified and interpreted by her intelligence. Thus, what she apprehends as she looks around her is not 'des femmes agenouillées ..., des paysans vautrés..., des gens prosternés...', but the de-personalized *agenouillements..., vautrements..., prosternement...*; this use of the verbal substantive in *-ment*, so frequent in certain types of passage that it becomes a real affectation on the Goncourts' part, is 'impressionistic' in the sense that, by comparison with the more conventional 'des femmes agenouillées', *des agenouillements de femmes...* may be said to reproduce the immediacy of the im-pression, or the sequence of successive impressions as apprehended by the mind (and more especially the mind acting 'mechanically' under the effect of shock, fatigue, or illness). Thus, in the dark interior of the church, the first impression received by Madame Gervaisais is the vague one of *des agenouillements*, to which are added, with gradually increasing precision, ...*de femmes* and ...*leur châle sur la tête*. Again, *pliées comme un paquet* represents the immediate visual impression, while *se cognaient le front contre le bois d'un banc* provides its interpretation. In the following lines, by a similar process, *des vautrements* assumes priority over *paysans*; while the epithet in *leurs yeux sauvages*, which might at first sight be accounted for in rational terms, as intensifying the derogatory implications of *paysans*, is perhaps rather to be taken as denoting a further sensory impression. The eyes appear *sauvages* because what registers at first is their glinting in the darkness, only sub-sequently identified as due to the *réverbération des cierges* (and we should note again that the vague abstraction of *réverbération* precedes the precision of *des cierges*); syntactically, moreover, *leurs yeux sauvages* is equated, by the parallel construction of the clauses, with another primarily *visual* impression in *l'énorme cloutis* (*des semelles de leurs souliers*).

The series of objects of the main verbal phrase continues with another impressionistic abstraction in *un prosternement général*— different from the preceding ones, however, in that there is no accompanying noun in the possessive case; on the analogy of *des agenouillements de femmes... qui... se cognaient...* or of *des vautre-ments de paysans enfonçant...*, one might expect 'un prosternement... de gens se disputant les dalles', but this time it is the abstract noun itself which becomes the subject of the gerundive *disputant*, and the elliptical construction is even more striking. Moreover, what has been said about the 'sequence of impressions' rendered by the preceding phrases applies even more forcefully here, for *un prosternement général* is left unqualified until the next phrase, when *des gens* is introduced, exactly as if it were in apposition to the missing possessive.

The Goncourts' predilection for this nominal construction (verbal substantive plus possessive) in place of the conventional verbal construction of relative clause or participial phrase (of the type 'des paysans qui se vautraient' or 'les semelles cloutées') can also be termed 'impressionist' in a second sense, which is here illustrated most clearly in *la réverbération des cierges*. Such a stylistic device, in that it gives priority to the vague abstraction of *réverbération* over the concrete precision of *cierges*, corresponds closely to the technique of the Impressionist painter, for in both cases a blurred impression of colour, or brightness, is preferred to the photographically precise representation of the object which is the source of that impression. Similarly, in the case of the last example analysed, the vague impersonality of *un prosternement général* could be said to be the counterpart, in literary terms, of the Impressionist painter's approach: in both cases, 'the artist is primarily interested in catching a fleeting movement or characteristic posture, and is only incidentally concerned with the individuals whom he happens to use as his models'.[2]

This impressionist approach to their subject-matter on the part of the authors, and the syntactical devices which result from it, are not the only features which give an individual stamp to the passage —nor is the impressionist approach consistently maintained throughout the piece. In the first place, we should note the striking phrase *dans l'obscurité pieuse*, whose concentration expresses the idea so much more successfully than if it were set out in full in the normal manner of prose description—but we should also observe that such concision is inevitably the product of conscious reflection, and contrasts rather sharply with the effect of spontaneous impression created by the paragraph as a whole. Again, the trio of *de toutes les espèces, de toutes les classes, de toutes les figures* suggests the rhetorical phrasing of the traditional, analytical prose style which the Goncourts, no less than Verlaine and the Symbolist poets, professed to be reacting against—and in any case this too indicates

[2] Cf. S. Ullmann, op. cit., p. 137.

an approach at variance with the dominant one in this first paragraph: analytical reflection instead of the 'mechanical' registering of sensory impressions. But it is the following lines which seem to conflict most markedly with what seems to be the primary intention of this passage in general: the description of the *prêtres à fin profil*, *le menton appuyé sur leurs mains jointes et leurs doigts noués*... creates an effective little vignette, but one whose clarity and precision are in sharp contrast to the impressionism of lines 1–8; and this effect is only heightened by the comparison drawn from the plastic arts, for the *donataires au bas d'un vitrail* evoke an image much too clear and concrete to be assimilated into a coherent, impressionist whole (just as, from another point of view, *le mouvement des donataires*... is very different in its effect from the grammatically similar phrases examined above: the banality of the verbal substantive *mouvement* makes this element of the phrase completely subordinate to what follows, and does not detract from the clarity or the immediacy of ...*des donataires au bas d'un vitrail*).

The remainder of the paragraph (ll. 11–16) contains two further striking examples of nominal construction, which restore the impressionist character of the opening phrases. The density and concision of *des prières rampantes de jupes de soie et de jupes d'indienne côte à côte*[3] can be measured if one considers what would be the normal way of expressing the idea it conveys: 'des femmes habillées de jupes de soie et de jupes d'indienne qui rampaient comme elles priaient côte à côte'; the depersonalization of the image is carried so far here that the word 'femmes' has been completely suppressed: it is the *jupes de soie et... d'indienne* to which the *prières rampantes* are attributed, and which, in the equally impressive phrase which follows, [*couchent*] *leurs génuflexions par terre*. Finally, the two parallel phrases *des prières de désespoir...*, *des prières enragées...*, even though the abstract noun is still personified (*des prières... qui viennent de quitter...*), reintroduce a note of analytical comment: the present tenses of the verbs *viennent...*, *veulent...*, *se cramponnent...* (the only finite verbs the passage has contained since *flambait* of l. 6) may be intended to make the scene more vivid, but the reader is more likely to take them as making generic statements about *kinds* of prayer—a generalizing comment on the

---

[3] *Indienne*: 'toile de coton peinte ou imprimée, que l'on a fabriquée primitivement dans l'Inde, puis à Rouen' (*Larousse*)—*cheap* skirts, therefore, compared with the more expensive ones made of silk.

authors' part rather than the character's reaction to her surroundings.

Whereas nominal constructions have characterized the first paragraph, the second opposes two sentences of contrasting character. In the first of these verbs predominate, creating the desired effect of incessant, rapid motion (*devenait...*, *prenait...*, *tombait...*, *se relevait*, *marchait...*, *déposait...*, *posait...*, *rebaisait...*, *trempait...*, *touchait...*) as the conventional practices of the worshippers are recorded as a series of ritual gestures. The almost mechanical effect is heightened by the repetitions and linking echoes which bind the series together: *entrer/à peine entré*; *eau bénite/bénitier*; *bénitier noir/ange blanc*; *tombait/se relevait*; *déposait/posait*; *baiser/rebaisait*. The second, in contrast with this, is a sentence without a main verb, in which the dominance of the noun is restored. Both sentences illustrate a characteristic tendency of the Goncourts' prose: the tendency towards a paratactic sentence-structure, suppressing where possible the conventional grammatical articulation of more traditional prose style. In the first case, the series of verbs governed by the relative (*un venant du dehors qui...*) are strung together loosely in parallel; and the absence of even the conjunction 'et' in its normal place before the last verb of the series helps to emphasize the 'dynamic' use of the same conjunction at the beginning of the next sentence.[4] The forceful ellipsis *Et rien que cela, et toujours...* (scil. 'On ne voyait rien que cela, et on le voyait toujours') 'pulls together', as it were, the string of verbs, and rounds off this graphic picture of human activity, against a background which is again represented as a series of depersonalized impressions (with the four abstract nouns *adorations, contemplations, attitudes, immobilités*); *adorations balbutiantes* is a particularly bold, and successful, condensation of the type analysed with reference to *prières rampantes* above. In the two following instances the combination of noun and epithet is less surprising, though the grammatical context indicates clearly enough the originality of the notion; while in the case of the fourth pair, it is the unusual use of *immobilités* in the plural (apparently as a graphic alternative for 'personnes immobiles', until we come to *...coupées de signes de croix*) that is striking, rather than the association of noun and epithet. Finally, the paragraph concludes with yet another instance of this stylistic

---

[4] Cf. a similar use of the conjunction in the Flaubert passage (p. 152) and comment (p. 160).

device, though the substitution of *l'idolâtrie des bouches* for 'les bouches (des personnes) qui l'idolâtrent' seems little more than *précieux* affectation—especially, perhaps, if taken in conjunction with the preceding phrase, here of course meant literally, though it is often used in a figurative sense ('adorer le joli pied d'une femme'). There is, too, something perhaps not wholly satisfactory in the juxtaposition of the abstract *idolâtrie* with the very concrete *décoller*.

The following paragraph constitutes a digression: it is devoted neither to narrative nor to description, but to reflective comment; though this is more clearly the case in the second sentence than in the first. Neither sentence contains a main verb: in both cases there is ellipsis of a hypothetical main clause with the verb *être* ('C'est un émouvant... sanctuaire que...'; 'C'est un lieu de vertige...'). In the first sentence, however, it is really only the first two of the series of nouns qualifying *sanctuaire* (*ce coin*, *cette chapelle*) that can be said to be congruous with the notion of 'sanctuary'; when the series continues with *l'apparence...*, *l'affadissante odeur...*, *ce qui reste dans l'air...*, the sentence degenerates into an anacoluthon from the logical, if not from the grammatical point of view, and what is most striking about this sentence is not the analytical comment but a new series of sensory impressions contained in it. New stylistic devices, reinforcing the characteristic dominance of the noun, include the oxymoron *d'ombre ardente* (whose effect is, however, perhaps diluted by the almost explanatory repetition of the idea in the following phrase *de nuit et d'or*) and the highly original phrase *ce grand marbre ranci*. This is interesting not only for the imaginative use of *ranci* quite out of its normal context, but also because, whereas *grand* suggests that *marbre* is here to be taken in its secondary sense of '(marble) monument', *ranci* equally strongly implies the primary sense, the substance 'marble': the two senses are not incompatible but rather complementary, and the phrase illustrates the element of poetic ambivalence sometimes to be seen in the Goncourts' handling of vocabulary.

The analytical comment proceeds from visual (*l'apparence...*) to olfactory (*l'affadissante odeur...*), and thence to auditory impressions, or the memory of them (*ce qui reste dans l'air d'une éternité de prières*); visual impressions are brought in again (*les souvenirs des murs*—i.e. the votive tablets, etc., *les images parlantes...*), to be followed by auditory (*ce silence chargé d'élans étouffés, la respiration...*, *un marmottage de foi*...), before the whole is summed up in a vaguer, more suggestive appeal to sensory experience in general (*ce qu'on sent flotter partout*...). This sentence thus adumbrates what is to develop into the central theme of the novel: the insidious effect of the accumulation of such sensory impressions on a hypersensitive temperament. What renders the chapel of Sant'Agostino an *émouvant et tremblant sanctuaire* is that the atmosphere is impregnated with *toutes les douleurs des entrailles de la femme*: a curiously conventional expression, *entrailles* being a stylized term evoking, euphemistically, the womb, and in a more general figurative sense, the seat of the emotions.

The second sentence is more openly analytical: it is almost rhetorical in its style, and contains none of the pictorial impressionism in which the passage has been so rich up to this point. This is replaced by oratorical devices such as the ternary phrasing of *sur un coin de terre, dans un temple, dans une église* or of *à la religion d'une statue, à une pierre, à quelque chose qui*..., or the antithesis between *monde* and *Ciel*; and by a vocabulary whose conventional abstraction echoes the clichés of eighteenth-century anti-religious pamphlets; though the link with the preceding sentence is maintained with *vertige*, here very precise in its meaning.

The change to a much simpler narrative style at the beginning of the penultimate paragraph has already been discussed. Characteristic features of sentence-structure are, however, still apparent: the series of verbs (*l'autre mère marcha*..., *se jeta*..., *mit*..., *colla*...) without connecting link, which gives the effect, as in paragraph 2, of rapid, automatic action; and the similar parataxis of the closing sentence. There are also two further examples of the Goncourts' partiality for the noun construction, but this time it is the adjective, not the verb, which is replaced by the noun: 'un petit enfant fiévreux' becomes *un petit fiévreux d'enfant*, and 'à l'or froid' becomes *au froid de l'or*. Otherwise, there is a marked contrast in style, and the only links with what has gone before are provided by significant items of vocabulary such as *mère... le pied de la Vierge... baiser... les chaises et les gens... l'autre mère... le pied baisé... sa bouche... colla son front... une prière;* and by the adjectival phrase *mue comme par un ressort*, given prominence at the head of the sentence, and which takes up the idea of *machinalement* (l. 1). Thus the crucial action—Madame Gervaisais's involuntary imitation of the other worshippers—is presented with the utmost economy: the authors have characteristically chosen to devote themselves to a painstaking, detailed evocation, using all the stylistic resources of their 'écriture artiste', of the state of mind preceding and justifying the action.

The final brief sentence closes the chapter on a 'minor cadence': the progressive shortening of the clauses (here one of nine syllables, followed by one of seven, then by one of five) creates an effect of incompleteness, even of suspense, throwing the reader's attention forward to what follows. And indeed, the next chapter opens: 'Deux jours après le docteur disait...' The crisis is over, and the child is on the way to recovery.

A passage such as this provides an excellent illustration of some of the ways in which the Goncourt brothers hoped to revitalize French narrative prose style. Here, the impressionistic writing is unusually well suited to the subject-matter: the impressionable heroine's reaction to her immediate environment is vividly conveyed by the syntax and figures of speech. While some of these devices may elsewhere be overdone, to the extent of becoming mere stylistic affectation, this passage is a highly successful example of the Goncourts' truly original manner.

20 Mallarmé

Victorieusement fui le suicide beau
Tison de gloire, sang par écume, or, tempête!
Ô rire si là-bas une pourpre s'apprête
A ne tendre royal que mon absent tombeau.

5   Quoi! de tout cet éclat pas même le lambeau
S'attarde, il est minuit, à l'ombre qui nous fête
Excepté qu'un trésor présomptueux de tête
Verse son caressé nonchaloir sans flambeau,

La tienne si toujours le délice! la tienne
10   Oui seule qui du ciel évanoui retienne
Un peu de puéril triomphe en t'en coiffant

Avec clarté quand sur les coussins tu la poses
Comme un casque guerrier d'impératrice enfant
Dont pour te figurer il tomberait des roses.

MALLARMÉ, *Vers et prose*
Date of first publication (in definitive
    form): 1893[1]
In *Œuvres complètes*, ed.
H. Mondor and G. Jean-Aubry
    (Paris: Gallimard, 1945), p. 68

---

[1] The poem was first published, in a version widely divergent from the final text, in Verlaine, *Hommes d'aujourd'hui*, No. 296 (Paris, 1886); cf. Mallarmé, *Œuvres complètes* (1945), p. 1481. Other earlier versions are to be found in *Les Poésies de Stéphane Mallarmé* (Paris, 1887–two variant readings, and minor differences of punctuation), and in *Album de vers et de prose* (Paris, 1887–definitive text except for omission of punctuation in ll. 4 and 8).

THIS poem belongs to the series of dense, hermetic sonnets in Mallarmé's second manner. One of the last great sonneteers, he regarded the sonnet as 'un grand poème en petit': 'Les quatrains et les tercets me semblent des chants entiers, et je passe parfois trois jours à en équilibrer les parties, pour que tout soit harmonieux et s'approche du Beau'. This poem is a regular French sonnet (ABBA ABBA CCD EDE); but the rigid, massive effect produced by Parnassian sonnets with their four distinct blocks is here softened by the continuous melodic line, especially in the last three stanzas. The first stanza has an impressive majesty, and the sestet displays a miraculous purity and serenity; but the second quatrain betrays in lines 5-6 a certain awkwardness. The poem has a kind of pure transparency, and its significance seems to shift subtly when it is viewed in different lights or from different angles. All its facets are equally important and form an indivisible whole. Hence the sparing use of punctuation, for 'les signes qui en sont absents ne serviraient qu'à diviser inutilement le tout'. The conclusion illustrates Mallarmé's conception of the 'chute' of a sonnet—'comme un écho vague et perdu de l'idée principale, une sorte de sonore cadence, de prolongement lumineux, de luxe inutile, une dernière pirouette, une queue de comète'. The poet shows his habitual concern for correct rhyming: all the rhymes are at least *suffisantes*, and two are *riches* (*lambeau-flambeau*, *tienne-retienne*). The poem seems, in fact, to have crystallized around its rhymes, for the drastically revised definitive text takes over from the first version all the words at the rhyme except for 'fête' (*tempête*) and 'poète' (*fête*). There is no metrical novelty here. Mallarmé exploits all the resources of the Alexandrine: some lines scan regularly, but the conventional rhythm of the Alexandrine is at times upset by the boldness of the *coupes*, and the musical flow of the lines often overruns the caesura, the rhyme, even the stanza. Mallarmé's Alexandrine has great flexibility; but he never ventures here beyond the 'vers brisé' of Hugo and the Parnassians. The versification is the least original feature of the poem, and it almost seems as if Mallarmé retained the traditional metre as a counterpoise to his audacious innovations in the realm of language, syntax, and imagery.

The poem begins with a line characteristically Mallarméan in its elliptic mystery. No opening could make a more striking impact than these few words—luminously clear in isolation, yet coming together to form what seems to be a sibylline incantation or cabbalistic formula. Syntactically, the line has to be construed as a kind of ablative absolute: the auxiliary of the verb *fui* ('participe absolu') has been suppressed, and the normal word order ('le beau suicide fui victorieusement') has been reversed so that *le suicide beau* stands at the end of the comma-less line and immediately introduces the four parts of line 2 which are in apposition to it. Metrically, an immense sense of liberation is conveyed by the 'enjambement sur la césure', and the scansion throws the main stress on the two monosyllables, enhancing them in the proximity of the two longer, intrinsically more dramatic words to which they are attached. *Beau* is also accentuated by its unusual inversion (after instead of before the noun). This monosyllabic 'finale vocalique', significantly the only word to be retained from the first version of the line, supplies an intense climax: its full, open vowel sound closes the series of short, sharp assonant *i*'s and forms a kind of counterweight to *Victorieusement*. The verbal transposition results in a pair of striking antitheses with positive and negative terms arranged in chiastic order, but with the positive values placed prominently at

A   B   B   A

the beginning and end of the line: *Victorieusement fui le suicide beau.* Honoured with a capital letter and filling out a whole hemistich, the sumptuous golden adverb *Vict-or-ieusement* rings out like a trumpet blast and sets the dominant mood of triumphant exultation. *Fui* suggests a paradox—a triumphant flight, an escape which snatches victory out of defeat. *Suicide beau* hints at another paradox—a splendidly heroic self-immolation. Taken in conjunction with the following line, *tout cet éclat* in line 5 ('tout ce coucher' in the first version) and *ciel évanoui* in line 10, *suicide beau* seems to be a dramatic periphrasis for a sunset ('désastre' in the first version) which is here assimilated to a glorious death-agony—'Hier, un soleil mort! une gloire dans l'ombre!'[2] Line 1 represents, therefore, the denouement of the 'drame solaire' which Mallarmé regarded as 'le grand et perpétuel sujet de la Mythologie',[3] and the paradoxical antitheses evoke the ambiguity of the sundown—tragedy and triumph, catastrophe and apotheosis. The sun fades away in a blaze of glory; but its *suicide beau* is the prelude to rebirth in a new dawn, and its diurnal cycle (light–darkness–resurgence of light) closely parallels Mallarmé's account of the poetic process: life, 'death' (depersonalization), luminous resurrection of the spiritual con-

---

[2] *Œuvres complètes*, p. 6.   [3] Ibid., p. 1169.

sciousness leading to the poetic reconstitution of the universe under the sign of Beauty. There exists for Mallarmé an analogy between himself and the sun, between the poetic act and the 'acte solaire', between 'la gloire ardente du métier' and 'les feux du pur soleil mortel'.[4] 'Il y a aise, et maturité,' he observes, 'à demander un soleil, même couchant, sur les causes d'une vocation.'[5] The sun probably symbolizes 'l'Idéal' or 'le Rêve', and the evening struggle of light and darkness ('désolé combat' in the first version) seems to suggest the mental agony, the desperate battle involved in creating 'l'Art pur'.

The emblematic sunset, a pure abstraction in line 1, is elaborated in the fiery, stormy splendour of line 2, another line of extraordinary incantatory and suggestive power. The exclamation-mark which intervenes in mid-sentence indicates the raised tone of voice, the emotional reaction of the poet to this colourful, dramatic spectacle of fire and gold, blood and foam.

The verbless line is a remarkable example of Mallarmé's nominal style, for apart from the two prepositions it consists of nothing but nouns, six nouns without articles or epithets. Even where an adjective ('tison glorieux') might have been used an abstract noun complement (*tison de gloire*) is preferred—no doubt because of its poetic sonority and its greater plenitude of meaning. All six nouns are stressed with heavy insistence, and the Alexandrine acquires thereby a massive weight. The main effect is 'de matérialiser, d'alourdir, de rendre épaisses comme des couleurs déposées au couteau, les nuées chaudes, les barres de feu sur un ciel de soir'.[6] The super-abundance of *coupes* dislocates the normal rhythm of the Alexandrine; but this dislocation is highly appropriate here to the furious, chaotic disorder of the sunset scene. Musically, the line abounds in sounds of a rich, deep resonance—[ɔ̃], [waːr], [ɑ̃], [ym], [ɔːr], [ɛːt]—and the two 'finales consonantiques' with their unelided mute *e* (*gloire*, *tempête*) reverberate in a kind of sonorous 'prolongement' which lends an infinite expansiveness to the seemingly endless line.

The sunset is not explicitly 'named', but rather evoked by a series of four metaphors or 'correspondances' conveying sharp, vivid sensations and impressions. The series stretches out in an open-ended enumeration, for there is no 'et' before *tempête* to close the

---

[4] *Œuvres complètes*, p. 54.   [5] Ibid., p. 646.

[6] A. Thibaudet, *Mallarmé* (Paris, 1926), p. 254.

list. The imagery once again expresses the ambiguity of the sunset:

    A   B   A   B

Tison de gloire, sang par écume, or, tempête!, and both A and B groups are organized 'par masses décroissantes' which suggest a gradual shrinking or fading away.

Tison de gloire: the sun is likened to a glowing firebrand. This somewhat Promethean image may evoke the metaphysical ambition of Mallarmé's poetry or perhaps the torch of immortal glory kindled by the afterglow of the Work. Echoing the idea of victory, *gloire* sounds like another triumphant fanfare—'le cri des Gloires'.[7]

Sang par écume picks up again the ideas of flight and suicide. *Par* is used here in the sense of 'dans' or 'à travers': the blood-red sun is sinking through a mass of foaming white clouds before vanishing from sight. Mallarmé claims that there is an etymological link between 'TO GLOW, *briller*, et BLOOD, le *sang*';[8] he also likens clouds to 'l'écume De l'Océan céleste';[9] finally, a passage of *Les Dieux antiques* describes 'la *Tragédie de la Nature*, — la bataille du Soleil avec les nuages qui se rassemblent autour de lui comme de mortels ennemis, à son coucher', and associates the sunset battle with an image of blood—'des ruisseaux de sang qui jaillissent du corps du mythe'.[10] Foam, however, is also a Mallarméan symbol of pure poetry—'Rien, cette écume, vierge vers...',[11] while *sang* might well represent likewise the bleeding of the poet-martyr— 'Und für sein denkbild blutend: MALLARMÉ'.[12]

The triumphant sound of the detached monosyllable *or* rings out in solitary power. It is the heart of the sunset glory, the luminous orb which glows like an incandescent disk of rich, golden metal. It is like the pure essence of the sun and, as such, an appropriate symbol of 'l'Art pur' which Mallarmé conceives as a sort of transmutation of words into alchemist's gold.

Tempête! forms a sonorous, dramatic climax of the line. The word has a tragic resonance suggestive of outward and inner catastrophe. It evokes sombre, stormy clouds churning around the setting sun; but it also recalls the storm in *Un Coup de dés*, the stubborn resistance of the world to Art ('Du sol et de la nue hostiles...'),[13] the

---

[7] *Œuvres complètes*, p. 75.   [8] Ibid., p. 919.

[9] H. Mondor, *Mallarmé lycéen* (Paris, 1954), p. 176.

[10] *Œuvres complètes*, p. 1216.

[11] Ibid., p. 27.

[12] Stefan George, 'Franken', *Der Siebente Ring* (Berlin, 1907), p. 18.

[13] *Œuvres complètes*, p. 70.

brainstorm caused by 'l'Impuissance' ('l'irascible vent des mots qu'il n'a pas dits').[14]

There is a pause after line 2; then the stanza concludes with a pair of lines linked by enjambment. There is a sense of great distance as if there had been a vast expansion of space, and *là-bas* ('sur l'horizon' in the MS. Lebey)[15] suggests a lofty, Olympian vantage-point. The triumphant *Ô rire* again illustrates Mallarmé's nominal style—a noun (='quelle plaisanterie') substituted for a main verb (='je ris'). *Absent* is another transposed epithet (before instead of after the noun), and *royal* is either an adjective separated from its noun (*tombeau*) or an adjective employed in an adverbial sense. The unusual position or usage throws both words into relief. *Une pourpre* probably refers to the band of purple clouds which finally form around the setting sun—'Les nuages violets couleur du soir semblent le consoler dans l'agonie de sa disparition.'[16] The clouds spread over the horizon and resemble a purple pall appropriately draping a royal sarcophagus. Death and its pomps are here amplified to a cosmic scale: the whole universe seems to be in mourning for the lord of light.

Mon (l. 4) indicates for the first time that the stanza is written in direct speech; but the problem then arises: who is the speaker? It could be the sun which is here personified and is speaking in the first person. His suicide is merely an illusion, for the Phoenix-Sun[17] will rise again; and he laughs at the royal obsequies which are being celebrated over his non-existent or empty (*absent*) tomb. On the other hand, Mallarmé could be identifying himself here with the sun, and his poetic destiny with the 'drame solaire'. The Poet is a 'prince intellectuel', and in an imaginary 'Fête du Poète' Mallarmé evokes him enthroned 'dans l'empyrée' and 'ceint de la pourpre que lui a le droit de porter'.[18] The royal tomb would therefore be as appropriate to the disciple of Apollo as to the sun. Then again, just as the sun 'dies' only to be reborn, so too the Poet 'dies' only to find luminous resurrection in the radiance of his poetry, and though as a 'vaine forme de la matière' he will literally die he will live on in the Work. As Mallarmé told J. Huret, 'le cas d'un poète, c'est le cas d'un homme qui s'isole pour sculpter son propre tombeau.' His physical remains will be consigned to the 'sépulcre solide où gît tout ce qui nuit, Et l'avare silence et la massive nuit',[19] but his

---

[14] *Œuvres complètes*, p. 54. [15] Ibid., p. 1481. [16] Ibid., p. 1216.
[17] Ibid., p. 68. [18] Ibid., p. 521. [19] Ibid., p. 55.

real tomb, the tomb of the Poet, will be the Work. If the tomb is here described as *absent* the epithet could be taken as signifying the pure notion of the Work, the Work conceived as a still unrealized possibility, and if Mallarmé laughs here at the funeral rites on the horizon it could mean that if he succeeds in creating the poem he will have conquered the tomb ('vaincre le tombeau' in the first version) and transcended death—'le seuil où des torches consument, dans une haute garde, tous rêves antérieurs à leur éclat répercutant en pourpre dans la nue l'universel sacre de l'intrus royal qui n'aura eu qu'à venir'.[20]

When the sun disappears into the night in a Mallarméan poem the succession often passes to the poet himself:

> Quand l'ombre menaça de la fatale loi
> Tel vieux Rêve, désir et mal de mes vertèbres,
> Affligé de périr sous les plafonds funèbres
> Il a ployé son aile indubitable en moi.[21]

It is as if the sun had to be analogically and ideally re-created in the rest of the poem. Mallarmé rises magnificently to his task here.

The first quatrain ends with a full stop rather than the exclamation-mark which might have been logically expected. Mallarmé perhaps considered that a full stop was emphatic enough, for the second sentence which begins in line 5 runs on for no less than ten lines. The speaker of the first four lines is strangely ambiguous; but from there on there is no doubt about the angle of vision. Everything is envisaged from the personal standpoint of the poet himself. The long second sentence hinges on the conjunction *Excepté que* and consists of a question at midnight answered by a glowing vision which dominates the second half of the poem. Mallarmé speaks somewhere of the 'terrible difficulté de combiner, dans une juste harmonie, l'élément dramatique hostile à la poésie pure et subjective, avec la sérénité et le calme de lignes nécessaires à la Beauté'. Here the sunset drama is linked with the luminous vision of calm, serene Beauty by a short transitional scene of midnight darkness, and the two main sections are harmonized by the series of 'correspondances' arising from the superimposition of the image of the golden head of hair upon that of the sunset glory.

In lines 5–6 total darkness has descended, and the scene has shifted from the horizon to a small, enclosed place. It seems to be one of

---

[20] *Œuvres complètes*, p. 289.   [21] Ibid., p. 67.

those vague, shadowy Mallarméan rooms—a 'milieu nul ou à peu près'.[22] These closed, nocturnal rooms are usually an empty space forming a 'Décor de l'absence'[23] and symbolizing, as it were, a psychological blank, a sort of microcosm of the universal Void. Their inhabitants seem to have become rarefied and to have lost their contours, and there is an atmosphere of doubt, questioning, expectation. Here the poet is present, and he is not alone. He has a companion with him as in 'Prose'—'Nous fûmes deux, je le maintiens...' The poem belongs to the Méry Laurent cycle, and with the mysterious *nous* of line 6 she makes a discreet entrance. The poet seems to be beside his mistress, and the room is perhaps a boudoir. Certainly Mallarmé's famous lamp, symbol of his nocturnal labours, is conspicuous by its absence; but the anguish usually attendant upon 'la nuit sans espérance' is here offset and counter-pointed by the 'fête amoureuse'. Has there been some desertion of 'le Rêve' for life, of Art for love, of Glory for happiness in obscurity? The hesitation and embarrassment of the contorted syntax suggests that the poet is torn between two options; there is an unresolved ambiguity of attitude which contrasts with Mallarmé's well-known declaration: 'Il n'y a que la Beauté et elle n'a qu'une expression parfaite — la Poésie. Tout le reste est mensonge— excepté pour ceux qui vivent du corps, l'amour... Pour moi, la Poésie me tient lieu de l'amour parce qu'elle est éprise d'elle-même, et que sa volupté d'elle retombe délicieusement en mon âme.' Certainly there is a strong contrast in mood between the exultant irony of lines 1–4 and the gravity of lines 5–6 which is reflected in the full, dark vowel sounds. Paradoxically *il est minuit* has a series of sharp, bright *i* sounds which seem positively to scintillate in the surrounding dark-ness.

The interjection *Quoi!* expresses astonishment tinged with dis-appointment and regret at the glorious vision faded. It introduces an indignant question not unlike that in 'Toast funèbre'—'Est-il de ce destin rien qui demeure, non?' *Tout cet éclat* replaces 'tout ce coucher' (the first version), and the substitution of this more vivid, but also more vague and allusive term seems to betray an intention to extend its meaning beyond that of the sunset splendour; *éclat*, thrown into relief at the hemistich by the inversion, contrasts with *lambeau* at the rhyme. *Lambeau* is used elsewhere by Mallarmé in a sunset image—'les lambeaux de la pourpre usée des couchants';[24]

[22] *Œuvres complètes*, p. 319.　　　[23] Ibid., p. 1483.　　　[24] Ibid., p. 269.

but here the word (qualified as 'cher lambeau' in the first version) seems to refer to a subjective as well as to an objective reality—the 'fragment' of the projected Work (Mallarmé differentiates by this term his actual poems from the unrealizable *Grand Œuvre*). *Lambeau* in this sense corresponds to 'relique' in 'Don du Poème', and *pas même le lambeau* is therefore an image of absence—the absence of the poem. The poem has not been created, and there is nothing left to show for Mallarmé's efforts. *S'attarde* is more gravely resonant than 'Ne reste' (first version); but the introduction of this longer verb forced Mallarmé to suppress the 'ne' (a characteristic Mallarméan ellipsis). *Il est minuit*, inserted right in the middle of line 6 between two strong *coupes*, is a parenthesis which resembles a whispered confidence or a meaningful reminder. It is the middle of the night; yet its bright vowels evoke not darkness, but light. It is the 'partage de minuit'—the half-way point between sunset and sunrise, between death and rebirth, the harbinger of luminous resurrection. Even *l'ombre* becomes a festive shade; for its opaque meaning and sound are mitigated by *fête*, a word paradoxically more appropriate to light than to shadow: 'La fête, c'est toujours chez Mallarmé le moment où s'allume une flamme, spirituelle ou amoureuse.'[25] *A l'ombre qui nous fête* seems, then, to be a significant variant, replacing the weak padding of the first version ('dans la main du poète'). Like the dark clouds around the setting sun the darkness of the room envelops a new radiance. There is no comma, as might have been expected, at the end of line 6, and there is consequently a direct introduction to the 'fête lumineuse' which follows.

From the second hemistich of line 6 to the end of the stanza the 'poésie sonore' takes on a new character. There is a sprinkling of consonants like [ʃ], *f* and *v* together with languid *l*'s and caressing, silky *s*'s which combine to suggest an almost tactile sensation of soft, voluptuous surrender. In line 7 the assonance in *é* is strengthened by *présomptueux* which replaces 'trop folâtre' in the first version; but the most striking feature of the line is the marked alliteration in *t* which prepares and emphasizes the final word *tête*. The consonant *t*, for Mallarmé, 'représente, entre toutes, l'arrêt', and he attributes to it a 'signification fondamentale de fixité et de stationnement'.[26] It is as if the *t*'s of *trésor présomptueux de tête* were already announcing the solid, massive 'casque d'or' of the final image. *Trésor*,

[25] J.-P. Richard, *L'Univers imaginaire de Mallarmé* (Paris, 1961), p. 183.
[26] *Œuvres complètes*, p. 953.

placed in the privileged position at the hemistich, has a rich, splendid sonority enhanced by the *-somptueux* element of the following epithet. There is 'enjambement sur la césure' in lines 7–8: in each line a noun and its epithet straddle the hemistich, but their order is exactly reversed in chiastic pattern—

$$\begin{matrix} \text{A} & \text{B} \\ \textit{trésor présomptueux,} \\ \text{B} & \text{A} \\ \textit{caressé nonchaloir.} \end{matrix}$$

There is also 'enjambement sur la rime', and the expressive *rejet* (*Verse*) imparts an appropriate impetus to the continuous flow of the lines which seems to reinforce the image of the glowing radiance streaming from the woman's golden hair.

Line 7 opens the series of subordinate clauses which make up the second half of the sentence and which, as often in Mallarmé, carry the essential meaning. As if in a casual afterthought the conjunction *Excepté que* introduces a qualifying clause containing a significant reservation. From here on the sonnet veers off in a new, unexpected direction, reproducing the dialectical movement of *Un Coup de dés*: 'RIEN... EXCEPTÉ... PEUT-ÊTRE... UNE CONSTEL-LATION.'[27] Of all the splendour nothing is left except for *un trésor présomptueux de tête* which emerges out of the shadow and hovers before the eyes of the 'solitaire ébloui de sa foi'.[28] Like one torch igniting another, the sun seems to have passed on its light to the hair which glows mysteriously in the darkness. A sun of the night has taken over from the sun of the day. The *trés-or* reflects the golden core of the poetic sun (*or*) and seems likewise to symbolize pure Beauty. It is as if the poem coming into radiant existence were effecting a triumphant reconciliation of Art and Love. The explosion of light seems to hint at a creative rebirth like the 'Résurrection' described in Mallarmé's letter of 31 December 1865: 'L'impuissance est vaincue et mon âme se meut avec liberté.' There is a sense of release, and from now on the smooth, easy flow of the verse confirms the impression of a poetic breakthrough.

Trésor de tête is a poetic conceit which illustrates the manner of 'Mallarmé le précieux' and supplies another example of his nominal style (noun for adjective). It possesses two distinct, but simultaneous meanings: (1) 'tête précieuse', (2) a rich splendour of golden hair (cf. 'tête d'or'). In the last sense it recalls the 'extase d'or, je ne sais quoi! par elle nommé sa chevelure'.[29] *Trésor* links the two images of the sunset and the hair, for it is a vague, general word

27 *Œuvres complètes*, pp. 474–7.   28 Ibid., p. 67.   29 Ibid., p. 269.

applied by Mallarmé to both alike (cf. 'une liquéfaction de trésor rampe, rutile à l'horizon').[30] The sunset is sometimes likened to hair spread across the sky; but here the hair image is superimposed upon that of the sunset: the woman's golden glory lends her a sun-like radiance. The image resembles that applied to Méry Laurent in 'O si chère de loin'—'très grand trésor et tête si petite' (cf. *puéril, enfant* and the variant of the MS. Lebey: 'La tienne, si toujours petite!'). But golden hair is an obsessional theme in Mallarmé, and its references transcend its particular possessor: 'La blondeur, c'est l'or, la lumière, la richesse, le rêve, le nimbe.'[31] Material, yet not fleshly, the hair seems to symbolize pure, disembodied Beauty, and its golden colour gives it a cold, metallic lustre which recalls 'Hérodiade aux cheveux froids comme l'or'—'Je veux que mes cheveux qui ne sont pas des fleurs... Mais de l'or... Observent la froideur stérile du métal.' This impression is reinforced here by the detachment of head and hair from the woman's body, with the part standing for the essence of her whole being (synecdoche). Thibaudet is reminded of some rare, precious 'objet d'art' from an eighteenth-century 'musée galant'; but might it not rather represent a 'fragment' of Beauty which is here manifesting itself in the proud glow of the woman's hair? The epithet *présomptueux* is one of those sonorous, evocative adjectives dear to Mallarmé. It advantageously replaces 'trop folâtre' (first version) and evokes a whole cluster of possible meanings: (1) 'une onde de fiers cheveux';[32] (2) the arrogant pride of its owner; (3) the presumptuous usurpation of the splendour of the poetic sunset; (4) a symbolic prefiguration of the coming dawn (cf. Latin *praesumere, praesumptio,*'to anticipate,' 'anticipation'). The verb *Verse* here means 'diffuses', as is clear from the first version: 'Y verse sa lueur diffuse ...' ('Y' = 'dans la main du poète', a phrase suppressed in the definitive text, though still implied in *caressé*). The hair is giving off a soft, gentle glow without heat. *Nonchaloir* (etymologically *non, chaloir*) suggests the absence of heat. This rare, archaic word was revived by Baudelaire ('La Chevelure') and adopted by the Symbolists. It is one of Mallarmé's few archaisms, and he applies it as here to the hair as well as to the sunset ('un grand nonchaloir chargé de souvenir!'[33]) The hair image is thus once more linked with that of the sun. *Nonchaloir* echoes *gloire*, and *flambeau* recalls

---

[30] *Œuvres complètes*, p. 398. [31] Ibid., p. 251.
[32] Ibid., p. 593. [33] Ibid., p. 33.

tison. Sans flambeau is another image of absence (=‘in the absence of, or without need of, any torch’). Like *trésor* and *nonchaloir* the torch image is applied by Mallarmé to the sunset (‘Torche dans un branle étouffée’)[34] and to flaming hair (‘une joyeuse et tutélaire torche.’)[35] The woman’s hair is itself a *flambeau*, i.e. not a reflection, but the only source of light in the dark room. This *trésor présomptueux de tête* which retains something of the poetic sunset has become Mallarmé’s sole illumination.

The first tercet is separated from the preceding quatrain only by a comma, and the two tercets are linked by strophic enjambment. There is also frequent enjambment (*sur la césure* and *sur la rime*) in lines 9–14, including another example of a pair of nouns and

$$\text{epithets straddling the hemistich in reversed chiastic order: } \overset{A}{ciel}$$
$$\overset{B}{\text{évanoui}}, \overset{B}{\text{puéril}} \overset{A}{\text{triomphe}}.$$

There is likewise a bare minimum of punctuation to impede the flow of the lines—just an exclamation-mark after *délice* which expresses excitement rather than a logical break or pause. From this point the long sentence flows on with no punctuation until the final full stop in line 14; but at the same time there is a gradual slowing down of the rhythm from the initial outburst of joyous delight to the immobility of the final tableau. In the first tercet there is a certain element of repetition: *La tienne* is repeated symmetrically at the beginning and end of line 9, and *tienne* is echoed in *retienne* (cf. *Oui, évanoui*). These echoes of words and sounds are not a simple refrain, but rather form a kind of musical structure with a leitmotif effect. This obsessive recurrence of thematic ideas is accompanied here by an abundance of *i* sounds which surround and enhance the piercing ecstasy of *délice!* At the same time there is a growing clarity of meaning. In lines 10–14 there is confirmation of the ‘relai lumineux’ hypothesis: the woman’s head-dress of light is the only thing to retain something of the sunset glory. This was even more explicit in the first version: ‘Seul gage qui...’, whereas in the final text the reader is left to imagine ‘gage’ for himself. Similarly the identity of Mallarmé’s companion becomes a little clearer: line 9 reveals that it is someone whom he is addressing directly. The warm, affectionate use of the second person singular suggests an intimate relationship, and *si toujours le délice!* recalls those other words addressed to Méry

[34] *Œuvres complètes*, p. 73.   [35] Ibid., p. 53.

Laurent—'si Délicieusement toi, Mary'.[36] Together with *caressé*
this exclamation directly alludes to the emotions aroused in the poet
by the golden hair of his mistress. It is as if he were surrendering
to a gentle, restful mood. Woman here seems no longer to be a
rival of Art, but 'un relai, un havre de grâce'.[37]

La tienne refers back to *tête* or perhaps, more subtly, to the idea
('la chevelure') implied in *un trésor de tête*. It is one of those pronouns which form landmarks in Mallarmé's labyrinthine syntax
and which he often uses in a long, complex sentence to indicate a
pause, a connecting link or a sudden leap forward. *Si toujours le
délice!* replaces 'si toujours frivole!' (first version). The *i* vowel is
more stressed in the sensual word *délice*, and the idea of youthfulness implied by 'frivole' is adequately conveyed by *puéril* and
enfant. The definitive version of the phrase involves once again
verbal transposition and nominal style (a noun used in an adjectival
sense; = 'always so delightful'). The transposition of *toujours*
throws the adverb into greater relief in this piece of Mallarméan
gallantry. *Oui seule*, as the *rejet* of line 9, is very emphatic. The *Oui*
is a strong affirmation, a kind of aesthetic profession of faith
(='je le maintiens'). *Seule* is more ambiguous: it conveys the idea
of precious rarity; but like the *Quoi!* of line 5 it may have a certain
tinge of disappointment. *Ciel évanoui*, thrown into prominence by
the inversion, brings back the haunting, obsessional image of the
literal and metaphorical sunset. *Ciel* is the Mallarméan symbol of
the infinite 'Rêve'—the 'ciel antérieur où fleurit la Beauté!'[38]
Ciel évanoui recalls the 'Le ciel est mort' of 'L'Azur' and is the
supreme image of Absence—the symbol of a meaningless world,
the symbol of the 'Absolu-Néant'. The original version contains a
tragic plural ('soirs évanouis'), as if every evening ended in a similar
disaster; but the MS. Lebey has another variant: 'cieux
évanouis' to which Mallarmé finally returned, though changing the
plural into the singular. His preference for the singular over the
plural is often revealed in his variants, and here in this poem it is
characteristic that of over twenty nouns only two are in the plural.
It is as if the plural expressed the Many, while Mallarmé is concerned
to capture the immutability of the One. *Puéril triomphe* replaces the
'désolé combat' of the first version which evoked the evening struggle

[36] *Œuvres complètes*, p. 61.
[37] E. Bonniot in *Revue de France*, IX (1929), p. 642.
[38] *Œuvres complètes*, p. 33.

of light and darkness. *Triomphe* still recalls the sunset victory; but *un peu de puéril triomphe* suggests some inadequacy in the analogy between the hair and the sun. Is Mallarmé expressing a wry dissatisfaction with the disparity between *tout cet éclat* and this charming, but somewhat frivolous image? Is he still feeling a lingering regret for the radiant 'Rêve' of which this poem is merely the *lambeau*? There may be a hint of this here; but he does not dwell on it. His mood is perhaps that of the letter of 3 May 1868: 'Après tout, des poèmes seulement teintés d'absolu sont déjà beaux, et il y en a si peu.' There may be only a trace of the *ciel évanoui* lingering in the woman's hair; but it is better than nothing. Besides, Love, embodied in the woman, brings a real compensation for any aesthetic disappointment, and her boyish triumph arouses a mood of playful irony in the poet. At this literal level *puéril* sums up the implications of 'folâtre' and 'frivole' in the first version: and *puéril triomphe*, with its faintly androgynous aggressiveness, forms an effective link between *trésor présomptueux* and *casque guerrier d'impératrice enfant*.

From *en t'en coiffant* onwards the rhythm begins to slow down, and the excitement gives way to a growing calm which is reflected in the more regular syntax and which culminates in the relaxed serenity of the final image. The pronoun *la* (l. 12) refers to *tête* or the implied 'chevelure': we see the woman laying her head upon the cushions with a languorous movement which recalls the *nonchaloir* of line 8. The *en* of *t'en coiffant* refers to *triomphe*, the victorious radiance of the sunset. The hair forms a halo or crown of light around the woman's head. The 'Avec grâce' of the first version is replaced by *Avec clarté* which, as the *rejet* of the first tercet, stresses the luminosity of the hair and recalls another association of blond hair and the sunset:

> ...avec du soleil aux cheveux, dans la rue
> Et dans le soir, tu m'es en riant apparue
> Et j'ai cru voir la fée au chapeau de clarté
> Qui jadis sur mes beaux sommeils d'enfant gâté
> Passait...[39]

In lines 13–14 an image of the eternal Hérodiade is superimposed upon that of Méry, for these two lines are taken almost verbatim from the rough drafts of the *Ouverture d'Hérodiade* and are unique

[39] *Œuvres complètes*, p. 30.

in being transferred without modification (apart from the suppression of a comma) from the first to the final version of the sonnet. This unexpected image with its graceful preciosity provides a highly decorative 'chute'. The quasi-Parnassian immobility of the casque is offset by the shower of roses; but there is no precise delineation of the woman's face. The helmet image has a peculiar shell-like vacuity which has to be filled in by the reader's imagination. It is as if, like the sun, the woman had vanished. The creature of flesh and blood seems to have been metamorphosed into a figuration in metal and flowers, into a sumptuous symbol of pure Beauty reigning over the darkness of Mallarmé's Void.

It was Mallarmé's boast that he had struck out the word *comme* from the dictionary; but it is used here to introduce the simile of line 13, and *pour te figurer* is employed as a somewhat cumbersome equivalent to present the rose image of line 14. *Casque guerrier* which again evokes the triumphant glow of the hair synthesizes several previous motifs: *Victorieusement, gloire, sang, or, tempête, trésor présomptueux, triomphe*. It is as if the woman's hair had solidified into a thick mass piled high upon the head and resembling a golden battle helmet. 'Casque d'or' is a term applied to this hair style, and Mallarmé himself speaks of Méry's 'mutin casque blond'.[40] Here too he playfully attributes to the woman a somewhat aggressive, belligerent appearance and attitude. *Impératrice enfant*: this description clearly fits Hérodiade, the young, hieratic princess to whom these lines were first dedicated, far better than Méry Laurent; but be that as it may the glowing hair rules over the darkness like a symbol of 'la beauté reine', and the woman's regal beauty corresponds to the royal tomb of the first stanza. The phrase is another example of nominal style (noun for adjective) and could have two senses: (1) child empress, (2) imperious child. *Enfant* could apply not only to Hérodiade but also to Méry, Mallarmé's 'grande enfant'. The point is that youthfulness, ingenuousness, playfulness, capriciousness are essential ingredients of Mallarmé's female ideal—'la femme-enfant'. At a deeper level *enfant* carries the same aesthetic implications as *puéril*, while in terms of the solar cycle the sequence *présomptueux-puéril-enfant-rose* can be interpreted as the promise of the rosy dawn ahead. *Pour te figurer* seems to mean literally 'pour représenter ta figure', and this etymological meaning is made explicit in a variant of one of the fragments of the *Ouverture*: 'D'où

---

[40] *Œuvres complètes*, p. 116.

pour feindre sa joue il tomberait des roses.' But in the context of the sonnet the flower are perhaps meant to take on a significances which transcends Méry's rosy charms. The Poet, says Mallarmé, 'isole parmi l'heure et le rayon du jour... ces fleurs dont nulle ne se fane'.[41] Flowers are for Mallarmé earthly images of Beauty, and roses are the most beautiful of flowers. Here we have not 'la Rose' of 'Toast funèbre', i.e. 'l'absente de tous bouquets', but simply 'des roses', i.e. poems celebrating the beauty of his stern, but gracious Muse; not the *Grand Œuvre*, but 'des poèmes seulement teintés d'absolu'.

Mallarmé's poems are the debris of his *absent tombeau*, the *lambeaux* of the unrealized masterpiece, imitations and not the Thing itself. He regarded these 'fragments' merely as 'études en vue de mieux', and his dying words—'Ce devait être très beau'— leave an ultimate impression of failure; but the poems expressing this defeat constitute a sort of victory in themselves: they exist. It is true, some of Mallarmé's works are notable mainly for the lapidary splendour of certain isolated lines; but 'Victorieusement fui...' stands out as an almost perfect whole and must be ranked among the finest and most serene of his poems. 'Fleur et bijou' is how Verlaine described it.

[41] *Œuvres complètes*, p. 55.

21 Régnier

Odelette

Un petit roseau m'a suffi
Pour faire frémir l'herbe haute
Et tout le pré
Et les doux saules
5 Et le ruisseau qui chante aussi;
Un petit roseau m'a suffi
A faire chanter la forêt.

Ceux qui passent l'ont entendu
Au fond du soir, en leurs pensées,
10 Dans le silence et dans le vent,
Clair ou perdu,
Proche ou lointain...
Ceux qui passent en leurs pensées
En écoutant, au fond d'eux-mêmes,
15 L'entendront encore et l'entendent
Toujours qui chante.

Il m'a suffi
De ce petit roseau cueilli,
A la fontaine où vint l'Amour
20 Mirer, un jour,
Sa face grave
Et qui pleurait,
Pour faire pleurer ceux qui passent
Et trembler l'herbe et frémir l'eau;
25 Et j'ai, du souffle d'un roseau,
Fait chanter toute la forêt.

HENRI DE RÉGNIER, *Les Jeux rustiques et divins*
Date of first publication: 1897
Éditions du *Mercure de France* (Paris, 1897), pp. 217-18

THE felicitous title of the *recueil* indicates the most obvious feature of this poem—the graceful alliance of conventional pastoral and natural paganism. Its manner is reminiscent of the slender Franco-Hellenistic vein which runs from Ronsard through Chénier to Leconte de Lisle; but this Neo-Classicism expresses itself in supple *vers libres*, and the verbal simplicity is combined with a musical incantation and a vague, evocative reverie of a somewhat Symbolist, but not excessively hermetic, nature. Régnier's style floats, as E. Raynaud remarks, 'comme une écharpe dénouée autour de la pensée', and his meaning is only lightly veiled. It is a poetry half-way between Verlaine's emotional impressionism and Mallarmé's intellectual symbolism—and on the way to the Neo-Classicism of Moréas. Régnier, however, subordinates his own Classical symbolism to the discreet expression of a modern, post-Romantic sensibility which is peculiarly his own. The harmonious blending of Ancient and Modern is the distinctive mark of his composite, yet original, minor talent. Régnier is entirely and uniquely himself in this brief, charming *odelette* in which he presents a subtle illustration of his poetic art.

He here resembles some Arcadian shepherd from an idyllic eclogue who is playing improvisations on his rustic pipe; but whether ancient or modern, he is engaged in the unchanging creative act. Evening, the favourite hour of the Symbolists, is drawing in, bringing with it its mysterious, languorous atmosphere. Wayfarers pass by; but the poet himself is alone in his sylvan retreat which is a refuge from life, a kind of poetic sanctuary. Nature here is charming, gracious, harmonious. There are no precise notations of colour, and the poem is like a faint silken tapestry rather than a vivid tableau. The accent is not upon the visual aspect of the natural background, but upon its sounds: rustling grass, sighing foliage, murmuring waters, the forest echoing the song of the pipe. Outwardly it is a descriptive, decorative Neo-Classicism; but Régnier's *odelette* has faintly elegiac undertones, and with the evocation of *Amour* a shadow passes over Arcady. It is neither realism nor pure fantasy. The sole reality here is that of the 'rêve intérieur'. Inner world and outer world, soul and nature, past and present are fused in a transfigured image reflected as in the rippling mirror of an enchanted fountain.

The various features of the setting, partly Neo-Classical, partly reminiscent of the Norman countryside around Régnier's native

Honfleur, are above all familiar emblems from the poet's imaginative world. The *ruisseau* and the *fontaine* exemplify his obsession with running water which symbolizes the universal flux of things:

> ...son onde, qui sans cesse
> Fuit, mire tour à tour
> Votre regard, ô Tristesse,
> Et votre visage, Amour ('Odelette', *Vestigia flammae*).

Régnier's special love of trees is also in evidence here. The willow, especially the weeping willow, with its pliant branches and its slender, drooping leaves, which is often reflected in the waters beside which it thrives, is a sad tree (cf. Psalm CXXXVII) and a traditional symbol of unrequited love (cf. *Othello*, IV, 3). The murmur of the gentle willow expresses an almost articulate sorrow: 'le frisson du saule, Incertain et léger, est presque une parole' ('Le Sang de Marsyas', *La Cité des eaux*). The forest too seems alive 'comme une âme, ombre et songe' ('Motifs de légende et de mélancolie', *Poèmes anciens et romanesques*), and the melancholy rustling of its branches and leaves sounds like a voice: 'C'est toute une forêt qui sanglote et qui tremble Tragique' ('Les Pins', *Les Jeux rustiques et divins*). Nature here is not a 'vain décor' but a mysterious, vital force with a soul and sentient faculties which allies itself with the poet's song. There is an intimate accord between Nature and humanity: men and things are transient, but the consoling beauty of Nature reconciles Régnier with the instability of life and love. Nature and love are harmoniously blended in the melancholy, narcissistic image of *Amour* in the fountain. This graceful personification seems to belong to the decorative mythology of Neo-Classicism. It is a literary convention which ennobles and generalizes the theme:

> Et vous ne saurez plus...
> Si c'est le vent qui rôde ou la feuille qui tremble,
> Ma voix ou votre voix ou la voix de l'Amour
> ('Élégie', *La Cité des eaux*).

There is not a direct confrontation, but a reflection in an undulating mirror: it is the discarnate, transparent essence of Love. Régnier's Eros, however, wears a grave, dolorous expression very different from the smiling face of the Classical deity. It is like a dream image welling up from the depths of memory. The tears merge with the weeping of the fountain; but the personal emotion is restrained and discreetly masked by the mythological veil. The poetry is equally far removed from rhetorical Romantic exhibitionism and from Symbolist despair. Régnier remains in control of his sensibility, but his emotion suffuses and enriches the conventional Neo-Classicism.

The poet seems to be offering us here an intuition of the ultimately spiritual nature of the universe; but does he really believe in the presence of vital forces behind natural phenomena or in the objective existence of mythical beings? His attitude is in fact entirely subjective: the world exists only as a reflection or echo in the mind. Myths are a creation of man's thought, and the spirituality of things emanates less from Nature than from the poetic imagination:

> Aucun de vous n'a donc vu...
> Que tout le grand songe terrestre
> Vivait en moi pour vivre en eux (*Médailles d'argile*, Prologue).

The basic tenet of Régnier's aesthetic is the primacy of subject over object, of mind over Nature, of Art over life. Life flows by incessantly; only its reflection in art endures. Art captures 'l'éternelle Beauté', and the poet's song lends expression to the diverse voices of Nature which mingle in a universal harmony. The function of poetry is to catch the sad music of life's transient beauty and to eternalize it. 'L'Art est tout.'

The central image from which the whole poem springs is accordingly the *petit roseau*. The shepherd's rustic pipe is the typical instrument of the Classical pastoral, and its wild, woodland notes appeal to Régnier more than the more formal, stately music of Apollo's golden lyre ('Le Sang de Marsyas', *La Cité des eaux*). The *roseau cueilli* is an instrument taken direct from nature, a simpler, more artless version of the flute. Régnier has explained their poetic identity in 'Péroraison' (*Aréthuse*):

> O lac pur, j'ai jeté mes flûtes dans tes eaux,
> Que quelque autre, à son tour, les retrouve, roseaux,
> Sur le lac pastoral où leurs tiges sont nées
> Et vertes dans l'Avril d'une plus belle Année.
> Que toute la forêt referme son automne
> Mystérieux sur le lac pâle où j'abandonne
> Mes flûtes de jadis mortes au fond des eaux.

Adapted to the expression of real, but discreet emotion, the light, delicate, yet solemn music of the reed-pipe is not unlike the elegiac tone of Régnier's poetry, and he often uses it as a symbol of poetic inspiration, associating it now with the song of the spring:

> J'ai retrouvé, ce soir, ma flûte d'autrefois.
> Elle est lisse et légère aux mains. Je me revois
> Comme jadis, debout et la tige à la bouche,
> Le dos contre le tronc d'un pin, près de la source
> Dont l'onde, en s'écoulant, guidait mon jeune jeu
> Si bien que ma chanson imitait peu à peu
> Son rythme, ses frissons, son murmure, sa voix
>
> ('La Flûte et la source', *La Sandale ailée*),

now with that of the forest:

> La chanson de sa flûte emplissait le bois sombre,
> O merveille, on eût dit que chaque arbre eût chanté!
> C'était vaste, charmant, mystérieux et beau
> Cette forêt vivante en ce petit roseau
> Avec son âme, et ses feuilles, et ses fontaines,
> Avec le ciel, avec la terre, avec le vent
>
> ('Le Sang de Marsyas', *La Cité des eaux*).

Régnier's humble instrument is frail and delicate, but its song is appealing in its apparent simplicity and naïveté. The little pipe performs the essential poetic operation and illustrates the incantatory power of music.

A modern Orpheus, Régnier effaces himself here behind the music of the pipe which has the power to move inanimate things. Stanza 1 evokes the startling effect of his song on Nature. Grass, meadow, willows, stream, and forest come alive, stir tremulously, and burst into song. It is as if there were some secret harmony between the human soul and the *anima mundi*. Stanza 2 introduces passers-by who seem to represent mankind in a sort of anonymous transience (*ceux qui passent*). The sound of the sylvan music catches the ear; but its main effect lies in the resonances which it stirs in other men's minds (*en leurs pensées, au fond d'eux-mêmes*), and the three tenses (*ont entendu, entendront, entendent*) indicate its lasting hold on the human soul. It lingers on indefinitely and echoes in the memory long after the actual sound has died away. Régnier's song becomes in this way that of all men. The poem is a variation on the old, eternal theme of a universal song—the mutability of all things and, in particular, the instability of love. Stanza 3 sums up all the motifs of the poem: the image of disappointed love; the melancholy song which disturbs nature and mankind; the theme of the *roseau*, symbol of poetic creation. This last motif, repeated at the beginning and end of Stanzas 1 and 3, is clearly the dominant theme.

The poem has a delightful freedom of form. Nothing could be more light and graceful than the musical fluidity of the supple lines and stanzas. There is also a perfect harmony of form and content, for what could be a more suitable vehicle for the song of a *petit roseau* than a short *odelette*? The poem opens the cycle of Régnier's numerous *odelettes*, a Neo-Classical form invented by Ronsard and revived by Nerval and Banville. Elegant brevity, sophisticated simplicity and exquisite delicacy are among its main characteristics; but the outstanding feature of Régnier's little ode is its sweet, subtle melodiousness à la Debussy. It has a light, gentle rhythm 'sans rien en lui qui pèse ou qui pose', and its musical suggestiveness is close to that of Verlaine:

> De la musique avant toute chose...
> Rien de plus cher que la chanson grise
> Où l'Indécis au Précis se joint...

Régnier is particularly fond of short enumerations and complementary notations linked by 'et' which succeed one another like ripples or waves of music (ll. 2–5, 10, 15–16, 23–4). Another element in the quiet, delicate music of his verse is the abundance of unelided final mute *e*'s which occur not only at the rhyme, but also within the body of the lines (ll. 4, 7, 8, 9, 14, 15, 16, 25, 26), and which are particularly effective when they cluster in twos and threes (ll. 2, 13, 21, 23). Only a sensitive reading of the poem can reveal all its musical resources; but it is at least immediately apparent that it possesses the clearly defined characteristics of a song. It owes this songlike quality above all to the exact or slightly modified repetition of the same words, phrases, or lines which recur like melodious refrains:

> Un petit roseau m'a suffi (ll. 1, 6)
> Il m'a suffi
> De ce petit roseau cueilli (17–18)

roseau (1, 6, 18, 25)
Pour faire frémir l'herbe haute (2)
Pour faire...
...trembler l'herbe et frémir l'eau (23-4)
...faire chanter la forêt (7)
Fait chanter toute la forêt (26)
chante (5, 16)
ceux qui passent (8, 13, 23)
l'ont entendu (8)... l'entendront... l'entendent (15)
Au fond du soir (9)... au fond d'eux-mêmes (14)
en leurs pensées (9, 13)
Dans le silence et dans le vent (10)
pleurait (22)... pleurer (23).

There are over a dozen repetitions in only twenty-six lines, and all these musical echoes merge together in a general harmony of extreme subtlety.

The language itself is not obscure, only its implications and associations. There are no rare or unusual terms, no neologisms, very few realistic or picturesque details. The style is in general eminently Classical—simple, lucid, reserved. What is less Classical is a certain preference for 'la grâce' over 'la beauté' and the marked tendency towards melodious diffuseness. The sentences are long, but are not heavy or dragging; they have a supple, sinuous structure, with pauses for breath and stress. The syntax of Stanza 2 almost gets lost in line 12, but it is picked up again by the repetition of *ceux qui passent* (l. 13). In the first and last stanzas the short co-ordinate main clauses (ll. 6-7, 25-6) carry the main burden of Régnier's song; the final two lines, in particular, are an affirmation of his poetic art.

The flexible stanzas vary in length, becoming steadily longer as the poem develops: Stanza 1 (7 lines), 2 (9), 3 (10). Their growing length is accompanied by an increasing range of musical suggestiveness. Stanza 1 with its predominance of consonants like *s*, *r*, *f*, and *l* seems to echo the murmur of grass, leaves, and stream, while the short, sharp vowels [i], [e], [y], introduce a light, dancing rhythm offset only by the longer, fuller [o], [ã], and [u] sounds. This contrasting note emerges more strongly in the second stanza which evokes the echoes stirred by the music in men's souls. The pastoral description fades away here before the reverie which prolongs and completes it, and the poetry takes on a graver resonance from the accumulation of the vowel sounds [a], [ã], [œ], [wa], [wɛ̃], [ɔ̃], and [u]. These vowels return in lines 19–22, which express the cause of the poet's melancholy; but the *petit roseau* and Nature are present again with their consoling, healing power in Stanza 3. Lines 17–18 and 24–6 echo lines 1–2 and 6–7, thus rounding off the unity of the poem. Their lighter music enframes as it were the melancholy emotion and lends it a serene, aesthetic distance. The final stanza is in this sense both thematically and musically the culmination and résumé of the whole poem.

The lines themselves do not wildly fluctuate in length; nor are there any *vers impairs* or *vers géants*. The only irregularity lies in the varying combinations of *octosyllabes* and four-syllable lines. The standard line is octosyllabic (seventeen out of twenty-six); but the admixture of shorter lines increases as the stanzas lengthen: Stanza 1 (2), 2 (3), 3 (4). The intermingling of the longer and shorter lines does not present any startling or revolutionary metric novelty, for the latter are exactly half the length of the *octosyllabes* and are smoothly integrated into the general harmony. The octosyllabic lines with variable *coupes* (mainly 4 + 4 or 5 + 3, occasionally 3 + 5 and rarely 6 + 2 or 2 + 6) are one of the freest and liveliest of French lyric metres; but it is the introduction of the shorter lines which is largely responsible for the supple grace of the verse, allowing it to expand or contract with the ebb and flow of mood and meaning. Two or three four-syllable lines may seem only typographically different from an *octosyllabe* or a Romantic *trimètre*; but in fact they slightly slow down the poetic flow and throw into sharper relief their verbal elements. In lines 11–12, for example, there is a certain echoing effect, with the 'points de suspension' adding a suggestion of indefinitely prolonged reverberation. In lines 3–4 there is a fond dwelling on certain features of nature followed by the enhancement by contrast of the succeeding longer line (l. 5). Similarly, the image of *Amour* is intensified in all its details by the slow, grave deliberateness of lines 20–2. The isolated four-syllable lines at the end of Stanza 2 and at the beginning of Stanza 3 correspond symmetrically; but their effect is exactly opposite: enjambment produces in both cases an enlargement of the preceding or following *octosyllabe*, but it is the shorter line which is appropriately thrown into prominence in Stanza 2, and the longer line in Stanza 3.

The combination of longer and shorter lines here is not really as capricious as the interplay of rhyme and assonance at the end of them. There is no attempt to alternate consistently masculine and feminine rhymes, and the rhyming comes under the Verlainian category of 'la rime assagie'. There are just two or three *rimes suffisantes* (ll. 8 and 11, 19–20, 22 and 26), several weak or banal rhymes (ll. 1 and 5–6, 9 and 13, 17–18, 24–5), certain cases of simple assonance (ll. 2 and 4, 15–16, 21 and 23); at times there is not even assonance (ll. 3, 7, 10, 12, 14). It is this together with the varying length of stanzas and lines which confers on the poetry the semi-irregular character of 'vers libres symbolistes'. Their soft, caressing music, which sounds like the faint music of running water heard through a screen of rustling foliage, derives from the subtle interweaving of internal harmonies. Freed from the severe confinement of rhyme the verse runs on melodiously from line to line like a meandering stream gliding between the soft reeds lining its banks and occasionally overflowing into the adjacent meadows.

Régnier's Arcadian dreamworld with its sophisticated, pastel-like charm and the light, delicate melancholy of its 'jeu de flûte' presents a sharp contrast with the urgent pressures and strenuous preoccupations of our time. Little read nowadays, Régnier practises an art in a minor key with an artificial, faintly *fin-de-siècle* atmosphere; but his refined grace can sometimes be 'plus belle encor que la beauté'.[1] In this graceful poem he lives on with his elusive personality, that strange compound of reflections and resonances. His little ode is the quintessence of all his poetry—'un espace pour ondes, une acoustique qui recueille, une eau qui reflète'.

---

[1] La Fontaine, *Adonis*, l. 78.

22 Alain-Fournier

La Rencontre

C'étaient deux femmes, l'une très vieille et courbée; l'autre, une jeune fille, blonde, élancée, dont le charmant costume, après tous les déguisements de la veille, parut d'abord à Meaulnes extraordinaire.

Elles s'arrêtèrent un instant pour regarder le paysage, tandis que 5
Meaulnes se disait, avec un étonnement qui lui parut plus tard bien grossier:

— Voilà sans doute ce qu'on appelle une jeune fille excentrique,
— peut-être une actrice qu'on a mandée pour la fête.

Cependant, les deux femmes passaient près de lui et Meaulnes, 10
immobile, regarda la jeune fille. Souvent, plus tard, lorsqu'il s'endormait après avoir désespérément essayé de se rappeler le beau visage effacé, il voyait en rêve passer des rangées de jeunes femmes qui ressemblaient à celle-ci. L'une avait un chapeau comme elle et l'autre son air un peu penché; l'autre son regard si pur; l'autre 15
encore sa taille fine, et l'autre avait aussi ses yeux bleus: mais aucune de ces femmes n'était jamais la grande jeune fille.

Meaulnes eut le temps d'apercevoir, sous une lourde chevelure blonde, un visage aux traits un peu courts, mais dessinés avec une finesse presque douloureuse. Et comme déjà elle était passée devant 20
lui, il regarda sa toilette, qui était bien la plus simple et la plus sage des toilettes…

Perplexe, il se demandait s'il allait les accompagner, lorsque la jeune fille, se tournant imperceptiblement vers lui, dit à sa compagne: 25

— Le bateau ne va pas tarder, maintenant, je pense?…

Et Meaulnes les suivit. La vieille dame, cassée, tremblante, ne cessait de causer gaiement et de rire. La jeune fille répondait doucement. Et lorsqu'elles descendirent sur l'embarcadère, elle eut ce même regard innocent et grave, qui semblait dire: 30

— Qui êtes-vous? Que faites-vous ici? Je ne vous connais pas. Et pourtant il me semble que je vous connais.

D'autres invités étaient maintenant épars entre les arbres, attendant. Et trois bateaux de plaisance accostaient, prêts à recevoir les
35 promeneurs. Un à un, sur le passage des dames, qui paraissaient être la châtelaine et sa fille, les jeunes gens saluaient profondément, et les demoiselles s'inclinaient. Étrange matinée! Étrange partie de plaisir! Il faisait froid malgré le soleil d'hiver, et les femmes enroulaient autour de leur cou ces boas de plumes qui étaient alors à
40 la mode...

La vieille dame resta sur la rive, et, sans savoir comment, Meaulnes se trouva dans le même yacht que la jeune châtelaine. Il s'accouda sur le pont, tenant d'une main son chapeau battu par le grand vent, et il put regarder à l'aise la jeune fille, qui s'était assise à l'abri. Elle
45 aussi le regardait. Elle répondait à ses compagnes, souriait, puis posait doucement ses yeux bleus sur lui, en tenant sa lèvre un peu mordue.

Un grand silence régnait sur les berges prochaines. Le bateau filait avec un bruit calme de machine et d'eau. On eût pu se croire
50 au cœur de l'été. On allait aborder, semblait-il, dans le beau jardin de quelque maison de campagne. La jeune fille s'y promènerait sous une ombrelle blanche. Jusqu'au soir on entendrait les tourterelles gémir... Mais soudain une rafale glacée venait rappeler décembre aux invités de cette étrange fête.

ALAIN-FOURNIER, *Le Grand Meaulnes*
Date of first publication: 1913
Nouvelle édition (Paris: Émile-Paul, n.d.),
pp. 89–91

THIS passage is an extract from the central and most important episode in the novel, Meaulnes's first encounter with Yvonne de Galais. 'La Rencontre' (Pt. I, ch. xv) is the final, 'edited' version of the most decisive event in Fournier's own life, the meeting of the eighteen-year-old schoolboy and the blonde Yvonne de Q. (Quiévrecourt) in her 'manteau marron' and 'chapeau de roses'—first, on Ascension Day (1 June 1905) at the Salon de la Nationale from where he followed her down the Cours-la-Reine on to a *bateau-mouche* and as far as her aunt's house in the Boulevard St.-Germain;

then again, on Whit Sunday (11 June) when he accosted her, pursued her to Mass at St.-Germain-des-Prés and later had with her 'la grande, belle, étrange et mystérieuse conversation'[1] as they walked together along the Seine. Yvonne was already engaged, and when they met again eight years later she was married and the mother of two children. Fournier did not remain entirely faithful to her memory; but he still worshipped her from afar with an impossible love. Her *beau visage effacé* haunted him; he had hallucinatory visions of her; he even wondered at times if he had not fallen in love with his own dream. In his imagination she became inseparably associated with the beloved countryside of his childhood, and in this way she finally became the catalyst of *Le Grand Meaulnes*: 'Je rêve d'un long roman qui tournerait tout autour d'elle, dans une campagne qui serait celle d'Épineuil ou de Nançay.'[2]

The novel presents a remarkable transposition of personal experience. The *Rencontre*, in particular, tallies in all essentials with the meeting in real life. Many elements are taken over, often verbatim, from Fournier's earlier accounts of his 'Belle Aventure'.[3] The setting, however, is transferred from Paris to the mysterious Domaine des Sablonnières, which is in many respects a glorified version of the Château de Loroy in the author's native Sologne. The aristocratic Yvonne de Q. changes her surname and is metamorphosed into the idealized figure of *la jeune châtelaine*. Finally, Fournier himself becomes, in one of his aspects, Augustin Meaulnes, the silent, solitary young peasant hero with his closely cropped hair and his black, belted blouse.

Meaulnes's adventure begins with his departure for the station at Vierzon on a freezing December afternoon. He falls asleep[4] in the trap, loses his way and shelters in a disused sheepfold. Here he recalls 'un rêve — une vision plutôt, qu'il avait eue tout enfant...; un matin, au lieu de s'éveiller dans sa chambre, ...il s'était trouvé dans une longue pièce verte... Près de la fenêtre, une jeune fille cousait, le dos tourné, semblant attendre son réveil...'(I, x). Next

---

[1] Isabelle Rivière, *Images d'Alain-Fournier* (Paris, 1938), p. 251.

[2] Ibid., p. 255.

[3] Rapid notes taken down almost immediately after the event and quoted in part by I. Rivière in *Vie et passion d'Alain-Fournier* (Monaco, 1963), pp. 12–20; the poem 'A travers les étés' (July 1905); 'La Belle Histoire' (Easter 1906) related to I. Rivière (*Images...*, pp. 245–55); Alain-Fournier, *Lettres au petit B* (Paris, 1949), pp. 135–41; the letter to Yvonne de Q. reproduced in *Vie et Passion...*, pp. 186–9.

[4] He also falls asleep on his way back from the Domaine, so that the strange dreamlike encounter will be rounded by two sleeps.

day he stumbles on an old, ruined domain with a white gate, a long, winding avenue, and a grey turret rising above a screen of fir trees. Convinced that 'son but était atteint' and that 'il n'y avait plus maintenant que du bonheur à espérer', he makes his way in and finds children organizing a fête. His arrival seems expected, and fancy-dress clothes are laid out for him. He dines with the other guests; he joins in the theatrical revels of 'la foule joyeuse aux costumes extravagants'; he comes across a room where 'une femme ou une jeune fille, un grand manteau marron jeté sur ses épaules, tournait le dos, jouant très doucement des airs de rondes et de chansonnettes... Ce fut comme son rêve de jadis. Il put imaginer longuement qu'il était marié, un beau soir, et que cet être charmant et inconnu, qui jouait du piano, près de lui, c'était sa femme' (I, xiv). Next morning he rises early and strolls outside in the mild, spring-like sunshine dressed in a 'costume d'étudiant romantique'. He breakfasts alone, inquires about the boat-trip arranged for that day, goes off in search of the landing-stage and, as he is wandering along the path around the pool, he hears 'des pas grincer sur le sable'.

It is Fournier's familiar device of introducing his characters by a premonitory sound which arouses expectation or suspense; they are heard before they are seen. Yvonne's arrival 'chez Florentin' (III, ii) will likewise be heralded by the sound of carriage-wheels grinding to a halt outside: 'La voici, c'est elle.' Here her identity is unknown; but she exactly resembles the Yvonne de Q. of 1905 and is also chaperoned by an old lady.[5] The opening sentence neatly registers Meaulnes's impressions in strict order of succession, with the most important element reserved till last so as to produce a more striking effect: (1) the vague perception of two female figures; (2) the rapid indication of their most conspicuous features by means of contrasting pairs of adjectives(*très vieille et courbée/blonde, élancée*); (3) Meaulnes's reaction to the girl's costume. The old lady is noted first, and the ignominies of age serve as a foil to set off the beauty of youth. She is summarily dismissed, and the final part of the sentence dwells at length upon the appearance of the girl. Meaulnes is first struck by her blond hair and slender figure; but what he finds spell-binding about her is her extraordinary costume. The girl's dress is not particularized until later ('le gracieux chapeau de roses et le grand manteau marron'). All that is described here is the effect produced by it upon Meaulnes himself. After the flamboyant

---

[5] *Images...*, p. 246.

fancy dress of the make-believe world of the *Fête étrange* the girl's costume makes her stand out among the rest, sets her in a class apart.

The two women stop for a moment to view the scenery; but Meaulnes has eyes only for the girl, and he goes on musing about the identity of this 'stunner'. His wonderment is plain enough, but *bien grossier* underlines the vulgar gaucheness of his initial reaction. He may be dressed up as a dandified student of 1830, but he remains at heart a sturdy, forthright peasant schoolboy with a stubborn, ingrained preference for naturalness and simplicity. The girl does not conform either to Meaulnes's own world or to that of the *Fête étrange*. She is foreign to his limited experience, and he cannot make her out. At first he concludes that she must be what censorious provincials would regard as *une jeune fille excentrique* with a taste for daring, showy fashions. Then he wonders if she might not be *une actrice qu'on a mandée pour la fête*, for he no doubt takes her for what in his innocence he imagines an actress to be like— fascinating, but also extravagant, provocative, meretricious. Like Fournier himself in 1905[6] Meaulnes here echoes the moral intransigence and social prejudice of his narrow environment.

Cependant has here its temporal sense, for Meaulnes wakes up out of his reverie as he realizes that the two women have moved on and have now drawn level with him. Their movement contrasts with his immobility. *Immobile*, emphatically placed and comma'd off, illustrates the power of the apt, isolated adjective (cf. *perplexe*, l. 23). The women are walking near him; but Meaulnes remains glued to the spot, lost in rapt contemplation of *la jeune fille*. Like Yvonne de Q. in 1905,[7] she seems unapproachable; but Meaulnes has now caught a close glimpse of her. The meeting of 1905 seemed like a predestined encounter of souls, a mysterious moment of destiny: 'Ma destinée; toute ma destinée, toute ma destinée'.[8] In the novel there is no excited rhetoric; the tone of the narrative remains perfectly flat and calm—perhaps because Meaulnes has not yet recognized in this marvellous apparition the long-awaited incarnation of the woman in his two premonitory dreams. In these dreams he had, after all, seen only her 'dos tourné'. This is the first time that he has had a full, direct view of her face. It is, however,

[6] *Images...*, p. 246.
[7] *Lettres au petit B*, p. 137.
[8] *Vie et passion...*, p. 14.

only a brief, fleeting vision, and subsequently her features will blur in the memory. Meaulnes's desperate attempts to recall the girl's elusive countenance are closely based on Fournier's own tortured experiences: 'O mes efforts de mémoire, les soirs! ...Ce rêve merveilleux et mélancolique et presque réel: des rangées de femmes jeunes, belles, qui passent. L'une a un chapeau comme elle, et l'autre son air penché et l'autre le "marron clair" de sa robe et l'autre le bleu de ses yeux, et pas une, pas une, aussi loin que je regarde, aussi longtemps qu'elles passent, n'est elle.'[9] *Désespérément* with its strongly affective force is a typical example of Fournier's fondness for the expressive adverb of manner (cf. *imperceptiblement, gaiement, doucement, profondément*). The enumeration of the women passing by in Meaulnes's dreams ends with an abrupt, sharp contradiction: *mais aucune de ces femmes n'était jamais la grande jeune fille.* She seems to be an elevated being who exists on a higher plane than the rest of her sex, out of reach and almost out of this world; but she alone measures up to the high demands of 'le grand Meaulnes'. The other women have just one of her characteristics; but none possesses all the qualities which go to make up her ideal perfection. However, the catalogue of their single features adds up to an oblique, composite portrait of the heroine herself: her hat ('le gracieux chapeau de roses'); *son air un peu penché* (the slightly drooping head is partly a consequence of her height, but like Yvonne de Q.[10] she acquires thereby a gentle maternal attitude very different from the bolder, more aggressive posture which might have been expected in *une jeune fille excentrique* or *une actrice*); *son regard si pur*[11] (mirror of the soul); *sa taille fine*[12] (suggestive of a certain frailty); *ses yeux bleus* (her eyes, like those of Yvonne de Q., recall the 'regard immensément bleu' of a Botticelli Madonna).[13]

After this digression the hero reverts to his immediate surroundings, and the action springs to life again with the sudden switch from the imperfect tense to the past definite: *Meaulnes eut le temps d'apercevoir...* As the girl walks past he glimpses as in a flash the very features which will later strike François Seurel: 'Une lourde chevelure blonde pesait sur son front et sur son visage, délicate-

---

[9] Alain-Fournier, *Correspondance avec Jacques Rivière* (Paris, 1948), I, p. 148.

[10] Cf. 'son air... un peu penché comme mon enfance' ('A travers les étés').

[11] Cf. 'ce regard si pur' of Yvonne de Q. (*Vie et passion...*, p. 12).

[12] Fournier's nickname for Yvonne de Q. was 'Taille-Mince' (*Lettres au petit B*, p. 141).

[13] Cf. *Correspondance...*, I, p. 171.

ment dessiné, finement modelé' (III, ii). In both passages the girl's face recalls that of Rossetti's *Beata Beatrix*, a portrait with which Fournier was familiar and with which he compares Yvonne de Q.[14] In the painting the hair is coppery rather than blond, but it forms a thick, heavy mass which half conceals the brow and ears; the features too seem *un peu courts* because the head is tilted; finally, the face of Rossetti's dead wife betrays the *finesse presque douloureuse* common to Yvonne de Q.[15] and to Yvonne de Galais. Like the excessive slenderness of her waist and ankles (I, xv) this is another indication of the girl's fragile delicacy. 'La plus frêle des femmes', she is like 'certains malades gravement atteints sans qu'on le sache' (III, ii).

After she has walked past, Meaulnes turns his attention to a closer study of her costume, and like Fournier in 1905[16] he has to admit that *sa toilette... était bien la plus simple et la plus sage des toilettes.*[17] Her dress has no doubt an aristocratic, not a peasant simplicity; hence Meaulnes's previous error. The main point is that the girl is in reality the only person not wearing a *déguisement*, and it is this fact which makes her stand out in the whimsical, unreal world of the *Fête étrange*. The 'points de suspension' indicate the tailing off of Meaulnes's thoughts as he is aroused from his reverie by the sudden realization that the two women are moving away from him.

The shy, adolescent intruder cannot decide what he should do next. He does not indeed make up his mind—it is made up for him. The girl addresses her companion, and Meaulnes seems to take her question about the boat for a discreet, indirect hint for him to follow, especially as she imperceptibly turns her head towards him as she speaks. Her words fade away into the suggestive silence of the 'points de suspension', and interpreting them as an invitation to some mysterious voyage into the unknown Meaulnes is galvanized into action: *Et Meaulnes les suivit.* This short sentence with its dynamic *Et* and its verb in the past definite nicely catches the sudden, impulsive movement. As he follows in the wake of the two women Meaulnes again notes at closer quarters the contrast between old age and youth. The frailties of the old lady are accentuated here even more harshly than before (*cassée, tremblante*), and the noisy

[14] Cf. *Correspondance..*, I, p. 171.
[15] *Images...*, p. 247.
[16] Ibid., p. 246.
[17] More evidence of Fournier's liking for adjectival 'redoublement'; cf. *une lourde chevelure blonde, ce même regard innocent et grave.*

gaiety of her ceaseless chatter and laughter introduces a frivolous jarring note into the seriousness of the scene and contrasts with the quiet replies of the girl who neither laughs nor even smiles here.[18] Similarly the glance which she casts at Meaulnes as she and her companion walk down to the landing-stage is at once *innocent* and *grave*, i.e. neither flirtatious nor indifferent. It seems that the attraction is not all on Meaulnes's side; but it remains possible that he is reading into her enigmatic gaze more than is warranted. What is certain is that the thoughts attributed to her here are words actually spoken by Yvonne de Q .[19] The girl's two questions express her curiosity about his identity (*Qui êtes-vous?*) and her surprise at the presence of this uninvited guest (*Que faites-vous ici?*); but the following words (*Je ne vous connais pas. Et pourtant il me semble que je vous connais*) state the crucial issue of this central episode in the novel. The implication seems to be that by some mysterious affinity their souls have been predestined for each other from all eternity, that each has been waiting for the other's arrival, and that they have now met; hence their strange mutual recognition.

At this point the interest shifts from the mental duel between Meaulnes and the girl, and a kind of poetic tableau is built up around them. For the first time since meeting the two women the hero becomes aware of the presence of other people. Guests, standing about under the trees, are also waiting for the boat to arrive. The scene is, in effect, a surrealistic transposition of the boat-ride of 1905. It is June in December; the Seine becomes the pool beside the Domaine; the massive Ponton de la Concorde with its garish advertisements changes into the simple rustic landing-stage; the large *bateau-mouche* splits into the three *bateaux de plaisance* or *yachts* (the precise nature of the craft is left vague, nor is there any reference to anyone sailing them); the old aunt and Yvonne de Q. are transformed into *la châtelaine et sa fille*. Meaulnes takes them to be such since as they go by *les jeunes gens saluaient profondément, et les demoiselles s'inclinaient*. It is like the ceremoniousness of an eighteenth-century *fête galante* in the manner of Nerval or Verlaine, and the following pair of lyrical exclamations sum up the mood of the hero: *Étrange matinée! Étrange partie de plaisir!* The repetition of *Étrange*, an obsessional key-adjective of Four-

---

[18] There was the same contrast between the 'vieille dame gaie' ('A travers les étés') and Yvonne de Q., 'grave et douce, sans sourire' (*Correspondance...*, I, p. 207).

[19] *Images...*, pp. 246, 249, 252; and *Lettres au petit B*, p. 138.

nier,[20] emphasizes the mysteriousness of the scene, and the 'position affective' of the epithet reflects Meaulnes's emotional reaction to his strange experience. The sun is shining brightly; but the air remains cold on this December morning, and—a period touch—the women are shown drawing more tightly round their throats the long feather boas which were fashionable in 189... A *partie de plaisir* would seem 'fort peu de saison, mais les enfants en avaient décidé ainsi, sans doute' (I, xv). The realistic description breaks off with the 'points de suspension', and almost as if in a somnambulistic state Meaulnes suddenly finds himself *sans savoir comment* on board the same boat as the girl. It is as if they were severing all links with reality and floating away on a dream voyage. The old lady who in 1905 accompanied Yvonne de Q. on the boat[21] is here left behind on shore. Holding on to his hat in the high wind like Fournier on the *bateau-mouche*,[22] Meaulnes here assumes his characteristic attitude of the Adventurer, while the girl equally characteristically *s'était assise à l'abri*. Like Fournier and Yvonne de Q.[23] each has a clear view of the other: he is able to study her at his ease, and *Elle aussi le regardait*. She smilingly replies to her companions, but she is really intent on him: *posait doucement ses yeux bleus sur lui* (note the repetition here of *doucement* and *ses yeux bleus*), *en tenant sa lèvre un peu mordue* (a habit shared with Yvonne de Q.).[24]

The dreamlike boat-trip continues in the final paragraph. The wind has now dropped, and profound stillness reigns over the *berges prochaines*[25] (*prochaines* = a poetic archaism for 'proches'). The only sound to be heard is that of the boat gliding across the lake, with its engine gently purring and the water washing from its bows.[26] The weather is a memory of the glorious June of 1905, an illusory summer day in the heart of winter. In this Romantic climate anything could happen, and Meaulnes rapidly slips into a dream within a dream. He imagines journey's end not unlike Fournier in 1905.[27] The boat is bound for the beautiful garden of

---

[20] Cf. *étrange fête*. This adjective recurs over twenty times in the novel.

[21] *Images...*, p. 247.

[22] Ibid.　　　　　　　　　　　　　　　　　[23] Ibid.

[24] Cf. *Lettres au petit B*. p. 136.

[25] Cf. 'Les berges de la Seine sont si tranquilles et si feuillues qu'on se croirait au cœur de la campagne, sur un lac solitaire' (*Images...*, p. 247).

[26] *Un bruit calme de machine et d'eau*: this detail is to be found verbatim in 'A travers les étés', *Images...*, p. 247 and *Vie et passion...*, p. 13.

[27] *Vie et passion...*, p. 13.

some *maison de campagne*; the girl will stroll about under a white parasol;[28] and *jusqu'au soir*[29] they will hear the moaning of turtle doves.[30] It is as if nothing could ever disrupt the idyllic beauty and calm happiness of this Other World. The 'points de suspension' produce the effect of a 'prolongement de rêve'. Meaulnes's imagination continues to wander until he is sharply brought back to earth by the threatening, harsh-sounding conclusion: *Mais soudain une rafale glacée venait rappeler décembre aux invités de cette étrange fête.* The icy gust is not simply a meteorological phenomenon, but rather seems to symbolize the cold blast of reality. It is as if the wind here were bringing an ominous presentiment of some impending disaster.

The episode of the *Rencontre* is very strange; but it is written in the simplest of styles. This passage is made up of nine of Fournier's 'petits paragraphes serrés et voluptueux'.[31] The two longest paragraphs contain eight and seven sentences respectively; but the majority are short and have four sentences or less (three consist of only one sentence). There are thirty-three sentences in all. Their length varies from forty-seven to two words; but twenty of them are composed of fifteen words or under, seven range between twenty-one and twenty-six words, and only two exceed forty words. They are preponderantly short in length and simple in structure, with only sparing use of subordination. The vocabulary is equally simple. There are no rare words; they are concrete rather than abstract; they come for the most part from the plain ordinary language of everyday speech. The verbs, in particular, are largely elementary[32] or commonplace,[33] and are often repeated. The style

[28] *Sous une ombrelle blanche*: this phrase is found in *Lettres au petit B*, p. 137, and is repeated like a refrain in 'A travers les étés'. 'La blancheur d'une ombrelle' often flits through Fournier's memories of Yvonne de Q.; cf. *Correspondance...*, I, p. 34; *Images...*, p. 246; *Vie et passion...*, p. 187.

[29] Cf. 'Elle va, lointaine et seule, méditer son attente. Elle sait qu'elle attend la plus douce et la plus pure soirée, au déclin de laquelle nous sommes sûrs d'aller l'un vers l'autre... Et notre amour ne sera rien autre chose que cette soirée, sa douceur à en pleurer sentie ensemble, ses horizons à en mourir désirés ensemble' (*Correspondance...*, II, p. 62).

[30] Cf. 'Une tourterelle ne cesse pas de roucouler. Vous savez, ce roucoulement qui rend les jours d'été si longs, si romanesques' (Letter to Marguerite Audoux, 19.vii. 1911). There is a reminiscence here of the 'Maison des Tourterelles' of Mme Benoist at Épineuil (cf. 'A travers les étés' and *Vie et passion...*, p. 13).

[31] *Correspondance...*, II, p. 371.

[32] *Être* (7 times), *avoir* (4), *aller* (3), *paraître* (3), *sembler* (3), *faire* (2), *pouvoir* (2), *se trouver*, *venir*.

[33] *Regarder* (5 times), *dire* (3), *passer* (3), *répondre* (2), *connaître* (2), *tenir* (2), *voir*,

reveals no pretentious inflation, no straining for effect. It is notable, on the contrary, for the plain, spare simplicity, the fresh, sensuous immediacy which swiftly captures gestures and movements, the artist's eye for the significant or suggestive detail, the frequent repetitions[34] which, though hardly noticed at a first reading, produce a haunting subconscious effect.

The main characteristic is a mysterious simplicity, for sensuous experience is here transfigured by the veiled intensity of the lyrical emotion and by the vaguely metaphysical resonances. It is like 'la simplicité du mystère' which Fournier admired in the Bible —a 'simplicité effrayante' which he sought to model on 'le style de saint Matthieu; *du français de Christ*'.[35]

---

apercevoir, demander, suivre, cesser, rire, descendre, attendre, recevoir, rester, savoir, sourire, poser, croire, entendre.

[34] *Jeune fille* (8 times), *l'autre* (5), *étrange* (3), *blonde* (2), *yeux bleus* (2), *doucement* (2), *fine/finesse, vieille* (2).

[35] *Correspondance...*, II, p. 339.

23 Proust

Le bœuf froid aux carottes fit son apparition, couché par le Michel-Ange de notre cuisine sur d'énormes cristaux de gelée pareils à des blocs de quartz transparent.

— Vous avez un chef de tout premier ordre, Madame, dit M. de
5 Norpois. Et ce n'est pas peu de chose. Moi qui ai eu à l'étranger à tenir un certain train de maison, je sais combien il est souvent difficile de trouver un parfait maître queux. Ce sont de véritables agapes auxquelles vous nous avez conviés là.

Et, en effet, Françoise, surexcitée par l'ambition de réussir pour
10 un invité de marque un dîner enfin semé de difficultés dignes d'elle, s'était donné une peine qu'elle ne prenait plus quand nous étions seuls et avait retrouvé sa manière incomparable de Combray.

— Voilà ce qu'on ne peut obtenir au cabaret, je dis dans les meilleurs: une daube de bœuf où la gelée ne sente pas la colle, et
15 où le bœuf ait pris parfum des carottes, c'est admirable! Permettez-moi d'y revenir, ajouta-t-il en faisant signe qu'il voulait encore de la gelée. Je serais curieux de juger votre Vatel maintenant sur un mets tout différent, je voudrais, par exemple, le trouver aux prises avec le bœuf Stroganof.

20 M. de Norpois, pour contribuer lui aussi à l'agrément du repas, nous servit diverses histoires dont il régalait fréquemment ses collègues de carrière, tantôt en citant une période ridicule dite par un homme politique coutumier du fait et qui les faisait longues et pleines d'images incohérentes, tantôt telle formule lapidaire d'un
25 diplomate plein d'atticisme. Mais, à vrai dire, le critérium qui distinguait pour lui ces deux ordres de phrases ne ressemblait en rien à celui que j'appliquais à la littérature. Bien des nuances m'échappaient; les mots qu'il récitait en s'esclaffant ne me paraissaient pas très différents de ceux qu'il trouvait remarquables. Il appartenait
30 au genre d'hommes qui pour les œuvres que j'aimais eût dit: 'Alors, vous comprenez? Moi, j'avoue que je ne comprends pas, je ne suis

pas initié', mais j'aurais pu lui rendre la pareille, je ne saisissais pas l'esprit ou la sottise, l'éloquence ou l'enflure qu'il trouvait dans une réplique ou dans un discours, et l'absence de toute raison perceptible pour quoi ceci était mal et ceci bien, faisait que cette 35 sorte de littérature m'était plus mystérieuse, me semblait plus obscure qu'aucune. Je démêlai seulement que répéter ce que tout le monde pensait n'était pas en politique une marque d'infériorité mais de supériorité. Quand M. de Norpois se servait de certaines expressions qui traînaient dans les journaux et les prononçait avec 40 force, on sentait qu'elles devenaient un acte par le seul fait qu'il les avait employées, et un acte qui susciterait des commentaires.

Ma mère comptait beaucoup sur la salade d'ananas et de truffes. Mais l'Ambassadeur, après avoir exercé un instant sur le mets la pénétration de son regard d'observateur, la mangea en restant 45 entouré de discrétion diplomatique et ne nous livra pas sa pensée. Ma mère insista pour qu'il en reprît, ce que fit M. de Norpois, mais en disant seulement au lieu du compliment qu'on espérait: 'J'obéis, Madame, puisque je vois que c'est là de votre part un véritable oukase'. 50

PROUST, *A l'ombre des jeunes filles en fleurs*
Date of first publication: 1918
A la recherche du temps perdu
(Paris: Gallimard, 1954),
I, 458–9

THE episode of the dinner-party given by the narrator's parents for the former ambassador, M. de Norpois, is a major set-piece, occupying a prominent place at the beginning of *A l'ombre des jeunes filles en fleurs*. The opening words of this volume of Proust's long novel are: 'Ma mère, quand il fut question d'avoir pour la première fois M. de Norpois à dîner...'; and the account of the evening, with its preliminaries, the digressions it gives rise to, and the 'post-mortem' held by Marcel's parents after the departure of the distinguished guest, only comes to an end over fifty pages later. It is the sort of episode, not infrequent in *A la recherche du temps perdu*, which is evidently not selected for treatment merely as an event important in itself, but also because of the scope it offers for the development of a number of continuous, interwoven narrative threads. It introduces a new character, Norpois, who although he is to remain a secondary figure, will make occasional appearances throughout later volumes, as his past relations with other characters are brought to light. Representing as he does a world of diplomacy, good taste, and aristocratic refinement, he opens up for the young Marcel, as do other acquaintances outside the family circle, interesting possibilities of escape from the narrow confines of his bourgeois upbringing; his standing in society enables him to set the seal of a man of the world's approval, albeit qualified, on the social aspirations of Madame Swann, at whose house he has dined on the previous evening—thereby providing a link with a central theme of the earlier volume, *Du côté de chez Swann*; and finally the views of this experienced connoisseur lead Marcel, who has just returned from a visit to the theatre to see La Berma play Phèdre, to modify his first self-conscious reactions—just as the boy's naïve enthusiasm for Romanesque architecture (one of the ostensible reasons for the choice of Balbec for a forthcoming holiday) is similarly modified by the great man's judicious preference for the later Gothic style.

M. de Norpois is an influential senior colleague of the narrator's father, and this (his first) visit to the house is something of a landmark. However, in the passage chosen for commentary, as throughout the whole episode, the way in which the subject is treated reveals a certain ambivalence. On the one hand, adopting the perspective of the narrator in so far as he is re-creating the past as it appeared to him as a young boy, we can see how the former ambassador personifies for Marcel's parents, as well as for the boy himself, a world of superior cultural and intellectual values, and how they regard him as a visitor whose breadth of experience and sureness of judgement call for deferential respect. On the other hand, however, it is just as clear that for the mature narrator Norpois has more than a touch of the pompous and ridiculous; and as so often is the case with Proust, it is the interplay of these two attitudes which gives the episode its particular character.

The passage selected for commentary is preceded first by a longish passage introducing M. de Norpois himself; then by an account of the matinée performance of *Phèdre* which had failed to come up to the expectations of the young Marcel; and finally by a preliminary conversation between Marcel's father and his guest in the boy's presence before dinner and as they take their places at table. These introductory pages consist for the most part of objective description of M. de Norpois, with some indication of the views of Marcel's parents; and although the opening conversational exchanges at the dinner-table contain a much larger element of direct speech, the effect is very similar: the impression we obtain of the ambassador remains on the whole quite neutral, where it is not positively favourable. For instance, his attitude compares favourably with that of Marcel's parents when we are told that Norpois asked the boy various questions 'sur ce qu'avaient été ma vie et mes études, sur mes goûts dont j'entendis parler pour la première fois comme s'il pouvait être raisonnable de les suivre...'. In short, although at an early point in the presentation of this character we have been told that 'la conversation de M. de Norpois était un répertoire complet des formes surannées du langage particulières à une carrière, à une classe et à un temps', in the immediate context this does not convey a pejorative implication, and there is hardly more than a hint of caricatural exaggeration in the portrayal of a predominantly sympathetic character.

When we come to the account of the dinner-party proper, however, the tone appears to have undergone a significant change, and from this point onwards Norpois joins the ranks of those larger-than-life figures which, although they are based on the accurate observation of social types, owe their existence to a creative process which dwells on selected attributes and magnifies them to the status of comic foibles. A. Feuillerat has examined the whole sequence of the 'dîner de M. de Norpois' in his comparison between the final version of *A l'ombre des jeunes filles en fleurs* and the original text, set up in proof in 1914 but never published.[1] Showing how the definitive text represents a considerable amplification of the pre-war original, he instances a number of passages from this episode, including—and this is surely very significant—virtually all the direct speech contained in the passage under consideration.[2] Whether or not the wider implications of Feuillerat's thesis are justified, there does seem here to be a remarkable 'sharpening' of the portrait in the direction of caricature. If the caricatural figure

[1] *Comment Marcel Proust a composé son roman* (Yale, 1934).

[2] The only remark originally put into the mouth of Norpois at this point was: 'Vous avez un chef de tout premier ordre, Madame.' The whole passage was originally much less extensive than in the final version; for instance, both the first and the fifth paragraphs represent later additions.

is one who in every situation produces a stock response, whose behaviour becomes almost predictable, then in the passage under discussion one can see the process of selection and exaggeration at work to achieve just this sort of caricatural effect.

The opening phrase of the passage brings with it an abrupt change of tone; following on from an analysis of La Berma's performance as Phèdre, it produces an almost bathetic descent from the sublime to the trivial. However, the banality of the reference to the *bœuf froid aux carottes* is deliberately relieved by certain stylistic features characteristic of Proust. This opening paragraph refers back to a passage which appears a dozen pages earlier, in which Françoise, the cook, had already been compared to Michelangelo; both passages represent post-1914 additions, and one can discern behind the selection of this highly contrived image a purpose in keeping with the spirit of all the additions relating to Norpois and the dinner-party: the desire to heighten reality. The opening lines of the passage are accordingly designed to produce a mock-heroic effect, and even the first phrase, in the context, can be seen to contribute to this: the *bœuf froid aux carottes* is personified, as it were, by the rather pompous expression *fit son apparition*. In the earlier reference to the preparation of the dinner, we have been told how Françoise has been put on her mettle, regarding the occasion as a challenge to her abilities; the menu had been devised, the food selected and bought, with especial care. What had earlier been expressed in the form of a simile, as an ingenious conceit:

> ...elle allait elle-même aux Halles se faire donner les plus beaux carrés de romsteck, de jarret de bœuf, de pied de veau, comme Michel-Ange passant huit mois dans les montagnes de Carrare à choisir les blocs de marbre les plus parfaits pour le monument de Jules II

is now presented more tersely as a metaphor: Françoise has now *become* 'le Michel-Ange de notre cuisine'. However, the image receives a further development in the combined metaphor and simile of lines 2–3: the term *cristaux*—a metaphor, since, although the chopped-up jelly can certainly assume a 'crystalline' appearance, it is impossible to speak literally of 'crystals' of jelly—forming the middle term of the comparison between *gelée* and *blocs de quartz*. In elevating the humble Françoise to the level of Michelangelo, and comparing the *bœuf froid aux carottes* on its bed of jelly with the materials used by a great sculptor (note the adjective *énorme* which assists the comparison), Proust is following the classical formula for the mock-heroic as established by Boileau and Pope: the treatment of ordinary, banal subject-matter by means of incongruously elevated diction. It is a formula particularly suited to his own highly cultured, ironic vision of the world.

When M. de Norpois begins to speak, everything suggests the great man who is used to holding forth in front of an audience of deferential listeners: the self-centredness, the clichés, the pompous oratorical phrasing; he speaks dogmatically, as one whose wide experience entitles him to bestow praise where it is deserved. The content of the first paragraph spoken by him is of course complimentary, but it is impossible not to detect a certain condescension in his manner: the assumption that his host is in a position to employ a 'chef de cuisine' instead of a female cook; the pompous egoism of *Moi qui ai eu..., je sais...*; the affected archaism of *maître queux*; and the conventional flattery of the last phrase—a meaningless cliché[3]—all contribute to this impression.

The interpolated paragraph of comment (ll. 9–12) serves principally as a reference back or reminder, since the fact that this is an occasion out of the ordinary has been made abundantly clear already; *sa manière incomparable de Combray* is an allusion to the first part of *Du côté de chez Swann*, in which we are told of the virtuosity shown by Françoise when all the family were gathered at Combray in the summer. In that volume, the rich affective associations of 'Combray' in the mind of the narrator as a child are minutely explored by the author's nostalgic reminiscences; here, Proust is content to make a summary reference without attempting to evoke a mood which would have clashed with the much more matter-of-fact tone of this whole passage. Towards Françoise herself, the author's attitude is generally somewhat ambivalent: if the young Marcel shows an affection tinged with anxious dependence, the mature narrator is much more detached and, on occasion, critical. Here, it is the detached narrator who is in control: the first half of the sentence, rising with a sort of exaltation to its climax at *...dignes d'elle*, has a touch of the mock-heroic of the first paragraph (*ambition..., semé de difficultés dignes d'elle*), whereas the second half,

---

[3] *Agape*, 'repas fraternel' (strictly, of the early Christian Church). Even when used familiarly (normally in the plural, as here), the term has the connotation of 'repas entre amis' (Robert), not—as the context would suggest here—of 'banquet'.

which falls away from the climax with a pleasing balance, contains alongside the undoubted praise (*sa manière incomparable de Combray*) an element of distinct criticism in *une peine qu'elle ne prenait plus quand nous étions seuls*. The phrase *sa manière incomparable...* serves to integrate the paragraph into the passage as a whole: it contains enough suggestion of the artist-virtuoso for the reader to recognize a continuation of the metaphor of the opening paragraph.

The tenses of the short 'interpolated' paragraph (*s'était donné, avait retrouvé*) make it clear that it contains the narrator's reflections 'on the side', which do not interrupt the self-satisfied flow of Norpois's compliments. He continues his rather condescending appreciation, embellishing the commonplaces he utters by stylistic tricks, such as the pompous emphasis of *...au cabaret, je dis dans les meilleurs*, and also, perhaps, in a different way, by the affectation of the familiar *cabaret* for 'restaurant': a *cabaret* is normally a fairly lowly establishment,[4] with which it would hardly be complimentary to compare one's hostess's cuisine—but here we may assume that the speaker's preference for this term represents current fashionable usage, a sort of upper-class 'slang'. (We may also possibly detect a similar 'fashionable' preference for the familiar term in line 4, where Norpois uses *chef* instead of the more accurate *chef de cuisine* or *cuisinier*.) The next phrases: *...où la gelée ne sente pas la colle, et où le bœuf ait pris parfum des carottes* show an orator's care for balance, in spite of the vulgarity of the first proposition (and the banality of the second, since the whole purpose of the slow, hermetic preparation of the 'bœuf en daube' is that the meat shall imbibe the flavour of the liquid in which it is cooked!) The self-centredness of the diplomat comes out graphically in the 'stage-direction' which accompanies his request for a second helping, while the following sentence takes his self-importance to new heights with the pronouncement about an appropriate test of the cook's resources, which he appears to assume the right, as well as the capacity, to judge.

At the same time, the pompous phraseology is brought to a climax with *votre Vatel* and *...aux prises avec le bœuf Stroganof*. These two expressions can be seen as illustrations of the critical intention behind Proust's caricature, since they are both figures of speech which further exemplify Norpois's self-important rhetorical

---

[4] 'Sorte d'auberge, de café d'un rang inférieur' (Littré); 'sorte d'auberge, de café d'un rang modeste' (Robert).

manner. The first is an example of antonomasia, the specific form of metonymy in which a proper name is used to represent a general class: here *votre Vatel* stands for 'votre chef de cuisine'.[5] The following observations by Antoine Adam show how Proust regarded Norpois's use of such mannerisms:

(Le langage Norpois) est enfin l'exemple éclatant de cette banalité prétentieuse dont tant de gens font une vertu littéraire. Marcel Proust avait pris de bonne heure, avec Lucien Daudet, l'habitude de s'en moquer. Les deux amis appelaient ces fausses élégances des louchonneries. C'était louchonnerie que de dire Albion, la verte Érin, nos petits soldats. Comme l'a très bien vu Lucien Daudet, le langage Norpois n'est rien d'autre que le langage louchon.[6]

Votre Vatel is an excellent example of a 'louchonnerie'; we may compare 'John Bull', 'l'oncle Sam' which occur in the conversation preceding the passage under discussion. The figure *aux prises avec le bœuf Stroganof* is a metaphor drawn from the sphere of military activities or athletic contests; it is another example of elevated diction applied to a lowly subject, and again takes up the 'heroic' image from the beginning of the passage, as the speaker pays ironic tribute to the skills and hard-earned triumphs of the culinary art.[7] However, whereas we are ready to accept the mock-heroic manner direct from the narrator's pen as an example of successful imaginative writing, here the same, or similar, features from the

[5] The 17th-C. Vatel was not strictly speaking a chef, but the *maître d'hôtel* or 'steward' of the Duc de Condé. History remembers him because, when the King was being entertained by Condé at Chantilly, he mistakenly believed that the fish he had ordered for a banquet had failed to arrive, whereupon his keen sense of honour, unable to face the disgrace, led him to take his own life.

[6] 'Le Roman de Proust et le problème des clefs', *Revue des sciences humaines*, VI (1952), p. 75. As Adam shows in this article, the multiplicity of reminiscences in the case of Norpois rules out the possibility of Proust's having had a single model in mind: the character is a composite amalgam of traits taken from various real-life representatives of his class and profession.

[7] While *Je serais curieux de juger... maintenant...* might seem to imply that the Baron is proposing a suitable conjunction of dishes in an ideal menu, the fact is that although *bœuf Stroganof* (strips of fillet beef sauté'd in butter and embalmed with mushrooms in a sour cream sauce) may call for a different kind of culinary expertise—this is the primary implication of the remark—it is too similar to *daube de bœuf* for it to be likely that the two dishes would ever be juxtaposed as successive courses on the same menu. It is more probable that *maintenant*, taken together with the tense of the main verb, means 'on another occasion'.

mouth of Norpois ring hollow, and are seen as a further indication of the character's reliance on facile clichés.

In the brief space of the two short paragraphs devoted to direct speech, the ambassador has been sketched in a most masterly manner. The caricatural exaggeration which has packed so many examples of his mannerisms of speech into these few lines only serves, like the comic characterization of the dramatist, to make him more lifelike, and Norpois already stands out as a character we feel we should have no difficulty in recognizing in real life. These are the sort of mannerisms which reveal a whole personality; and even if Proust had not commented on the 'formes surannées du langage particulières à une carrière, à une classe et à un temps', we should still have been able to identify the speaker as a pompous representative of a world different from that of Marcel and his parents (*Moi qui ai eu à l'étranger à tenir un certain train de maison...*) self-consciously 'playing up' to the idea that his hosts have of him (*...un parfait maître queux..., au cabaret, je dis dans les meilleurs...*), a man whose speech habits are marked on the one hand by a certain 'déformation professionnelle' (his various tricks of oratory) and on the other by a sort of slang peculiar to his class and generation (*agapes, cabaret, Vatel*). All this is recorded 'direct' by the narrator, the mature Marcel; there is no need for comment, as Norpois gives himself away each time he opens his mouth—if not to the young Marcel and his parents, at least to the reader, to whom Proust clearly presents him as a source of amusement, albeit amusement of a civilized, indulgent nature.

While the long fifth paragraph still contributes to the overall characterization of M. de Norpois, it contains none of the ambassador's own phrases; and whereas the reader is aware that the direct pronouncements of the earlier paragraphs have been selected and presented with ironical detachment by the author/narrator, keeping Norpois in the centre of the picture, the new paragraph explores the effect of the latter's remarks on the young Marcel. The perspective is therefore quite different: here we are dealing with the relationship between two characters at the dinner-table, or more particularly with the boy's reaction to the eminent visitor—the whole being 'edited' and presented at second hand, as it were, by the grown narrator. There is no sharp break at line 20, however; indeed, the first sentence of this paragraph makes a very effective transition, as regards both style and content: *l'agrément du repas* carries on the idea of the previous paragraphs, and although it appears at first sight as though this expression is to be interpreted quite simply in the sense that the ambassador's anecdotes provide intellectual 'agrément', we immediately see that in fact it forms part of a sustained metaphor, together with *nous servit* and *régalait*: by a pleasant conceit, Norpois appears on this occasion not only to be vying with Françoise in contributing to the success of the dinner-party but also to be in the habit of feasting (*régalait*) his friends in the same way. The effect of the metaphor is surely to bring Norpois down from his exalted position as privileged guest: not only does the phrase *pour contribuer lui aussi...* bring him down to the same level as Françoise but it makes his 'contribution' seem less solid and worth-while than hers.

From this point onwards (l. 22), the metaphor is dropped, and the style becomes more abstract and analytical; though some assistance is given to the expression of the idea by the contrast in length and structure between the two phrases beginning with *tantôt*. Whereas the first is rather lacking in shape and character, with the emphasis falling on the abstract epithets *ridicule... coutumier du fait... longues... incohérentes*, the second—suiting the style to the content— has an incisive, almost 'lapidary' quality, with the more expressive *lapidaire* and *atticisme* brought into relief. It is not until the end of the second sentence of the paragraph that the change of subject-matter is made clear: the young Marcel makes his entry with the pronoun of *j'appliquais* at line 27, and the connection is established between the ambassador's ideas of good and bad in oratory and the spoken word (*ces deux ordres de phrases*) and Marcel's own notions of good and bad in literature.

To begin with, the young listener is quite disorientated: as he attempts, unsuccessfully, to subject the ambassador's anecdotes to the test of his own standards of literary appreciation, there is at first no suggestion that the fault lies elsewhere than in the inade-quacy of these standards. The *nuances* escape him; the objects of Norpois's raillery and of his admiration 'appear' indistinguishable to him: the narrator seems to justify the diffidence felt by his younger self, faced with the ambassador's greater experience and superior judgement; and just as the latter would have had to confess his inability to understand the kind of literature which appealed to Marcel (for instance, the 'poetic prose' of the novelist Bergotte, as related in *Du côté de chez Swann*), so the boy acknowledges his inability to fathom the subtleties of the style which Norpois admires. Again, the phrasing at this point, with the simple rhetorical balance of *l'esprit ou la sottise, l'éloquence ou l'enflure, dans une réplique ou dans un discours*, seems to point to the oratorical nature of this style—one that is not at all subtle in fact; hence the baffling paradox that this kind of literature should have its own 'mystère', and should appear to the impressionable boy to be *plus obscure qu'aucune*. The next sentence continues in the same vein, analysing the dilemma from the same point of view with the diffident *Je démêlai seulement...*; but although ostensibly the young Marcel is confessing the inadequacy of his own judgement *vis-à-vis* that of the ambassador, we can here see the double perspective at work clearly enough, and *répéter ce que tout le monde pensait... supériorité* surely shows the ironical vision of the mature narrator. In the last sentence of the paragraph this change of perspective is even more apparent: *certaines expressions qui traînaient dans les journaux* is a pejorative intensification of *ce que tout le monde pensait*, and *les prononçait avec force* gives away the secret of the 'confidence trick' —though as lines 41-2 show, it is a confidence trick that succeeds. While what really distinguishes Norpois's pronouncements is their emphatic *manner* (*avec force*), the prestige of his personality is such that they acquire the status of authoritative texts (the diplomatic-legal terminology of these closing phrases is of course a pointer to the context in which this prestige operates).

The juxtaposition of the two angles of vision—that of the young Marcel, bewildered by this first contact with the representative of a generation, and a culture, so different from his own, with a set of values that he is just as unable to understand as Norpois is to appreciate his own enthusiasms; and the other, the ironic viewpoint of the mature narrator, which encroaches on the first in the penultimate paragraph of the passage, and takes over completely in the last sentence—this cleverly-arranged juxtaposition enables us to make up our minds quite unambiguously about M. de Norpois. From this point onwards, we are able to see through him; we recognize in him a man of social charm and presence, but whose judgement, especially on matters of literary taste, is conventional and superficial. It is essential to Proust's purpose that the reader should be able to make up his mind in this way, in anticipation of a new development a few pages later, towards the close of the dinner-party episode, when Marcel has the temerity to ask the great man for his opinion of Bergotte as a writer, and the boy is utterly discomfited as the ambassador delivers a scathing appraisal which covers nearly two pages; for now no intervention from the narrator is necessary in order to correct the perspective of the vision of the youthful Marcel. We have been forewarned, and can read between the lines, and interpret the boy's self-deprecating remarks as an ironical commentary on the old-fashioned, inadequate views that Norpois represents.

The short concluding paragraph restores a balance to the passage, focusing again on the narrative of the dinner-party after the somewhat discursive analysis of lines 20–42. The transition is made with another of the brusque changes of subject which Proust the comic writer evidently enjoyed: like the opening phrase of the passage, *Ma mère comptait beaucoup sur la salade d'ananas et de truffes* produces a comic effect of incongruity when taken with the phrase which precedes it. The sentence originally followed on immediately after ...*sa manière incomparable de Combray* of line 12, while the whole passage ended at ...*sa pensée*: it will be seen how much richer the later additions have made the account of the dinner, even if this has resulted in a certain loss of compactness and unity, both as regards subject-matter and style. Here, the mock-heroic tone of the opening paragraph returns—at Norpois's expense this time—with the pompous expressions *après avoir exercé sur le mets la pénétration de son regard d'observateur, ...entouré de discrétion diplomatique, ...ne nous livra pas sa pensée*. The passage in general conjures up a highly conventional stereotype of the traditional diplomat, shrewd and penetrating, but tight-lipped and inscrutable; while the first phrase contains an explicit echo of the opening paragraph of the dinner-party episode: 'il exerçait sur chaque nouveau venu ses facultés d'observateur afin de savoir de suite à quelle espèce d'homme il avait à faire.' The incongruity of these attributes being brought into play by the *salade d'ananas et de truffes* is of course highly comic. The final polite formula is another comic 'mot-clef': *oukase* belongs, like *agapes* and *Vatel*, to the kind of expression with which a man like Norpois seasons his speech in order to give an elevated tone to the conversation; expressions which are esoteric in origin, but which become debased by use until they are finally so many empty clichés. This closing example would in any case hardly be flattering if taken literally: derived from the Russian word for 'edict', the term usually retains, as does its English counterpart 'ukase', the implication of an arbitrary decree ('Fig. et ironiquement: décision arbitraire, ordre impératif'—Robert).

Once more, this final remark reveals the nature of the author's comic vision. Proust's aim in putting these 'formes surannées du langage...' into Norpois's mouth was not merely the objective characterization of that milieu. Taken singly, such expressions may have objective validity as illustrations of period usage; but their very concentration, and the fact that the character's speech is almost entirely reduced in places to a string of these mechanical clichés, shows that in the figure of Norpois he was trying to create a quintessential, larger-than-life representative of this class and period. 'Il n'y a que les types excentriques qui m'amusent et qui m'instruisent,' he was to write later; and here—particularly if we bear in mind the differences between the earlier states of the text and the final version—we can clearly see the caricatural process at work in a most successful example of Proust's comic invention.[8]

[8] 'The pompous pronouncements that flow smoothly from the lips of M. de Norpois are a veritable patchwork of administrative clichés, typical, yet, in the universe of Proust's novel, characteristic only of him. Norpois's language reveals in a most specific way the intellectual vacuum behind the ambassador's imposing façade, a very general characteristic of society people in Proust's world. After a reader has encountered M. de Norpois a couple of times, he knows just what to expect' (Germaine Brée, *The World of Marcel Proust* (London, 1967), p. 187).

24 Colette

Ma Mère et les bêtes

Mais à seize ans, revenant en Puisaye après une quinzaine de
théâtres, de musées, de magasins, je rapporte, parmi des souvenirs
de coquetterie, de gourmandise, mêlés à des regrets, à des espoirs,
à des mépris aussi fougueux, aussi candides et dégingandés que
moi-même, l'étonnement, l'aversion mélancolique de ce que je 5
nommais les maisons sans bêtes. Ces cubes sans jardins, ces logis
sans fleurs où nul chat ne miaule derrière la porte de la salle à
manger, où l'on n'écrase pas, devant la cheminée, un coin du chien
traînant comme un tapis, ces appartements privés d'esprits familiers,
où la main, en quête de cordiale caresse, se heurte au marbre, au 10
bois, au velours inanimés, je les quittai avec des sens affamés, le
besoin véhément de toucher, vivantes, des toisons ou des feuilles,
des plumes tièdes, l'émouvante humidité des fleurs...

Comme si je les découvrais ensemble, je saluai, inséparables, ma
mère, le jardin et la ronde des bêtes. L'heure de mon retour était 15
justement celle de l'arrosage, et je chéris encore cette sixième heure
du soir, l'arrosoir vert qui mouillait la robe de satinette bleue, la
vigoureuse odeur de l'humus, la lumière déclinante qui s'attachait,
rose, à la page blanche d'un livre oublié, aux blanches corolles du
tabac blanc, aux taches blanches de la chatte dans une corbeille. 20

COLETTE, *La Maison de Claudine*
Date of first publication: 1922
Œuvres complètes (Paris: Flammarion,
1949), VII, 52–3

THIS passage is introduced by an initial paragraph in which
Claudine recalls two earlier visits to Paris. At the age of six she had
briefly passed through the city, and her recollections consist solely

of harsh auditory impressions ('Une série de bruits brutaux, le train, les fiacres, les omnibus'). Five years later she had spent a week there, and the memories of her stay are a nightmare of disagreeable physical sensations: 'chaleur sèche', 'soif haletante', 'fiévreuse fatigue', the fleas in the hotel bedroom in the Rue Saint-Roch, the oppressive height of the houses. During the following five years she is caught up again in the life of her province, with hardly a thought of the metropolis.

Her third visit to Paris and her return home are evoked in the next two paragraphs which form the passage under examination. Her unfavourable recollections of her previous encounters with Megalopolis were based on vivid sensory impressions, but they were brief and highly selective in the manner of childhood memories. This time she has spent a whole fortnight in the capital, and the longer stay enables her to form a closer, more detailed judgement. She is now between childhood and womanhood, and her growing maturity allows her to comprehend more clearly her essentially sensuous reactions to the big city. Sixteen is an impressionable age, and she vividly conveys the impact of the bustling life of Paris with its heady, confusing whirl of novel, lively activities. For a young provincial girl whose life has been bounded by her home, her school, and the countryside around Saint-Sauveur[1] it has been a fortnight packed with excitement. However, Paris ultimately disappoints. She rejects its superficial attractions and returns home with a new awareness of the difference between the febrile, artificial city life and the tranquil, simple existence in the country. The underlying theme of the whole passage is indeed the contrast between modern urban civilization and Nature, between the *maisons sans bêtes*, the *cubes sans jardins* and the *logis sans fleurs*, on the one hand, and [*sa*] *mère, le jardin et la ronde des bêtes*, on the other. Her aversion to Paris and her preference for her provincial home spring basically from her sensuous response to the world. Her senses, especially those of sight, smell, and touch, are peculiarly acute, and these are starved in Paris. The city is arid, hard, cold, lifeless, unnatural. It cannot offer a permanent appeal to a child of nature brought up close to the soil with animals and plants all round her. She is glad to leave behind its grey drabness and return to the

---

[1] Saint-Sauveur-en-Puisaye is a small, obscure village in Burgundy, about twenty miles from Auxerre and some 100 miles from Paris. Colette lived here at No. 3 Rue de l'Hospice from 1873 to 1891.

warm, colourful intimacy of her home with its flower-garden and innumerable pets prowling around, under the presiding genius of her mother, the incomparable Sido.

Claudine is here in many respects a double of the author herself. Colette is an accomplished stylist with a highly professional technique; but her sensibility retains a fresh immediacy, and her essentially sensory memory has here recaptured the lost paradise of her own youth. Her natural, vivacious style evokes with sensuous precision the sights, colours, and scents of the enchanted childhood world which she loved so much and in which she so often sought refuge in adult life.

The first sentence is very skilfully constructed. First Claudine briefly establishes the time and place: she is sixteen and has just returned home to Puisaye. Then there is a swift flashback to her fortnight in Paris, with her activities listed in a short accumulation of concrete nouns organized in a ternary pattern: *de théâtres,/de musées,/de magasins*. There is no 'et' to close the series, and the open-ended enumeration combines with the spritely rhythm to suggest the tumultuous, breathless rush to cram into the fortnight as much as possible. The main verb *je rapporte* arrives next; but it is separated from its direct objects by a whole swirling cloud of memories recalling the girl's lively, uninhibited response to 'la vie parisienne' and presenting a vivid, if unflattering self-portrait. These memories fall into two successive groups of abstract nouns—a binary group of singular nouns (*de coquetterie,/de gourmandise*) and a ternary group of plurals (*à des regrets,/à des espoirs,/à des mépris*). Both groups reveal marked symmetries: the nouns have the same number of syllables and are governed by the same prepositional forms. Once again there is in neither case an 'et' to link or close the series of nouns which come tumbling out in this lively evocation of Claudine's youthful peccadilloes together with the welter of her confused, contradictory emotional reactions. The second string of nouns is symmetrically balanced by a ternary group of qualifying adjectives which nicely catch the passionate ardour and gauche candour of raw adolescence: *aussi fougueux,/aussi candides/et dégingandés que moi-même*. Monotony is avoided by the omission of *aussi* before *dégingandés*, and the series is this time appropriately closed by *et*. At the same time this final accumulation is organized 'par masses croissantes' which round off the medley of reminiscences. From here on the lively movement of the sentence begins to slow down, and the excited jumble of memories is succeeded by a calm, cool, critical judgement. The skilfully delayed objects of *je rapporte* form the climax of the sentence and take on an enhanced importance as the girl's emphatic, definitive impression of the city: *l'étonnement, l'aversion mélancolique de ce que je nommais les maisons sans bêtes.*

Her repugnance towards this lifeless, unnatural phenomenon is further elaborated and more closely analysed in the second sentence; but this leads to an almost chiastic reversal of the syntactic pattern. This time the series of direct objects with their dependent phrases and long relative clauses comes first, while the main verb *je les quittai* is long delayed, and its sudden arrival marks a sharp break with the whole way of life previously described. Paris consists not of homes, but of *cubes, logis, appartements,* and the girl's distaste is underlined by the contemptuous demonstratives accompanying all three terms. Once again there is an overall ternary pattern ; but the second group is expanded by two parallel relative clauses introduced by *où* and the third is also accompanied by a similar dependent clause which in turn culminates in the familiar ternary rhythm (*au marbre,/au bois,/au velours inanimés*). Claudine is implicitly contrasting Paris with Saint-Sauveur here, and the long series of skilfully varied negatives emphasizes the absence of all those features which she associates with her home: *cubes sans jardins ; logis sans fleurs où nul chat ne miaule..., où l'on n'écrase pas... un coin du chien ; appartements privés d'esprits familiers ; au marbre, au bois, au velours inanimés.* She misses here the presence of a vital animal and plant life. She misses the garden with its colourful flowers, but she misses above all the mewing cat and the dog lying by the fire. Domestic pets are friendly *esprits familiers* which respond to the touch with a *cordiale caresse.*[2] They are the warm, living furniture of a home. The dog, for example, is described as stretched out *comme un tapis*; but unlike a carpet it reacts when trodden on! Parisian flats are insulated from nature and cluttered with lifeless marble, wood, and velvet. It is with an intense feeling of relief that she finally reaches the main verb *je les quittai*. The slow, mournful description of Paris is now over, and the pace begins to quicken as the girl looks forward with impatient eagerness to her return home. All her

---

[2] The epithet placed before the noun acquires greater emotive force. Cf. *émouvante humidité, vigoureuse odeur, blanches corolles.*

senses, and especially her tactile sense, have been starved in the city, and she leaves Paris with the urgent need for reinvigoration by direct physical contact with the warm, vital life of nature in all its forms—animals and plants, birds and flowers. The ternary rhythm returns here at the end of the sentence which tails off in 'points de suspension' suggestive of infinite yearning: *toucher, vivantes,*[3] *des toisons ou des feuilles,/des plumes tièdes,/l'émouvante humidité*[4] *des fleurs...*

Claudine is carried away on the wings of desire, and by the beginning of the second paragraph she is already back in Saint-Sauveur. The first short sentence describes her homecoming, and her delighted contemplation of the familiar[5] scene is like a sudden discovery of Sido's communion with Nature, which illuminates the mysterious vital link uniting men, animals, and plants. She here finds the plenitude which she had missed in Paris. The end of the sentence breaks again into a ternary rhythm as she joyously greets [*sa*] *mère,/le jardin/et la ronde des bêtes* which she recognizes as if for the first time as a harmonious whole (*ensemble*), as an indivisible, living unity (*inséparables*).

She had arrived home at six o'clock, the time when her mother always watered the garden, and the scene has remained vividly and indelibly fixed in her memory (*je chéris encore*). The passing hour is given artistic permanence as she fondly evokes the green watering-can, the stains on her mother's blue sateen dress,[6] the strong, invigorating smell of the leaf-mould feeding new life, the rose-pink light of the setting sun tinting the page of a book, the leaves of a tobacco-plant, the white spots of the cat in its basket. The ternary pattern with its swelling rhythm and its skilful variation of the prepositional forms re-emerges for the last time here at the end of the paragraph: *à la page blanche d'un livre oublié,/aux blanches corolles du tabac blanc,/aux taches blanches de la chatte dans une corbeille.* All the primitive innocence of Claudine's childhood world seems to be symbolized here by the intense, pure whiteness evoked

---

[3] The power of the detached epithet is also exploited in the last paragraph; cf. *inséparables* and especially *rose*.

[4] Cf. 'J'aime l'humidité... Il faut croire... qu'elle satisfait ce qu'il y a en moi de végétal' (cit. M. Goudeket, *Près de Colette* (Paris, 1956), p. 128).

[5] The familiarity of the scene is abundantly indicated by the long series of definite articles in the second paragraph.

[6] On Sido's famous blue dress, see M. Raaphorst-Rousseau, *Colette, sa vie et son art* (Paris, 1964), pp. 31–2, 135.

by the fourfold repetition of the adjective of colour and especially by the chiastic arrangement of *blanches corolles du tabac blanc*. The whiteness is itself suffused with the soft glow of the *lumière déclinante* which magically transfigures the whole scene and creates as it were the luminous, colourful harmony of some Impressionist painting.

All the elements are drawn from reality, a humble, commonplace reality. No mysticism or transcendentalism is involved; but from this everyday material the author has distilled her characteristic form of poetry—a 'poésie à ras de terre'.

25 Mauriac

Du fond d'un compartiment obscur, Thérèse regarde ces jours purs de sa vie — purs mais éclairés d'un frêle bonheur imprécis; et cette trouble lueur de joie, elle ne savait pas alors que ce devait être son unique part en ce monde. Rien ne l'avertissait que tout son lot tenait dans un salon ténébreux, au centre de l'été implacable, — sur ce canapé de reps rouge, auprès d'Anne dont les genoux rapprochés soutenaient un album de photographies. D'où lui venait ce bonheur? Anne avait-elle un seul des goûts de Thérèse? Elle haïssait la lecture, n'aimait que coudre, jacasser et rire. Aucune idée sur rien, tandis que Thérèse dévorait du même appétit les romans de Paul de Kock, les *Causeries du Lundi*, l'*Histoire du Consulat*, tout ce qui traîne dans les placards d'une maison de campagne. Aucun goût commun, hors celui d'être ensemble durant ces après-midi où le feu du ciel assiège les hommes barricadés dans une demi-ténèbre. Et Anne parfois se levait pour voir si la chaleur était tombée. Mais, les volets à peine entrouverts, la lumière pareille à une gorgée de métal en fusion, soudain jaillie, semblait brûler la natte, et il fallait, de nouveau, tout clore et se tapir.

Même au crépuscule, et lorsque déjà le soleil ne rougissait plus que le bas des pins et que s'acharnait, tout près du sol, une dernière cigale, la chaleur demeurait stagnante sous les chênes. Comme elles se fussent assises au bord d'un lac, les amies s'étendaient à l'orée du champ. Des nuées orageuses leur proposaient de glissantes images; mais avant que Thérèse ait eu le temps de distinguer la femme ailée qu'Anne voyait dans le ciel, ce n'était déjà plus, disait la jeune fille, qu'une étrange bête étendue.

En septembre, elles pouvaient sortir après la collation et pénétrer dans le pays de la soif: pas le moindre filet d'eau à Argelouse; il faut marcher longtemps dans le sable avant d'atteindre les sources du ruisseau appelé la Hure. Elles crèvent, nombreuses, un bas-fond d'étroites prairies entre les racines des aulnes. Les pieds nus des

jeunes filles devenaient insensibles dans l'eau glaciale, puis, à peine secs, étaient de nouveau brûlants. Une de ces cabanes, qui servent en octobre aux chasseurs de palombes, les accueillait comme naguère
35 le salon obscur. Rien à se dire; aucune parole: les minutes fuyaient de ces longues haltes innocentes sans que les jeunes filles songeassent plus à bouger que ne bouge le chasseur lorsqu'à l'approche d'un vol, il fait le signe du silence. Ainsi leur semblait-il qu'un seul geste aurait fait fuir leur informe et chaste bonheur. Anne, la
40 première, s'étirait — impatiente de tuer des alouettes au crépuscule; Thérèse, qui haïssait ce jeu, la suivait pourtant, insatiable de sa présence. Anne décrochait dans le vestibule le calibre 24 qui ne repousse pas. Son amie, demeurée sur le talus, la voyait au milieu du seigle viser le soleil comme pour l'éteindre. Thérèse se bouchait
45 les oreilles; un cri ivre s'interrompait dans le bleu, et la chasseresse ramassait l'oiseau blessé, le serrait d'une main précautionneuse et, tout en caressant de ses lèvres les plumes chaudes, l'étouffait.

MAURIAC, *Thérèse Desqueyroux*
Date of first publication: 1927
Ed. C. Jenkins (London: U.L.P., 1964),
pp. 63–5

Thérèse Desqueyroux is a novel notable for its craftsmanship, its compulsive power, its all-pervasive atmosphere of a dark fatality. The setting, the narrative technique, the highly personal style, the haunting character of the heroine herself make it probably one of the most representative of Mauriac's works. Thérèse is presented by the author as a familiar, exemplary figure of the world of Bordeaux and the Landes: 'Que de fois, à travers les barreaux vivants d'une famille, t'ai-je vue tourner en rond, à pas de louve; et de ton œil méchant et triste tu me dévisageais' (p. 48). The materialistic, bourgeois society to which she belongs by birth and marriage is petty, smug, pharisaical, conformist, oppressive. Her need for freedom, self-fulfilment, and happiness is thwarted at every turn, and her thirst for a profound, all-consuming love, in particular, remains unslaked. Her frustration takes a destructive turn, and she tries to break out of her stifling, claustrophobic prison. Her husband Bernard inadvertently takes a double dose of Fowler's solution, and she does not warn him. He has come to symbolize her imprisonment in an empty, loveless marriage, and from here on she drifts half unconsciously, half lucidly into an unsuccessful attempt to poison him. The victim commits perjury at the trial, and the honour of the Family is saved. Thérèse is acquitted, and the scandal is more or less hushed up. Now, however, the 'puissante mécanique familiale' is mounted against her, and she is virtually sentenced to solitary confinement for life in the depths of the Landes. Her health deteriorates so seriously that Bernard becomes frightened and agrees to an 'amicable' separation. A small income is settled on her, and like some wild bird ailing in captivity she is released from her cage. Left to her own devices, she escapes to Paris, and we last glimpse her mingling with the anonymous crowd on a Parisian street.

The longest and most important section of the novel (chs. ii–viii) consists largely of a series of flashbacks ranging kaleidoscopically over Thérèse's past life and darkly illuminating the configuration of a destiny. As she drives in the victoria from the court-house at Bordeaux to the station at Nizan, then in the dark compartment of the slow train to Saint-Clair, and from there by trap to Argelouse where she will confront her husband, she moves forward through space towards an uncertain future; but simultaneously she makes another journey back through time as she relives certain moments of her life and tries to 'regarder en face l'acte qu'elle a commis'. Her examination of conscience is sincere enough; but the omniscient author hints that the heroine is implicated in some obscure hereditary fatality: 'Où est le commencement de nos actes? Notre destin, quand nous voulons l'isoler, ressemble à ces plantes qu'il est impossible d'arracher avec toutes leurs racines. Thérèse remontera-t-elle jusqu'à son enfance? Mais l'enfance est elle-même une fin, un aboutissement' (p. 59). She looks back nostalgically to the lost innocence of her youth ('L'enfance de Thérèse: de la neige à la source du fleuve le plus sali'); but she is quick to ask herself whether it is not the contrast with 'cette ineffaçable salissure des noces' (p. 59) which makes her schooldays seem now more pure than they actually were. 'Ces lointains étés d'Argelouse... ces beaux étés... c'est vers eux qu'il faut que sa pensée remonte, si elle veut voir clair. Incroyable vérité que dans ces aubes toutes pures de nos vies, les pires orages étaient déjà suspendus' (p. 60).

The passage under examination, which comes from chapter iii, evokes Thérèse's adolescence and, in particular, her summer holidays at Argelouse.[1] There is no minute description in the realist manner, and there are only a few rare colour notations (the *canapé de reps rouge*, the base of the pines reddened by the sunset, the green meadows watered by the springs, the blue sky above the rye-field); but what is lost in variety and picturesqueness is made up for by concentration, intensity, and a certain inward ardour, and an almost physical sensation of the locale is conveyed by the author's extraordinary power of sensuous perception. It is the familiar Mauriac country—the shuttered house with its slightly old-fashioned décor and dark interior; the fierce sun which creates a torrid 'climat de feu' and reduces all life below to a state of suffocating, listless torpor; the scorched, arid landscape of the Landes with its pine forests and sandy soil; the strange cloud-formations drifting across the stormy sky; the 'palombières' from which in the autumn the hunters will stalk their prey; the immense silence which enhances the sense of human solitude and unnaturally heightens the slightest sound (the scraping of the cicada, the song of the lark, the report of the gun). It is a real world with which the author is intimately acquainted; but it is also and above all a country of the mind, a world within a world, an almost mythical setting built up by means of a series of violent contrasts—light/darkness, heat/coolness, desert/water, innocence/cruelty, joy/pain. Argelouse with its prodigious silence and its parched environment (pp. 96, 112, 134) seems to be 'une extrémité de la terre; ...quelques métairies sans église, ni mairie, ni cimetière, disséminées autour d'un champ de seigle' (p. 61). It is here at the end of the world that Thérèse goes to stay with Tante Clara, spending as much time as she can with Bernard's half-sister, Anne de la Trave. On the surface there is little in common between the 'lycéenne raisonneuse et moqueuse' and 'sa dévote amie', 'cette couventine à l'esprit court' (pp. 56, 57, 71). Simple, ingenuous, active, extrovert, Anne seems the opposite of Thérèse, and the contrast between her passion for Jean Azévédo and Thérèse's relations with Bernard will later arouse her friend's jealousy and exacerbate her despair. Here Anne is still the 'chère petite idiote' (p. 71), turning over the family album, roaming the Landes, hunting birds, and riding her jingling bicycle.

[1] Argelouse is a village south of Bordeaux; but Mauriac is here writing about another hamlet in the same region where he sometimes spent his summer holidays on a family property—'ce quartier perdu de Jouanhaut que j'ai décrit dans *Thérèse Desqueyroux* sous le nom d'Argelouse' (*Écrits intimes* (Geneva, 1953), p. 21). The name Argelouse was perhaps preferred because of its harmonious softness.

Structurally, this flashback to the school holidays falls into two parts which evoke respectively high summer (paras. 1 and 2) and September (para. 3). In both parts there is a parallel of afternoon and evening which produces an effect of contrasting symmetry. The friendship of the two girls and their various activities are described in the passage under consideration; the remainder of the flashback illuminates the heroine's essential loneliness — even with Anne, and especially when she is left with her deaf old aunt.

The association connecting past and present is the recurrent darkness motif: *compartiment obscur, salon ténébreux, demi-ténèbre,* the scene at dusk on the edge of the field, the hunting cabin. The dimly lit compartment is almost an image of the darkened soul of the heroine, for as she sits meditating in the train she is seeking light in her darkness. The immediate surroundings fade out; the tense switches from present to past; Thérèse's reverie takes over in the abrupt flashback from her joyless, sunless existence to the happier, brighter days of her youth (*éclairés, lueur de joie*). At once remote and familiar (cf. the insistent demonstratives—*ces jours, cette trouble lueur, ce canapé, ce bonheur*), the past is viewed in the light of what has happened since, and the ambiguity of the third-person narrative ('elle-sujet'/'elle-objet') allows Mauriac himself to intrude with absolute, extra-temporal remarks: *elle ne savait pas alors que... Rien ne l'avertissait que...* Thérèse's life is presented by the omniscient author *sub specie aeternitatis,* but the heroine herself remains ignorant of her tragic destiny. Her youth is seen first as a time of unalloyed purity (*ces jours purs de sa vie*); but this is at once qualified: *purs mais éclairés d'un frêle bonheur imprécis.* Whether there is some incompatibility implied here between purity and happiness is unclear. The frail happiness referred to is itself mysteriously vague (*imprécis*) and will remain so (*informe bonheur*). As for the *lueur de joie* its brightness is offset by the disturbing epithet *trouble,* and the cruel, categorical ending of the sentence stresses that this joy will be short-lived: *ce devait être son unique part en ce monde.* It is a narrowly confined, sheltered happiness: *tout son lot tenait dans un salon ténébreux, au centre de l'été implacable.* The drawing-room is a refuge from the torrid heat of midsummer. The two epithets somewhat dramatize the atmosphere: *ténébreux,* a favourite adjective of Mauriac, is more intense and suggestive than 'obscur', while the hyperbolic character of *implacable* almost results in the personification of the summer as a violent, living adversary. The second sentence is built around this central contrast between the dark interior and the blazing sunlight outside. Hitherto general and abstract, the language becomes henceforward more concrete and physical. The description narrows down from the larger area (*salon ténébreux*) to pinpoint a few smaller details which take on an enhanced particularity—the *canapé de reps rouge*, Anne's *genoux rapprochés*, the *album de photographies*.[2] It is as if the girls' pleasure in each other's company were concentrated in this brief tableau. Their happiness resides in physical proximity, in a passive immobility, in a long, siesta-like repose. But if this is clear to author and reader it is less so to Thérèse, for at this point the perspective shifts back to the mind of the heroine, and a brief passage of interior monologue begins with the largely unanswered question: *D'où lui venait ce bonheur?* Thérèse cannot understand her adolescent emotions, and her relationship with Anne seems to her now to have been very superficial. In a series of short, impatient sentences she disparages her young friend, minimizing the closeness of their rapport by the incredulous question: *Anne avait-elle un seul des goûts de Thérèse?* and by the insistent repetition of the two successive negatives: *Aucune idée sur rien... Aucun goût commun...*[3] In the *maison de campagne* of the typical middle-class family of Bordeaux books did not figure very prominently, and Thérèse had to dig them out of the cupboards in order to satisfy her omnivorous and somewhat undiscriminating passion for reading matter, ranging from popular fiction (Paul de Kock) to literary criticism (Sainte-Beuve) and history (Thiers). The naïve, domesticated Anne had none of Thérèse's disturbing intellectual curiosity: *Elle haïssait la lecture, n'aimait que coudre, jacasser et rire.* The two girls had nothing in common save the *goût... d'être ensemble durant ces après-midi où le feu du ciel assiège les hommes barricadés dans une demi-ténèbre.* It is as if they were driven together by the fiery climate, were united against the common foe—the implacable sun which turns the Landes into a furnace and imprisons men indoors. The sun motif re-emerges here in a grandiose, quasi-apocalyptic image, bringing with it another powerful contrast of light and darkness (*feu du ciel/demi-ténèbre*). A hostile, destructive force, the sun is

---

[2] The family album has a special significance in this novel. The erring grandmother, Julie Bellaude, and the other black sheep of the family are excluded from it. Thérèse herself will one day be 'ainsi effacée, anéantie' (pp. 51, 95, 111).

[3] These elliptical phrases are very appropriate here to the swift flashes of thought characteristic of the interior monologue.

presented in the form of an extended military metaphor: *feu, assiège, barricadés*. The closed shutters are like barricades warding off the attack of the sun. The strong, dynamic verb lends energy to the image, and the switch to the present tense confers upon it greater generality. This unexpected, dramatic touch forms the transition to the impressive climax of the paragraph with its evocation of extreme light and heat. The dynamic 'et' (*Et Anne...*) indicates not only the abrupt conclusion of Thérèse's musing and the return to the narrative, but also a sudden, impulsive movement amid the universal lethargy. From here on the almost cosmic image of the sun's assault contracts to the *salon ténébreux* with its two occupants. The bare description is confined to only three details—the shutters, the single, narrow shaft of white-hot sunlight, the mat. The rhythm here begins to gather speed as Anne, the more active and restless of the girls, gets up to see if the heat has abated. The final sentence with its condensed syntax (*les volets à peine entrouverts, soudain iaillie*) and its strong, violent verbs (*jaillie, brûler*) hastens, in energetic spurts, to its climax (*la natte*), and then, owing chiefly to the interpolation of *de nouveau*, it gradually slows down again and ends in immobility. The light image here takes the form of an extended simile (*pareille à, semble*). The sunlight is likened to a stream of hot, molten metal which suddenly pours into the room and seems to scorch the mat. Anne has only half opened the defences of the house; but such is the sun's power that she has to close the shutters again and return to cover. *Se tapir*, a favourite metaphor of Mauriac, suggests that the two girls are like animals lying low from their pursuer. They are trapped in darkness by the fierce, consuming sun of the Landes. It is the first intimation of the hunting theme.

The second paragraph forms a contrast with the violent climax of the first. The scene abruptly changes: the girls are out of doors, and dusk is closing in. With the gradual abatement of the sweltering heat the style itself becomes calmer, with fewer dynamic verbs, less dramatic epithets and less overpowering imagery. The sentences themselves are harmoniously balanced—an elegant chiasmus in the one simple sentence (*nuées orageuses/glissantes images*), and a similar syntactic pattern in the other complex sentences (one or two subordinate clauses followed by the gently descending movement of the main clause). There is no attempt at precise localization (*des pins, les chênes, du champ*)—the reader's familiarity with the landscape is tacitly assumed. The sun is already low on the horizon, for its red glow is staining only the base of the pines. The cicada too is *tout près du sol*, and the evening silence is broken solely by the furious scraping of this belated insect. The inversion of the second temporal clause which contrasts almost chiastically with the normal order of the first has the effect of suddenly springing on the reader the only verb of sound in the paragraph (*s'acharnait*) as well as appropriately throwing into relief the delayed subject (*une dernière cigale*). The sun is declining; but *même au crépuscule* the stagnant heat trapped beneath the oaks remains oppressive, and the girls therefore stretch out beside the open field—the nearest thing to a cool lake in the vicinity of Argelouse. The mannered subjunctive (*Comme elles se fussent...*) is characteristic of Mauriac's highly literary style (cf. *songeassent*). There is once again a focusing down from the wider scene to the edge of the field with the two girls, and their recumbent posture (*assises, s'étendaient*) recalls the previous situation in the *salon ténébreux*. But here the tableau is open to a stormy sky, and the final sentence with its sombre touches seems to form a premonitory climax to the paragraph. The clouds assume strange, fleeting shapes. Anne glimpses a *femme ailée*, but by the time Thérèse looks up the angel has turned into *une étrange bête étendue*. This image seems to suggest the swift tarnishing of youthful purity,[4] and the sprawling beast is like a reflection of the monster dormant in human nature.

In the third paragraph time has moved on. It is September now, and there is a certain sense of liberation from the deluge of fire. There is no siesta this time, and after a light afternoon meal (*collation*) the girls set out on an expedition deep into the Landes. The long summer drought has taken its toll, and the parched countryside is described in nominal style (noun complement for adjective) as *le pays de la soif*. At this point the narrative gives way to another passage of brief, selective description. This time the proper names (*Argelouse, la Hure*[5]) firmly anchor the scene in a definite locality; but once again the description proceeds from the general wider area (the vast, sandy wasteland) to close in upon particular details—*les sources du ruisseau, un bas-fond d'étroites prairies, les racines des aulnes,*

---

[4] Cf. 'Un garçon de vingt ans se décompose, se dissout, se colore, s'obscurcit comme un beau nuage; et ce qu'hier nous adorions en lui, aujourd'hui est effacé' (*Le Jeune Homme* (Paris, 1926), p. 27).

[5] The name of a real stream which often recurs in Mauriac's childhood memories (cf. *Commencements d'une vie*), and which also figures in *Le Mystère Frontenac*, where it is described as the 'plus secret ruisseau des Landes'.

les pieds nus des jeunes filles. A brief, elliptic phrase (*pas le moindre filet d'eau...*) elaborates *le pays de la soif*; then a couple of sentences in the present tense evoke the sandy tract and, like an oasis in the middle of a desert, the myriad springs of la Hure which water the verdant, low-lying meadows and the roots of the elders. Sand is for Mauriac a symbol of desiccation and privation; clear, living water is a sign of purification and renewal. This recall of the journey to the limpid headsprings of la Hure is like a return to the pure waters of childhood which will be all too soon polluted by the muddy contamination of later life. Another intense sensation recalls that the sun is still very hot. The girls bathe their feet in the icy water. One minute their feet are numb with cold, *puis à peine secs*, they are *de nouveau brûlants.* The friends seek refuge in the shade of a 'palombière'.[6] This cabin will figure again in the story—Thérèse will later recall that she first met Jean Azévédo at 'cette palombière abandonnée où je goûtais naguère auprès d'Anne et où je savais que, depuis, elle avait aimé rejoindre cet Azévédo' (p. 89). Here it is explicitly likened to the dark drawing-room of the first paragraph. The situation is basically identical. Two elliptical phrases (*Rien à se dire; aucune parole...*) stress once again the absence of common interests; but there is no boredom—*les minutes fuyaient de ces longues haltes innocentes.* There is a similar absence of movement; but here it is adapted to the hunting motif by the comparison with the stillness of *le chasseur lorsqu' à l'approche d'un vol, il fait le signe du silence.* It is as if the slightest gesture would have made *leur informe et chaste bonheur* fly away like a bird. However, the prolonged repose is once again disturbed, and as before Anne is the first to become restless. Two parallel main clauses with their similar rhythm catch the successive movements of the two girls: *Anne, la première, s'étirait* (a sudden, impetuous movement contrasting with the immobility of the preceding lines); *Thérèse, qui haïssait ce jeu, la suivait pourtant* (a slower, more reluctant, yet compulsive movement). Both clauses culminate in long, expressive adjectival phrases which explain and symmetrically contrast the different reasons for the two movements: *impatiente de tuer des alouettes au crépuscule/insatiable de sa présence.* The hunting theme[7] now emerges fully into the open

---

[6] A touch of local colour which deftly reintroduces the hunting theme. For more details about these cabins and the hunting customs of the Landes see *Thérèse Desqueyroux*, ed. Jenkins, pp. 147–8.

[7] Mauriac's novels often convey the relentless atmosphere of the chase. The sun pursues men; men stalk animals; lovers hunt their prey; God himself is the Hunter

and will form the startling climax of the paragraph. In the arid Landes 'rien n'est vivant, hors les oiseaux qui passent' (p. 111); yet thousands of larks and other birds are shot or trapped every year. Thérèse *haïssait ce jeu*; but like her half-brother Bernard ('cet Hippolyte mal léché') Anne has hunting in her blood and she here turns suddenly into *la chasseresse*—a chaste, cruel Diana figure. From here on the narrative moves quickly, and the point of view seems to shift from Thérèse back to the author, who here presents his heroine from outside (*son amie*). Anne takes down the gun—a *calibre 24* with no recoil, but not the less lethal for that. The vivid scene which follows conforms to the descriptive technique already noted. From the bank on which Thérèse is standing there is a commanding view of the rye-field with Anne in the middle of it; then, immediately after the gunshot, there is the extraordinary close-up of Anne's face and the wounded bird. As if provoking the violence which is to follow, the baleful sun makes its last appearance here as Anne points her gun at it *comme pour l'éteindre*. The final sentence with its rapid succession of verbs (*se bouchait, s'interrompait, ramassait, serrait, caressant, étouffait*) has a dramatic swiftness. It is all over in a flash, and the deed is done before we realize what is happening. We do not actually hear the report of the gun, nor do we see the bird fall. The shot is evoked indirectly in its effect (*Thérèse se bouchait les oreilles*), and the wounding of the bird is likewise indicated by the immediate suppression of its rapturous song (*un cri ivre s'interrompait dans le bleu*). Then the binary rhythm gives way to a swelling ternary movement which is reinforced by the three symmetrical nouns, each qualified by a following epithet (*oiseau blessé, main précautionneuse, plumes chaudes*). The sentence with its soft, caressing alliteration culminates unexpectedly in the sharp, brutal finality of *l'étouffait*. Isolated by the comma and thrown into relief by the preceding phrase, this climax is very deliberate and calculated. The combination of kindness and cruelty is all the more shocking because it is a young girl, the pure, devout Anne, who here reveals herself to be a killer.

---

laying his toils for the unsuspecting soul. Sometimes the roles are reversed, and the hunter becomes the quarry.

Bibliography

Albalat, A. *Le Travail du style* (Paris, 1905).

Alonso, A. 'The Stylistic Interpretation of Literary Texts', in *Modern Language Notes*, LVII (1942), pp. 489-96.

Antoine, G. 'Stylistique des formes et stylistique des thèmes, ou le stylisticien face à l'ancienne et à la nouvelle critique', in *Les Chemins actuels de la critique*, ed. G. Poulet (Paris, 1968).

Art of Criticism, The, ed. P. H. Nurse (Edinburgh, 1969).

Auerbach, E. *Mimesis; the Representation of Reality in Western Literature* (Berne, 1946; English translation, Princeton, 1953).

Bally, C. *Traité de stylistique française*, 3rd ed. (2 vols., Geneva, 1951).

Barat ,E. *Le Style poétique et la révolution romantique* (Paris, 1904).

Berry, F. *Poets' Grammar* (London, 1958).

'Bibliographie de l'explication française', in *Les Études classiques* (Namur, 1948), pp. 112-74, 247-309.

Boillot, F. *Quelques heures de français dans une université anglaise* (Paris, 1923).

The Methodical Study of Literature (Paris, 1924).

Psychologie de la construction dans la phrase française moderne (Paris, 1930).

Bremond, H. *Les Deux Musiques de la prose* (Paris, 1924).

Brooks, Cleanth. *The Well Wrought Urn* (New York, 1947).

Brown, Huntington. *Prose Styles: Five Primary Types* (Minneapolis, Minn., 1966).

Bruneau, C. *Petite Histoire de la langue française* (2 vols., Paris, 1955-8).

Brunot, F., & Bruneau, C. *Histoire de la langue française* (20 vols., Paris, 1907-53).

Cahiers d'analyse textuelle (Paris, 1959–   ; published annually).

Chassé, C. *Styles et physiologie* (Paris, 1928).

Cherel, A. *La Prose poétique française* (Paris, 1940).

Cortat, R. *L'Explication de texte* (Paris, 1957).

Cressot, M. *Le Style et ses techniques* (Paris, 1947).

Cruickshank, J. *Critical Readings in the Modern French Novel* (London, 1961).

Davidson, H.M. *Audience, Words and Art* (Columbus, Ohio, 1965).

Delbouille, P. *Poésie et sonorités* (Paris, 1961).

Deloffre, F. *La Phrase française* (Paris, 1967).
 Le Vers français (Paris, 1969).

Derche, R. *Études de textes français* (6 vols., Paris, 1966).

Dorchain, A. *L'Art des vers* (Paris, 1905).

Empson, W. *Seven Types of Ambiguity* (London, 1930).

Encyclopedia of Poetry and Poetics, ed. A. Preminger (Princeton, 1965).

Estève, C. *Études philosophiques sur l'expression littéraire* (Paris, 1938).

Étienne, S. *Défense de la philologie* (Liège, 1933).
 Expériences d'analyse textuelle en vue de l'explication littéraire (Liège, 1935).

Explication de texte, ed. J. Sareil (Englewood Cliffs, N.J., 1967).

Fiser, E. *Le Symbole littéraire* (Paris, 1941).

Gandon, Y. *Le Démon du style* (Paris, 1938).

Germain, F. *L'Art de commenter un texte* (Paris, 1965).

Godin, H. J. G. *Les Ressources stylistiques du français contemporain* (Oxford, 1948).

Gourmont, R. de. *Esthétique de la langue française* (Paris, 1899).
 Le Problème du style (Paris, 1902).

Grammont, M. *Le Vers français* (Paris, 1904; revised edition, 1937).
 Petit Traité de versification française, 15th ed. (Paris, 1955).
 Essai de psychologie linguistique (Paris, 1950).

Guiraud, P. *La Stylistique* (Paris, 1954).
 (and others) *Style et littérature* (The Hague, 1962).

Hatzfeld, H. *Literature through Art* (New York, 1952).
 A Critical Bibliography of the New Stylistics (Chapel Hill, N.C., Vol. I, 1953; Vol. II, 1966).
 Initiation à l'explication de textes français (Munich, 1957; revised edition, 1966).

Hough, G. *Style and Stylistics* (London, 1969).

Jones, P. Mansell. *The Assault on French Literature* (Manchester, 1963).

Kayser, W. *Das sprachliche Kunstwerk* (Berne, 1948).

Krafft, J.-G. *Essai sur l'esthétique de la prose* (Paris, 1952).
  Poésie, corps et âme (Paris, 1961).
Langue et littérature: Proceedings of the VIIIth Congress of the Fédération Internationale des Langues et Littératures Modernes (Paris, 1961).
Lanham, R. A. *A Handlist of Rhetorical Terms* (Berkeley, Calif., 1968).
Lanson, G. *L'Art de la prose* (Paris, 1909).
  'Quelques mots sur l'explication de textes', in *Méthodes de l'histoire littéraire* (Paris, 1925), pp. 38–57.
Lausberg, H. *Elemente der literarischen Rhetorik*, 2nd ed. (Munich, 1963).
Le Hir, Y. *Esthétique et structure du vers français* (Paris, 1956).
  Commentaires stylistiques de textes français modernes (Paris, 1959).
  Rhétorique et stylistique, de la Pléiade au Parnasse (Paris, 1960).
  Analyses stylistiques (Paris, 1965).
Lewis, C. Day. *The Poetic Image* (London, 1947).
Littérature et stylistique: Cahiers de l'Association Internationale des Études Françaises, no. 16 (Paris, 1964).
Lucas, F. L. *Style* (London, 1955).
Marouzeau, J. *Précis de stylistique française*, 2nd ed. (Paris, 1946).
Martin, E.-L. *Les Symétries du français littéraire* (Paris, 1924).
Martinon, P. *Les Strophes* (Paris, 1912).
Michaud, G. *L'Œuvre et ses techniques* (Paris, 1957).
Morier, H. *Le Rythme du vers libre symboliste* (3 vols., Geneva, 1943–4).
  La Psychologie des styles (Geneva, 1959).
  Dictionnaire de poétique et de rhétorique (Paris, 1961).
Mornet, D. *Histoire de la clarté française* (Paris, 1929).
Murry, J. Middleton. *The Problem of Style* (Oxford, 1922).
Nardin, P. *Le Commentaire stylistique aux rendez-vous littéraires* (Dakar, 1958).
Paulhan, J. *Les Fleurs de Tarbes* (Paris, 1941).
Poem Itself, The, ed. S. Burnshaw (London, 1964).
Pouget, P. *L'Explication française* (Paris, 1952).
Raleigh, W. *Style* (London, 1897).
Rawlinson, D. H. *The Practice of Criticism* (Cambridge, 1968).

Richards, I. A. *Principles of Literary Criticism*, 3rd ed. (London, 1928).

Practical Criticism (London, 1929).

The Philosophy of Rhetoric (London, 1936).

Rose, C. Brooke. *A Grammar of Metaphor* (London, 1958).

Roustan, M. *Précis d'explication française* (Paris, 1911).

Textes français commentés et expliqués (Paris: Delaplane, n.d.).

Rudler, G. *L'Explication française* (Paris, 1902).

Sayce, R. A. *Style in French Prose* (Oxford, 1953).

'Literature and Language', in *Essays in Criticism*, VII (1957), pp. 119–33.

Schlumberger, B. *L'Explication littéraire* (London, 1951).

Souriau, M. *L'Évolution du vers français au xviie siècle* (Paris, 1893).

Spitzer, L. *Stilstudien* (2 vols., Munich, 1928).

Romanische Stil- und Literaturstudien (2 vols., Marburg, 1931).

Linguistics and Literary History (Princeton, 1948).

A Method of Interpreting Literature (Northampton, Mass., 1949).

Spoerri, T. *Französische Metrik* (Munich, 1929).

Suberville, J. *Histoire et théorie de la versification française* (Paris, 1946).

Ullmann, S. *Style in the French Novel* (Cambridge, 1957).

The Image in the Modern French Novel (Cambridge, 1960).

Language and Style (Oxford, 1964).

Vianey, J. *L'Explication française* (Paris, 1912).

Vigneron, R. 'Explication de textes', in *Modern Language Journal*, XLII (1927), pp. 19–35.

Vinaver, E. 'Le Chêne et le roseau', in *Modern Languages*, XLII (1961), pp. 1–8.

Vivier, R. 'De l'explication en poésie', in *Romanica Gandensia*, IV (1956), pp. 7–29.

Wartburg, W. von. *Évolution et structure de la langue française*, 3rd ed. (Berne, 1946).

Wellek, R. & Warren, A. *Theory of Literature* (London, 1949).

Wimsatt, W. K. 'Explication as Criticism' in *Explication as Criticism*: Selected Papers from the English Institute (New York, 1963) pp. 1–26.